STRUCTURAL STEEL DESIGN-LRFD

STRUCTURAL STEEL DESIGN-LRFD

Thomas Burns

Delmar Publishers

I ⓣ P An International Thomson Publishing Company

Albany • Bonn • Boston • Cincinnati • Detroit • London • Madrid • Melbourne
Mexico City • New York • Pacific Grove • Paris • San Francisco • Singapore • Tokyo
Toronto • Washington

Notice to the Reader

Publisher does not warrant or guarantee any of the products described herein or perform any independent analysis in connection with any of the product information contained herein. Publisher does not assume, and expressly disclaims, any obligation to obtain and include information other than that provided to it by the manufacturer.

The reader is expressly warned to consider and adopt all safety precautions that might be indicated by the activities described herein, and to avoid all potential hazards. By following the instructions contained herein, the reader willingly assumes all risks in connection with such instructions.

The publisher makes no representations or warranties of any kind, including but not limited to, the warranties of fitness for particular purpose or merchantability, nor are any such representations implied with respect to the material set forth herein, and the publisher takes no responsibility with respect to such material. The publisher shall not be liable for any special, consequential or exemplary damages resulting, in whole or part, from the reader's use of or reliance upon this material.

Delmar Staff
Senior Editor: Mark Huth
Associate Editor: Kimberly Davies
Editorial Assistant: Donna Leto
Developmental Editor: Kimberly Davies

Project Editor: Patricia Konczeski
Production Coordinator: Karen Smith
Art/Design Coordinator: Cheri Plasse

Copyright © 1995
By Delmar Publishers Inc.   .

An International Thomson Publishing Company
ITP® The logo is a trademark under license
Printed in the United States of America

For more information, contact:

Delmar Publishers Inc.
3 Columbia Circle, Box 15015
Albany, New York 12203-5015

International Thomson Editores
Campos Eliseos 385, Piso 7
11560 Mexico D F Mexico

International Thomson Publishing
Berkshire House 168–173
High Holborn
London, WC1V7AA   England

International Thomson Publishing GmbH
Konigswinterer Strasse 418
53227 Bonn   Germany

Thomas Nelson Australia
102 Dodds Street
South Melbourne 3205   Victoria, Australia

International Thomson Publishing Asia
221 Henderson Bldg. #05-10
Singapore 0315

Nelson Canada
1120 Birchmont Road
Scarborough, Ontario   Canada, M1K 5G4

International Thomson Publishing-Japan
Kyowa Building, 3F
2-2-1 Hirakawa-cho
Chiyoda-ku, Tokyo 102   Japan

CONTENTS

PREFACE

This text has been written for students of civil engineering technology, building construction, architecture, and related technical disciplines, who are taking their initial course in structural steel design, or the steel portion of a structural systems sequence. It was written to provide students, at both the associate and bachelor-degree levels, with fundamental knowledge of structural steel design using the Load and Resistance Factor Design (LRFD) method This text reflects the latest provisions of the second edition (1994) of the American Institute of Steel Construction's *(AISC) LRFD Manual of Steel Construction.*

The author has attempted to provide easy-to-read, yet extensive, coverage of the most essential topics that are normally covered in the length of a semester. The text provides the necessary information required for tha students of the aforementioned programs to successfully grasp the design and behavior of structural steel members. Chapters 1 through 3 introduce the student to the concepts of LRFD, the behavior of steel as a material, and the process of design. I have found that these chapters ultimately form the groundwork for a first understanding of steel design. Many times design will intimidate students because they are confused about what the LRFD method is actually trying to accomplish. Hopefully, these chapters will give the student some insight on the design process, rather than just design problems. After this introduction, the text begins (in chapters 4 through 11) to focus on the basic elements of steel design. Tension members, compression members, rolled beams, plate girders, and connections are discussed, among other topics. Coverage on these items is thorough, with many examples and homework problems to aid the students in their development. The text also includes a capstone design chapter (chapter 12), which integrates the fundamentals learned in the previous chapters into an example focusing on all aspects of the structural design process, I have found such a chapter to work extremely well in finishing off the students'exposure to steel design, and it may serve as the model for several different design projects.

The text assumes that the student has a thorough background in statics strength of materials, and construction practices, although it requires only a solid foundation in algebra and trigonometry. The derivations of most formulas are left to the discretion of more advanced texts on this subject, since they are typically not essential to the use of such design formulas. The text provides many of the section tables (in both U.S. and SI units) in Appendix B as well as some of the common AISC column load tables in Appendix C. Therefore, the text can be fully utilized without the AISC reference, although it is recommended that students have access to the LRFD manual as a means to more fully complement this text.

The examples are presented in the U.S. customary system with the SI equivalents found next to these, in parenthesis. This was done in order to prepare the student in the use of SI units which will evolve in the U.S. Steel industry in the upcoming future. The exercise problems in the back of each chapter will utilize each system, although slightly more emphasis is placed on the traditional U.S. system. These examples and exercises strive to convey the fundamental ideas found in the design process. Therefore, a detailed, step-by-step, procedure is given in every example to facilitate the students' understanding of basic design concepts. Again, the author's emphasis on providing a tool of learning is paramount in the structure of the text.

Appendix A contains an overview of simplified frame analysis using the moment distribution method. This was placed into the text to provide the student with an abbreviated guide to analyze simple rigid frames. This may be useful as the fundamentals of steel design are applied to a more detailed problem or course project.

In closing, I have always believed that the good designer must be able to grasp the "big picture," while being able to set that "picture" as a sum of its simpler parts. I hope that this text succeeds in helping the student grasp the big picture of the design world, while being able to explain each of the simpler structural components. There are many people whom I wish to thank for their help in making this book possible. I will always be grateful to my Mom and Dad for teaching me the value of education, I would also like to thank my colleagues in the Civil Engineering Technology program for being collectively the finest group of educators I have ever had the pleasure of knowing. Also, my gratitude is extended to my editor, Kimberly Davies, for her work in making this text a reality. Finally, I would like to thank my wife, Kim, and my children, Allison and Michael, for helping me to see both the "big picture" and the simple things that life is all about.

Acknowledgments

The following persons reviewed the manuscript and offered their suggestions and guidance. Their contribution is appreciated.

Weilin P. Chang
School of Building Construction
University of Florida

Ronald E. Gallagher
Engineering Design Department
University of Toledo

Irving Ingel
School of Architecture
Washington University

Raymond Issa
School of Building Construction
University of Florida

David C. McLaughlin
Construction Steel Department
Chippewa Valley Technical College

William Charles Patrick
Moorehead State University

Wally Simmons
Bakersfield College

Stuart Wood Jr.
Central Piedmont Community College

1

STEEL AND STEEL DESIGN

1.1   Introduction to Steel

Steel is an alloy, which is a metal made from various elements. The two main elements that comprise steel are iron and carbon. Iron is by far the main ingredient in terms of percentages, usually making up roughly 98% of all the components found in steel. Carbon typically will comprise less than ½% of steel but is very important because it affects the steel's strength and hardness. In mild carbon steels, an increasing carbon content will produce stronger and harder steels. At the same time, this increase in the carbon content will also produce a reduction in ductility. This loss of ductility is sometimes referred to as brittleness, which is not an advantageous quality for any structural material.

Other alloying elements such as silicon, nickel, manganese, and copper can also be added to steel in varying amounts to enhance certain properties such as strength, hardness, and corrosion resistance. These elements, like carbon, also comprise a very small percentage of steel's chemical composition. The American Society of Testing Materials (ASTM) specifies chemical limits for these elements which are permitted in different types of steel.

The most common structural steel used in bridges and buildings is designated A36 by the ASTM. The chemical requirements for A36 steel, as specified by the ASTM, is shown in Table 1–1. Many other types of steel are also commonly produced when certain properties are considered to be necessary by the designer. The advantageous properties of other common steels are briefly outlined in Table 1–2. A typical example of a special design condition requiring special properties may be a corrosive environment, commonly found in saltwater regions. Such a severe environment may require that a designer specify a steel such as A588 since its corrosion resistance is approximately four times better than that of A36 steel. Another common example that requires special steel properties would be the use of high strength steel, such as A572, in long-span or multi-story structures. Steels of higher strength will commonly be specified in structures where the dead load is a major portion of the total design load, because the judicious use of these steels will lead to an overall reduction of both cost and weight. In these applications, the cost savings of high strength steel may not just be found in the reduction of actual steel weight but also in other areas such as the foundation.

Today, and in the future, designers will have at their disposal an ever increasing number of steels to fit their special needs.

Table 1–1   ASTM Chemical Requirements for A36 Steel

Product	Shapes[a]	Plates					Bars			
Thickness, in.	All	To ¾ Incl.	Over ¾ to 1½ Incl.	Over 1½ to 2½ Incl.	Over 2½ to 4 Incl.	Over 4	To ¾ Incl.	Over ¾ to 1½ Incl.	Over 1½ to 4 Incl.	Over 4
Carbon, max, %	0.26	0.25	0.25	0.26	0.27	0.29	0.26	0.27	0.28	0.29
Manganese, %	–	–	0.80-1.20	0.80-1.20	0.85-1.20	0.85-1.20	–	0.60-0.90	0.60-0.90	0.60-0.90
Phosphorus, max%	0.04	0.04	0.04	0.04	0.04	0.04	0.04	0.04	0.04	0.04
Sulfur, max, %	0.05	0.05	0.05	0.05	0.05	0.05	0.05	0.05	0.05	0.05
Silicon, %	-	–	–	0.15	0.15-0.40	0.15-0.40	–	–	–	–
Copper, min, % when copper steel is specified	0.20	0.20	0.20	0.20	0.20	0.20	0.20	0.20	0.20	0.20

Source: Copyright ASTM. Reprinted with permission.
[a]Manganese content of 0.85-1.35%, and silicon content of 0.15–0.40%, is required for shapes over 426 lb/ft.

Table 1–2 Mechanical Properties of Structural Steels

ASTM Designation	Minimum Yield Stress, F_y	Ultimate Tensile Strength, F_u	Description
A36	36 Ksi	58–80 Ksi	Most common type of steel used in construction. All general structural purposes.
A242	42–50 Ksi	63–70 Ksi	High-strength, low-alloy steel. Better corrosion resistance, mainly used in bridges. Superseded by A709.
A588	42–50 Ksi	63–70 Ksi	Typically referred to as "weathering" steels because they are left unpainted in their final condition. High-strength, low-alloy steel. Corrosion resistance about four times greater than that of A36. Generally superseded by A709.
(36)	36 Ksi	58–80 Ksi	Bridge designated steels.
A709 (50)	50 Ksi	70 Ksi	Quenched and tempered high-strength, low-alloy steels. Can be produced as weathering steels, having high corrosion resistance.
(100)	100 Ksi	110–130 Ksi	

1.2   Important Design Properties of Steel

The property of steel that is most important to the understanding of design concepts is its stress-strain behavior. This behavior is best typified in the standard tensile test usually performed in most strength of materials courses. An ideal stress-strain curve for a mild-carbon structural steel is shown in Figure 1–1.

There are three important regions of this curve that are vital for the designer to understand. The first region is the straight-line portion of the graph between the origin and point A. This region is referred to as the **elastic range**. In the elastic range, this linear relationship implies that some increase in stress (psi), will lead

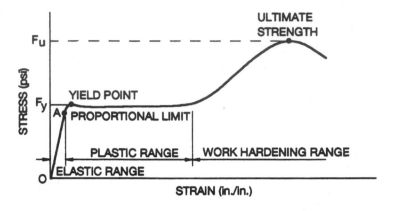

Figure 1–1 Typical Stress-Strain Diagram for Mild Carbon Steels

to some specific, corresponding increase in strain (in./in.). The ratio of this linear relationship determines a material's **modulus of elasticity, E,** which is typically taken as 29×10^6 psi for steel. This straight line relationship exists until the proportional limit. Soon after the proportional limit is surpassed the material will reach its elastic limit and then its yield point. This yield point corresponds to a stress level referred to as the material's **yield stress, F_y.** The yield stress of a material is a stress level that is very important in structural design because it serves as a limiting value of a member's usefulness.

After a material reaches its yield stress, the material strains uncontrollably with practically no corresponding increase in stress. This region is typically referred to as the **plastic region,** the second important region on the curve. Once a material is stressed past its elastic limit, it can never return to its original length. This is referred to as plastic deformation and can be disastrous for a structural member. (Could you imagine what would occur every time a heavy truck crossed a bridge if the beams were allowed to be plasticly deformed?)

Although having a steel member enter the plastic region should always be avoided in design, once the steel member has entered this region, its plastic deformation is an important asset in signalling potential collapse. The length of the elastic and plastic region in essence can be viewed as a measure of the material's ductility. If a material is ductile, it will strain or deflect a large amount before actually breaking. In terms of a structural behavior, it is highly advantageous for a material to exhibit distress before it actually collapses because of the potential warning it provides. Many structural problems can be remedied by quick action after a member distress is first noticed. Such distress may include sagging or leaking roof systems, cracked slabs, or even displaced door and window frames. After a mild carbon steel passes through its plastic region it enters the third important region—the **strain hardening region.** In the strain hardening region, steel undergoes an ability to increase its stress-carrying capability. This is due to the fact that as the steel deforms, the internal structure of the metal is being dislocated.[1] These dislocations increase as the plastic deformation increases and in turn make it harder for the future dislocations to occur. This concept is easily seen by trying to break a coat hanger by repeatedly bending it back and forth. Doesn't the hanger get "tougher" to bend the last two or three times before it breaks? The last important point in the stress-strain diagram is the highest stress point on the curve, the **ultimate tensile stress, F_u.** This is an important material property that indicates the maximum stress level a member can withstand before breaking. This stress level is also used in portions of steel design.

1.3   Manufacture and Fabrication of Rolled Steel Shapes

The term **rolled** refers to the process whereby structural steel sections are manufactured today. A rolled steel section actually starts out as a large block of red hot steel called an ingot. This block is passed through a successive series of rollers whereby it is gradually formed into its final shape. The properties of the steel section can be further enhanced by additional processes, such as quenching and tempering, which may take place after the initial rolling. Quenching is a rapid cooling of the steel section and tempering is the reheating of the steel to roughly 1150°F. These processes change the microstructure of steel, leading to increases in both strength and hardness.

The first steel I-beams in the United States were rolled in the late 1800s[2]. Today, there are a wide variety of beams and other sections that are commonly rolled (Figure 1–2). These other sections include angles, channels, tees, zees, tubes and plates. Information regarding typical rolled shapes can be obtained from the American Institute of Steel Construction (AISC) *Manual of Steel Construction, Load and Resistance Factor Design*[3]. This manual gives detailed information about section shapes, design examples, design aids, and specifications. References will be made throughout this text to the second edition of the LRFD manual, published in 1994, and it will be advantageous for the student to have access to this manual.

Since this book deals with the basics of steel design, much of the discussion will center about the wide flange shape (W-section) which is the most common structural shape used for beams and columns. (Figure 1–3)

The wide flange section is a shape with the outer edge of its flange approximately parallel to the inner edge. This facilitates the process of connecting members together with high strength bolts. The abbreviation used when calling out a certain W-section on plans or drawings would be as follows:

W 12 × 50

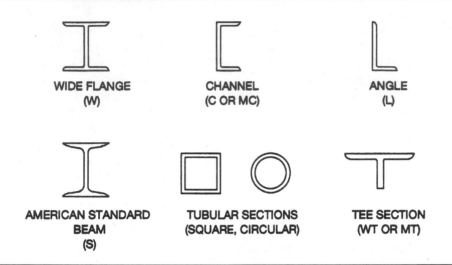

Figure 1–2   Common Rolled Steel Shapes Used in Construction

which means that the rolled shape is a wide flange section, approximately 12 inches in depth, and weighs 50 pounds per foot of length. The depth and weight given are particularly important pieces of information to designers because they are constantly concerned with clearance height, dead weight, and cost per pound of the structure. As the student is required to know more about the cross-sectional properties of specific rolled shapes, they will be referred to the tables in the LRFD manual or an applicable rendition thereof.

Manufactured steel shapes change over time depending on demand. If there is little interest in a certain size, it may be discontinued. On the other hand, if the steel industry recognizes a demand, new standard shapes may be added. An example of this can be found by referring back to the eighth edition of the AISC's *Manual of Steel Construction, Allowable Stress Design*[4], in which the largest W-section was a W 36 × 300 at the time of publication in 1978. Today, because of

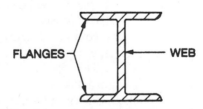

Figure 1–3   The Wide-Flange Section

demand for larger sections, there are a number of W-sections larger than a W 36 × 300, with the heaviest being a W 36 × 848.

Fabrication of rolled steel sections and plates involves the cutting, welding, and drilling of these shapes to facilitate their erection in a steel structure. Fabrication of steel occurs in what is commonly referred to as a *fabricating shop*. Such shops are involved in a variety of activities, all of which aim to prepare the raw steel shapes into their final form.

Some of the activities in a fabricating shop include: the welding together of steel plates to form *plate girders* used in many long-span applications, the drilling of bolt holes in their exact locations for connection purposes, and the cutting of shapes to achieve their proper length and angle of fit.

1.4   SI Unit Usage in the Steel Industry

The International System of Units, the SI System, was adopted in 1960 by the international scientific community to standardize a particular metric system for use around the world. This was done in order to avoid confusion over quite a number of different metric systems which had been used in different countries over the last two hundred years. Although the Metric Conversion Act, passed in 1975, was meant to increase metric usage by the U.S. public, little substantial progress was made until recently.

Likewise, the use of SI units in the U.S. construction industry was virtually nonexistent. However, many federal and state agencies are beginning to mandate metric usage in the development of all their construction documents. An example of this trend is the mandatory use of metric units in all construction projects for the U.S. government's General Services Administration (GSA) starting in 1994. Because of this trend, the American Institute of Steel Construction has published two versions of the second edition of the *Manual of Steel Construction, Load and Resistance Factor Design*, one version using the U.S. customary units and the other based on the International System of Units (SI System).

Much confusion seems to surround the SI System. A major problem seems to be language-related, especially with regard to terms such as *kilogram*.[5] The older metric systems used the term kilogram for both mass and weight applications. The SI System changed the fundamental units of length and mass from centimeter and gram to meter and kilogram. The kilogram is a unit of mass and the new unit of force is referred to as a newton. The newton is defined as:

Unit Force = Unit Mass × Unit Acceleration
1 Newton = 1 Kilogram × 1 meter/second^2

The difference between the U.S. customary system and the SI System is that the U.S. system is based on gravity, where force (pounds, kips, etc.) is the basic unit. The SI System is an *absolute system,* where mass (kilogram) is the basic unit. In order to calculate an object's weight (or force) the SI System multiplies the object's mass by the Earth's gravitational acceleration constant, which is 9.81 meters per second squared (m/sec²). This book displays the example problems in U.S. customary units and displays the SI units in parentheses where applicable. The exercise problems contain many SI unit problems as well. As the student becomes more familiar with the SI System, its usage will seem much less cumbersome. The SI System employs prefixes with their basic units that represent factors of ten. These common prefixes are shown in Table 1–3.

The typical quantities that steel designers utilize are those relating to length, force, and stress. U.S. customary units and their SI counterparts are shown in Table 1–4 along with the conversion factor from U.S. to SI units. This will help the modern designer in the crossover between both systems. The metric equivalents of the many standard steel sections are also included in the tables found in Appendix B. If a complete listing of these metric equivalents is desired, the student is referred to the AISC publication on metric shapes.[6]

Table 1–3 Common SI System Prefixes

Factor	Prefix	Symbol
$.000001 = 10^{-6}$	micro	μ
$.001 = 10^{-3}$	milli	m
$1000 = 10^3$	kilo	K
$1000000 = 10^6$	mega	M
$1000000000 = 10^9$	giga	G

1.5   Types of Steel Structures

Because of its superior strength, quality control, and ease of fabrication, steel is an ideal material for a variety of structure types. Practically every type of structure imaginable has been or can be built with steel. The following paragraphs and Figure 1–4 briefly outline some of the more common structures made from steel.

Wall bearing construction typically utilizes steel members which frame into, or sit on top of, concrete or masonry walls. The steel members are typically rolled-beam sections or perhaps, open web steel joists. These steel members will form the framing of a roof or floor system. A common example of this type of structure is the steel beam located in the basement of many houses, which spans across the foundation and is pocketed into the concrete foundation wall.

Table 1–4 SI System Conversions

Quantity	U.S.	SI	Conversion Factor from US to SI	Conversion Factor from SI to US
Length	Foot	meter	.3048	3.281
	Inch	meter	.0254	39.37
Force	Pound	newton	4.448	.224
	KIP	kilonewton	4.448	.224
Stress	psi	Pascal (N/m²)	6895.	.00145
	ksi	Megapascal	6.895	.145
	psf	Kilopascal	.0478	20.92
Area	sq. in.	sq. mm.	645.2	.00155
Moment of Inertia	in.⁴	mm⁴	416,231	.0000024

Skeleton-frame construction is a common steel building system, and was first used in the erection of the Home Insurance Building in Chicago in 1885. This type of construction consists of multiple numbers of floors and bays and is normally associated with multi-story or office-tower construction. Steel beam members form the support systems for the individual floors, while the steel columns support these beams.

Long-span construction with steel is normally handled by plate girder-, truss-, or arch-type construction systems. Plate girders are most commonly seen as beams on many bridge overpasses. These beams consist of three or more rolled steel plates which are welded together to form the I-section. The depth of a plate girder increases as the span length increases to give the girder more moment resisting capacity. Truss-type structures are very common in bridges and long span roof framing. A truss is made from individual steel members which, ideally, are loaded in only tension or compression. Similar to a plate girder, a truss will generally become deeper as a span length increases to give the truss more load carrying capability. Steel arch structures are more elaborate in design and fabrication than the other types of steel structures, and are typically relegated to bridge structures or structures dependent on aesthetics. An arch is ideally in full compression along its entire length, although other stresses such as bending exist due to other factors in a real arch.

Figure 1–4a Skeleton Frame Construction, Georgia Railroad Bank and Trust Building, Atlanta, Georgia. (Courtesy Bethlehem Steel Corporation.)

Figure 1–4b Plate Girder Construction, Madison Square Garden, New York, New York. (Courtesy Bethlehem Steel Corporation.)

Figure 1–4c Steel Truss Construction, Hawk Falls Bridge, Pennsylvania. (Courtesy Bethlehem Steel Corporation.)

Figure 1–4d Steel Arch Construction, Lewiston-Queenston Bridge, New York. (Courtesy Bethlehem Steel Corporation.)

1.6 Failure in Steel Structures

When most people consider failure of a steel structure, they envision a cata-strophic collapse such as the Tacoma-Narrows Bridge failure outside of Tacoma, Washington in 1940. Practically all engineering students have seen the five minute movie[7] that captured the failure of this immense structure, where the gently swaying superstructure rapidly turned into a violently twisted mass of steel and concrete, resulting in catastrophic collapse.

Although the early theories behind this bridge's collapse dealt with wind turbulence and resonant motion types[8], recent arguments reject these ideas and today's debate now points to self-excitation or nonlinear behavior.[9] In either case, the bottom line is that some unknown or unseen design factor led to this failure. Collapse is not the only type of design failure that occurs—in fact, it might be the least likely in terms of quantity that actually happens. Far more frequent, it is the design failure that affects a project's schedule or the service-ability of a completed structure. Items such as excessive deflection, temperature effects, or ease of erection all can lead to problems that do not cause collapse but will give the designer a multitude of headaches. This leads the designer to face three key points:

1. **Serviceability** of a steel structure is dependent upon the yield point, F_y, of its key members. The stress on a member usually must not surpass this point because that will lead to permanent deformation, and the member will be considered to have failed.
2. The design of a structure must consider **all possible loading cases and other facets of the project.** Stresses imposed by wind, temperature, and seismic activity must be incorporated into the design and the structure must mesh with architectural, mechanical, and environmental aspects of the project. To neglect these concerns may lead to delays and cost overruns, which constitute a design failure.
3. The design must be **practical.** If the structure is only able to be built on paper it is of little use and has again failed due to the poor design.

Adherence to these principles will help the inexperienced designer become a success. The experience and insight of other professionals and construction personnel should always be listened to and evaluated. The hardest of problems can sometimes be solved by the simplest of means.

1.7 The Load and Resistance Factor Design (LRFD) Philosophy

Today, there are two widely recognized philosophies that are being used in the design of steel structures. These are the **Allowable Stress Design (ASD)** method and the **Load and Resistance Factor Design (LRFD)** method, which is the focus of this text.

The most common method for designing steel structures until the late 1980s was the Allowable Stress Design (ASD) method because of its simplicity and proven track record in providing the basis for safe and reliable designs. The ASD philosophy is based on keeping the stresses in a member below some fraction of a specified stress in the steel. By keeping the actual stress levels under a fraction of some specified stress (such as the yield stress, F_y), the ASD method typically provides conservative results. The Allowable Stress Design method has been the primary steel design philosophy used since the introduction of steel as a building material. However, with the AISC's adoption in 1986 of the Load and Resistance Factor Design (LRFD), there is an accepted and increasingly popular alternative.

Introduction to LRFD

Over the last 25 years, the structural design community has been very interested in developing a design procedure which uses probability-based rationale. With the adoption (1986) of the AISC *Load and Resistance Factor Design Specification*, the steel design industry has given its endorsement for such a method. Although Load and Resistance Factor Design (LRFD) has not received the quick and overwhelming acceptance that some in the design community would like [10], many expect this philosophy to achieve greater usage by designers in the near future.

A simplified view of structural mechanics states that when members are loaded they respond by resisting that load. The failure of a member can occur because either the loads on a member are larger than those for which it was designed or because the resistance of the member is smaller than what was anticipated. If we contemplate loads and member resistances, we begin to realize that they are indeed variable over the life of a structure.

As will be discussed in Chapter 2, loads on structures may consist of, among others, dead loads (D), live loads (L), wind loads (W), earthquake loads (E), and snow loads (S). These loads are very different in terms of predictability. The uncertainty of a dead load should be relatively small as compared to the variability associated with the wind loads or earthquake loads. As a designer of a structure, one should have a good handle on the major components of dead load such as self weight, but possibly be less certain of the live load requirements to be placed on the structure 20 years into the future. Therefore, one must logically state that live loads are more unpredictable than dead loads. (The reader should remember that in the ASD methodology a distinction between the type of loads was never discussed as part of the design process.)

The resistance of a member to applied loads is also a variable based on manufacturing, age, and dimensions. When designers specify A36 steel, this means that it is *supposed* to have a minimum yield strength (F_y) equal to 36 ksi. But there is some small percentage of A36 steel members with a yield strength less than 36 ksi. The resistance of some steel members may also decrease with age because of processes such as corrosion which may reduce the effective cross-sectional area of resistance.

The LRFD method approaches structural steel design using a probabilistic approach, incorporating the variability of loads and member resistance, to arrive at a more rational and (hopefully) cost effective solution.

Basic Concepts of Probability and Failure

Probability is the chance or likelihood that a predefined occurrence will actually happen. The frequency of a variable event is the number of times it occurs in a set of observations. Any variable event can be looked at in terms of probability, whether that event is winning the lottery, selecting an ace out of a deck of cards, or having a structure collapse.

The probability of a random event occurring can be mathematically defined by an equation referred to as a probability function. A probability function can be graphically depicted as a curve, relating the frequency of an event occurring with a particular value of a random variable. For instance, when rolling a pair of dice there are 36 possible combinations which may occur. If one was interested in rolling a combination equal to two, they would realize that only one possible combination exists to give that value. Therefore, the frequency that the event (rolling the dice) at that particular value (the value of two) would have a 1 out of 36 probability of occurring. Likewise, if the designer is interested in a probabilistic approach to design, a solid foundation of the most basic probability function must be understood.

One of the most common probability distributions in statistics is the **normal distribution curve** or the **normal curve**. The graph of this curve is very important in the field of probability because it has been found to accurately represent the frequency of occurrence in almost all random variables. When defining the normal distribution curve it is imperative that the student have some familiarity with terms such as mean, standard deviation, median and mode. The **mean** is the average value (or the value of the random variable with the highest probability of occurring) in a set of observations (Figure 1–5). The mean can essentially be thought of as the *expected value* of the random variable, although it will not always be the value that the variable assumes (Figure 1–5). The **standard deviation** of a probability function measures the spread or scatter of the random variable values away from the mean value. A probability function can take on many different shapes which represent the different "spreads" or "scatter" of data about the mean, although they may have the same mean value (Figure 1–6). The **median** is the value in a set of data which separates the lower half from the upper half and the **mode** is the value which is repeated most often in the set.

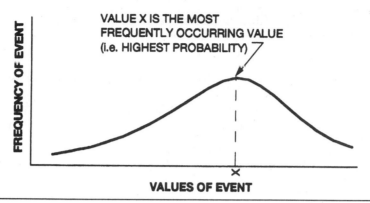

Figure 1–5   Typical Probability Function

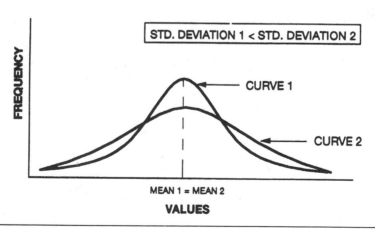

Figure 1–6   Different Probability Functions with the Same Mean

The normal distribution curve is unique because it not only accurately represents the frequency of occurrence in many random events but also has the following features (See Figure 1–7).

- Symmetrical about the x-axis with the mean, mode, and median occurring at its peak.
- Asymptotically approaches the x-axis in each direction.
- Area under the curve equals one.

These unique features of the normal distribution curve are used as the basis of many probabilstic models and the random variables associated with each, but how does this relate to the design of structural steel members?

If we think of the failure mechanism in structures we can begin to see it depends on two different factors, the strength or **resistance** of a member and the **loads** acting on that member. From a statistical perspective the two factors can be viewed independent random variables neither being time dependent. In reality, the resistance of a member generally decreases with time while loads tend to increase.[11] Failure can be simplified by being viewed as occurring when the structural resistance of a member is exceeded by the load effects on that member. In Figure 1–8 we see two normal curves representing the **structural resistance, R,** and **load effects, Q.** The reader must realize that in the realm of probability, a chance exists for a member's resistance to occur anywhere along the R curve and that a load effect can likewise occur anywhere along the Q curve. When an event occurs whereby $Q > R$, there is no margin of safety and the member can be considered to have failed. The probability of failure can be viewed as a function of the area under the load (Q) and resistance (R) curves. Realizing that normal curves are asymptotic to the x-axis, the student should be aware that the curves **always** intersect. The shaded area below the intersection of the two curves in

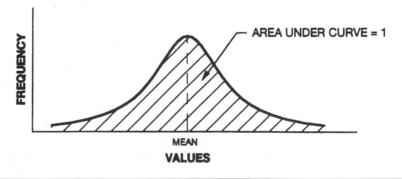

Figure 1–7 Representation of the Normal Probability Function

Figure 1–8 represents failure, and this possibility of failure exists because no matter how strong our member, there is some chance (however infinitely small) that failure might occur.

Limit States

When a member no longer functions as it was designed, it is said to have exceeded a limit state. In the LRFD approach (as in ASD), there are two types of limit states which are discussed—strength limit states and serviceability limit states. Designers are primarily concerned with strength limit states such as load carrying capability (which may specifically refer to moment capacity, shear capacity, or plastic hinge formation). Serviceability limit states refer primarily to deflection, vibration, and drift. The focus of most codes is on the strength limit states because of the great concern for public safety. Serviceability requirements will deal with the quality of acceptable behavior of a member and depend greatly on the designer's judgment as well as the specific needs of the individual project.

In LRFD the general strength limit state, which should not be exceeded, is referred to as the safety margin Z. If the following equation accurately describes structural capacity,

$$Z = R - Q$$

where R = resistance function

Q = load function

then a limit state is violated when $Z < 0$.

Limit state violations in Allowable Stress Design (ASD) were expressed in terms of a factor of safety against a particular failure. From a design perspective, the major shortcoming with the ASD philosophy is that the factors of safety for various behaviors (bending, shear, etc.) all have different values. These values emerged from years of practical design experience and not from a rational basis.

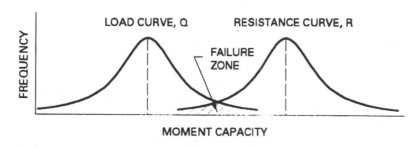

Figure 1–8   Probabilistic Representation of Structural Adequacy

This has led to designs in which identical members experiencing different conditions (such as different loading types) would actually be very different in terms of a safety margin against failure. This is not to say that the ASD method has worked poorly; on the contrary, it has worked well. But the philosophy, while working well in terms of public safety, is providing nonuniform reliability to all members.

In the LRFD method, a measure of structural integrity called the **reliability index** ß is used in place of the traditional factor of safety. The reliability index, ß, is the number of standard deviations where the mean value of a combined resistance and loading probability curve (expressed as $ln(R/Q)$) lies away from the point of failure (where $Z < 0$). The higher this reliability index becomes is essentially equivalent to a wider spread between failure and the mean value of $R - Q$ (or $ln(R/Q)$). A typical strength limit state violation can then be regarded as a probability of the safety margin, Z, being less than zero. This combined normal curve can be seen in Figure 1–9.

One of the main goals of the LRFD philosophy is the establishment of uniform reliability (or safety margin) between all types of members subjected to all types and combination of loads.

Load and Resistance Factor Design Philosophy (LRFD)

LRFD is unique as a philosophy because it establishes a uniform reliability for all members in a structure based on a probabilistic approach to load factors and resistances. Pioneered by Galambos[12,13], the LRFD method strives to achieve the proper emphasis on both loads and different structural behaviors so as to design more cost-effective and reliable structures.

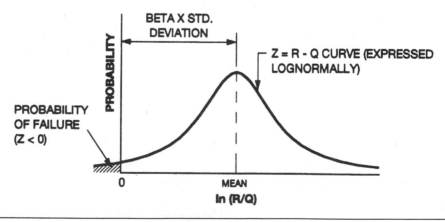

Figure 1–9   Probabilistic Representation of Structural Adequacy on a Combined Resistance-Load Function

The design method for LRFD boils down to one general equation:

Design Strength $\geq$ Required Resistance

or

$$\phi R_n \geq \Sigma \delta_i Q_i$$

where

ϕ = resistance factor ($\phi < 1$)

R_n = nominal resistance of member

δ_i = Load factors ($\delta_i > 1$)

Q_i = different load effects

The required resistance is computed using the highest of several different load combinations as set forth in the LRFD specifications. These load combinations will be discussed further in the next chapter. The required resistance will be the factored moment, shear, or axial load which are applied to a particular member.

The load factors used for the required resistance by the AISC specification were developed by the American National Standards Institute[14] (ANSI A58.1, now ASCE 7–88) for the purpose of specifying minimum acceptable load criteria for buildings. The load factors for individual load types (dead, live, wind) stem from the previously mentioned reliability index. Target levels for ß range from 3.0 for members under dead and live loads to 1.75 for members under these loads combined with earthquake loading.

The nominal resistance of a member is the calculated strength based on standard techniques that will be developed fully in the following chapters. It should be realized that member capacities will utilize full material strengths (such as F_y) rather than using allowable levels.

The resistance factors are developed based on the variability of each resistance with the goal of establishing a uniform reliability between members. For example, the ø factors will be different between columns and beams, because column behavior is more sensitive to factors such as initial crookedness and, therefore, will be given a lower resistance factor. These resistance factors will be unique to each type of behavior for which we are designing and also help to calibrate member resistance in LRFD to the more traditional ASD values.

Advantages of LRFD

The following items are some of the main advantages of using the LRFD method for designing steel structures:

- The probabilistic approach provides a more uniform reliability in all structures subjected to many types of loading conditions. The method does away with many arbitrary practices, such as treating dead and live loads as equivalent, thereby leading to a more rational design.

■ Provides steel designers with an option that is similar to the strength design method presently used in reinforced concrete design. This flexibility will give designers another tool in their search for a safe and economical design.

■ Typically provides better economy as the dead loads make up a greater percentage on a given structure. Because dead loads are less variable by nature than live loads, a lower load factor is used. This may lead to a reduction in member size and therefore better economy. This cost effectiveness depends on the particular member, structure type, and span length but is generally better than the ASD method as dead loads increase.

■ Provides designers a greater degree of flexibility in handling special cases. Unusual load cases or special design situations may call for designers to modify the usual design procedures. Such cases can be handled easily by modifying the load or resistance factors at the designer's judgment. Also resistance factors and load factors may be changed easily as future research dictates the necessity thereof.

1.8   Summary

Steel has been widely used in the construction industry throughout this century because of its strength, durability, and economy. Many different steel shapes are rolled to satisfy the demands of the steel construction industry and new shapes are developed every year. Design of steel structures focuses on providing safety, practicality, and economy for a wide array of buildings and structures. The Load and Resistance Factor Design (LRFD) method for structural steel design was adopted by the AISC in 1986 as the first probabilistic design method used in steel design. This method views the loads on a member and the member's capacity as random variables that change throughout the structure's lifetime. By using probability-based logic, the LRFD method assigns load and resistance factors to structural members in order to arrive at a safe and rational design.

EXERCISES

1. Investigate the uses of an American Standard beam (S-section) and list the difference between this shape and a wide flange shape. Why is the wide flange shape preferred over the S-section in modern construction?

2. List the meanings of these different designations.

—— C 15 × 50

—— L 7 × 4 × ½

—— HP 14 × 117

—— WT 12 × 47

3. How does the element carbon affect the quality of steel? What is the usual percentage of carbon in mild carbon steel members?
4. Why is the plastic region on steel's stress-strain curve important? What impact does this region have on steel's behavior as it begins to fail?
5. Compare the LRFD method of steel design to the Strength Design method which is presently used in reinforced concrete design. How long has the American Concrete Institute endorsed this method? How is the Strength Design method different from the LRFD method?
6. Research live load to dead load ratios (L/D) involved in using the LRFD method for various behaviors. In general, what L/D ratio do the LRFD method and the ASD method become approximately equivalent?

REFERENCES

1. Van Vlack, Lawrence, *Elements of Material Science and Engineering,* Addison-Wesley Publishing, Reading, MA, 1980, p. 204.
2. McGuire, W., *Steel Structures,* Prentice-Hall, Inc. Englewood Cliffs, NJ, 1968, p. 19.
3. AISC. *Manual of Steel Construction, Load and Resistance Factor Design,* Second Edition, Chicago, American Institute of Steel Construction, 1994.
4. AISC. *Manual of Steel Construction, Allowable Stress Design,* Ninth Edition, Chicago, American Institute of Steel Construction, 1989.
5. Everett L. Boyd, "Pounds, Kilos and Newtons," *Civil Engineering,* September 1991, pp. 72–73.
6. AISC. *Metric Properties of Structural Shapes with Dimensions According to ASTM A6M,* Chicago, American Institute of Steel Construction, 1992.
7. "Tacoma Narrows Bridge Collapse," Franklin Miller, Ohio State University, Department of Photography, Motion Picture Division, 1963.
8. Farquharson, F. B., "Aerodynamic Stability of Suspension Bridges," University of Washington Engineering Experiment Station, Bulletin No. 116, 1941.
9. Berreby, David, "The Great Bridge Controversy," *Discover,* February 1992, pp. 26–33.
10. Aine Brazil, Robert DeScenza, and Thomas Scarangello, "LRFD: Still Waiting," *Civil Engineering,* July 1991, pp.46–48.
11. R. E. Melchers, *Structural Reliability Analysis and Prediction,* Ellis Horwood Limited Publishers, New York, 1987, p. 32.
12. Theodore Galambos and M. K. Ravindra, "Proposed Criteria for Load and Resistance Factor Design," *Engineering Journal,* AISC, 1981, Vol. 18, No. 3 pp. 74–82.
13. M. K. Ravindra and Theodore Galambos, "Load and Resistance Factor Design for Steel", *Journal of the Structural Division,* ASCE, September 1978, pp.1337–1353.

14. ASCE, *American Society of Civil Engineers Minimum Design Loads for Buildings and Other Structures,* ASCE 7–88 (formerly ANSI A58.1), ASCE, New York, 1990.

2

SPECIFICATIONS, BUILDING CODES, AND TYPES OF LOADS

2.1   Introduction

Before a designer begins the design process, a good knowledge of the requirements which govern building construction is required. The designer must be fully
aware of the laws and regulations that are enforced in a particular locality, as
well as the design requirements when using a particular type of material. The
application of these regulations when constructing a building is one of the
designer's primary duties and one of the most important regulations for a
structural designer is the knowledge of how to design a building under the
application of different loading cases. These topics will be the focus of the
upcoming sections.

2.2   Specifications

Many organizations exist, both in the U.S. and around the world, to promote the
use of a particular material in the construction market. These organizations
strive to improve and advance the use of their material through extensive
research into its engineering properties and behavior. The usual end result of this

research is the publication of a specification for the convenience of designers and engineers.

These specifications typically contain suggested design methods that hopefully will ensure a safe and economical design. They also promote the information that the organization believes to be the best engineering practice at the time of publication. The evolvement of these practices will take place continuously over a number of years. The prudent designer should allow these specifications to guide his or her judgment and make a serious effort to understand the principles behind the equations found in a particular specification. The judgment of a good designer is still the most important factor in design because no specification will cover every possible situation. The responsibility of designing a safe structure rests solely with the design engineers and their supporting staff. A specification is not a magic shield for the designer to hide behind if problems occur, it simply represents the best design information which the promoting organization has to offer.

For structural steel design of buildings in the U.S., the principal design specification is the American Institute of Steel Construction's (AISC) *Manual of Steel Construction*. This manual contains not only the AISC design specifications, but also many other useful design tools such as tables and charts. Other commonly used specifications in the U.S. are listed below. These organizations represent the best body of knowledge for a design engineer to utilize in their respective areas.

American Concrete Institute (ACI), P.O. Box 19150 Redford Station, Detroit, MI, *Building Code Requirements for Reinforced Concrete*.

American Association of State and Highway Transportation Officials (AASHTO), 444 North Capitol Street, N.W., Washington, DC, *Standard Specification for Highway Bridges*.

American Railway Engineering Association (AREA), 50 F Street, N.W., Washington, DC, *Manual for Railway Engineering*.

American Institute of Timber Construction (AITC), 333 West Hampden Avenue, Englewood, CO, *Timber Construction Manual*.

American Welding Society (AWS), P.O. Box 351040, Miami, FL, *Structural Welding Code*.

2.3   Building Codes

Building codes, in contrast to specifications, are wide ranging documents covering many areas of a project such as design loadings, occupancy limits, plumbing, electrical requirements, and fire protection. Building codes are adopted by states, cities, or other governmental bodies as a legal means for protecting the public's health and welfare. The building code for a particular state, city, or county will constitute a broad set of rules by which all construction must adhere. Because of this, a designer must be knowledgeable of the applicable building codes as a project begins.

Many times, a particular locality will have more than one code to which construction must conform. It is not unusual to have a project located within city limits that must conform to, not only the city's building code, but also the county and state building codes as well.

Although there is no single national building code, there are organizations whose purpose is to write **model building codes**. These model codes are sometimes integrated, fully or partially, by many state or local building codes. The most common model codes are listed below.

Building Officials and Codes Administrators International Incorporated (BOCA), *National Building Code*[1].

International Conference of Building Officials, *Uniform Building Code*[2].

Southern Building Code Congress International, *Standard Building Code*[3].

2.4   The Purpose of Design Loads

Almost all building codes provide chapters dedicated to the proper assignment and application of minimum design loads and load combinations on a structure. These design loads are usually referred to as **service loads** and are provided to ensure that, under normal conditions, the structure will be both safe and serviceable. The magnitude of these service loads might seem to be rather large and conservative, but the building must be designed to resist the maximum load as forecast over a certain period of time. It would be foolish to design a structure using loads that are considered to be typical everyday loads. Aren't we glad when the wind gusts to 45 mph during a (rather typical) spring storm, that structures were not designed for an everyday wind gust of 15 mph? The designer hopes the structure remains serviceable and functioning even in the event of the loads reaching (or exceeding) these service values. An event such as an overload condition is a case when the size of the safety margin may be reduced (see Chapter 1) and, therefore, proper member design becomes extremely important.

Many maximum design live loads, used in building codes, are based on a return period of 50 to 100 years. This suggests that these maximum loads are expected to occur once every 50 or 100 years. An excellent guide to design loads and their application is the American Society of Civil Engineer's *Minimum Design Loads for Buildings and Other Structures* (ASCE 7–88)[4].

2.5   Types of Loads

Building structures are designed to resist many types of loads such as dead loads, live loads, wind loads, snow loads, and earthquake loads. The complete design must consider all effects of these loads, both individually and in combination with one another. A short explanation of these loads and their influence in design is explored in the following paragraphs.

Dead Loads

Dead loads are all permanent loads imposed on a structure. Such loads include the structure's selfweight, piping, conduit, permanent equipment, and permanent furniture.

Dead loads are estimated in the preliminary design phase and are set as the design is completed. Although dead loads are not precisely known as the design process begins, an experienced designer can estimate section sizes and structure weight based on previous designs. After a structure is built, these dead loads should not change radically over a structure's life unless a renovation of the structure is undertaken. In steel design, the calculation of self weight is made even easier by the standard designations of rolled shapes. If it is known that a building frame consists of 300 lineal feet of W 12 × 87's, the calculation of the approximate weight of that steel frame is as follows;

300 ft. × 87 lbs./ft. = 26,100 lbs.

It is imperative that the designer has the ability to calculate the applied dead loads in a structure due to the weight of the various building materials. The weights and densities of various construction materials can be found in the Appendix of most building codes. An abbreviated list is shown in Table 2–1. The following example will demonstrate the calculation of dead loads on a rolled beam.

Table 2–1   Typical Recommended Dead Loads for Construction Materials.

Densities		Weights	
Steel	490 #/ft³	Asphalt shingles	2 #/ft²
Reinforced concrete	150 #/ft³	Four-ply felt and gravel	
Dry soil	90–120 #Ift³	composition roof	5.5 #/ft²
Brick masonry	100–130 #/ft³	20-gauge metal deck	2.5 #/ft²
Stone Masonry	140–175 #/ft³	Plywood (per 1/8" thickness)	.4 #/ft²
Water	62.4 #/ft³	7/8" hardwood flooring	4 #/ft²
Seasoned wood (pine)	37 #/ft³	2 × 8 floor @ 16" spacing,	
Seasoned wood (oak)	47 #/ft³	unplastered	5 #/ft²
Ceramic tile	150 #/ft³	2 × 10 floor @ 16" spacing	6 #/ft²
Plywood	36 #/ft³	Drywall	4 #/ft²
		2 × 4 wall, unplastered	4 #/ft²
		Ceramic tile on 1" mortar bed	23 #/ft²

EXAMPLE 2.1

Calculate the dead load per foot on the rolled steel section as shown below. The beam in question has a 6 foot wide distributive floor area loading it.

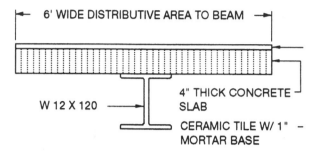

The load on the beam as shown comes from three sources: the self weight of the beam, the 4" thick concrete slab, and ceramic tile on the 1" mortar base. The calculation per foot of beam length can be performed as follows:
Steel beam:

 120 lb. per lineal foot = 120 lb./ft.

Concrete slab:

 6 ft. wide × (4 in./12 in./ft.) × 150 lb./ft.^{3} = 300 lb./ft.

Ceramic Tile on 1" Base:

 6 ft. wide × 23 lb./ft.^{2} = 138 lb./ft.

 Total Dead Load = 120 + 300 + 138 = 558 lb./ft.

Live Loads

Live loads are simply instantaneous or moveable loads, produced in a structure by the occupancy of people or mobile equipment, such as furniture. Such loads can vary in magnitude, location, and duration. Actual values of live load are hard to predict, so most building codes will assign a minimum live load for floor or roof areas (in pounds per square foot, psf) based on intended use of a building. A typical building code might assign live load values as shown in Table 2–2.

 Most of these live loads have been developed as a result of practical experience over the last century, because they have proven to yield safe and serviceable results when correctly applied. The designer should consult the local building code for a tabular listing such as the one shown in Table 2–2. Remember that the building code will suggest these loads as the *minimum,* leaving the use of higher values to the discretion of the designer, should the increase be deemed necessary.

Table 2–2 Suggested Values for Minimum Uniformly Distributed Live Loads. (Reprinted from the ASCE's *Minimum Design Loads for Buildings and Other Structures*, ASCE 7–88, with permission from the American Society of Civil Engineers.)

Occupancy or Use	Live Load (lb/ft²)	Occupancy or Use	Live Load (lb./ft.²)
Air-conditioning (machine space)	200 *	Kitchens, other than domestic	150*
Amusement park structure	100*	Laboratories, scientific	100
Attic, nonresidential		Laundries	150*
Nonstorage	25	Libraries, corridors	80*
Storage	80*	Manufacturing, ice	300
Bakery	150	Morgue	125
Balcony		Office buildings	
Exterior	100	Business machine equipment	100*
Interior (fixed seats)	60	Files (see file room)	
Interior (movable seats)	100	Printing plants	
Boathouse, floors	100*	Composing rooms	100
Boiler room, framed	300	Linotype rooms	100
Broadcasting studio	100	Paper storage	**
Catwalks	25	Press rooms	150*
Ceiling, accessible furred	10#	Public rooms	100
Cold storage		Railroad tracks	‡‡
No overhead system	250‡	Ramps	
Overhead system		Driveway (see garages)	
Floor	150	Pedestrian	
Roof	250	Seaplane (see hangars)	
Computer equipment	150*	Rest rooms	60
Courtrooms	50–100	Rinks	
Dormitories		Ice skating	250
Nonpartitioned	80	Roller skating	100
Partitioned	40	Storage, hay or grain	300 *
Elevator machine room	150*	Telephone exchange	150 *
Fan room	150 *	Theaters:	
File room		Dressing rooms	40
Duplicating equipment	150 *	Grid-iron floor or fly gallery	
Card	125 *	Grating	60
Letter	80*	Well beams, 250 lb/ft per pair	
Foundries	600*	Header beams, 1000 lb/ft	
Fuel rooms, framed	400	Pin rail, 250 lb/ft	
Garages—trucks	§	Projection room	100
Greenhouses	150	Toilet rooms	60
Hangars	150§	Transformer rooms	200 *
Incinerator charging floor	100	Vaults, in offices	250 *

Source: Reprinted from ASCE, "Minimum Design Loads for Buildings and Other Structures," ASCE 7–88, with permission from the American Society of Civil Engineers.

*Use weight of actual equipment or stored material when greater.

EXAMPLE 2.2

Using the same beam as in Example 2.1, calculate the total live and dead load per foot of beam length if the beam is part of the floor in the projection room of a movie theater.

The dead loads remain the same as in Example 2.1 at 558 lb/ft. The live load can be found in Table 2–2 as 100 psf. Therefore, the live load per foot is calculated as:

100 psf × 6 ft. = 600 lb./ft.

The total dead and live load is:

600 lb./ft. + 558 lb./ft. = 1158 lb./ft.

Wind Loads

An understanding of wind loads is important for all types of structures, but is extremely important as structures increase in height with respect to their lateral width. Structures that are tall and slender, such as skyscrapers, chemical tanks, and cooling towers for power plants, are very likely to have their design influenced by wind loadings. The behavior of wind forces on structures having unusual shapes or site conditions warrant special consideration and may possibly be recommended for wind tunnel investigation. Some studies have suggested that wind pressures may be amplified by a factor of 2.0 on structures under certain site conditions such as a low building in the presence of taller, adjacent building.[5]

The wind pressure on a structure is assumed to be of uniform intensity based on the velocity pressure (in psf) obtained from the **basic wind speed**, V, which is taken at a distance of 33 feet (10 meters) above the ground. Although wind pressures can be measured at various locations, many building codes use a distance of 33 feet as a standard distance above the ground for measuring wind speed. These speeds are taken from a chart such as that shown in Figure 2–1. The typical expression for wind pressure is calculated from the following equation:

$$q_z = .00256 \, K_z (IV)^2$$

where

q_z = pressure at height z above ground, psf

V = basic wind speed (100 year wind) taken from Figure 2–1 or similar chart

I = structure importance factor

K_z = velocity pressure coefficient

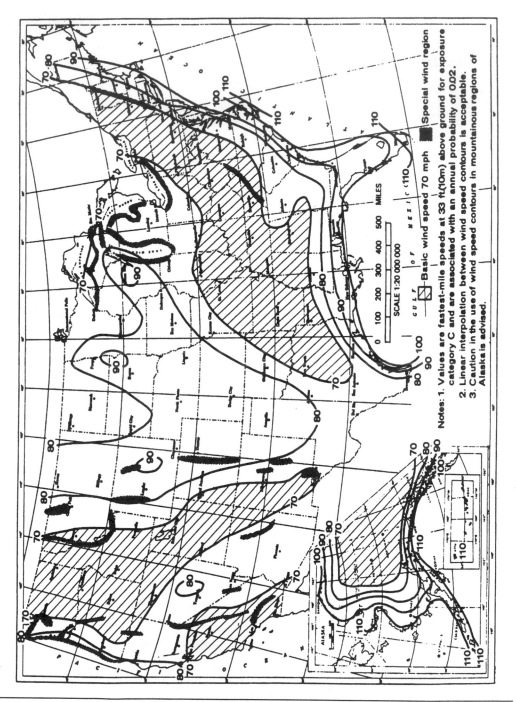

Figure 2–1 Basic Design Wind Speeds in the United States. (Reprinted from the ASCE's *Minimum Design Loads for Buildings and Other Structures*, ASCE 7–88, with permission from the American Society of Civil Engineers.)

The **importance factor** I is used to assign a value that corresponds to a structure's basic function. Building codes generally categorize structures in terms of its function and assign a factor based on this criterion (See Table 2–3 and Table 2–4). Those structures that are considered essential facilities (hospitals, fire stations, etc.) will have a higher importance factor assigned and therefore will be designed to more stringent load cases.

The **velocity pressure coefficient,** K_z, is based on the exposure provided by the surrounding terrain and is given in Table 2–5. The four conditions of exposure represent conditions of diminishing shelter from wind forces, with *Exposure B* and *Exposure C* used by most building codes. Exposure B represents surrounding terrain that have buildings or forests of 20 feet or more in height, covering at least 20% of the area in a distance of 1 mile from the site. Exposure C represents sites that have a generally open and flat terrain for a distance of a half mile or more. The following example illustrates the calculation of the basic wind pressure using the above technique.

EXAMPLE 2.3

Calculate the basic wind pressure for the state of Kentucky on a structure at an elevation of 20 feet above the ground. The structure is a hospital located in flat, open terrain.

To begin with, we must find the basic wind speed for the state of Kentucky from Figure 2–1. This shows a basic wind speed of 70 miles per hour. Next, the importance factor for this structure should be found. A hospital is a Category III structure, and since it is located away from an oceanline, the importance factor is 1.07 as shown in Table 2–4. The velocity pressure coefficient is based on the structure's exposure condition, which for this hospital corresponds to Exposure C. The velocity pressure coefficient at 20 feet can be found from Table 2–5 as 0.87. Based on this information we can find the basic wind pressure at 20 feet, q_{20}. "As shown at the top of page 33."

$V = 70$ mph
$I = 1.07$
$K_{20} = 0.87$
$q_{20} = .00256(0.87)[(1.07)(70)]^2 = 12.5$ psf

It should be noted that the values found in the above tables are from the References[4] and are subject to local state and governmental modifications.

Other factors that influence this basic pressure include coefficients for wind gust and shape factor. The basic wind pressure is assumed to act uniformly along the walls of a structure, generally pressing against the windward wall and causing suction on the leeward wall. The basic wind pressure on the roof can be either upward or downward depending on the roof shape, structure shape, and

Table 2–3 Classification of Structures for Wind, Snow, and Earthquakes Loads. Reprinted from the ASCE's *Minimum Design Loads for Buildings and Other Structures*, ASCE 7–88, with permission from the American Society of Civil Engineers.)

Nature of occupancy	Category
All buildings and structures except those listed below	I
Buildings and structures where the primary occupancy is one in which more than 300 people congregate in one area	II
Buildings and structures designated as essential facilities, including, but not limited to:	III
Hospital and other medical facilities having surgery or emergency treatment areas	
Fire or rescue and police stations	
Structures and equipment in government	
Communication centers and other facilities required for emergency response	
Power stations and other utilities required in an emergency	
Structures having critical national defense capabilities	
Designated shelters for hurricanes	
Buildings and structures that represent a low hazard to human life in the event of failure, such as agricultural buildings certain temporary facilities, and minor storage facilities	IV

Table 2–4 Importance Factors, *I* (Reprinted from the ASCE's *Minimum Design Loads for Buildings and Other Structures*, ASCE 7–88, with permission from the American Society of Civil Engineers.)

Category*	*I*	
	100 miles from hurricane oceanline and in other areas	At hurricane oceanline
I	1.00	1.05
II	1.07	1.11
III	1.07	1.11
IV	0.95	1.00

*See Table 2–3

NOTES:
(1) The building and structure classification categories are listed in Table 1.
(2) For regions between the hurricane oceanline and 100 miles inland the importance factor *I* shall be determined by linear interpolation.
(3) Hurricane oceanlines are the Atlantic and Gulf of Mexico coastal areas.

Table 2–5 Velocity Exposure Coefficient, K_z. (Reprinted from the ASCE's *Minimum Design Loads for Buildings and Other Structures,* ASCE 7–88, with permission from the American Society of Civil Engineers.)

Height above ground level, z (feet)	K_z			
	Exposure A	Exposure B	Exposure C	Exposure D
0 – 15	0.12	0.37	0.80	1.20
20	0.15	0.42	0.87	1.27
25	0.17	0.46	0.93	1.32
30	0.19	0.50	0.98	1.37
40	0.23	0.57	1.06	1.46
50	0.27	0.63	1.13	1.52
60	0.30	0.68	1.19	1.58
70	0.33	0.73	1.24	1.63
80	0.37	0.77	1.29	1.67
90	0.40	0.82	1.34	1.71
100	0.42	0.86	1.38	1.75
120	0.48	0.93	1.45	1.81
140	0.53	0.99	1.52	1.87
160	0.58	1.05	1.58	1.92
180	0.63	1.11	1.63	1.97
200	0.67	1.16	1.68	2.01
250	0.78	1.28	1.79	2.10
300	0.88	1.39	1.88	2.18
350	0.98	1.49	1.97	2.25
400	1.07	1.58	2.05	2.31
450	1.16	1.67	2.12	2.36
500	1.24	1.75	2.18	2.41

Note: Linear interpolation for intermediate values of height z is acceptable.

direction of loading (Figure 2–2). Generally, it is assumed that on roofs of steeper slopes, the wind pressure will push on the windward side and cause suction on the leeward side, while on a roof of a smaller slope the wind forces will cause a suction over its entire length. The influence of these factors on the basic wind pressure are not within the scope of this text; however, extensive coverage of wind behavior is cited in References 9 and 10 at the end of the chapter.

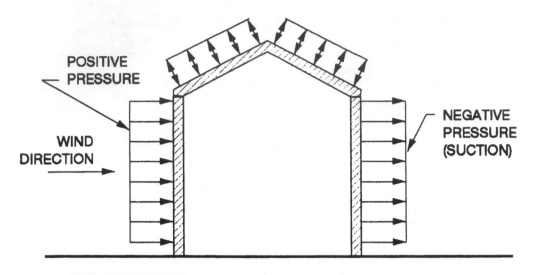

Figure 2–2   Typical Wind Pressures on a Structure.

Snow Loads

Snow loads are handled much in the same way as wind loads; that is, the basic value (termed ground snow load) is taken from isolines on a map such as the one shown in Figure 2–3. This ground snow load value can then be modified by coefficients that account for exposure, structure importance, and whether the building is heated or otherwise. For example, if a building is located in open terrain, the basic ground snow value would be reduced because of the probability that winds would prevent a large accumulation of snow. For more information on these modifiers, refer to the ASCE *Minimum Design Loads for Buildings and Other Structures*.

Other factors that must be taken into account are the slope of the roof and profile of adjacent roofs or structures. Both of these items can affect the depth of snow accumulation due to the possibility of snow drifts. Steeper roofs accumulate less snow, but lower adjacent roofs have severe snow drift potential. Parapet wall and other roof projections also can lead to severe drifting. Most codes take

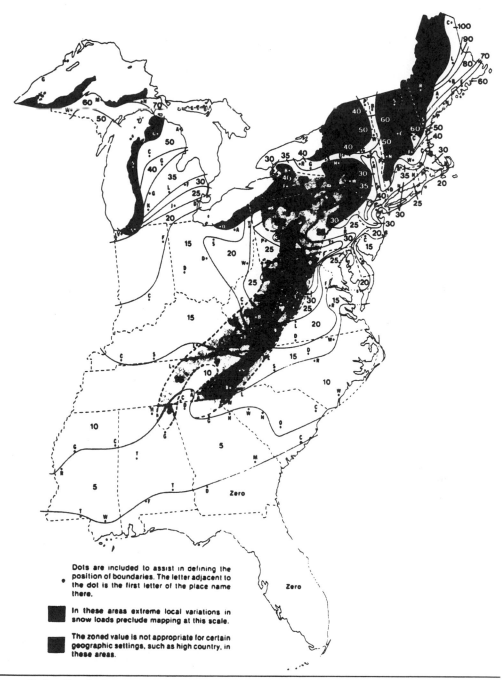

Dots are included to assist in defining the position of boundaries. The letter adjacent to the dot is the first letter of the place name there.

In these areas extreme local variations in snow loads preclude mapping at this scale.

The zoned value is not appropriate for certain geographic settings, such as high country, in these areas.

Figure 2–3 Basic Design Snow Loads for the Continental United States (in pounds per square foot). (Reprinted from the ASCE's *Minimum Design Loads for Buildings and Other Structures,* ASCE 7–88, with permission from the American Society of Civil Engineers.)

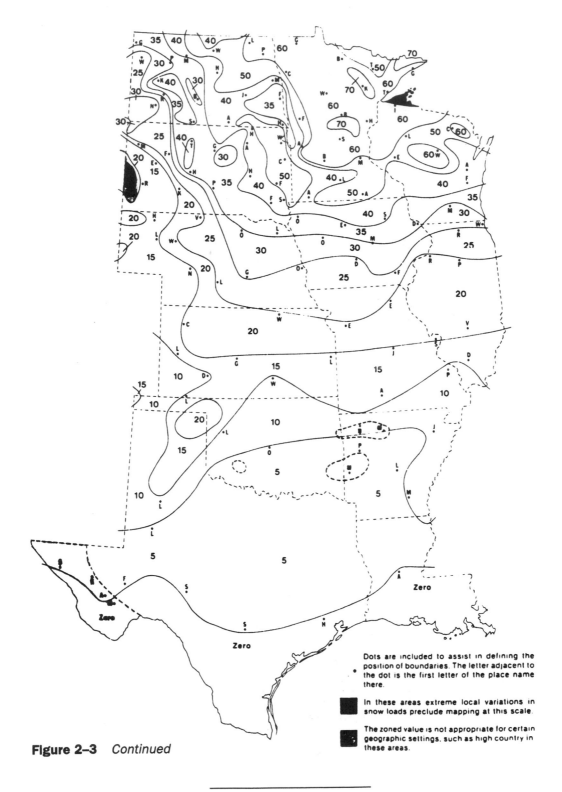

Figure 2–3 *Continued*

Dots are included to assist in defining the position of boundaries. The letter adjacent to the dot is the first letter of the place name there.

In these areas extreme local variations in snow loads preclude mapping at this scale.

The zoned value is not appropriate for certain geographic settings. such as high country in these areas.

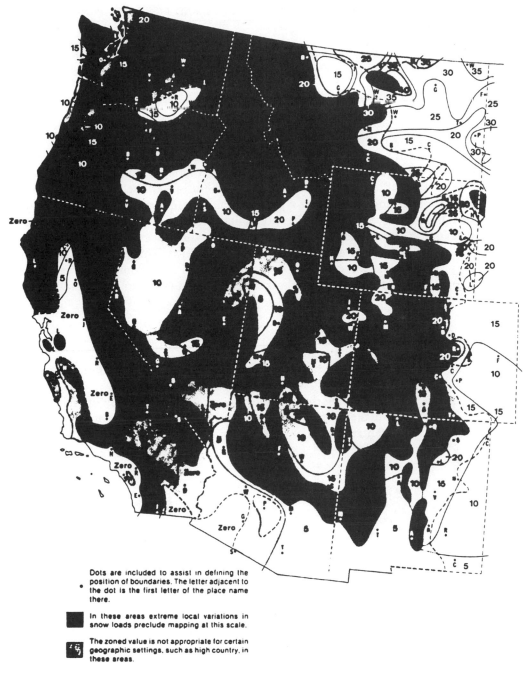

Dots are included to assist in defining the position of boundaries. The letter adjacent to the dot is the first letter of the place name there.

In these areas extreme local variations in snow loads preclude mapping at this scale.

The zoned value is not appropriate for certain geographic settings, such as high country, in these areas.

Figure 2–3 *Continued*

this into account by placing a snow "surcharge" in these particular areas (Figure 2–4).

Earthquake Loads

Although severe earthquakes have been recorded throughout history, the building code requirements regarding the structural design to resist earthquakes is a rather recent phenomena.[6]

An earthquake is a sudden release of energy along a fault line. This release of energy sets off both horizontal and vertical vibrations of the ground. The vertical vibrations or shock waves are typically counteracted through the gravity loads of the building's self weight. The horizontal movements are of greater concern because they tend to move the base of the structure out from underneath it, thus causing what is referred to as base shear (Figure 2–5). This base shear is typically approximated as an equivalent static lateral load in building codes to simplify the analysis. This lateral base shear is calculated in the following formula:

$$V = \frac{ZIC}{R_w} W$$

where

V = total base shear to be distributed as lateral loads over floor levels as per code.

Z = factor reflecting the possible peak ground acceleration of an earthquake occurring in a particular region. A higher number representing a greater acceleration. For example much of California is

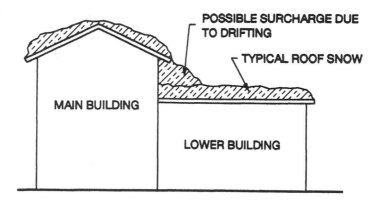

Figure 2–4 Additional Load from Potential Snow Drifts on Lower Adjacent Roofs.

located in Zone 4 (See Figure 2–6) which is assigned the highest acceleration coefficient in any building code.

I = Factor representing the importance of the structure. Hospitals, fire stations and other critical emergency structures are given a higher factor.

C = Coefficient relating to the structure's natural frequency and soil conditions. Building with smaller frequencies tend not to match the frequencies of a normal earthquake, and this is desirable because resonant behavior is avoided.

R_w = Response modification factor reflecting the reduction of a structure's response due to damping and inelasticity.

W = The structure's dead weight under seismic conditions

For a look at the coefficients assigned to each of these earthquake factors, refer to your state building code.

The application of a static load gives only a rough approximation of the forces applied to a structure by an earthquake. Other methods, called *dynamic methods,* have been developed to more closely approximate the true force of an earthquake. A common dynamic method of analysis is termed the spectrum technique that focuses on the earthquake's energy applied to a building and how that building will absorb this energy. While dynamic methods are more exact with respect to the true response of the structure, they are also more rigorous to perform. The analysis of eartquake forces requires a rather extensive analysis background and therefore is outside the scope of this fundamental text.

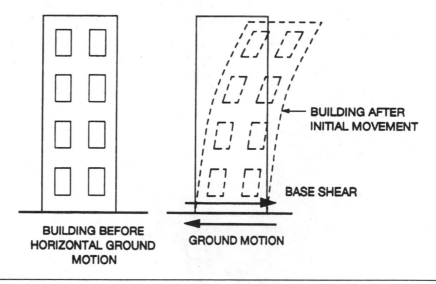

BUILDING BEFORE HORIZONTAL GROUND MOTION

BUILDING AFTER INITIAL MOVEMENT

BASE SHEAR

GROUND MOTION

Figure 2–5   Base Shear on Buildings under Earthquake Forces.

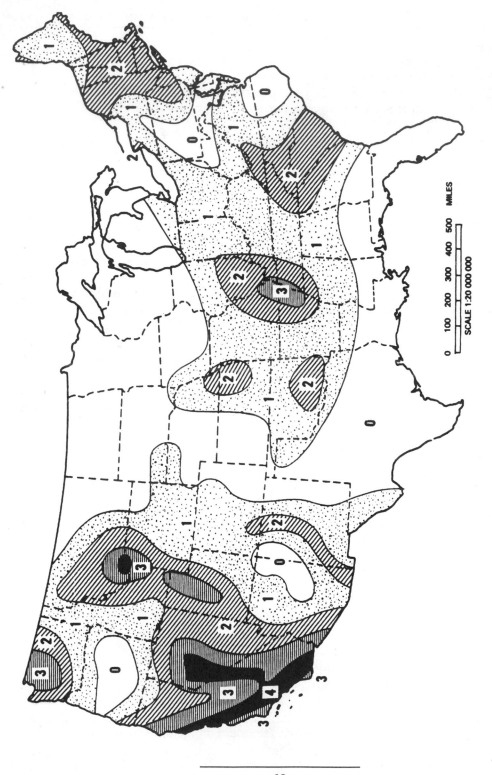

Figure 2–6 Seismic Zones for the Continental United States. (Reprinted form the ASCE's *Minimum Design Loads for Buildings and Other Structures*, ASCE 7–88, with permission from the American Society of Civil Engineers.)

Although the actual analysis is complex, an understanding of the factors that influence a structure's behavior provides a good foundation for the student to proceed further on this topic.

Miscellaneous Loads

Other loads that the structure has to tolerate, can sometimes be overlooked by the inexperienced designer. Construction loads will always be present during the erection of a structure, and many times these loads can be far greater than any live load placed on the structure in everyday operation. The effect of the load can be exaggerated due to the structure's "incompleteness" during the construction phase. A good example of this can be seen in Figure 2–7, which shows the cantilevered portions of a plate girder bridge before erection was completed. Certainly, the designer must have taken into account the behavior of this structure during the construction phase. A structure during construction may be extremely vunerable to standard design loadings and therefore items such as stability, temporary bracing, or shoring must be considered by at least some member of the design team.

Finally, special loadings due to impact, uplift, and even temperature change must be a source of concern in design. Impact refers to the increased stress that a structure or member feels due to a sudden and dynamic load. Impact loading from vehicles or equipment may increase static stresses on members from 20 to 100 percent. Uplift loads from water and wind might be a concern in certain structures subject to unusual wind loads or structures located in floodplains. Temperature stresses caused by improper expansion joints or even temperature variations in members can cause unusual problems for the designer[7].

The complete design will address all potential loadings in a manner consistent with a particular geographic location. This is a vital necessity for a safe and prudent design.

2.6   Load Combinations for LRFD

Much work in probabilistic load criteria[8] has culminated in the publication of the ASCE standard[4] that was referenced previously. LRFD uses the basic load combinations as suggested by this standard as the minimum requirements for load carrying structures. As already mentioned, the LRFD specification states that the design strength of a member has to be greater than or equal to the required resistance. The required resistance is the effect (moment, shear, axial force, etc.) caused by the highest factored load combination as stated in the ASCE publication or in section A4.1 of the AISC specification. The designer will choose the highest load combination as the controlling basis for a member's design and calculate the "load effect" that arises from this controlling combination. These load combinations, with their respective load factors, are as follows:

Figure 2–7 Erection of the Quinnipiac River Bridge in Connecticut Demonstrates the Importance of Construction Loads in Design. (Courtesy Bethlehem Steel Corporation.)

(A4–1) $1.4D$
(A4–2) $1.2D + 1.6L + 0.5(L_r \text{ or } S \text{ or } R)$
(A4–3) $1.2D + 1.6 (L_r \text{ or } S \text{ or } R) + (0.5L \text{ or } 0.8W)$
(A4–4) $1.2D + 1.3W + 0.5L + 0.5(L_r \text{ or } S \text{ or } R)$
(A4–5) $1.2D \pm 1.0E + 0.5L + 0.2S$
(A4–6) $0.9D \pm (1.3W \text{ or } 1.0E)$

With D = gravity dead loads
$\quad L$ = gravity live loads
$\quad L_r$ = roof live loads
$\quad W$ = wind load
$\quad E$ = earthquake load
$\quad S$ = snow load
$\quad R$ = load to initial rainwater of ice

A load combination may have up to three separate parts that can consist of: the factored dead load effect, the 50 year maximum live load effect, and a possible live load effect labelled as an **arbitrary-point-in-time (APT)** value. Such APT values are typically only a fraction of their design values, since this would reflect a small probability that they would occur simultaneously with the other 50 year maximum live loads and full gravity loads. The following example demonstrates the calculation of the LRFD load combinations on a typical roof beam.

EXAMPLE 2.4

Calculate the maximum load effect on a 15 foot long beam that is part of a roof framing system. The service dead loads for the roof are 25 psf, the service live loads are 15 psf, and the wind load is 8 psf (downward). The beams are spaced at 8 feet on center and all other effects are negligible.

For this solution we will list the individual effects in terms of pounds per lineal foot of beam length as follows:

D = 25 psf × 8 ft width = 200 lb/ft
L_r = 15 psf × 8 ft width = 120 lb/ft
W = 8 psf × 8 ft width = 64 lb/ft

Calculating separate load combinations:

(A4–1)   1.4(200 lb/ft) = 280 lb/ft
(A4–2)   1.2(200 lb/ft) + 0.5(120 lb/ft) = 300 lb/ft
(A4–3)   1.2(200 lb/ft) + 1.6(120 lb/ft) + 0.8(64 lb/ft) = 483.2 lb/ft
(A4–4)   1.2(200 lb/ft) + 1.3(64 lb/ft) + 0.5(120 lb/ft) = 383.2 lb/ft
(A4–5)   1.2(200 lb/ft) = 240 lb/ft
(A4–6)   0.9(200 lb/ft) – 1.3(64 lb/ft) = 96.8 lb/ft
          0.9(200 lb/ft) + 1.3 (64 lb/ft) = 263.2 lb/ft

Therefore the maximum load case used for calculation of the factored load effect would be A4–3 and the factored load would be 483.2 lb/ft. This factored load effect would then be used to analyze the maximum effects (moment, shear, tension, etc.) which would occur on any on the roof elements.

2.7   Summary

Specifications exist to provide a designer with the most current information concerning the use and application of a particular construction material. Building codes are written to protect the public's safety and guide a designer as to the proper application of design loads and other building requirements. Building codes are legally adopted by a city, state, or other governmental body. A designer will use the design loads from the applicable building code and calculate the total loads to be applied to a structure. This total load will be used in conjunction with all applicable load combinations to calculate the maximum factored load effect for which the structure should be analyzed.

EXERCISES

1. Explain the differences between a building code and a specification. How are they similar?
2. Read the Foreword of the AISC *Manual of Steel Construction* and list the objectives of this organization. How do these differ from the objectives of a building code.
3. Review your state building code's chapter on structural loads and list the values of ground snow load, basic wind speed, and seismic zone in regards to your school's geographic location. How might you modify these values if you were designing an identical structure with respect to the importance factor, exposure factor, and other possible modifiers.
4. Again reviewing your state building code, determine the applicable live loadings for your school. Is there more than one live load which may be applied in this structure?
5. Calculate the basic wind pressure at 30 feet above grade for a structure located in flat, open terrain under the following conditions. The structure is
    a. hospital in Pittsburg, Pennsylvania
    b. school in Austin, Texas
    c. gas station in Billings, Montana
    d. restaurant in Athens, Georgia
    e. all of the above in your city
6. For the beam shown below, calculate the factored weight per foot applied to the beam using the information regarding dead and live loads given earlier in this chapter. The service live load is 40 psf.

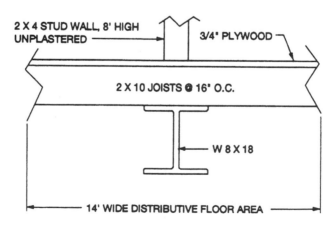

2 X 4 STUD WALL, 8' HIGH UNPLASTERED — 3/4" PLYWOOD

2 X 10 JOISTS @ 16" O.C.

W 8 X 18

14' WIDE DISTRIBUTIVE FLOOR AREA

7. A roof system has an applied service dead load of 40 psf, a snow load of 17 psf, and a downward wind pressure of 15 psf. Using the LRFD load combinations, calculate the controlling factored load in terms of pounds per square foot.

8. A stack room of a library is supported by a framing system consisting of W 10 × 49 beams that are 15 feet long and situated at 8 feet on center. Calculate the maximum factored load effect on a beam if the floor is a 6" reinforced concrete slab.

9. Redo problem #7 with the dead load at 15 psf and the wind pressure upwards (suction) on the roof.

10. Determine the controlling factored axial load effect on a column located in a warehouse has the following service axial forces applied to it:
Dead Load = 170 kips
Live Load from Floor = 140 kips
Roof Live Load = 35 kips
Wind Load = 28 kips

11. If a beam has a maximum factored load applied to it of 500 lbs/ft and load combination A4–2 controls its design, find the magnitude of service dead load and live load if the ratio of live to dead load is 1.0. How would this change if the ratio of live to dead load was 3.0?

REFERENCES

1. Building Officials and Code Administrators International, *The BOCA National Building Code*, Country Club Hills, IL, 1990.

2. International Conference of Building Officials, *Uniform Building Code,* Whitter, CA, 1991.

3. Southern Building Code Congress International, *Standard Building Code*, Birmingham, AL, 1991.

4. American Society of Civil Engineers, *ASCE Standard Minimum Design Loads for Building and Other Structures,* ASCE 7–88 (formerly ANSI A58.1), New York, NY, 1990.

5. Billington, David P. and Abel, John F., "Design of Cooling Towers for Wind", *Methods of Structural Analysis*, Proceedings of the National Structural Engineering Conference, Volume 1, ASCE, New York, 1976, p. 242.

6. Berg, Glen V., "Historical Review of Earthquakes, Damages, and Building Codes," *Methods of Structural Analysis,* Proceedings of the National Structural Engineering Conference, Volume 1, ASCE, New York, 1976, p. 387.

7. Fintel, Mark and Gosh, S. K., "Distress Due to Sun Camber in a Long-Span Roof of a Parking Garage," *Concrete International,* July 1988, pp. 42–50.

8. Galambos, Theodore V., Ellingwood, Bruce, MacGregor, James G., Cornell, C. Allin, "Probability Based Load Criteria: Assessment of Current Design

Practice," *Journal of the Structural Division*, ASCE, Volume 108, May 1982, pp. 959–977.

9. Simiu, Emil, and Scanlan, Robert H., *Wind Effects on Structure*, Second Edition, John Wiley and Sons, New York, 1986.

10. Lui, Henry, *Wind Engineering*, Prentice-Hall, Englewood Clifts, New Jersey, 1991.

3

THE DESIGN AND PROBLEM-SOLVING PROCESSES

3.1 Introduction

The process of solving problems is a process that contains both individual and universal characteristics. The characteristic of identifying a problem to begin with is a rather universal characteristic, although what follows may in large part be a function of an individual's judgment. Structural design can also be viewed as a problem solving and, therefore, it is worth discussing some of the items that are important in the *understanding* of the design process.

3.2 The Design Model

In the simplest sense, structural design is the process in which a design problem is solved. In this process the designer determines how resources, such as available wide-flange shapes, are to be allocated in a structural framing system. To do this, the designer will utilize knowledge of engineering principles and materials to arrive at the optimum solution. The optimum solution will be economical and safe, yet take into account the individual needs that are specific to a particular project. The design process is largely a function of the designer's ability, experience, and judgment. But how does this process really take shape?

There are a variety of problem-solving concepts that exist in many different fields of learning such as business, information science, and psychology. Many people have developed these concepts into "design models" that can theoretically be applied to any particular problem. Structural design also has a number of models that try to explain the steps taken by the structural designer to solve a particular problem.

Some design models[1] portray problem-solving as a spiral process, in which the problem-solver utilizes certain tools that stem from a large body of general knowledge and focuses down to a solution that is needed to solve a specific problem (Figure 3–1).

Other design models[2] view problem-solving in "input-output" terms, whereby certain information containing the specific requirements of the problem is input and, by utilizing various methods, the solution comes forth as the output. In this solution process, there is often reference made to the designer's "black-box" thought processes (Figure 3–2). The description of such thought processes as a black-box is meant to signify the individuality associated with design solutions because of the creative nature of this process. Although the designer uses specifications and codes for guidance, the process relies heavily on judgments made by the individual designer. The inner workings and steps of any design will vary with the design engineer.

The events that occur inside the black-box are difficult to explain since they are unique to the structural designer. There are common elements that occur in

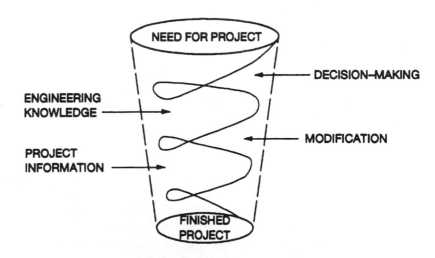

(PLANS, SPECIFICATIONS, COMPUTATIONS)

Figure 3–1   Spiral Design and Problem-Solving Process

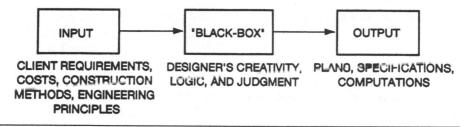

Figure 3–2   Black-Box Design Process

each design process, and we will attempt to highlight some of these in the following paragraphs.

Every design process starts with **problem identification**, where the designer must "focus in" on all the design aspects with which he or she will be involved. For example, a column design will not merely involve the actual column design but will also involve baseplate design, beam connection design, and connection of other appurtenances. To exclude these other facets of column design would not only be unwise, but potentially disastrous. A good designer will always be mindful of how the member fits in with the complete project.

The design process involves **trial-and-error techniques**; in fact, many times the most economical member is found by an iterative, trial-and-error approach. Although a trial-and-error approach may seem to be rather non-technical, many famous structures from ancient times were actually "refinements" of similar structures that had succeeded or failed. A good historical example of this trial-and-error approach in an ancient structure is the Bent Pyramid at Dashur. This pyramid, located in Egypt, is well known because at approximately midheight the angle of its side slope changes from 52° to 43.5°. This angle change is extremely unusual to have occurred during the construction of such a structure and has been attributed to the apparent failure of the nearby Meidum Pyramid.[3] It seems that when the news of the failure at the Meidum Pyramid reached the builders of the Bent Pyramid, they opted to reduce the slope in order to achieve (what they thought would be) a more stable design. Although many previously-built pyramids had been built using the 52° side angle, this one failure has been shown to influence later designs by what amounts to a trial-and-error approach. A good design will utilize trial-and-error techniques, not only in refinements of particular components, but also by way of previous engineering experiences. Many times we, as an engineering community, can learn more from out mistakes than our successes.

Finally, all design processes will involve **computations**, that are a set of clearly written and precise design calculations. Computations are more than just formulas we use in the determination of certain structural components. Computations are the mathematical verification of the designer's judgments and serve as a record of the design process. These computations should include all of our assumptions, specification references, and justifications that have been made during the design process. These computations are as close to a description of the events that occur inside the designer's black-box as there can be. Computations are immensely important because they serve as a designer's historical reference. This reference is important in providing the designer with the assumptions that were made and the design steps utilized while working on a specific type of project.

Although a good set of computations is vitally important, it is usually one of the hardest talents for a young designer to acquire. As a general rule, the author believes that if a designer can stop working on a particular set of design computations for two weeks and then resume work with a minimum amount of time for start-up, then the designer has a relatively complete set of design computations.

In closing, the aforementioned items are only some of those involved in a structural design process. Many other aspects will vary on the individual designer and the type of project that is being designed. However, the idea of structural design as a problem-solving process is extremely important because it reinforces that design is based on logic, creativity, and sound engineering principles.

3.3   The Assumption of Load Path and Floor Loading

One of the first assumptions made by the structural designer is the path across which the forces travel as they move throughout a structure. Loads (or forces) will travel through a structure along what is referred to as a **load path**. The location of the assumed load path could be conveniently found by answering the question, "How do the loads on the structure get transferred to the supporting soil?".

Structures may be viewed as mechanisms by which loads are distributed to their individual members, such as beams, columns, and floor slabs. It remains up to the structural designer to make judgments on the amount of load distributed to individual members and the manner in which loads will travel throughout the structure.

Many times a structural designer will assume a distribution of loads to particular members based on the concept of **distributive area**. This concept typically considers the area that a member has to support as being halfway bewteen the next closest, similar member. To illustrate, Figure 3–3 shows that the steel floor beam located at 48" on center is assumed to carry the dead and live loads placed in the area 24" to the right of the beam.

The distributive area technique works very well in normal floor framing under standard dead and live loads. A typical steel framing plan for a supported

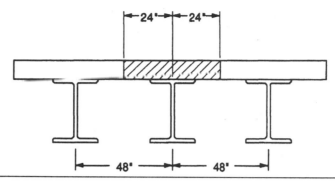

Figure 3–3   Distributive Area in a Structural Floor System

floor system may be found in Figure 3–4. In this illustration, we can see that the floor beams at 6 feet on center are tied into larger floor girders. These girders are then connected to the columns located at each of the four corners of the bay. (A *bay* typically refers to the area bounded by structural columns, usually in a square or rectangular arrangement. In Figure 3–4, one bay is bounded by

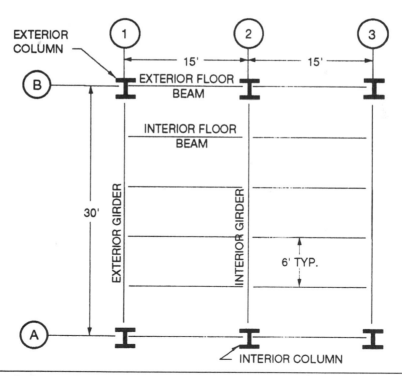

Figure 3–4   Typical Floor Framing System

columns A1–A2–B2–B1 and the other bay is bounded by columns A2–A3–B3–B2). Under the distributive area technique, the designer will assume that each of the floor beams carry the loads in their area and these loads are then transferred as concentrated loads to the larger girders which in turn distribute their loads to the columns.

The following example illustrates how the distributive area technique may be used to approximate, not only the amount of load on individual members, but also the load path which exists.

EXAMPLE 3.1

Calculate the loads on each member (floor beams, girders, and columns) shown in the framing plan of Figure 3–4 using the distributive area method. The floor live load is 100 psf (4788 Pa) and the dead load is 120 psf (5745.6 Pa). The dead load includes slab and member selfweight.

Initially, the designer must realize that there is a big difference in quantity of load applied to the interior (or center) beams, girders, and columns as opposed to the exterior (or edge) beams, girders, and columns. This difference is attributed to a larger amount of distributive area for these interior members.

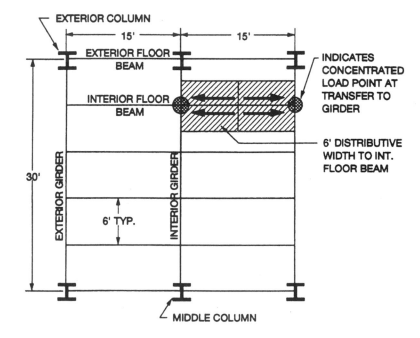

For the Interior Floor Beams (spaced at 6 ft. o.c.)

Distributive area is 6 feet (1.83 m); therefore, each interior beam feels the application of (6 ft. × 220 psf) or 1320 pounds per lineal foot (19,276.5 N/m). If each beam is assumed to be a simply supported over its 15 foot length (4.57 m), the reaction placed on the floor girder from each interior floor beam is as follows:

$$R_{ig} = R_{eg} = wl/2 = (1320 \text{ lbs./ft.})(15 \text{ ft.})/2 = 9900 \text{ lbs.}$$
$$(= (19,276.5 \text{ N/m})(4.57 \text{ m})/2 = 88,094 \text{ N or } 88.1 \text{ KN})$$

where

R_{ig} = Reaction to interior girder

R_{eg} = Reaction to exterior girder

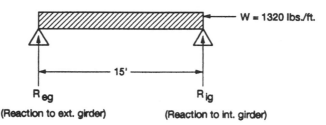

W = 1320 lbs./ft.

15'

R_{eg}
(Reaction to ext. girder)

R_{ig}
(Reaction to int. girder)

For the Exterior Floor Beams (which frame directly into the columns)

Distributive area is 3 feet (.9 m); therefore, each exterior beam feels the application of 660 pounds (3 ft. × 220 psf) per lineal foot (9638.3 N/m) over its 15 foot (4.57 m) length. Assuming the simple support conditions, the reactions applied directly to the columns would be as follows:

$$R_{ec} = R_{mc} = wl/2 = (660 \text{ lbs. per ft.})(15 \text{ ft.})/2 = 4950 \text{ lbs.}$$
$$(= (9638 \text{ N/m})(4.57 \text{ m}) = 44,066 \text{ N or } 44.1 \text{ KN})$$

where

R_{ec} = Reaction to exterior column

R_{mc} = Reaction to middle column

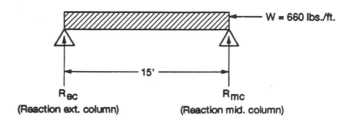

W = 660 lbs./ft.

15'

R_{ec}
(Reaction ext. column)

R_{mc}
(Reaction mid. column)

For the Interior Floor Girder

The reaction of 9900 pounds (44,035 N) from the floor beams is applied every 6 feet in the locations shown as shown in diagrammatic form below. Remember that for the interior girder the floor beams frame in from each side, so the total applied load at the four points shown is doubled. These loads are then transferred to the middle column.

$$R_{mc} = 4(P)/2 = 4(19,800 \text{ lbs})/2 = 39,600 \text{ lbs}$$
$$(= 4(88,070 \text{ N})/2 = 176,140 \text{ N or } 176.1 \text{ KN})$$

where

R_{mc} = Reaction to middle column

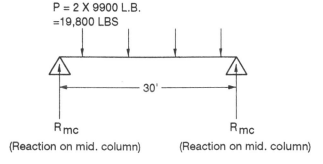

For the Exterior Floor Girder

The reaction of 9900 pounds (44,035 N) from the floor beam frames in from one side only; therefore, the load is only 9900 pounds (44,035 N) at each location. As shown below, the reaction at the exterior columns would therefore only be half as much.

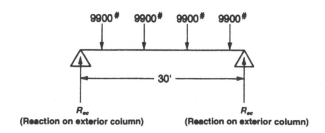

$$R_{ec} = 4(P)/2 = 4(9900 \text{ lbs.})/2 = 19,800 \text{ lbs.}$$
$$(= 4(44,035 \text{ N})/2 = 88,070 \text{ N or } 88.1 \text{ KN})$$

where

R_{ec} = Reaction to exterior column

For the Middle Columns (R_{mc})

The load applied to the middle column (P_{mc}) from the two exterior floor beams (each side of column) and the interior girder reaction results in a total load as follows:

$$P_{mc} = 2(R_{mc})_{\text{ext.fl.beams}} + (R_{mc})_{\text{int.gird.}}$$
$$= 2(4950 \text{ lbs.}) + (39,600 \text{ lbs.}) = 49,500 \text{ lbs.}$$
$$(= (44,035) + 176,140 = 220,175 \text{ N})$$

For the Exterior Columns

The load applied to the exterior column (P_{ec}) from the one exterior floor beam and the exterior girder is as follows:

$$P_{ec} = (R_{mc})_{\text{ext.fl.beams}} + (R_{mc})_{\text{ext.gird.}}$$
$$= (4950 \text{ lbs.}) + (19,800 \text{ lbs.}) = 24,250 \text{ lbs.}$$
$$(= 22,017 \text{ N} + 88,070 \text{ N} = 110,087 \text{ N})$$

3.4   The Process of Member Evaluation

Since we have discussed (at some length) the concepts of the problem-solving process, let us begin to focus our attention on the particular problems that occur in structural design. Only two general catagories of structural design problems exist in the realm of engineering—**evaluation problems** and **design problems**. If the inexperienced designer can establish the type of problem that is under consideration, the solution process can be clearly defined. In this section, we will discuss the problem-solving process contained in member evaluation problems; while the following section will present the solution process in design problems.

Evaluation problems require the structural designer to evaluate an existing member under an existing or proposed loading. Evaluation problems may ask the designer to answer one of the following questions:

■ Is the member adequate under the specified load?
■ Will the member meet specification criteria?
■ Is the member safe for public usage?

When using the Load and Resistance Factor Design method, all the above questions can be grouped into one general question that lies at the heart of the LRFD philosophy: Is the member's design strength greater than or equal to the required strength due to the factored load conditions? If the designer's answer to this question is yes, the member is adequate and the evaluation problem for that behavior is ended. Should the answer to this question be no, the designer must initiate design changes to correct the deficiency.

The evaluation problem always has an existing member with specific dimensions and material properties. If the designer is fortunate, there will be access to an existing set of plans or specifications that will document the member's dimensions and properties. However, on many older structures, a set of plans or specifications may no longer exist. Therefore, detailed inspection and testing will have to be performed to attain the member size and material properties.

In addition to knowing (or being able to attain) the member size and properties, in an evaluation problem the designer will usually know the load or loadings for which the evaluation shall be completed. Knowing this information, the designer can always calculate the load capacity that a particular member can hold. The two most common load capacity formulas that the designer will utilize are manipulations of the *direct stress* formula and the *bending stress* formula. The common load capacity formulas used in LRFD are listed below:

$$P_n = F \times A \qquad \text{(Direct Stress)}$$
$$M_n = F \times Z_x \qquad \text{(Bending Stress)}$$

where

P_n = Nominal Axial Load Capacity

M_n = Nominal Moment Capacity

F = Critical Stress Level, usually the yield stress (F_y)

A = Cross-sectional Area

Z_x = Plastic Section Modulus (to be discussed further in Chapter 6, typically about a section's x-axis)

Upon calculating the nominal load capacity of a member, the designer will apply a reduction factor to determine the member's **design capacity** or **design strength**. These manipulations of the direct stress and bending stress formulas are used repeatedly throughout structural design to calculate such items as tensile capacity, compressive capacity, and moment capacity.

After calculating a member's capacity, the designer will then use the specific knowledge of the problem and the controlling load combination to calculate the required capacity. The comparison of member's capacity (or design strength) to the required capacity (or required strength) can then be readily accomplished and will be used extensively in the upcoming chapters.

3.5   The Process of Member Design

Design problems are usually considered to be the harder of the two types that face the structural designer. This is because the structural designer is required to choose a particular section that will provide sufficient strength, serviceability, and fit into the architectural system for which it is designed. It is much easier to consider the adequacy of a given member (with all of its dimensions and properties known) than to be given general requirements and asked to design.

The problem-solving process of design problems can be somewhat simplified if a designer can focus attention on what is really trying to be solved. In general, the solution to all design problems is finding the most suitable (and economical) member area. The member selected will actually be expressed as an area (in^2 or mm^2) or as some function of area (moment of inertia, in^4 or mm^4, section modulus, in^3 or mm^3). The most suitable member will provide a design capacity equal to (or possibly a little greater than) the required capacity, and that will also satisfy other design criteria such as clearance heights and availability. If the designer chooses an actual member size that provides a design capacity equal to the required capacity, the member is (in theory) as economical as it can be without exceeding the specified critical stress level.

Therefore, the two most commonly used design formulas are still the direct stress equation and the bending stress equation. However, the designer is now solving for an area (or a function of area) and the stress level that he or she is using is the maximum allowed per specification (the critical stress for that particular behavior). The reworked direct stress and bending formulas used in design are now as shown below:

$A_{min} = P_u / \phi F$ (Direct Stress)

$Z_{min} = M_u / \phi F$ (Bending Stress)

where

ϕF = the critical design stress level to be used (many times this critical stress level will be a threshold stress for a particular behavior. For instance, when yielding of the steel would be a limit state, the obvious critical stress is a function of F_y).

A_{min} = minimum area which will work

Z_{min} = minimum plastic section modulus

P_u = required or factored load

M_u = required or factored moment

The student will find that the design process involves more choices and is usually more challenging. Design should be viewed as a continuous problem that will not be solved on the very first try. In fact, many trials (and errors) are usually needed to refine the problem into its final form. In many ways, the structural design process is similar to the process in which music might be composed. Although there are only a few notes on the musical scale (and only a few types of structural members) there can be an infinite number of ways to put them together.

3.6   The Importance of Design Details

The construction of any structure, from a house to an eighty-story skyscraper, involves a seemingly infinite number of "small" items to which attention must be paid. These small items are typically referred to as *details,* although they are not in any way insignificant!

Design details are not the major structural components (such as beams and columns) that we typically think of when we consider the process of design. Rather, design details may focus on more subtle design items such as connection details between members, expansion and contraction devices, stairway and handrail framing, and mechanical system support. Design details are numerous and may literally outnumber the design of the "major" structural components by a wide margin.

To a structural designer, design details may sometimes seem unglamorous. For instance, when a bridge is designed how many people notice the expansion joint system as opposed to the main supporting trusses? Although the general public may never notice the expansion joint, its proper design and correct detailing is probably every bit as important to maintaining the bridge's longevity. Every design detail, although time-consuming and tedious, must be fully considered and correctly accomplished to ensure the safety and serviceability of every structure.

One of the most catastrophic examples involving the failure of a design detail was the collapse of two suspended walkways in the Hyatt Regency Hotel in Kansas City, Missouri on July 17, 1981 (Figure 3–5). This disaster, which killed 114 people and injured more than 200, resulted from a failure of the box beam-hanger rod connection (Figure 3–6).

The collapse occurred during an early evening dance being held in the hotel's atrium and was believed to have initially occurred in the middle box beam on the fourth floor walkway. The collapse mechanism was probably initiated when the nut assembly of the hanger rod pulled through the box beam that led to similar failures at the other fourth floor connection points.[4] As the fourth floor walkway lost support, it collapsed on the second floor walkway below, resulting in "the most devastating structural collapse ever to take place in the United States"[5].

Although much of the discussion following the collapse involved a change that was made to the original hanger rod detail, the following important points have been made:

Figure 3–5   Scattered Wreckage in the Aftermath of the Kansas City Hyatt-Regency Collapse. (Courtesy of World Wide Photos)

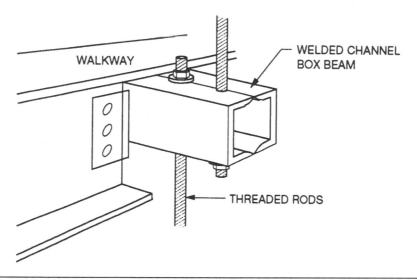

Figure 3–6   Schematic Illustration of Box Beam- Threaded Rod Connection involved in Walkway Collapse.

■ The loads acting on the fourth floor box beam-hanger rod connection at the time of the collapse were substantially less than those required under the Kansas City Building Code. The maximum load believed to be acting on the fourth floor connections was approximately 21.4 kips while the minimum design load per building code criteria was 40.7 kips. This would make the loads acting on the critical fourth floor connections at the time of the collapse only 53% of those required by the Kansas City Building Code. [4]

■ An investigation by the Deutsch Commission (which was to rule on a complaint filed by the Missouri State Board to revoke the licenses of the engineers involved) revealed that no original design calculations regarding this connection were found.[5]

■ Communication failure between the structural designer and the steel fabricator regarding the responsibility for the failed connection design was a major contributing factor in the collapse.[6]

How did this design detail slip between the cracks? Was it lost among the "more important" structural design items? Although we cannot attempt to answer these questions, this collapse underscores the importance of all pieces in the puzzle that we refer to as design.

3.7 Computers in Structural Design

Computers, and the software that provides the commands for the computer to process, have invaded practically every facet of our business and personal lives. Structural engineering and design is no exception. As early as 1958 the American Society of Civil Engineers convened a conference to discuss the use and potential of computers in structural engineering. Although the original computers were huge, relatively slow machines that would require extensive setup time by the user, these machines were the pioneers of the revolution that we commonly refer to as the computer age.

Advances and improvements in hardware and software have been especially dramatic in the last decade. Hardware advances have led to the use of personal computers by everyone in the structural design field. Personal computers have become more affordable, while also becoming faster and more powerful in their ability to assimilate data. Software advances have also accelerated. Many structural analysis programs provide the user with interactive design modules that essentially prompt the user with specific questions concerning design. Computer-aided drafting (CAD) software has rapidly advanced to the point where many analysis software packages have the ability to produce framing plans and other structural drawings. Other software on the market contain typical structural details known as "library symbols" that can be modified to suit a particular design and transferred or "imported" via transfer files into the actual CAD software that is being used.

The software industry has begun to refine this transfer mechanism (using DXF, IGES, or DXB files) and is expected to do so for the foreseeable future. The ability to transfer files from one type of software to another is an extremely powerful tool because it allows greater flexibility in the design process. A designer can now draw a "wire-frame model" of a structure to be analyzed in the earliest stages of preliminary design and continue to refine and modify this model until the design is complete. After this, the designer can use this model as the basis for his or her structural plans and through the use of other detailing software produce a complete set of structural plans.

Although the use of computer technology in structural design is expanding, it is important for the student to remember the following:

- ■ The computer and its software are the only tools that the designer uses. Although some would tend to think that a computer can design, in actuality, the computer can only process data. Always check the results that the computer presents. Although some people would like to think that computers are infallible, in structural design, this would be potentially a disastrous assumption.

- ■ The most important function of a designer is the ability to communicate and justify the design that has been selected. Although some of the results that are received from the computer may be used in a designer's justification, the computer alone cannot provide the justification of a design.

- ■ Do not be intimidated by computers or their software. The only way to learn about a piece of software is to spend many hours working with the software and gathering knowledge regarding its intricaties. Learn about all different types of software, from design and analysis, to CAD software, and even word-processing software. This will greatly increase your marketability and expertise.

3.8   Summary

Structural design is a problem solving process that is more than just calculating numbers. Design should begin with identification of the key components and encompasses trial and error techniques as well as utilizes the designer's judgment in arriving at the optimum solution. Details should always be considered and never overlooked. The use of computers to analyze and support the design process is expanding at an ever increasing rate. The designer should use the computer as a tool and always question the results that it produces.

EXERCISES

1. Calculate the load per lineal foot of beam length (N/m) for a W 310 x 74 steel beam with a concrete slab above it measuring 0.2 meters in thickness. The density of the concrete is 2400 Kg/m^3 and the live load is 5.75 KPa.

2. The cross section shown below is the framing for a 70 foot long simply supported bridge. Using the distributive area method, calculate the dead load (per foot) carried by an interior and exterior girder. Assume the parapet and railing to be distributed equally among all girders. The areas and densities of the materials are as follows:

$\gamma_{concrete}$ = 150 pcf

Area of parapet = 3 ft.^{2}

Area of beam = 7.8 ft.^{2}

1" thick future wearing surface, γ = 120 pcf

Guardrail = 15 pounds per foot

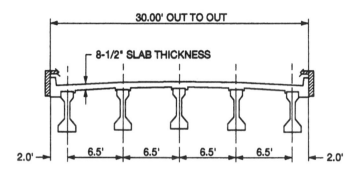

3. Given the framing plan shown below, calculate loads distributed from the floor loads to the columns. The floor dead load including selfweight is 150 psf and the floor live load is 175 psf.

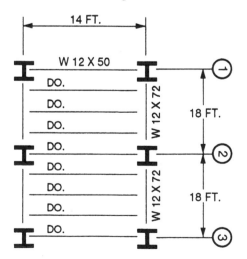

4. Investigate your house or apartment's framing system. Roughly sketch a floor plan and decide how loads travel throughout this structure from the roof to the foundation.

5. A pedestrian walkway is made up of two simple spans each 40 feet long as shown. Calculate the loads distributed to the abutments and the pier if the applied loads are as follows:

> Area of 1 parapet = 4.3 ft.^{2} (Density = 150 pcf)
> Area of slab = 10 ft.^{2} (Density = 150 pcf)
> Beams = W 12 × 120

Pedestrian Fence = 35 pounds per foot

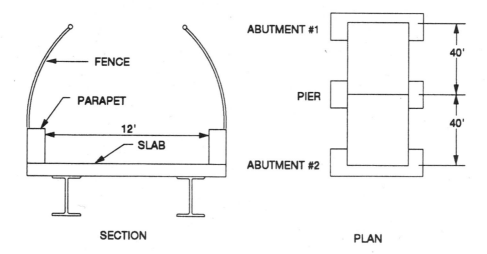

SECTION   PLAN

6. Give another specific example of trial and error design of some type of historical structure. (Hint: Gothic cathedrals, early railroad bridges, the Parthenon of ancient Greece.)

REFERENCES

1. James M. Becker, "A Structural Design Process," Proceedings of the National Structural Engineering Conference, *Methods of Structural Analysis, Volume 2,* ASCE, 1976, p.341.
2. William Addis, *Structural Engineering, The Nature of Theory and Design,* Ellis Horwood Limited, London, 1990, p.37.
3. Mario Salvadori, *Why Buildings Stand Up,* W. W. Norton and Company, New York, 1980, p.38.

4. "Investigation of the Kansas City Hyatt Regency Walkways Collapse," Center for Building Technology National Engineering Laboratory, National Bureau of Standards, U.S. Department of Commerce. p.233.

5. E. O. Pfrang and R. M. Marshall, "Collapse of the Kansas City Hyatt Regency Walkways", *Civil Engineering,* July 1982, p.65–68.

6. E. A. Banset and G. M. Parsons, "Communications Failure in Hyatt Regency Disaster," *Journal of Professional Issues in Engineering,* July 1989, p.273–288.

CHAPTER

4

TENSION MEMBER DESIGN

4.1 Introduction to Tension Members

The use of steel tension members is found throughout building and bridge construction today. The bottom chord members of simply-supported bridge and roof trusses, as well as the cables used in a variety of suspended bridges and walkways, are all tension members. (Figure 4–1)

Tension members may be cables, rods, angles, channels, wide flange sections, plates, or any number of sections that are built-up from these individual shapes. When built-up sections are used, they may be held together by tie bars or lacing bars located at certain intervals along the member's length to hold the individual pieces in correct alignment. The type of tension member used is largely a function of its end connections. A cable or circular rod might be an ideal tension member, although its physical shape may require special detailing in its connection to other members.

4.2 Modes of Failure and Formula Usage

The design of tension members in this book will follow the Load and Resistance Factor Design philosophy as previously mentioned. In this method, we aim to keep the design capacity of our member above the required capacity that is set

Figure 4–1 Example of Cables as Tension Members in the George Washington Suspension Bridge. (Courtesy of Bethlehem Steel Corporation.)

forth by the LRFD specification. The direct stress formula for calculating axial capacity will be our most useful equation when dealing with tension members. The student will soon realize that every problem in tension member design uses some form of the direct stress formula. This equation, which is the cornerstone of the curriculum in strength of materials, is $f = P/A$.

where

f = actual stress, psi or ksi
P = load, pounds or kips
A = resisting area, square inches

Before learning how to apply this equation in tension member design, it is necessary to consider the common modes of failure that might occur when a member is stressed in tension. These can be summarized as follows:

- Member fails where there are no holes
- Member fails where there are holes for bolted or riveted connections
- Member fails due to inadequate bolt spacing

The third method of failure should be the least likely to occur since chapter J in the LRFD specification specifies typical maximum and minimum requirements for distances between bolts and edge spacings. A good engineer or structural detailer will know these requirements and the student will further touch upon these specific criteria in Chapter 9 of this book. At this time, if the students are so inclined, they are referred to section J3 of the AISC *Manual for Steel Construction*, where these requirements are located. Other modes of failure sometimes associated with tension members, such as bolt shear and bearing, are considered by this author to be more closely identified with connection failure and, therefore, are the subject of Chapter 9.

The first two methods of failure, mentioned above, truly constitute the basis of what the designer is trying to prevent in tension member design. Failure through the member in a location where there are no holes is typically referred to as failure in the gross area; while failure through the plate in the area of bolt holes is referred to as failure in the net area. The gross and net area are radically different in their individual behaviors and their modes of failure. Therefore, it is imperative that both of these areas must be understood fully. In *every* case (excluding rods), both the gross and net area must be checked to determine which of the two is most critical.

The LRFD philosophy, as stated in Chapter 1, is simply the following:

Design Strength ≥ Required Strength

For tension members, this philosophy can be rewritten specificly as is shown below:

$$\phi_t P_n \geq P_u$$

where

ϕ_t = strength reduction factor for tension

(ϕ_t = .90 for gross, ϕ_t = .75 for eff. net area)

P_n = nominal tensile strength

P_u = factored tensile load applied to member

The nominal tensile strength, P_n, is calculated based on the direct stress formula (Load = Stress × Area), and will be discussed further in the upcoming section.

As mentioned earlier, the direct stress equation can be used in a number of ways to either determine a member's adequacy per AISC requirements or to design the member. In design, the direct stress formula can be used to determine the minimum required cross-sectional area for the member (A_{min}). This is the smallest area (hence the most economical) that would still meet the LRFD criteria of the LRFD specification. The formula for the minimum required area is simply accomplished by dividing the maximum ultimate load, P_u, by the tensile strength reduction factor (ϕ_t) and the critical stress limit (F) as shown below:

$$A_{min} = P/(\phi_t F)$$

(The critical stress level for the different tensile behaviors will be fully developed in the following section).

To evaluate an existing member, the direct stress formula can again be used to determine the member's adequacy. The design tensile capacity that a member can hold ($\phi_t \times P_n$) can be calculated and compared to the required (factored) capacity on the member. If the design capacity is greater than the required capacity, the member is indeed adequate.

This method of investigating the member's adequacy by the direct stress formula is shown in the following formula:

$$\phi_t P_n \geq P_u$$

or

$$\phi_t \times (A \times F) \geq P_u$$

where

ϕ_t = tensile reduction factor

F = Critical stress level for failure mechanism

A = Area used to resist force

(Note: Nominal Load Capacity = Area × Critical Stress)

Since the student now understands the methods behind the formula usage for tension members, the following section will be devoted to the understanding of the anticipated behavior of tension members, as well as the solution of common problems.

4.3   Tension Member Behavior: Gross vs. Net Area

The **gross area** is the cross sectional area of the tension member that has no bolt or rivet holes (Figure 4–2). This is the area away from the connection that is resisting the tensile stress. The actual stress in this location is very well approximated by the standard direct stress equation, $f = P/A$. The failure mechanism of tension members across the gross area is relatively simple, it would occur due to the **yielding of the steel**. Since the stress over the gross area is relatively uniform, yielding of all individual fibers of the cross section is anticipated to occur at the same time. Therefore, the failure we are trying to prevent, with regard to the

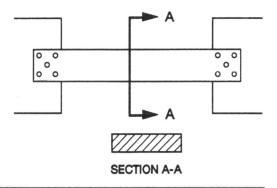

SECTION A-A

Figure 4–2   Illustration of Gross Area in a Tension Member.

gross area, is a yielding type of failure. The student could imagine this failure as occurring by the the member stretching out in an uncontrollable fashion, never able to regain its original length. (Remember the stress-strain diagram?)

The LRFD specification in section D1 sets the design tensile strength ($\phi_t P_n$) over the gross area for rolled members as follows:

$$\phi_t P_n = \phi_t (F_y A_g) \qquad\qquad\qquad \text{(Eq. 4–1)}$$

where

$\phi_t = .90$

F_y = steel yield stress

A_g = gross area

This means that the specification is considering the limit state for this behavior to be the yield stress of the particular steel being used. This is rather logical since the mode of failure at this location is a yielding mechanism.

Stresses on a tension member over the **net area** (i.e. vicinity of bolt holes) are extremely complex and studies in experimental stress analysis have shown stresses immediately adjacent to holes may be 2 to 4 times greater than those across the gross section.[1] In order to produce failure over this section, it must be remembered that the full cross-section must fail by the same mechanism. Although the full gross area failed by reaching its yield stress, the net area has stresses that are very uneven over its cross section. Since the areas directly adjacent to the bolt holes are much more highly stressed, these areas begin to yield long before the other areas of the net cross section. However, since much of the cross-sectional area is not even close to reaching its yield stress, the section will not fail by yielding at this time.

As stresses continue to build in the net area, the locations that have reached yield stress initially (the areas adjacent to the bolt holes) are now approaching the steel's ultimate tensile strength, F_u. At this time, cracking occurs at the holes and

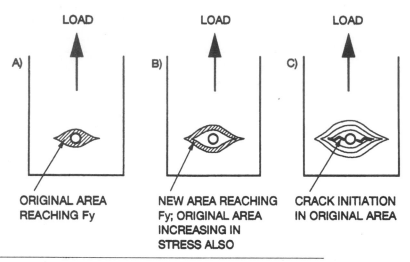

Figure 4-3 Failure Propagation around Bolt Holes

quickly propagates outward resulting in a fracture of the member (Figure 4–3). Some redistribution of stresses does occur, but the mode of failure across the net area is a fracture type of failure. Therefore, in design, we try to prevent this cracking failure from occurring at the net area.

Because of this behavior, the LRFD specification in its section D1 sets the design tensile strength over the net area as follows:

$$\phi_t P_n = \phi_t (F_u A_e) \qquad \text{(Eq. 4–2)}$$

where

$\phi_t = 0.75$

F_u = steel's ultimate tensile stress

A_e = effective net area

Notice that because the limit state is now a fracture type of behavior, the critical stress level is set to the steel's ultimate tensile strength. This will be fairly typical when the limit state involves cracking or fracture-type of mechanisms. The calculation of net area also has more factors to consider than those for the gross area. In the easiest sense, the net section is the gross area minus the area for the bolt holes in the section considered. Actually, there may be two or three net areas to be considered when a multiple bolt layout is used. This will be discussed in Section 4.5.

Before subtracting the holes from the gross area, one must remember that bolt holes have to be made a bit larger than the bolts so erection is not hampered. Generally, the method for making holes in steel is a process of subpunching and reaming which causes little damage to the sides of the holes. This process is typically faster[2] and more cost effective than drilling. If this process is used, a standard (nominal) hole will be approximately 1/16 of an inch larger than the bolt.

The area of a bolt hole is considered to be its rectangular projection on the proposed failure plane. The AISC specification considers the width of the actual bolt hole to be 1/16 inch larger than the *nominal* diameter of the hole, which is 1/16 inch larger than the bolt. This makes the actual width of the bolt hole simply the bolt diameter plus 1/8 inch. This makes the area of a hole simply the diameter of the bolt plus 1/8 of an inch multiplied by the thickness of the plate (Figure 4–4). Therefore, the net area across the assumed failure plane can be found by the following:

Net Area = Gross Area – [(number of bolts) ×
(diameter of bolt + 1/8") × (plate thickness)]   (Eq. 4–3)

The following examples introduce the student to the methodology used in solving tension member problems. Remember it is imperative to check both the gross and net areas in every problem.

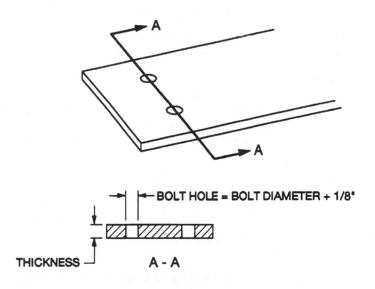

Figure 4–4   Illustration of Net Area in a Tension Member

EXAMPLE 4.1

The tension member shown below is subjected to a factored load of 85 kips (378.1 KN). Calculate the member's adequacy across the gross and net area and check per AISC requirements. The steel is A36 and the bolts are 3/4 inch (19.1 mm) in diameter.

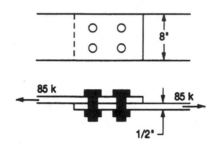

(In this problem we are asked to evaluate a given member under a given load. Remember, the typical method of evaluation is to calculate design tensile capacity and compare to the required capacity of 85 kips.)

The tension member is a plate; therefore, calculate the gross and net areas as follows:

$A_{gross} = 8" \times 1/2" = 4$ in.^{2} (2581 mm^2 or 0.00258 m^2)

$A_{net} = 4$ in.$^2 - 2(3/4" + 1/8")(1/2") = 3.125$ in.^{2} (2016 mm^2)

Now, using the Equations 4–1 and 4–2, calculate the design capacity across the gross and net areas and compare these values to the required capacity.

Gross Area

$\phi_t P_n = \phi_t(F_y \times A_g)$

$\quad = .90 (36 \text{ ksi} \times 4 \text{ in.}^2) = 129.6 \text{ kips} > 85 \text{ kips} — \text{OK}$

$\quad (= .90 (248.2 \text{ MPa} \times .00258 \text{ m}^2) = .576 \text{ MN or } 576 \text{ KN} > 378.1 \text{ KN})$

Net Area

$\phi_t P_n = \phi_t(F_u \times A_e)$

$\quad = .75 (58 \text{ ksi} \times 3.125 \text{ in.}^2) = 135.9 \text{ kips} > 85 \text{ kips} — \text{OK}$

$\quad (= .75 (399.9 \text{ MPa} \times .002016 \text{ m}^2) = .604 \text{ MN or } 604.5 \text{ KN} > 378.1$
$\quad \text{KN})$

Since the member is adequate at both gross and net areas, the member will work per LRFD specification.

EXAMPLE 4.2

Design the thickness of the flat plate tension member shown below if the service load needed to be supported is 55 kips (244.6 KN). The load is 50% live load and 50% dead load. The bolt is 3/4" diameter (19.1 mm) and the steel is A36.

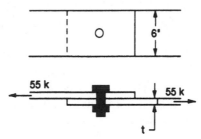

(This is a design problem since thickness of a plate is a function of its area. Remember to consider both gross and net areas.)

To begin with we must calculate the required capacity (P_u) that is to be applied to this member. Referring back to the standard load combinations from Chapter 2 (or Section A4.1 in the specification), we find that combination A4–2 controls and is as follows:

$P_u = 1.2$ (27.5 kips) $+ 1.6$ (27.5 kips) $= 77$ kips (342.5 KN)

Rearranging the formulas as given in Eq. 4–1 and 4–2, we can solve for area as follows;

Gross Area

$A_{g\,min} = 77$ kips$/(\phi_t F_y)$

$= 77$ kips$/(.90 \times 36$ ksi$) = 2.376$ in.^{2}

$(= .3425$ MN$/(.90 \times 248.2$ MPa$) = .00153$ m^2 or 1530 mm$^2)$

Since thickness = area/width = 2.376 in.^{2}/6 in.

Thickness = .396" (10.1 mm)

Net Area

$A_{n\,min} = 77$ kips$/(\phi_t F_u)$

$= 77$ kips$/(.75 \times 58$ ksi$) = 1.77$ in.^{2}

$(= .3425$ MN$/(.75 \times 399.9$ MPa$) = .00114$ m^2 or 1142 mm$^2)$

Express net area in terms of thickness t as follows:

Net area $= 6t - (1)(0.75" + 1/8")(t) = 5.125t$

1.77 in.$^2 = 5.125^t$

$.345$ in. $(8.76$ mm$)$ or $3/8" = t$

We have calculated two thicknesses (one for the gross and one for the net area) but the critical thickness would be 0.396" (over the gross area) because, although a 0.345" thick plate would work for the net area, it would be too small for the gross area.

(Author's note: In striving to present a simplified example to the beginning designer, I have shown an tension member design example with a connection of one bolt. This connection would undoubtedly fail in bolt shear and provide no structural redundancy in case of material deficiency or other potential failure catalysts.)

4.4 Effective Net Area, A$_e$

The student may have noticed that, up to now, all the illustrations and examples on tension members have dealt only with flat plates. This was purposely done in the initial discussions to simplify the subject of net area. Flat plates are ideal tension members with regard to their net area because all of their net area lies in the plane of loading. Therefore, all of a flat plate's net area is assumed to be active in resisting the tensile stress. This is not the case with rolled shapes whose full cross-section does not lie in the plane of the loading.

Previously, in the discussion on net area, it was revealed that the net section has an extremely uneven stress distribution. The magnitude of this stress distribution is increased dramatically if all of the net area is not effective in contributing to the resistance of tension stress. To measure a rolled shape's effectiveness of net area, the AISC introduces a term A_e, which is called the **effective net area.** The effective net area, A_e, is simply a member's net area multiplied by a **reduction coefficient U.** This is shown as follows:

$$A_e = A_{net} \times U \qquad \qquad \text{(Eq. 4–4)}$$

This reduction coefficient, U, approximates the increase in stress near the connection due to shear stress concentration when the full net area is not effective in transferring the applied load. The approximation of increased stress is actually done by decreasing the amount of area available. Hence, the term *effective net area.*

The value of U can most easily be found in section B3 of the commentary in the LRFD specification or taken from Table 4–1. These values reflect an approximate estimate of effectiveness in a rolled section based on items such as the type of section, the stockiness of the section, and the length of connection. The only elaboration needed on the information found in Table 4–1 is the explanation of the number of "bolts per line". A line of bolts refers to the fasteners spaced in a line along the length of the member, **not** across the net section.(Figure 4–5). The greater number of bolts per line ensures a longer connection area, thus helping to create a more effective net area.

Table 4–1 Standard AISC Reduction Coefficients, U

Description		Requirements	U
1. W, M, S shapes connected to flanges, and structural tees cut from these shapes	$b_f \geq (2/3)d$	3 bolts per line minimum	.90
2. W, M, S shapes and builtup members not meeting 1, and all other members meeting the requirements		3 bolts per line minimum	.85
3. All members having only 2 bolts per line			.75

Note: Values to be used unless larger values can be justified by testing.

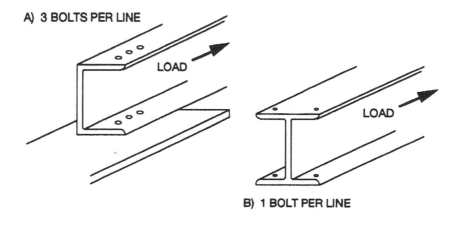

A) 3 BOLTS PER LINE

LOAD

LOAD

B) 1 BOLT PER LINE

Figure 4–5 Illustration of "Bolts per Line"

The direct stress formula for calculating either minimum required cross sectional area or the maximum factored load over the effective net area can be written as:

$$A_{net\ min} = P_u/(U \times \phi_t \times F_u) \qquad \text{(Eq. 4-5)}$$
$$P_u = \phi_t(F_u \times A_e)$$

where

$A_{net\ min}$ = minimum net cross sectional area of member to be designed

A_e = Effective net area (UA_n)

P_u = Maximum factored load from load combinations or maximum factored load on the member

F_u = Ultimate tensile stress of steel

The following examples will illustrate the use of this reduction coefficient, U, as it relates to the effective net area as used in the LRFD method.

EXAMPLE 4.3

The angle shown below is a $5 \times 5 \times 1/2$ ($127 \times 127 \times 12.7$) and is under a service tensile load of 48 kips (213.5 KN). Assume the distribution of load to be 50% live load and 50% dead load. The 7/8 inch diameter bolts are connected to the gusset plate as shown and all steel is A36. Calculate the adequacy of this member per AISC requirements.

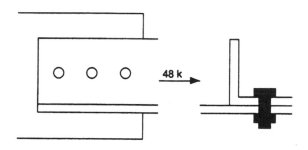

Again this is an evaluation problem to check the adequacy of a known member under a given load. To begin, let us calculate the maximum required capacity of this member or the maximum factored load it has to withstand.

P_u = 1.2(24 kips) + 1.6(24 kips) = 67.2 kips (Load combination A4–2 controls, see Section 2.6)

A_g = 4.75 in² (3060 mm²) From shape table in Appendix B

Calculating design capacity over the gross area using Eq. 4–1:

$\phi_t P_n = \phi_t (F_y A_{gross})$

$\phi_t P_n = .90 \ (36 \ \text{ksi} \times 4.75 \ \text{in.}^2) = 153.9 \ \text{kips}$

$(= .90 \ (248.2 \ \text{MPa} \times .00306 \ \text{m}^2) = .684 \ \text{MN or } 684 \ \text{KN})$

Since the design capacity is greater than the 67.2 kips of required capacity, the gross area is OK per AISC specification.

Check the Effective net area:

$A_e = U A_n$

$A_{net} = 4.75 \ \text{in.}^2 - (1)(7/8" + 1/8")(1/2") = 4.25 \ \text{in.}^2$

$U = .85$ (not a W, M, or S shape and 3 fasteners per line)

$A_e = .85 \times 4.25 \ \text{in.}^2 = 3.61 \ \text{in.}^2 \ (.002329 \ \text{m}^2)$

Calculating design capacity per Eq. 4–2;

$\phi_t P_n = .75 \ (3.61 \ \text{in.}^2 \times 58 \ \text{ksi}) = 157.1 \ \text{kips}$

$(= .75 \ (.002329 \ \text{m}^2 \times 399.9 \ \text{MPa}) = .698 \ \text{MN or } 698 \ \text{KN})$

Since the design capacity is greater than 67.2 kips, the effective net area is adequate per AISC specification and since both areas meet AISC criteria, member is adequate.

EXAMPLE 4.4

Design a W12 section to hold a factored load of 250 kips (1112 KN). The connection is to be made by ¾" bolts, through the flanges as shown below. There are at least 3 bolts per line and the steel is A36.

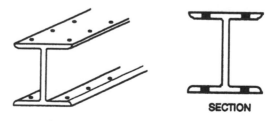

SECTION

(This is a design problem in which we are trying to determine the minimum area of a W12 section that will work. Since there are at least 3 bolts per line, we should know that the reduction factor, U, is either 0.85 or 0.90 based on the flange width to depth criteria.)

To begin, design for gross area realizing that the required capacity of 250 kips must be less than or equal to the design capacity ($\phi_t P_n$).

A_{min} = 250 kips/(.90 × 36 ksi) = 7.72 in.^{2}

(A_{min} = 1.112 MN/(.90 × 248.2 MPa) = .00497 m^2 or 4978 mm^2)

After looking in the section tables at the smallest possible W12 to meet this criteria we would try a W 12 × 30 (A = 8.79 in.^{2} or 5670 mm^2).

Check the effective net area based on a W 12 × 30

From Table 4–1 the reduction factor for a W12 × 30 (connected as shown) would be equal to 0.85, since 2/3 × depth (8.23") exceeds the flange width (6.52") and there are three bolts per line. Therefore calculate minimum net area per Equation 4–5 as follows:

$A_{net\ min}$ = 250 kips/.75 (58 ksi × .85) = 6.76 in.^{2}

(= 1.112 MN/.75 (399.9 MPa × .85) = .004361 m^2 or 4361 mm^2)

Because we have already incorporated the reduction factor, U, in the above calculation we can simply compare that net area to the actual net area of a W 12 × 30.

A_{net} = 8.79 in.^{2} – (4)(.75 in. + 1/8 in.)(.44 in.) = 7.25 in.^{2}

(= 5670 mm^2 – (4)(19.1 mm + 3.2 mm)(11.2 mm) = 4671 mm^2)

Since our actual net area is greater than the minimum net area of 6.76 in.^{2} (4361 mm^2), the W 12 × 30 will indeed be OK.

EXAMPLE 4.5

Calculate the design capacity of a 6 × 6 × 1/2 angle connected as shown below. The bolts are 7/8 inch diameter and the steel is A36.

From the section tables located in Appendix B this angle has a gross area of 5.75 in.^{2} (3710 mm^2). Calculate the design capacity over the gross area as follows by Eq. 4–1:

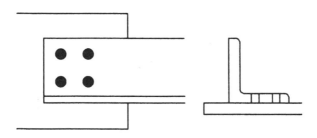

$$\phi_t P_n = \phi_t (F_y A_{\text{gross}})$$
$$\phi_t P_n = .90(36 \text{ ksi} \times 5.75 \text{ in.}^2) = 186.3 \text{ kips}$$
$$(= .90(248.2 \text{ MPa} \times .00371 \text{ m}^2) = .829 \text{ MN or } 829 \text{ KN})$$

Check the Effective net area:

$$A_e = UA_n$$
$$A_{\text{net}} = 5.75 \text{ in.}^2 - (2)(7/8 \text{ in.} + 1/8 \text{ in.})(1/2 \text{ in.}) = 4.75 \text{ in.}^2$$
$$U = .75 \text{ (only 2 fasteners per line)}$$
$$A_e = .75 \times 4.75 \text{ in.}^2 = 3.56 \text{ in.}^2 \ (.002299 \text{ m}^2)$$

Calculate design capacity as follows per Eq. 4–2;

$$\phi_t P_n = .75(3.56 \text{ in.}^2 \times 58 \text{ ksi}) = 154.9 \text{ kips}$$
$$(= .75(.002299 \text{ m}^2 \times 399.9 \text{ MPa}) = .689 \text{ MN or } 689 \text{ KN})$$

The design capacity is therefore equal to 154.9 kips (689 KN).

4.5   Multiple Bolt Configurations

In the discussion of effective net area's failure mechanism, we have implicitly considered the fracture to occur only directly across the member. That is, we have considered the cracking to occur only perpendicular to the direction of stress. This cracking failure, however, does not always have to occur straight across the member, but rather will occur in the path of least resistance. This path of least resistance is the path that traverses the smallest effective net area.

In Figure 4–6, the bolt arrangement shown has a layout consisting of multiple lines and spacings. Therefore, it is not readily apparent if failure would occur in the net area at section A–A or at section B–B. Although the failure line in

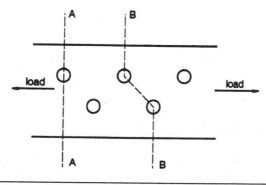

Figure 4–6   Potential Failure Paths with Multiple Bolt Layouts

section B–B is much longer, it also traverses two bolt holes instead of the one that section A–A would fail through. Which is the critical net area?

Although there are theoretical formulas that consider the shear stress effect along the diagonal failure line between bolt holes, tests show little is gained from using these complicated formulas over the empirical formula that the AISC proposes[3]. This empirical formula merely takes the net area (as we previously calculated) and adds in the additional diagonal areas by using the term $S^2/4g$. In this expression S is the longitudinal spacing of bolt holes (center-to-center) and g is the gage distance that is the center to center bolt spacing across the width of the member (Figure 4–7). Students should think of the $S^2/4g$ term as the diagonal distance between bolt holes, although they should remember that it is empirical by nature (that means it cannot be derived strictly by mathematical theory).

Therefore, when calculating the net area across a section containing diagonal areas the net area formula could be written:

$$A_{net} = A_{gross} - [(\# \text{ of holes})(\text{diameter} + 1/8)(\text{thickness})] +$$
$$[(\# \text{ of diagonals}) (S^2/4g)(\text{thickness})] \qquad \text{(Eq. 4–6)}$$

The above formula is based on all diagonals being of equal length. Should a net area contain diagonals of different lengths, each should be calculated separately. Every plausible net area should be calculated to determine what is critical. It should be noted that the $S^2/4g$ term is an approximation that the AISC gives for plates and angles. When dealing with more complex shapes such as channels, wide flanges and built-up members the engineer's judgment should be used regarding the various possibilities of critical net area.

The following example will illustrate the determination and use of critical effective net area in a standard tension member problem.

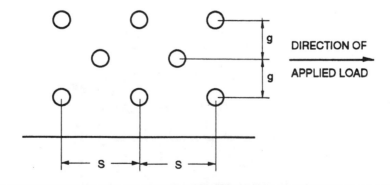

Figure 4–7   Representation of "s" and "g" for use in the s2/4g Term

EXAMPLE 4.6

Determine the adequacy of the plate shown below if it is made from A36 steel. Be sure to calculate the effective net area in the plate shown below considering sections through A–B, A–C–B, and A–C–E. The plate thickness is 1/2" and the bolt diameter is 5/8".

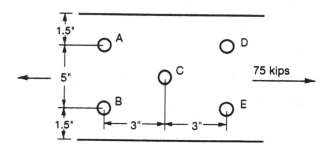

(In this evaluation problem we will determine adequacy by calculating the design capacity and comparing it to the factored load of 75 kips. Since we are dealing with a flat plate the reduction factor, U, for the effective net area is equal to 1.0)

Consider gross area

$$\phi_t P_n = \phi_t (A_g \times F_y) \quad A_g = 8" \times 1/2" = 4 \text{ in.}^2$$
$$\phi_t P_n = .90(4 \text{ in.}^2 \times 36 \text{ ksi}) = 129.6 \text{ kips}$$

Since 129.6 kips is greater than the factored load of 75 kips, the member is OK across gross area.

Consider the effective net area

(Remember since $U = 1.0$, effective net area is simply the net area)
In this problem, $s = 3"$ and $g = 2.5"$ therefore $s^2/4g = .90$
Calculate the different net areas as follows:

A–B: $4.0 \text{ in.}^2 - (2)(.75 \text{ in.})(.5 \text{ in.}) = 3.25 \text{ in.}^2$

A–C–B: $4.0 \text{ in.}^2 - (3)(.75 \text{ in.})(.5 \text{ in.}) + (2)(.90)(.5 \text{ in.}) = 3.77 \text{ in.}^2$

A–C–E: $4.0 \text{ in.}^2 - (3)(.75 \text{ in.})(.5 \text{ in.}) + (2)(.90)(.5 \text{ in.}) = 3.77 \text{ in.}^2$

The critical (smallest) net area is across section A–B and is 3.25 in².
The design capacity across the effective net area (using net area = 3.25 in.²) can be calculated as follows:

$\phi_t P_n = .75 \ (3.25 \text{ in.}^2 \times 58 \text{ ksi}) = 141.38 \text{ kips.}$

Since the design capacity (141.38 kips) is greater than the required capacity of 75 kips, the member is adequate across the effective net area.

Since the member meets AISC criteria across both gross and effective net area, member is adequate.

4.6   Pin-Connected Members and Rods

Many older truss bridges in use today have pin-connected members, instead of being bolted or welded into gusset plates. This was the usual configuration for bridges until the advent of bolting and welding. Today pin-connected members may still be used in special circumstances such as utility hangers, but in reality they are not used very often. Pin-connected tension members have different critical stress considerations as found in section D3 of the AISC specification. These will be briefly outlined in the following paragraphs.

The design capacity on the net effective area of the pin-connected tension member is shown below, although bearing and shear capacities on the effective area must also conform to AISC criteria found in section D3. These bearing and shear capacities will be further discussed in Chapter 9.

Design tensile capacity on net effective area:

$$\phi_t P_n = .75(2t\, b_{eff} F_u) \tag{Eq. 4-7}$$

where

$\phi_t = .75$

t = plate thickness

b_{eff} = effective width which is equal to $2t + .63''$ but not more than the actual distance from the hole edge to the edge of the part

F_u = steel's ultimate tensile strength

Threaded rods are also used in many hanger-type applications, from suspended walkways to sag rods in roof systems. The design capacity that the AISC specifies in Table J3.2 over the major diameter of a rod is as follows:

$$\phi_t T_n = .75(A_b \times .75 F_u) \tag{Eq. 4-8}$$

where

$\phi_t = .75$

A_b = nominal rod area

F_u = steel's ultimate tensile strength

This nominal rod capacity, T_n, is the criterion to prevent fracture, but slenderness criteria deflection criteria may also be important. The student is referred to section D2 and Chapter L of the LRFD specification for information regarding permissible slenderness and deflections respectively.

The following example will illustrate the use of the LRFD specifications as they pertain to threaded rods.

EXAMPLE 4.7

Design the diameter of a threaded rod to hold a service load of 15 kips. Assume live load is 2/3 and dead load is 1/3 of total. The steel is A36 (F_y = 36 ksi and F_u = 58 ksi).

Required capacity is as follows:

$$T_u = 1.2(5 \text{ kips}) + 1.6(10 \text{ kips}) = 22 \text{ kips (97.9KN)}$$

Designing the diameter of a rod is actually a function of area; therefore, design per the fracture criteria as listed in Equation 4–8:

Design area:

$$A_{min} = T_u/.75(.75F_u)$$
$$A_{min} = 22 \text{ kips}/.75(.75 \times 58 \text{ ksi}) = .674 \text{ in.}^2$$
$$(= .0979 \text{MN}/.75 \ (.75 \times 399.9 \text{MPa}) = .000435 \text{ m}^2 \text{ or } 435 \text{ mm}^2)$$

Since the rod is circular, $A = \pi/4 \times (d)^2$ and solving for diameter gives us a diameter equal to 1" (.785 in.^{2}).

4.7   Summary

Tension members are relatively common in steel contruction, being utilized in trusses, frames and various cable and rod applications. The LRFD method specifies that the tension member's design capacity ($\phi_t P_n$) is greater than or equal to the required capacity (P_u).

The tension member being considered must always be checked or designed over the gross area and the effective net area. The gross area is the section's full cross-sectional area, while the effective net area is the section with the bolt holes taken out. Sometimes the effective net area is reduced further to account for the ineffectiveness in transferring stress to adjoining members. The limit state that is probable over the gross area is yielding while the probable limit state over the effective net area is fracture.

EXERCISES

1. Find the maximum factored load permitted on a 6" wide × 3/4" thick plate with 1/2" diameter bolts as shown below. The steel is A36.

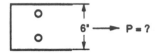

2. Find the design tensile capacity of a plate measuring 150 mm × 12.7 mm if it is made from A36 steel. The plate has two holes for 19.1 mm diameter bolts per cross-section.

3. Find the design tensile capacity of a 8" wide × 3/4" thick plate subjected to an factored axial tensile load of 85 kips. The plate has three 3/4" diameter bolt holes arranged in one row across the plate. The steel is A36. Is this acceptable per AISC criteria?

4. Design the thickness of a 127 mm wide plate with two 19.1 mm bolts arranged in a single row across the plate. The steel is A36 and the factored tensile load is 240 KN.

5. Design the thickness of a 8" wide steel plate with the bolt layout as shown below. The bolts are 3/4" diameter and the steel is A242 (F_y = 50 ksi and F_u = 70 ksi).

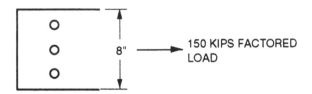

6. The W 12 × 50 shown below is used as a tension member and is bolted through its flanges as shown with 3/4" diameter bolts. Determine the maximum factored load. Steel is A36.

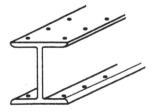

7. Determine the design capacity of a C 10 × 30 connected as shown in Figure 4–5 with 7/8" bolts. The steel is A242.

8. Find the design tensile capacity for a 4 × 4 × 1/2 angle connected as shown by the 5/8" diameter bolts. The angle has a service load of 45 kips (LL = 50% and DL = 50%) and the steel is A36. Compare to AISC specifications. Does this angle work?

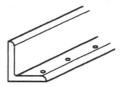

9. Rework problem 8 with the member being a 127 × 127 × 19.0 angle made from A242 steel.

10. Determine the critical net area through the plate shown below. The plate is 8 in. wide × 1 in. thick and the bolts are 1/2" diameter.

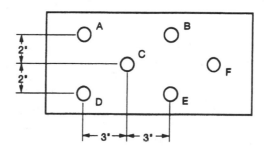

11. If the above plate has a 160 kip tensile service load on it (75% LL, 25% DL), is it adequate per AISC standards? Steel is A36.

12. Design a single angle tension member to carry a service dead load of 50 kips and a service live load of 55 kips. The angle is made from A36 steel and is connected with three 5/8" diameter bolts in one leg, these bolts arranged in one line.

13. Design the most economical W 12 section to hold a service tensile load of 400 kips. The bolts and connection details are the same as in problem# 6. Steel is A36. Assume dead and live loads are 50% of the service load each.

14. Design an economical angle to hold a factored load of 1100 KN. The angle is connected with 19.1 mm bolts situated as shown below and the steel is A36.

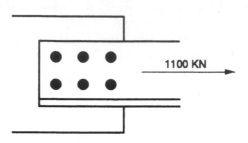

15. Design the most economical 4 × 4 angle to hold a service tensile load of 135 kips (50% LL, 50% DL). The angle has one line of 3/4" diameter A490 bolts with 3 bolts in this line. Steel is A242 (F_y = 50 ksi and F_u = 70 ksi).

16. Design a single angle tension member to resist a factored load of 155 kips. The steel is A36 and is to be connected with one line of three 3/4" diameter bolts.

17. Design a W 250 member to resist a factored load of 3000 KN. The member is to be connected through its flanges with four 19.1 mm bolts per cross-section and three bolts per line. Steel is A36.

18. Calculate the maximum factored load that can be placed on a 1-1/8" diameter threaded rod if the rod is made from A36 steel. What is this rod's design capacity?

19. Calculate the design capacity on the 7 × 4 × 1/2 double angles placed long legs back-to-back. The bolts are 3/4" diameter and are placed as shown. Steel is A36.

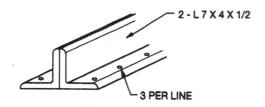

20. For the truss shown below, calculate the tensile loads on members AB, CD and FC and design single angle members to resist such loads. Steel is A36 and the angles are connected by one line of four 7/8" bolts. All loads shown are factored.

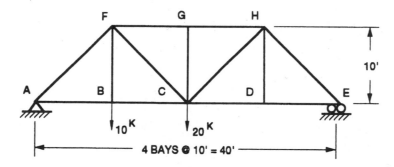

REFERENCES

1. Olsen, Gerner A., *Elements of Mechanics of Materials,* Englewood Cliffs, NJ: Prentice-Hall, 1974, p. 520.
2. Dowling, Patrick, Knolwes, Peter, and Owens, Graham, *Structural Steel Design,* London: The Steel Construction Institute, 1988, p.156.
3. Salmon, Charles G., and Johnson, John E., *Steel Structures Design and Behavior,* New York, Harper and Row, 1980, p. 70.

5

COMPRESSION MEMBER DESIGN

5.1 Introduction

Compression members are found in all types of construction from the skeleton framing of a building to the massive pier towers of the Golden Gate Bridge (Figure 5–1). If compression members are set vertically they are commonly referred to as *columns*. The student should note that the terms, *compression members* and *columns,* will be used interchangeably throughout this chapter.

The importance of compression members cannot be underestimated, they are extremely important in the overall design in buildings or bridges. The student must remember that if a column fails, everything supported above that column will most probably collapse.

This chapter will present the AISC technique for concentric compression member design using the Load and Resistance Factor Design (LRFD) method. Discussion will include column instability and the factors relating this behavior to the AISC equations.

It should be stated that columns are rarely, if ever, loaded concentrically in the real world. They are more typically subjected to some bending moment either through eccentric axial loads, beam reactions, lateral loadings, or a combination thereof. When such situations induce bending stresses into the axially loaded compression member, these members are typically referred to as *beam-columns.* This topic will be the focus of chapter 8.

Figure 5–1 The Golden Gate Bridge, San Francisco. (Courtesy Bethlehem Steel Corporation.)

5.2   Potential Modes of Column Failure

Column behavior is notably different than that of tension members. Whereas the tension member under stress tends to "straighten out" in the direction of the load, a column tends to "move out" of the plane of loading. This tendency to "move out" is referred to as **buckling** and is a serious concern in column design. Buckling constitutes failure because the column is unstable and cannot accept any additional load.

Another method of column failure is the **yielding** (crushing) of the material due to the actual stress on the member being greater than the yield. It is evident that as columns get longer, the failure mode that dominates is buckling. Only very short columns will fail due to yielding, and the intermediate length column will fail by a combination of these two types of behavior (Figure 5–2).

This intermediate behavior occurs because these columns do not buckle until stresses have reached a sufficiently high level, thereby initiating some yielding of the fibers. The vast majority of columns fall into the category of intermediate behavior.

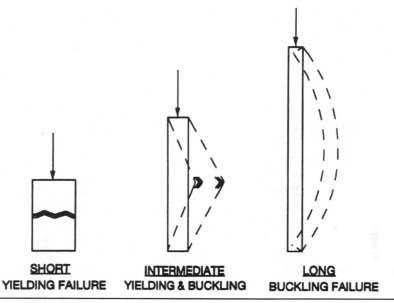

Figure 5–2   Various Failure Modes relative to Column Length.

5.3   Column Behavior

The understanding of columns and the use of today's design equations can be traced back to a Swiss mathematician, Leonard Euler. In the mid-eighteenth century, Euler studied column buckling and derived a formula to predict the load that would cause a column with rounded ends to buckle [1]. This formula is the basis of all modern day column equations and is shown below:

$$P = \frac{\pi^2 EI}{l^2}$$

where

P = Buckling load
E = Material's modulus of elasticity
I = Moment of inertia
l = Length of column between points of zero moment

Usually this formula is written in terms of buckling stress (P/A) by substituting Ar^2 for the moment of inertia, I. We can then express Euler's equation in terms of buckling stress as follows:

$$\frac{P}{A} = \frac{\pi^2 E}{(l/r)^2}$$

where
r = radius of gyration about the buckling axis

From Euler's equation the student can see that buckling is dependent on basically two factors; the l/r term (typically referred to as **slenderness ratio**) and the column's **modulus of elasticity**. The student should study Euler's equation and realize that as the slenderness ratio (l/r) increases, the buckling stress decreases. This would mean that as a column gets longer (therefore, more "slender"), the stress to initiate buckling becomes smaller.

Because of the incorporation of the modulus of elasticity in the Euler equation, its use was limited by the fact that it would describe only buckling that occurred in the material's elastic region. When buckling in the elastic region occurs it is referred to as **elastic buckling**. This phenomena of elastic buckling is limited to long, slender columns that buckle under low stress levels.

This limitation made this equation accurate in predicting buckling behavior for only a small number of columns. Columns that are of intermediate length do not buckle elasticly, and therefore, Euler's equation tended to overestimate their capacity. (Figure 5–3) Buckling for intermediate length columns occurs at higher stress levels, and this type of buckling is referred to as **inelastic buckling**, since some fibers will have yielded as buckling commences. Because many typical columns are of intermediate length, the Euler equation was ignored for many years[2] while engineer's searched for a single equation to describe buckling over all column lengths.

A single column equation defining column behavior over all ranges of slenderness ratios has never been developed. In lieu of this absence, modern day column design equations are based on the fact that there are two types of buckling that occur: elastic and inelastic. Elastic buckling occurs as stresses on a

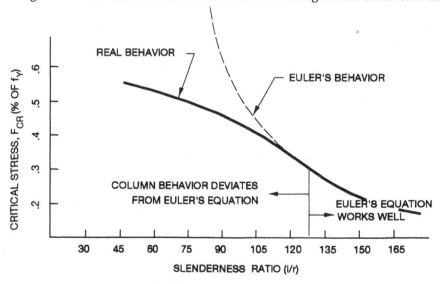

Figure 5–3 Actual Column Behavior versus Euler Behavior

column are rather low and still under the material's proportional limit. Inelastic buckling occurs at higher stress levels and cannot be well defined by the original Euler equation. The AISC recognizes this fact and, therefore, recommends two column equations (one for elastic and one for inelastic behavior) for use in design. We will discuss these AISC equations further in section 5.5.

5.4   Effective Length

The degree of fixity at the ends of a column is known to dramatically affect a column's buckling resistance. Because of this, there has been some modification of Euler's original equation because his testing dealt only with one type of end-restraint condition. Actually, columns may have many types of end-restraint conditions, so a modification factor that estimates effective length of the column has been introduced. This modification factor is referred to as the **effective length factor, K.**

This effective length factor approximates the length over which a column actually buckles. This buckling length can be longer or shorter than the actual length of the column based on end-restraints of the column and/or whether the column is subjected to lateral movement. The student should realize that as the length of a column is reduced, the column actually increases its resistance to buckling; conversely, as the column length is increased, the resistance to buckling decreases. End-restraint conditions on a column will dramatically influence the buckling length or **effective length, Kl,** of this member. The effective length factor, *K*, is an attempt to accurately describe the true buckling length of the column (Figure 5–4).

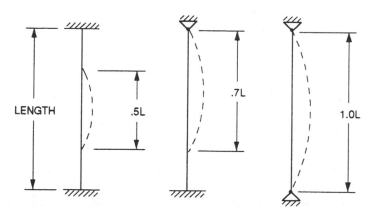

Figure 5–4   Effect of End Restraint Condition on Buckled Length

Much research has been devoted to the investigation of K factors in both braced and unbraced frames. The following chart (Figure 5–5) contains widely recognized K values for *ideal* end-restraint conditions (pin, fixed, free, etc.). The AISC recognizes that in real practice there are no ideal conditions, therefore, recommended K values are also shown. Notice the recommended values are always greater than or equal to the theoretical values.

The following example illustrates the power of the effective length factors as they are taken from this chart. Keep in mind that a column's effective length and its critical stress will be shown to have an inversely proportional relationship. That is, as a column becomes "shorter", the calculated critical stress will increase.

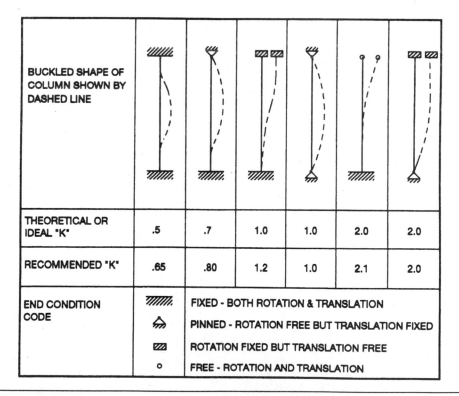

Figure 5–5 Typical Values of "K" for Idealized End Conditions

EXAMPLE 5.1

Calculate the effective length, *Kl*, of a 20 foot long column under the following three end-restraint conditions. Use the recommended values from the chart.

1. pin-pin
2. pin-fixed
3. fixed-fixed

The effective length should be calculated as follows:

1. Since the recommended *K* value for a pin-pin end condition is 1.0, the effective length, *Kl*, of this value is 1.0 × 20' = 20'
2. The recommended *K* value for a pin-fixed end condition is .80, therefore the effective length is .80 × 20' = 16' (Essentially because of its end conditions this column behaves similarly to a 16' long column with pin-pin end conditions).
3. With the recommended *K* value equal to 0.65, the effective length is equal to 0.65 × 20' = 13' (Again, the column has essentially the same behavior as a 13' long column with pinned ends).

5.5 AISC Column Design Philosophy Using LRFD

The AISC formulas for column design are the result of research committed to finding a formula that accurately predicts column behavior in all slenderness ranges. There have been many formulas proposed, including the *Gordon-Rankine,* the *parabolic,* and the *secant* formulas. The AISC recommends using a parabolic formula in the inelastic range and a hyperbolic Euler formula in the elastic range.

The AISC philosophy recognizes that the behavior of a column changes from the elastic to the inelastic range. Because of this the AISC sets a value of a **slenderness parameter** λ_c as the dividing line between the two aforementioned ranges. The value of this slenderness parameter is actually a ratio of yield stress to Euler buckling stress and can be written as shown below:

$$\lambda_c^2 = F_y/F_{euler}$$

where

$$F_{euler} = \pi^2 E/(Kl/r)^2$$

or

$$\lambda_c = (Kl/r\,\pi)\,\sqrt{F_y/E} \qquad\qquad \text{(Eq. 5–1)}$$

The parabolic formula that reasonably describes inelastic buckling was developed by the Structural Stability Research Council[4] (SSRC), and using the slenderness parameter this formula becomes:

$$F_{cr} = (1 - \lambda_c^2/4) \, F_y \text{ for } \lambda_c \leq \sqrt{2}$$

where

F_{cr} = critical buckling stress

At $\sqrt{2}$ you will notice that this equation's value of critical stress becomes $0.50 \, F_y$ which is indicative of AISC use of 50% F_y as the stress level delineating inelastic from elastic behavior. The reasoning for using a value of only 50% of F_y to delineate elastic from inelastic buckling is due to the effect of residual stress in rolled members. Residual stresses are those stresses that are "built-in" rolled members due to uneven cooling during the manufacturing process. Residual stresses can be as high as $20 - 30\%$ of F_y and these stresses can lead to intermediate columns buckling at stresses below their theoretical critical load. [3]

When $\lambda_c \geq \sqrt{2}$, elastic buckling behavior controls, and the SSRC formula is based on the Euler equation. It is presented as follows:

$$F_{cr} = (1/\lambda_c^2)F_y$$

The LRFD specification has slightly modified the aforementioned SSRC formulas in the following manner to reflect an initial out-of-straightness in the magnitude of 1/1500. For elastic buckling, when $\lambda_c > 1.5$, the critical stress is given by the following LRFD formula:

$$F_{cr} = (.877/\lambda_c^2)F_y \qquad\qquad\qquad \text{(Eq. 5–2)}$$

where

F_{cr} = critical buckling or column stress

The 0.877 is a modifier to Euler's equation to account for a column's reduced strength associated with initial crookedness and which is magnified by increased column length. This modifier is closely related to the variable safety factor in the denominator of AISC equation E2–1 of the ASD specification. The nominal safety factor in the allowable stress method was 5/3, but this increased to 23/12 due to column crookedness. To remain consistent with ASD, the LFRD method multiplies the elastic formula, LRFD E2–3, by approximately 5/3·23 /12.

For inelastic buckling stress, when $\lambda_c \leq 1.5$, the LRFD specification presents the following formula for critical buckling stress:

$$F_{cr} = (.658^{\lambda_c^2}) \, F_y \qquad\qquad\qquad \text{(Eq. 5–3)}$$

The reader should notice that equations 5–2 and 5–3 become equal when the slenderness parameter, λ_c, equals 1.5. At this point both equations become equal to $0.39 \, F_y$ and, therefore, if the stress in the column (P_u / A) exceeds $0.39 \, F_y$ the column is assumed to behave inelasticly. This AISC philosophy is outlined below in Figure 5–6.

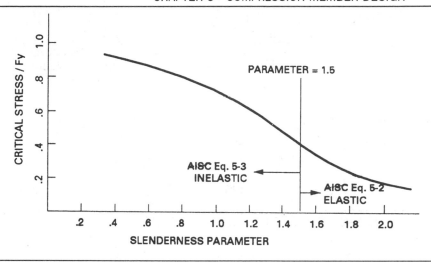

Figure 5–6   Use of AISC Column Equations relative to Behavior

5.6   Braced Columns

We have already discussed how columns will behave as the stress on them becomes increasingly large. So far in design, we realize that to carry more load we can always increase a member's area. But can we increase the load carrying capacity of these columns without using a larger rolled section?

Yes, with columns we can accomplish an increase in strength be reducing the effective length, *Kl*, through the use of bracing. Bracing of columns can take various forms such as steel X- bracing, the framing in of beams, or the bracing effects due to a floor system (Figure 5–7). All of these will reduce the overall buckling length of column, and as this length is reduced, the stress that the column is allowed to carry will increase (Figure 5–8).

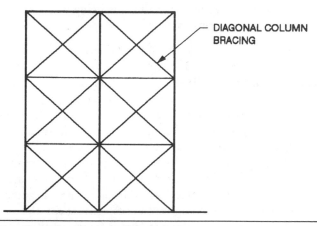

Figure 5–7   Bracing of a Structural Frame

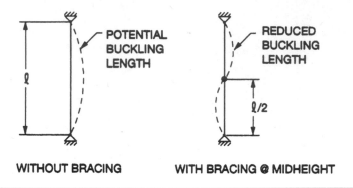

Figure 5–8   Bracing Effect on Column Buckling

The location of this bracing is also very important to the load carrying capacity of the column. The student will remember the buckling load formulas all incorporate the λ_c term known as the *slenderness parameter*. If we look again at the equation for this parameter:

$$\lambda_c = Kl/r\pi\,(\sqrt{F_y/E}\,)$$

we see that the only variable, once column heights, effective length factors and steel grades have been decided upon, is the radius of gyration, r. The radius of gyration is an elastic property of the individual rolled section based on the axis under consideration and is given by the formula:

$$r = \sqrt{I/A}$$

where

    I = moment of inertia about the axis being considered, in.^{4} (mm^4)
    A = the cross-sectional area of the shape, in.^{2} (mm^2)

As you view the section property tables, notice that r_y is always less than r_x for wide-flange sections. Therefore, for an unbraced wide-flange column, the slenderness ratio Kl/r_y will always be larger than Kl/r_x (assuming that K remains the same about both axes). This means that buckling of an unbraced column will always occur about the weak or y–y axis because the column is more slender in this direction. By bracing the column in the weak direction (y–y), we also reduce the Kl/r_y value to produce a larger critical stress. By lowering Kl/r_y, we might even reach the point where the weak axis no longer controls ($Kl/r_y < Kl/r_x$).

The design equations for columns with bracing are exactly the same as outlined in the previous section, although when bracing is used, the student cannot assume that buckling will necessarily occur about the weak axis. When bracing is used or if the effective length factor is different between the x and y axis, the slenderness parameter about the strong and weak axis must both be calculated. The higher of these two slenderness parameters will control the design, since the higher of the two will lead to a smaller value of critical stress.

5.7 Column Design Problems per LRFD

The LRFD method for columns follows the same format that was discussed in the previous chapters which is simply stated as follows:

Design Strength ≥ Required Resistance

For columns in particular this general format will take the specific form as shown below:

$$\phi_c P_n \geq P_u$$

where

$\phi_c = .85$, column reduction factor

$P_n = A_g F_{cr}$, nominal column strength

P_u = maximum factored column load

As we have stated before, there are two general types of problems encountered in steel design. In the evaluation problem you will be given a member and corresponding load, and asked to determine its adequacy. In a design problem you will be given loads and asked to design the member size.

The evaluation problem is very easy to perform and the following examples will attest to this. All that is necessary is to compare design strength $(\phi_c P_n)$ to factored load (P_u). The following examples will provide some insight to these problems.

EXAMPLE 5.2

Calculate the maximum factored load (P_u) that a W 14×53 (W 360×79) column can hold if it is 20 feet long (6.1 m) with a K = 1.0. Steel is A36.

The W 14×53 has the following:

$A = 15.6$ in.^{2} (10,100 mm^2)

$r_x = 5.89$ in.

$r_y = 1.92$ in. $(r_y = 48.9$ mm)

Because the column is not braced, the weak axis (r_y) will control.

$Kl/r_y = 1.0 \times 20 \times 12/1.92 = 125$

Calculating the controlling slenderness parameter from Eq. 5–1 we find:

$$\lambda_c = (Kl/r\pi) \sqrt{F_y/E}$$

$$\lambda_c = (125/\pi) \sqrt{36000/29 \times 10^6} = 1.401$$

Since $\lambda_c = 1.401 < 1.5$ we will use Eq. 5–3 to calculate the critical buckling stress F_{cr} as follows:

$$F_{cr} = (.658^{\lambda_c^2}) F_y$$

$$F_{cr} = (.658^{1.401^2})36 \text{ ksi} = 15.81 \text{ ksi}$$

$$(F_{cr} = (.658^{1.401^2}) \, 248.2\text{MPa} = 109\text{MPa})$$

Calculating the design capacity of the section, $\phi_c P_n$, we find:

$$\phi_c P_n = \phi_c A_g F_{cr}$$
$$.85 \times 15.6 \text{ in.}^2 \times 15.81 \text{ ksi} = 209.6 \text{ kips}$$
$$(.85 \times .010100 \text{ m}^2 \times 109\text{MPa} = .93\text{MN or } 930\text{KN})$$

Since the design capacity of the section represents the maximum factored load on the column, P_u is equal to 209.6 kips.

When bracing is used the slenderness parameters λ_c, about both the strong and weak axis should be checked with the larger controlling the design. Example 5.3 illustrates this type of problem.

EXAMPLE 5.3

Calculate the maximum factored load, P_u, for a W 24 × 104 that is 20 feet long with a K = 0.80. Then recalculate if the column is braced at midheight in the weak axis (still assume K = 0.80). Use A36 steel.

Part a

The W 24 × 104 has the following properties:

$A = 30.6 \text{ in.}^2$ $(19,800 \text{ mm}^2)$
$r_x = 10.1 \text{ in.}$
$r_y = 2.91 \text{ in.}$

Being unbraced, the weak axis will control and calculating the slenderness ratio about this axis we find

$$Kl/r_y = .8(20 \text{ ft.} \times 12 \text{ in./ft.}) / 2.91 \text{ in.} = 65.98$$

Using Eq. 5–1 the slenderness parameter can then be calculated as follows:

$$\lambda_c = (Kl/r\,\pi)\,\sqrt{F_y/E}$$

$$\lambda_c = (65.98/\pi)\,\sqrt{.00124} = .7399 < 1.5$$

Since the slenderness parameter is less than 1.5, inelastic behavior controls and Eq. 5–3 is used to find the critical buckling stress.

$$F_{cr} = (.658^{\lambda_c^2})F_y$$

$$F_{cr} = (.658^{.7399^2})36 = 28.62 \text{ ksi}$$

$$(= (.658^{.7399^2})248.2\text{MPa} = 197.4 \text{ MPa})$$

Calculating the design capacity of the section, $\phi_c P_n$, we find;

$$\phi_c P_n = \phi_c\,A_g\,F_{cr}$$
$$= .85 \times 30.6 \text{ in.}^2 \times 28.62 \text{ ksi} = 744.4 \text{ kips}$$
$$(= .85 \times .0198 \text{ m}^2 \times 197.4\text{MPa} = 3.33\text{MN or } 3332\text{KN})$$

Since the design capacity of the section represents the maximum factored load on the column, P_u is equal to 744.4 kips in this case.

Part b Column braced midheight in weak direction

Calculating the slenderness ratio, we find that the weak axis still controls in this scenario.

$$Kl/r_x = .8(20 \text{ ft.} \times 12)/10.1 \text{ in.} = 19.01$$
$$Kl/r_y = .8(10 \text{ ft.} \times 12)/2.91 \text{ in.} = 32.99$$

Using Eq. 5–1 the slenderness parameter can then be calculated as follows:

$$\lambda_c = (KL/r\,\pi)\,\sqrt{F_y/E}$$

$$\lambda_c = (32.99/\pi)\,\sqrt{.00124} = .369 < 1.5$$

Since the slenderness parameter is again less than 1.5, inelastic behavior controls and Eq. 5–3 is used to find the critical buckling stress.

$$F_{cr} = (.658^{\lambda_c^2})F_y$$
$$F_{cr} = (.658^{.369^2})36 = 34 \text{ ksi}$$
$$(= (.658^{.369^2})248.2 \text{ MPa} = 234.5 \text{ MPa})$$

Calculating the design capacity of the section, $\phi_c P_n$, we find:

$$\phi_c P_n = \phi_c A_g F_{cr}$$
$$= .85 \times 30.6 \text{ in.}^2 \times 34 \text{ ksi} = 884.4 \text{ kips}$$
$$(= .85 \times .0198 \text{ m2} \times 234.5 \text{ MPa} = 3.945\text{MN or } 3945\text{KN})$$

Since the design capacity of the section represents the maximum factored load on the column, P_u is equal to 884.4 kips in this case. Therefore, bracing increases capacity $884.4 − 744.4/744.4 = 18.8\%$.

Should the designer encounter a situation where different unbraced lengths occur on the same column, the unbraced length with the largest slenderness parameter would control the section. The largest slenderness parameter will translate into a lower critical stress, thereby reducing the section's design capacity. Example 5.4 will address this occurrence.

EXAMPLE 5.4

Calculate the design capacity of a W 12 × 79 column (W 310 × 117) whose length is 20 feet (6.1 m). The column is braced along its weak axis at five from the top and bottom of the column and the steel is A36. $K = 1.0$ and assume the braces are likewise.

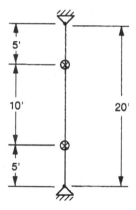

In this case, the unbraced lengths along the weak axis are 5 feet at the ends and 10 feet in the middle while the unbraced length along the strong axis is 20 feet. The effective length along the weak axis to be used for comparison with the strong axis is the larger of the following:

$Kl_y = 1.0(5 \text{ ft.}) = 5 \text{ ft.}$
$Kl_y = 1.0(10 \text{ ft.}) = 10 \text{ ft. } (3.05 \text{ m})$ — controls

Calculating the slenderness ratio, we find that the strong axis begins to control this scenario.

$Kl/r_x = 1.0(20 \text{ ft.} \times 12 \text{ in./ft.})/5.34 \text{ in.} = 44.9$
$Kl/r_y = 1.0(10 \text{ ft.} \times 12 \text{ in./ft.})/3.05 \text{ in.} = 39.3$

Using Eq. 5–1 the slenderness parameter can then be calculated as follows:

$$\lambda_c = (Kl/r\pi) \sqrt{F_y/E}$$

$$\lambda_c = (44.9/\pi) \sqrt{.00124} = .503 < 1.5$$

Since the slenderness parameter is again less than 1.5, inelastic behavior controls and Eq. 5–3 is used to find the critical buckling stress.

$$F_{cr} = (.658^{\lambda_c^2}) F_y$$

$$F_{cr} = (.658^{.503^2})36 = 32.4 \text{ ksi}$$

$$(F_{cr} = (.658^{.503^2})248.2\text{MPa} = 223.4\text{MPa})$$

Calculating the design capacity of the section $\phi_c P_n$ we find:

$$\phi_c P_n = \phi_c A_g F_{cr}$$
$$= .85 \times 23.2 \text{ in.}^2 \times 32.4 \text{ ksi} = 638.9 \text{ kips}$$
$$(= .85 \times .015 \text{ m}^2 \times 223.4 \text{ MPa} = 2.84\text{MN or } 2840\text{KN})$$

Design problems are, as usual, a little more difficult than the evaluation problems. To begin with, we will proceed on the assumption the student does not have the many design tables that might actually be at his or her disposal. This initial design procedure is a trial and error approach, but is found to be very quick using LRFD. If the reader realizes that the relationship between critical stress, F_{cr}, and the slenderness parameter, λ_c, is inversely proportional, then the process can begin by assuming a reasonable value for design stress, $\phi_c F_{cr}$. Typically this value may be approximately 25–30 ksi, tending to be larger when the slenderness parameter is small and vice versa. Once a value of design stress is assumed a trial section can be selected based on the following formula:

$$A_{g \text{ trial}} = P_u / \phi_c F_{cr}$$

This trial section can then be checked for its design capacity, $\phi_c P_n$, relative to the applied factored load on the column, P_u. If the design capacity is equal to or just a bit larger than the required (factored) capacity, then the trial section is good. If the trial section's design capacity is smaller than or much greater than the required capacity, then the section should be resized accordingly. The step by step process might be listed as follows:

1. Assume a design stress, $\phi_c F_{cr}$, typically around 25–30 ksi
2. Using an assumed $\phi_c F_{cr}$, calculated $A_{g \text{ trial}}$
3. Choose trial member based on $A_{g \text{ trial}}$
4. Calculate F_{cr} of trial member & compare $\phi_c P_n$ to P_u
5. If $\phi_c P_n = P_u$ or just a bit larger, the section is perfect
   If $\phi_c F_{cr} A_g \ggg P_u$, choose a smaller section
   If $\phi_c F_{cr} A_g < P_u$, choose a larger section

Table 5–1 Design Stress, ic Fcr, for A36 Steel. (Courtesy of the American Institute of Steel Construction, Inc.)

$\frac{Kl}{r}$	$\phi_c F_{cr}$ (ksi)	$\frac{Kl}{r}$	$\phi_c F_{cr}$ (ksi)	$\frac{Kl}{r}$	$\phi_c F_{cr}$ (ksi)	$\frac{Kl}{r}$	$\phi_c F_{cr}$ (ksi)	$\frac{Kl}{r}$	$\phi_c F_{cr}$ (ksi)
1	30.60	41	28.01	81	21.66	121	14.16	161	8.23
2	30.59	42	27.89	82	21.48	122	13.98	162	8.13
3	30.59	43	27.76	83	21.29	123	13.80	163	8.03
4	30.57	44	27.64	84	21.11	124	13.62	164	7.93
5	30.56	45	27.51	85	20.92	125	13.44	165	7.84
6	30.54	46	27.37	86	20.73	126	13.27	166	7.74
7	30.52	47	27.24	87	20.54	127	13.09	167	7.65
8	30.50	48	27.11	88	20.36	128	12.92	168	7.56
9	30.47	49	26.97	89	20.17	129	12.74	169	7.47
10	30.44	50	26.83	90	19.98	130	12.57	170	7.38
11	30.41	51	26.68	91	19.79	131	12.40	171	7.30
12	30.37	52	26.54	92	19.60	132	12.23	172	7.21
13	30.33	53	26.39	93	19.41	133	12.06	173	7.13
14	30.29	54	26.25	94	19.22	134	11.88	174	7.05
15	30.24	55	26.10	95	19.03	135	11.71	175	6.97
16	30.19	56	25.94	96	18.84	136	11.54	176	6.89
17	30.14	57	25.79	97	18.65	137	11.37	177	6.81
18	30.08	58	25.63	98	18.46	138	11.20	178	6.73
19	30.02	59	25.48	99	18.27	139	11.04	179	6.66
20	29.96	60	25.32	100	18.08	140	10.89	180	6.59
21	29.90	61	25.16	101	17.89	141	10.73	181	6.51
22	29.83	62	24.99	102	17.70	142	10.58	182	6.44
23	29.76	63	24.83	103	17.51	143	10.43	183	6.37
24	29.69	64	24.67	104	17.32	144	10.29	184	6.30
25	29.61	65	24.50	105	17.13	145	10.15	185	6.23
26	29.53	66	24.33	106	16.94	146	10.01	186	6.17
27	29.45	67	24.16	107	16.75	147	9.87	187	6.10
28	29.36	68	23.99	108	16.56	148	9.74	188	6.04
29	29.28	69	23.82	109	16.37	149	9.61	189	5.97
30	29.18	70	23.64	110	16.19	150	9.48	190	5.91
31	29.09	71	23.47	111	16.00	151	9.36	191	5.85
32	28.99	72	23.29	112	15.81	152	9.23	192	5.79

To aid the designer in the efficient utilization of the Equations 5–2 and 5–3, the LRFD manual provides many different design charts. One such helpful chart is Table 3–36 shown below in Table 5–1. This table lists design stresses ($\phi_c F_{cr}$) for varying slenderness ratios. By simply multiplying the tabular value by the section's area, the designer can quickly calculate the column's design capacity ($\phi_c P_n$). The following examples will illustrate the design of compression members using LRFD.

TABLE 5–1 Continued

$\dfrac{Kl}{r}$	$\phi_c F_{cr}$ (ksi)	$\dfrac{Kl}{r}$	$\phi_c F_{cr}$ (ksi)	$\dfrac{Kl}{r}$	$\phi_c F_{cr}$ (ksi)	$\dfrac{Kl}{r}$	$\phi_c F_{cr}$ (ksi)	$\dfrac{Kl}{r}$	$\phi_c F_{cr}$ (ksi)
33	28.90	73	23.12	113	15.63	153	9.11	193	5.73
34	28.79	74	22.94	114	15.44	154	9.00	194	5.67
35	28.69	75	22.76	115	15.26	155	8.88	195	5.61
36	28.58	76	22.58	116	15.07	156	8.77	196	5.55
37	28.47	77	22.40	117	14.89	157	8.66	197	5.50
38	28.36	78	22.22	118	14.70	158	8.55	198	5.44
39	28.25	79	22.03	119	14.52	159	8.44	199	5.39
40	28.13	80	21.85	120	14.34	160	8.33	200	5.33

'When element width-to-thickness ratio exceeds λ_r, see Appendix B5.3.

EXAMPLE 5.5

Find the most economical W 12 section to hold a compressive service load of 120 kips. Steel is A36, K = 1.0, l = 16 feet. Live load to dead ratio equals 1.0 and the column is unbraced. Assume load combination A4–2 (see Section 2.5) controls the design.

To start, let's calculate the factored load, P_u. Since the dead and live loads are evenly split, we find that

$$P_u = 1.6(60) + 1.2(60) = 168 \text{ kips } (747.3 \text{KN})$$

Since the effective length, Kl, is 16 feet, we will start by assuming a design stress of 25 ksi. The trial area can then be calculated as follows:

$$A_{g \text{ trial}} = 168 \text{ kips}/25 \text{ ksi} = 6.72 \text{ in.}^2$$

Therefore, we would tend to select a W 12 × 26 (A = 7.65 in.² or 4930 mm²) as our trial member. From here we can calculate the section's slenderness ratio as:

$Kl/r_y = (1)(16 \text{ ft.} \times 12)/1.51 \text{ in.} = 127.1$

Using Eq. 5–1 the slenderness parameter can then be calculated as follows:

$\lambda_c = (Kl/r\,\pi)\,\sqrt{F_y/E}$

$\lambda_c = (127.1/\pi)\,\sqrt{36000/29 \times 10^6} = 1.42 < 1.5$

Since the slenderness parameter is again less than 1.5, inelastic behavior controls and Eq. 5–3 is used to find the critical buckling stress.

$F_{cr} = (.658^{\lambda_c^2})\,F_y$

$F_{cr} = (.658^{1.42^2})\,36 \text{ ksi} = 15.4 \text{ ksi}$

$(F_{cr} = (.658^{1.42^2})\,248.2\text{MPa} = 106.1\text{MPa})$

Calculating the design capacity of the W 12 × 26 section, $\phi_c P_n$, we find:

$\phi_c P_n = \phi_c A_g F_{cr}$
$\quad\quad = .85 \times 7.65 \text{ in.}^2 \times 15.4 \text{ ksi} = 100.1 \text{ kips}$
$\quad\quad (= .85 \times .00493 \text{ m}^2 \times 106.1 \text{ MPa} = .444 \text{ MN or } 444 \text{ KN})$

Since the design capacity of this section is less than the required capacity, we need a bigger section.

Try

W 12 × 40 A = 11.8 in.² (7600 mm²)

Calculating this section's controlling slenderness ratio as follows:

$Kl/r_y = (1)(16 \text{ ft.} \times 12)/1.93 \text{ in.} = 99.5$

Using Eq. 5–1 the slenderness parameter can then be calculated as follows:

$\lambda_c = (Kl/r\,\pi)F_y/E$
$\lambda_c = (99.5/\pi)36000/29 \times 10^6 = 1.116 < 1.5$

Since the slenderness parameter is again less than 1.5, inelastic behavior controls and Eq. 5–3 is used to find the critical buckling stress.

$F_{cr} = (.658\lambda_c^2)\,F_y$

$F_{cr} = (.658^{1.116^2})\,36 \text{ ksi} = 21.37 \text{ ksi}$

$(F_{cr} = (.658^{1.116^2})248.2\text{MPa} = 147.4\text{MPa})$

Calculating the design capacity of the W 12 × 40 section, $\phi_c P_n$, we find:

$\phi_c P_n = \phi_c A_g F_{cr}$
$\quad\quad = .85 \times 11.8 \text{ in.}^2 \times 21.37 \text{ ksi} = 214.3 \text{ kips}$
$\quad\quad (= .85 \times .0076 \text{ m}^2 \times 147.4 \text{ MPa} = .953 \text{ MN or } 953 \text{ KN})$

Since the W 12 × 40 has a design capacity greater than the required capacity it works. At this point the reader might decide that a section smaller than a W 12 × 40 might work since there seems to be a sizeable gap between the required strength (168 kips) and the design strength. Try a W 12 × 35. You'll find this will not work and therefore the W 12 × 40 is most economical.

EXAMPLE 5.6

Design an economical W section to hold a factored load (P_u) equal to 795 kips. The column is 20 feet long and is assumed to have pin-pin end conditions. The column is braced at midheight in the weak direction and is made of A36 steel.

Again we will use the above trial procedure to design the proper column in this example. Since the column is braced at midheight in the weak direction, the effective length is 10 feet in the weak direction and 20 feet in the strong direction. Let's assume a design stress of 30 ksi. The trial area can then be calculated as follows:

$$A_{g\ trial} = 795 \text{ kips}/30 \text{ ksi} = 26.5 \text{ in.}^2$$

Therefore, looking at the section tables we may tend to select a W 14 × 90 (A = 26.5 in.² or 17,100 mm²) as our trial member. From here we can calculate the section's slenderness ratio as:

$$Kl/r_y = (1)(10 \text{ ft.} \times 12)/3.70 \text{ in.} = 32.4$$
$$Kl/r_x = (1)(20 \text{ ft.} \times 12)/6.14 \text{ in.} = 39.1 — \text{controls}$$

Using Table 5–1 the design stress for a slenderness ratio of 39.1 is found to be 28.23 ksi. This would make the design capacity of this section:

$$\phi_c P_n = (\phi_c F_{cr}) A_g$$
$$= (28.23 \text{ ksi}) 26.5 \text{ in.}^2 = 748.1 \text{ kips}$$

Since the design capacity (748.1 kips) of this section is just a bit less than the required capacity (795 kips), a W 14 × 90 will not work and we need a bigger section. Therefore let's try a W 14 × 99.

$$Kl/r_y = (1)(10 \text{ ft.} \times 12)/3.71 \text{ in.} = 32.34$$
$$Kl/r_x = (1)(20 \text{ ft.} \times 12)/6.17 \text{ in.} = 38.9 — \text{controls}$$

Using Table 5–1 the design stress for a slenderness ratio of 38.9 is found to be 28.27 ksi. This would make the design capacity of this section:

$$\phi_c P_n = (\phi_c F_{cr}) A_g$$
$$= (28.27 \text{ ksi}) 29.1 \text{ in.}^2 = 822.6 \text{ kips}$$

This section's design capacity is just a little higher than the required capacity, therefore it works very well.

In addition to the "from-scratch" procedure outlined previously, the AISC provides column load tables in Part 2 of its LRFD manual. (A partial listing of these load tables is found in Appendix C.) These tables contain much information, the foremost of which is the concentric design axial strength which can be carried based on a given effective length (kl) about the weak axis on a given section. Example 5.7 is a repeat of the previous example utilizing the information given in the column load tables.

EXAMPLE 5.7

Rework the design of the column from Example 5.6 using the LRFD column load tables.

On page 109 we see a column design chart that we will be using in this example. From the information given in Example 5.6 we know the following information:

$kl_x = 20$ ft.

$kl_y = 10$ ft.

Looking at the 10 ft. effective length line on the Figure, we would find that a W 14 × 99 has a design axial strength of 843 kips about the weak axis. However, since the r_x/r_y ratio is only 1.66 for this section and the length in the strong direction is two times greater than in the weak, the column is critical about the strong direction. The chart must be manipulated to give an equivalent weak axis effective length. This can be done as follows:

$kl_{y\,equiv} = kl_y\,[(kl_x/kl_y)/1.66]$

$\qquad = 10$ ft. $[(20$ ft./10 ft.)$/1.66] = 12.04$ ft.

Entering the chart with an equivalent kl of 12.04 feet and interpolating, we find that the design axial capacity of a W 14 × 99 is approximately 821 kips.

Should the weak axis control, the column load tables can be entered and a value for design capacity, $\phi_c P_n$, taken directly from the table without the manipulation needed in the prior example.

COLUMNS
W shapes
Design axial strength in kips ($\phi = 0.85$)

| F_y = 36 ksi |
| F_y = 50 ksi |

Designation		W14								
Wt./ft		132		120		109		99		90	
F_y		36	50	36	50	36	50	36	50[†]	36	50[†]
Effective length in ft KL with respect to least radius of gyration r_y	0	1190	1650	1080	1500	979	1360	890	1240	810	1130
	6	1160	1600	1060	1460	960	1320	873	1200	795	1100
	7	1160	1590	1050	1450	950	1310	867	1190	789	1080
	8	1150	1570	1040	1430	946	1300	860	1180	783	1070
	9	1140	1550	1030	1410	937	1280	852	1160	775	1060
	10	1120	1530	1020	1390	927	1260	843	1150	767	1040
	11	1110	1510	1010	1370	917	1240	833	1130	758	1030
	12	1100	1480	999	1350	905	1220	823	1110	749	1010
	13	1080	1450	985	1320	893	1200	811	1090	738	989
	14	1070	1420	971	1290	880	1170	799	1060	728	969
	15	1050	1390	956	1270	866	1150	787	1040	716	947
	16	1040	1360	940	1240	852	1120	773	1020	704	925
	17	1020	1330	924	1210	837	1090	759	991	691	902
	18	997	1300	906	1180	821	1060	745	965	678	878
	19	978	1260	888	1140	804	1030	730	938	664	853
	20	958	1220	870	1110	787	1000	714	911	650	828
	22	916	1150	831	1040	752	943	682	854	620	776
	24	872	1070	791	973	715	880	648	796	589	723
	26	826	997	749	902	678	815	614	737	558	670
	28	780	920	706	832	639	751	578	679	525	616
	30	733	844	663	762	600	688	542	621	493	564
	32	686	769	620	694	561	627	507	565	460	512
	34	639	697	577	629	522	567	471	511	428	463
	36	593	627	535	565	483	509	436	458	396	415
	38	547	563	494	507	446	457	402	411	365	372

Properties											
U		1.34	1.48	1.35	1.49	1.35	1.49	1.36	1.50	1.37	1.51
P_{wo} (kips)		196	272	173	240	148	205	125	174	109	151
P_{wi} (kips/in.)		23	32	21	30	19	26	17	24	16	22
P_{wb} (kips)		520	613	399	471	281	331	222	261	165	195
P_{fb} (kips)		215	298	179	249	150	208	123	171	102	142
L_p (ft)		15.7	13.3	15.6	13.2	15.5	13.2	15.5	13.4	15.4	15.0
L_r (ft)		73.6	49.6	67.9	46.2	62.7	43.2	58.2	40.6	54.1	38.4

A (in.²)		38.8		35.3		32.0		29.1		26.5	
I_x (in.⁴)		1530		1380		1240		1110		999	
I_y (in.⁴)		548		495		447		402		362	
r_y (in.)		3.76		3.74		3.73		3.71		3.70	
Ratio r_x/r_y		1.67		1.67		1.67		1.66		1.66	

[†]Flange is noncompact; see discussion preceding column load tables.

5.8   Local Buckling

Another concern with regard to compression members is that the individual components of the section do not fail before the member reaches its capacity. Buckling of individual pieces of the compression member (the web and/or flanges) before the whole section buckles is referred to as *local buckling*. In section B.5 of the LRFD specification, the criteria to prevent local buckling for stiffened and unstiffened compression elements is set. An element can meet the AISC criteria against local buckling in one of two ways, either by being "compact" or "noncompact". An element is said to be **compact** if the section can reach significant plastic deformation before buckling would occur, and it is said to be **noncompact** if the section can reach at least its yield strength before buckling would occur. Compactness will be discussed further in Chapter 6.

The LRFD specification categorizes stiffened elements as those that are supported in two edges parallel to the load, while unstiffened elements are those supported only along one edge. For a standard wide flange shape, the flange is assumed to be an unstiffened element since a half of it "cantilevers" out from its point of fixity at the web. The web is assumed to be a stiffened element, since it is fixed at its junction with both flanges. (Figure 5–9)

The stiffened and unstiffened portions of a wide flange section behave similarly to a column because as their "slenderness ratio" becomes smaller it is harder for the element to buckle. For local buckling we refer to this slenderness

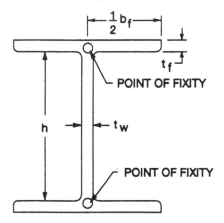

STIFFENED ELEMENT = WEB; WIDTH/THICKNESS RATIO = h/t_w
UNSTIFFENED ELEMENT = FLANGE; WIDTH/THICKNESS RATIO = $1/2 \, b_f/t_f$

Figure 5–9   Stiffened and Unstiffened Elements on a Rolled Beam

Table 5-2 Compactness Limits for Wide Flange Sections in Compression

Description of element	b/t Ratios	Limiting width/thickness ratios	
		Compact λ_p	Noncompact λ_r
Flanges of I-shaped rolled beams and channels in flexure	$b_f/2t_f$	$65/\sqrt{Fy}$	$141/\sqrt{Fy-10}$
Flanges of I-shaped sections in pure compression and plates projecting from compression elements	$b_f/2t_f$	NA	$95/\sqrt{Fy}$
All other uniformly compressed stiffened elements	h_c/t_w	NA	$253/\sqrt{Fy}$

ratio as the element's **width to thickness ratio** or **b/t ratio**. The AISC has set limits for an element's b/t ratio to ensure that local buckling will not occur before the section fails due to compact or noncompact behavior. The limit for compact behavior is referred to as λ_p and the limit for noncompact behavior is referred to as λ_r. These limits are outlined in Table 5–2.

All rolled wide flange sections subject to axial compression meet the compactness criteria shown in Table 5–2 and therefore, local buckling is practically nonexistent. However, if students deal with plate girders or other built-up sections, they should be aware that the critical stress may have to be reduced to ensure safety against this mode of failure.

5.9   Alignment Charts for Determining Effective Length

In real life situations, columns are not singular members (as they have been portrayed in this chapter so far) but are elements that are part of a structural frame. There are two basic categories of a structural frame; those that are **braced** against sidesway and those that are **unbraced** against sidesway. Frames can be braced against this lateral swaying in a number of ways, ranging from steel cross bracing to masonry shearwalls (Figure 5–10). However the question remains: In these real life design situations, how is the effective length factor, K, estimated?

The most commonly used method that estimates the effective length factor, K, for these cases is known as the **alignment chart method**. This method estimates a K value based on the rigidity of the members that frame into the end of the column.

Figure 5-10 Use of Structural Bracing. Alcoa Building, San Francisco. (Courtesy Bethlehem Steel Corporation.)

These alignment charts estimate the K factors based on the stiffness of all beams and columns that make up the framing to which the column is attached. This means that the end-restraint of the column is largely due to the rigidity of the members at that end of the column. The AISC has published an alignment chart for frames subjected to sidesway (sidesway uninhibited) and frames subjected to no sidesway (sidesway inhibited). The most widely used charts for sidesway inhibited behavior are the result of work by the Structural Stability Research Council [4]. The alignment charts for both cases are reproduced below with permission from the AISC (Figure 5-11).

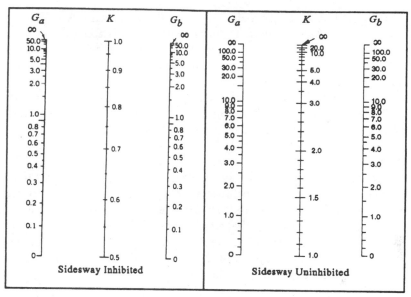

Figure 1.   The subscripts A and B refer to the joints at the two ends of the column section being considered. G is defined as

$$G = \frac{\Sigma\ (I_c/L_c)}{\Sigma\ (I_g/L_g)}$$

in which Σ indicates a summation of all members rigidly connected to that joint and lying in the plane in which buckling of the column is being considered. I_c is the moment of inertia and L_c the unsupported length of a column section, and I_g is the moment of inertia and L_g the unsupported length of a girder or other restraining member. I_c and I_g are taken about axes perpendicular to the plane of buckling being considered.

For column ends supported by but not rigidly connected to a footing or foundation, G is theoretically infinity, but, unless actually designed as a true friction free pin, may be taken as "10" for practical designs. If the column end is rigidly attached to a properly designed footing, G may be taken as 1.0. Smaller values may be used if justified by analysis.

Figure 5–11   Standard Alignment Charts. (Courtesy of the American Institute of Steel Construction, Inc.)

The use of these alignment charts involves calculating a stiffness factor, G, at both ends of the column under consideration using the following formula:

$$G_a = \Sigma(I_c/L_c)/\Sigma(I_g/L_g) \qquad\qquad\qquad \text{(Eq. 5–4)}$$

where

G_a = stiffness at end "a" of the column

The values I_c and I_g are the moment of inertias for the columns and girders respectively and L_c and L_g are their respective lengths. The summation must only include those members rigidly connected to that joint and lying in the plane for which buckling is being considered. The following example will demonstrate the basic use of these alignment charts in the calculation of the effective length factor, K. Also remember when using these charts, I_c and I_g are taken about axes perpendicular to the plane of buckling that is under consideration. Therefore, this text will assume using the moment of inertias about a column's strong axis, unless buckling is to occur about the weak axis. (In real world situations, an analysis involving the frame in the plane of both the strong and weak axis would probably be performed to calculate the "weakest" direction.)

Another topic which should be mentioned concerning the alignment charts is the **stiffness reduction factors** (SRF) found in Table 3–1 of the LRFD manual and shown below (Figure 5–12). The use of these factors is to modify K values pulled off the alignment charts if inelastic buckling controls. This modification is based on work by Joseph Yura[5] and is warranted because the alignment charts were developed for stresses in the elastic region. Since the inelastic region has a reduced modulus of elasticity, the K values should be likewise reduced.

The following example will demonstrate the utilization of both the alignment charts and the stiffness reduction factor.

\multicolumn{5}{c}{**Stiffness Reduction Factors (SRF) for Columns**}				
P_u/A ksi	F_y		P_u/A ksi	F_y	
	36 ksi	**50 ksi**		**36 ksi**	**50 ksi**
42	—	0.03	26	0.38	0.82
41	—	0.09	25	0.45	0.85
40	—	0.16	24	0.52	0.88
39	—	0.21	23	0.58	0.90
38	—	0.27	22	0.65	0.93
37	—	0.33	21	0.70	0.95
36	—	0.38	20	0.76	0.97
35	—	0.44	19	0.81	0.98
34	—	0.49	18	0.85	0.99
33	—	0.53	17	0.89	1.00
32	—	0.58	16	0.92	↓
31	—	0.63	15	0.95	
30	0.05	0.67	14	0.97	
29	0.14	0.71	13	0.99	
28	0.22	0.75	12	1.00	
27	0.30	0.79	11	↓	

— indicates not applicable.

Figure 5–12 Table of Stiffness Reduction Factors. (Courtesy of the American Institute of Steel Construction, Inc.)

EXAMPLE 5.8

In the unbraced frame shown below, calculate the adequacy ($\phi_c P_n \geq P_u$) of column #1. Calculate the effective length factor, K, from the alignment charts. Steel is A36 and assume the column's weak axis is continually braced such that out-of-plane buckling is prevented. The footing that is attached to the column end is properly designed and rigid.

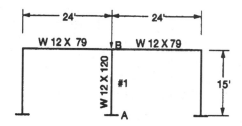

The first topic to look at in this problem is whether the column stresses will be in the inelastic range of behavior. From our earlier discussion in Section 5.5, we know that if $P_u/A \geq .39F_y$ inelastic behavior controls and stiffness reduction factors (SRF) must be used. In our present example, $P_u = 590$ kips and therefore the stress can be calculated as:

$P_u/A = 590$ kips$/35.3$ in.$^2 = 16.71$ ksi

Since 16.71 ksi is greater than .39 F_y (14.04 ksi), stiffness reduction factors must be used. Entering Figure 5–12 we find that the stiffness reduction factor equals 0.90.

Since column end "a" is fixed in a properly designed footing we will assume the stiffness $G_a = 10$ per the alignment charts guidelines of Figure 5–11. Stiffness as end "b" is:

$G_b = \Sigma(I_c/L_c)/\Sigma(I_g/L_g)$ (Eq. 5–4)

$\Sigma (I/L)$ for the columns at end "b" (1 – W 12 × 120)

   $= 1070$ in.$^4/15$ ft. × 12 in./ft. $= 5.94$

$\Sigma (I/L)$ for the girders at end "b" (2 – W 12 × 79's)

   $= 662$ in.$^4/24$ ft. × 12 in./ft. $= 2.30 \times 2 = 4.6$

Therefore the stiffness factor at end "b" is as follows:

$G_b = 5.94/4.6 = 1.29$

This value must then be modified by the appropriate stiffness reduction factor, 0.90, which yields:

$G_b = 1.29 \times 0.90 = 1.16$

Entering the chart for unbraced frames with G_a equal to 10 and G_b equal to 1.16 we find that $K \approx 1.9$ (see figure below). The value of G_a is not reduced because it is a value that was assumed to estimate the rigidity of the footing. The value is assumed to be 10 because that is a conservative estimate and to maintain this conservatism we will leave it at 10.

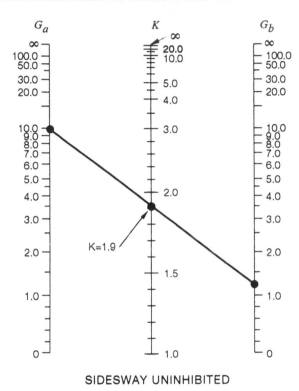

SIDESWAY UNINHIBITED

After solving for the effective length factor, the calculation of the column's design stress follows. First, let's calculate the slenderness ratio of the column about its strong axis (since we are considering buckling in this direction):

$Kl/r_x = 1.9(15 \text{ ft.} \times 12 \text{ in./ft.})/5.51 \text{ in.} = 62.06$

With this slenderness ratio we can solve for the design stress, $\phi_c F_{cr}$, from Table 5–1 is as follows:

$\phi_c F_{cr} = 24.98 \text{ ksi}$

Calculating the column's design capacity we find:

$$\phi_c P_n = (\phi_c F_{cr}) A_g$$
$$\phi_c P_n = 24.98 \text{ ksi} \times 35.3 \text{ in.}^2 = 881.8 \text{ kips}$$

Since 881.8 kips > 590 kips, the column works.

EXAMPLE 5.9

Calculate the effective length values for column #1 in the unbraced frame (sidesway uninhibited) shown below and calculate its design capacity. Steel is A36 and assume the column's weak axis is continually braced such that out-of-plane buckling is prevented. Assume no stiffness reduction factors are needed.

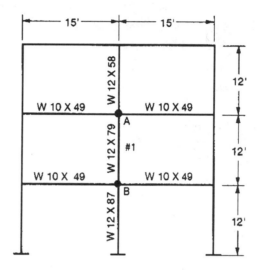

Begin by calculating the stiffness factor, G_a, at end "a" of the column in question. At joint "a" the sum of the (I/L)'s for all the columns at this end would be:

W 12 × 79 (the column itself)

$I/L = 662 \text{ in.}^4/144 \text{ in.} = 4.60$

W 12 × 58 (the column above)

$I/L = 475 \text{ in.}^4/144 \text{ in.} = 3.30$

$\Sigma (I/L)$ for the columns at end "a" yields;

$(\Sigma I/L)_{\text{columns}} = 4.60 + 3.30 = 7.90$

The sum of the (I/L)'s for all the girders at joint "a" would be :

The two W 10 × 49's

$I/L = 272$ in.^{4}/180 in. = 1.51

$\Sigma(I/L)$ for the girders at end "a"

$(\Sigma I/L)_{\text{gird}} = 2 \times 1.51 = 3.02$

Therefore G_a can be calculated as

$$G_a = \Sigma(I_c/L_c)/\Sigma(I_g/L_g) \qquad\qquad \text{(Eq. 5–4)}$$
$$= 7.9/3.02 = 2.62$$

Likewise, the stiffness at joint "b" can be found as follows:

W 12 × 79 (the column itself)

$I/L = 662$ in.^{4}/144 in. = 4.60

W 12 × 87 (the column below)

$I/L = 740$ in.^{4}/144 in. = 5.14

$\Sigma(I/L)$ for the columns at end "b" yields:

$(\Sigma I/L)_{\text{columns}} = 4.60 + 5.14 = 9.74$

Since the girders framing into joint "b" are of the same shape and length as at joint "a", the sum of I/L's for the girders will be the same as before, or 3.02. Therefore, the stiffness at joint "b" is as follows:

$G_b, = 9.74/3.02 = 3.23$

By entering these values for G_a and G_b in the alignment chart for sidesway uninhibited and connecting these values with a line (see figure below), the student can pick off an effective length factor, K of ≈ 1.81.

After solving for the effective length factor, the calculation of the column's design stress follows. First, let's calculate the slenderness ratio of the column about its strong axis (since we are considering buckling in this direction):

$Kl/r_x = 1.81(12 \text{ ft.} \times 12 \text{ in./ft.})/5.34 \text{ in.} = 48.8$

With this slenderness ratio we can solve for the design stress, $\phi_c F_{cr}$, from Table 5–1 is as follows:

$\phi_c F_{cr} = 26.86$ ksi

Calculating the column's design capacity we find:

$\phi_c P_n = (\phi_c F_{cr}) A_g$

$\phi_c P_n = 26.86 \text{ ksi} \times 23.2 \text{ in.}^2 = 623.1$ kips

Therefore the column's design capacity is 623.1 kips.

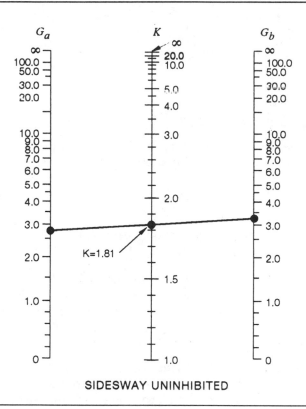

SIDESWAY UNINHIBITED

5.10 Axially Loaded Column Baseplates

In a steel frame, columns typically transmit their loads to the column directly beneath them, such that the most heavily loaded columns are on the basement or bottom floor. At this stage, the column will then transmit its load into a footing or foundation system that is commonly made of concrete. Since the compressive strength of concrete is much smaller than steel, the load from the column must be spread out over a larger area of the foundation. This is accomplished through the use of a steel **baseplate** that is typically bolted or welded to the bottom of the column.

The bearing stress that Volume II of the AISC specification recommends for the concrete surface depends on the area of the bearing plate (referred to as A_1) and the area of the concrete support (referred to as A_2). The LRFD specification recognizes the limit state of the concrete bearing capacity and presents its familiar design philosophy as follows:

$$\phi_c P_p \ge P_u$$

where

ϕ_c = .60 for bearing

P_p = nominal concrete bearing strength as follows

P_u = factored axial load

If the area of the bearing plate A_1 is equal to the area of concrete support A_2 the nominal concrete bearing stress P_p, is as follows:

$$P_p = .85 f_c' A_1 \qquad \text{(Eq. 5–5)}$$

where

f_c' = specified concrete strength, psi or ksi

A_1 = baseplate area, in.^{2}

Should the concrete support area be larger than the baseplate area, which is very typical, the nominal capacity is given as shown in Eq. 5–6. Notice the upper limit of this formula is given as $1.7 f_c' A_1$ or twice that as given by Eq. 5–5.

$$P_p = .85 f_c' A_1 \sqrt{(A_2/A_1)} \le 1.7 f_c' A_1 \qquad \text{(Eq. 5–6)}$$

The area of the baseplate, A_1, can simply be found by rearranging the aforementioned equations 5–5 and 5–6. By setting the design bearing capacity equal to the factored axial load, equations 5–5 and 5–6 can be solved for the area of the baseplate, A_1, as follows:

$$\phi_c P_p = P_u$$
$$P_p = P_u / \phi_c$$

If $A_1 = A_2$, Eq. 5–5 can be rearranged to solve for A_1 as follows:

$$.85 \ f_c' A_1 = P_u / \phi_c$$
$$A_1 = P_u / (\phi_c \ .85 f_c') \qquad \text{(Eq. 5–7)}$$

If $A_2 > A_1$, Eq. 5–6 can be rearranged to solve for A_1, choosing the **larger value** as is calculated:

$$1.7 f_c' A_1 = P_u / \phi_c$$
$$A_1 = P_u / (\phi_c 1.7 f_c') \qquad \text{(Eq.5–8)}$$

or

$$.85 f_c' A_1 \sqrt{(A_2/A_1)} = P_u / \phi_c$$
$$A_1 = [P_u / (0.6)(.85 f_c')]^2 / A_2 \qquad \text{(Eq. 5–9)}$$

The specification does limit the area of the baseplate, A_1, to at least the value of the depth of section multiplied by its flange width. This baseplate would need to be somewhat larger than the perimeter of the column section since room is needed for the connection of the plate to the concrete by anchor bolts. The larger of the baseplate areas is always used and this will be shown in the next example.

The other limit state of axial baseplate design involves the selection of the appropriate thickness of the plate itself. This thickness is based on the bending behavior of the plate caused by moments that tend to "curl up" the plate along its cantilevered edges (Figure 5–13). Based on this behavior, formulas have been developed to calculate plate thickness. The values referred to as "m", and "λn," are the cantilevered distances of the baseplates that are subjected to the maximum bending stresses. These distances are shown in Figure 5–14. The formula to calculate plate thickness is as follows:

$$t_{\text{"reg"}} = l \sqrt{\frac{2P_u}{0.9\,F_y BN}}$$

(Eq. 5–10)

$t_{\text{"reg"}}$ = calculated plate thickness

P_u = Factored axial load

N = length of baseplate, approximately equal to $\sqrt{A_1} + \Delta$

$\Delta = .5(0.95\text{d} - 0.80b_f)$

B = width of baseplate, equal to A_1/N

n = cantilevered plate distance, equal to $[B - 0.80b_f]/2$ (See Figure 5–14)

m = cantilevered plate distance, equal to $[N - 0.95\text{d}]/2$ (See Figure 5–14)

F_y = Yield stress of baseplate steel

$\lambda n' = \lambda \sqrt{db_f/4}$

$\lambda = 2\sqrt{x}/1 + \sqrt{1 - x} \leq 1$

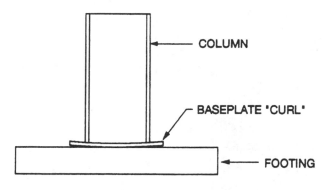

Figure 5–13 Baseplate "Curl"

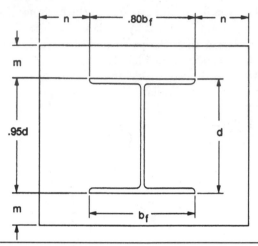

Figure 5–14   Baseplate Design Nomenclature

$$x = \left[\frac{4db_f}{(d + b_f)^2}\right] \left[\frac{P_u}{\phi_c P_p}\right]$$

l = larger of m, n, λn'

The following example illustrates the use of these equations in a typical baseplate design.

EXAMPLE 5.10

Design a square baseplate made from A36 steel for a W 12 × 65 column that rests on a 3' × 3' concrete footing. The column is under an factored axial load of 350 kips and the concrete has a 28 day concrete compressive strength of 3 ksi (f_c' = 3 ksi).

To begin let's get the maximum size of the steel baseplate that will be required by assuming that the concrete area (3 ft. × 3 ft.) is larger than the baseplate area. Using the larger area from Equations 5–8 and 5–9 we find the following:

$A_1 = P_u/(\phi_c 1.7 f_c')$ (Eq. 5–8)

   350 kips/((0.60)(1.7)(3 ksi))

   = 114.4 in.^{2}

$A_1 = [P_u/(0.6)(.85f_c')]^2/A_2$ (Eq. 5–9)

   [350 kips/(0.60)(2.55 ksi)]^2/(36 in.)^2

   = 40.4 in.^{2}

Choosing the larger A_1, we find it equals 114.4 in.^{2}. However, A_1 has to be at least equal to the column's flange width times its depth. For a W 12 × 65 this would be:

$A_1 = b_f d$

$\quad = (12.0 \text{ in.})(12.12 \text{ in.}) = 145.4 \text{ in.}^2 \text{ (Controls)}$

Choosing the larger area, we can now design a baseplate as follows:

$A_1 = B \times N$

$N \approx \sqrt{145.4} \text{ in.}^2 + \Delta$

where $\qquad \Delta = .5(0.95d - 0.80b_f)$

$\qquad\qquad = .5(0.95(12.12) - 0.80(12.0))$

$\qquad \Delta = .96 \text{ in.}$

$N \approx \sqrt{145.4} \text{ in.}^2 + .96 \text{ in.} = 13.02 \text{ in., use } 14 \text{ in.}$

Typically $B = A_1/N$, although since it was stipulated that this plate was to be square the width, B, is also 14 inches.

Next we can solve for the thickness of the plate by calculating Equation 5–10, choosing the larger of m, n, and $\lambda n'$. Before using equation 5–10 we must find the cantilevered distances, m, n, and $\lambda n'$. This is shown below:

$m = [N - 0.95d]/2$

$m = [14" - .95(12.12")]/2 = 1.24"$

$n = [B - 0.80b_f]/2$

$n = [14" - .80(12.00")]/2 = 2.20"$

$$x = \left[\frac{4(12.12)(12)}{(24.12)^2} \right] \left[\frac{350 \text{ kips}}{600 \text{ kips}} \right] = 58$$

$$\lambda = \frac{2\sqrt{.58}}{1 + \sqrt{1 - .58}} = .92 < 1$$

$$\lambda n' = \frac{.92\sqrt{(12)(12.12)}}{4} = 2.77 \text{ in.}$$

The largest value of m, n, and $\lambda n'$ is 2.77" and the thickness is given by Equation 5–10:

$$t_{req} = 2.77 \sqrt{\frac{2\ (350\ \text{kips})}{(.9)(36\ \text{ksi})(14)(14)}} = .92\ \text{in.} \hspace{2cm} \text{(Eq. 5–10)}$$

Therefore the plate is $14" \times 14" \times 1"$.

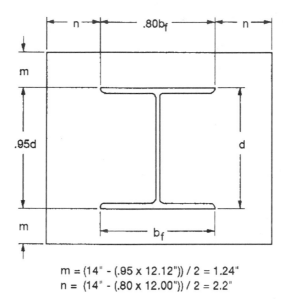

$$m = (14" - (.95 \times 12.12")) / 2 = 1.24"$$
$$n = (14" - (.80 \times 12.00")) / 2 = 2.2"$$

5.11 Singly Symmetrical and Unsymmetrical Members in Compression

Up to now, the discussion of compression members has only dealt with the doubly symmetrical shape of the wide flange section. This type of section is rather nice because it typically fails by flexural buckling, and is not prone to torsional related failures. The calculation of torsional resistance for compression members is a long and complicated procedure that is beyond the scope of this text. Unfortunately, other singly symmetrical or unsymmetrical shapes are sometimes used in compressive situations. Such shapes may include angles, double angles, structural tees, and built-up sections. Singly symmetrical sections, such as the double angle, and unsymmetrical sections, such as angles, are very susceptible to a failure known as flexural-torsional buckling.

Flexural-torsional buckling is a very complicated behavior, and it is aggravated by the fact that loading eccentricities among such unsymmetrical shapes are very prevalent. Therefore, if the singly symmetrical or unsymmetrical shapes that have been mentioned are to be used as compressive elements, both flexural buckling and flexural-torsional buckling must be checked for proper adequacy. If the reader should encounter such situations, there are many advanced design texts that address this topic.

5.12 Summary

Columns, and compression members in general, are some of the most important elements in the scope of structural design. Failure of such members primarily occurs due to an out-of-plane bending which is referred to as buckling. Buckling of a column is very dependent on the length of the member that is quantified in LRFD design by the concept of a slenderness parameter, λ_c. Another important element contained in the slenderness parameter is the effective length factor, K. This factor takes into account the column's end-restraint effect and is used to estimate the actual buckling length.

The LRFD specification considers two potential types of buckling behavior for steel columns; elastic and inelastic. When columns become shorter in length (and less slender) they will tend to fail due to inelastic buckling and, therefore, the LRFD specification will use an increasingly larger critical stress. Conversely, as a column becomes longer it will be more likely to fail due to elastic buckling and, therefore, proper use of the specifications will lead to a smaller critical stress.

EXERCISES

1. Using Equations 5–2 and 5–3, construct a graph for the column curves that describes the AISC philosophy of column behavior. Use slenderness parameters from .10 to 1.80 in increments of .10.

2. Discuss the reason why the recommended values on the effective length factor for idealized conditions are always equal to or higher than the theoretical values. Is this conservative?

3. How does the presence of residual stresses affect the buckling strength of columns? How do accidental eccentricities or crookedness of a column affect the buckling strength?

4. Given an unbraced W 10×49 column 20 feet long, pinned at both ends, calculate its design capacity, $\phi_c P_n$. Steel is A242 ($F_y = 50,000$).

5. Given an unbraced W 360×196 colum that is 8 meters long, calculate its design capacity, $\phi_c P_n$. The column ends are assumed to be fixed and the steel is A36.

6. An unbraced W 12×79 column is 15 feet long and carries a service load of 149 kips. If the $K = 1.0$, and the column is made from A36 steel, determine if it is adequate. Assume a L/D ratio equal to 1.0.

8. Calculate the design capacity, $\phi_c P_n$, of a W 12 × 79 column if it is 20 feet long and braced in its weak direction at the 5 feet and 13 feet from one end. Steel is A36. Assume $K = 1.0$.

9. Design an economical W section to carry a concentric factored load of 375 kips. The column is pin-fix at its ends and is unbraced. The column is limited to a depth of no more than 17 inches due to space requirements. Steel is A36 and the column is 20 feet long.

10. Design an economical column that is 7.5 meters long and unbraced. The column has pinned ends and carries a factored load of 1250 KN. Steel is A36.

11. Design the most economical W 10 section to hold a factored load of 240 kips, if it is 13 feet long and unbraced with a $K = 1.0$. Steel is A242 ($F_y = 50$ ksi)

12. Rework problem 9 if the column is braced at mid height in the weak axis. Assume both segments to have K = .80.

13. Rework problem 10 if the column is braced at third points along its weak axis. Assume the braces to be pinned supports.

14. Calculate the ultimate load, P_u, on a W 12 × 40 column that is 10 feet long with pinned end conditions, if it is braced at midheight in the strong direction. Steel is A36.

15. Calculate the ultimate load, P_u, on a W 310 × 86 column that is 5 meters long if it is braced at midheight in the strong direction and at third points in the weak direction. Ends are assumed to be pinned and the steel is A36.

16. Repeat problem 14 if the column height is increased to 17 feet.

17. In the braced frame shown below calculate the effective length factors for all the columns shown. The footings are properly designed and rigid and the factored load on all columns is assumed to be 280 kips. Steel is A36. Assume column buckling to occur in the plane of the strong axis and frame is braced against sidesway.

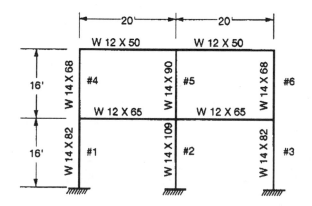

18. In the unbraced frame shown below, calculate the effective length factors for columns #1, #2, and #3 using the appropriate alignment charts. Using this information, calculate the maximum factored load that each column can carry. Remember to include stiffness reduction factors where applicable. The factored load on all columns is 300 kips and the steel is A36. Assume column buckling to occur in the plane of the strong axis and frame is braced against sidesway.

19. Rework problem 18 if sidesway is inhibited due to lateral bracing. How does this increase your design strength of these columns? Calculate the percentage increase.

20. Calculate the design capacity, $\phi_c P_n$, of a 4 x 4 x 1/2 steel tube whose ends are assumed to be pinned. The column is 20 feet long and is unbraced. Use steel with an $F_y = 46$ ksi.

21. Calculate the design capacity, $\phi_c P_n$, of a 89 x 89 x 6.4 steel tube that is 8 meters long. Its ends are pinned and the steel has an $F_y = 317.2$ MPa.

22. Design an unbraced column from a rectangular steel tube to hold a factored axial load of 400 kips if the column is 15 feet long with pinned end conditions. Use steel with an $F_y = 46$ ksi.

23. The columns (A36 steel) in the frame shown below are part of a typical 15' x 20' bay in a proposed warehouse. Assuming an equal load distributive based on distributive area and neglecting bending induced from the beams, design the lightest W section to hold the following loads:

1. Self weight of all members
2. Service live load of 600 psf plus service dead load of 400 psf

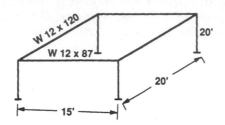

24. Design a square baseplate under a W 12 × 79 column carrying a factored axial load of 475 kips. The baseplate rests on a 30" × 30" concrete footing with an f'_c = 4000 psi. Steel is A36.
25. Design a baseplate under a W 14 × 90 column carrying a factored axial load of 395 kips. The baseplate is resting on a concrete pier wall that is 15 inches wide. The steel is A36 and the concrete has an f'_c = 3600 psi.

REFERENCES

1. L. Euler, with English translation by J. A. Van den Broek, "Euler's Classic Paper 'On the Strength of Columns'", *American Journal of Physics*, January 1947, p.309–318.
2. Jack McCormac, *Structural Steel Design,* Harper and Row, New York, 1981 p. 84.
3. Patrick Dowling, Peter Knowles, and Graham Owens, *Structural Steel Design,* The Steel Construction Institute, London, 1988, p.156.
4. Bruce G. Johnston, ed., Structural Stability Research Council, *Guide to Stability Design Criteria for Metal Structures,* 3rd edition, Wiley and Sons, New York, 1976.
5. Joseph A. Yura, "The Effective Length of Columns in Unbraced Frames," *Engineering Journal*, American Institute of Steel Construction, April 1971, p.37–42.

6

ROLLED-BEAM
DESIGN IN LRFD

6.1   Introduction and Review of Beam Theory

This chapter will explore the fundamental concepts behind the LRFD philosophy concerning the design of rolled steel beams. A firm grasp of the fundamentals is needed before any discussion can occur on more complex design topics such as plate girders and composite beams. As more advanced topics such as these are explored, the student will find that a solid knowledge of rolled-beam design is extremely helpful.

Beams, girders, stringers, purlins, and joists are all terms that describe members that may support loads applied perpendicular to their longitudinal axis. These members are integral pieces of all structures, from the steel beams that support the floor framing of buildings to the large steel girders supporting major interstate bridges. (Figure 6–1).

The stresses involved in the bending of beams should have been thoroughly covered in the student's strength of materials course. However, a brief review of the basic concepts will follow in the next few paragraphs.

When a beam is subjected to applied loadings it has to develop two primary stresses in order to maintain its integrity. In order to keep from ripping apart, the beam develops shear stresses to resist the shear resulting from the applied loads. Also, in order to keep from deflecting or rotating excessively, the beam must

Figure 6–1 Steel Girder Construction on the Passaic River Bridge, New Jersey. (Courtesy Bethlehem Steel Corporation.)

develop internal bending stresses to resist the applied bending moments caused by the loads (Figure 6–2). If the beam cannot develop resisting stresses to offset the stresses that result from the applied loading, failure will occur. A brief review of these stresses is presented below.

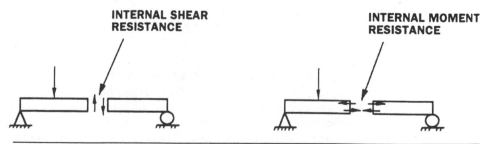

Figure 6–2 Internal Beam Resistance to Shear and Bending Forces.

SHEAR STRESSES

The actual shear stress, f_v, developed by a beam has to be equal to the shear stress applied to the beam. This shear stress is typically calculated from the formula:

$$f_v = \frac{VQ}{Ib}$$

where

f_v = shear stress on beam at that location, ksi or psi

V = shear force at point under consideration, kips or lbs.

Q = Static moment of area, in.^{3}

I = Moment of inertia of beam, in.^{4}

b = Width of beam at point under consideration, in.

Because the shear stresses in the vicinity of the flanges will be very low, the AISC allows a designer to use an easier calculation for the average shear stress in the web. The formula for average shear stress in the web is as follows:

$$f_v = \frac{V}{dt_w}$$

where

f_v = average shear stress

V = shear force on beam

d = depth of the beam

t_w = thickness of web

Typically this formula for average shear stress will yield somewhat lower results; although, since shear is typically not the controlling design behavior on steel beams, this difference can usually be neglected.

The reader should remember that the shear stress over the beam's cross-section will always be the maximum at the neutral axis. This fact is further magnified on a steel beam section since the width at the neutral axis is only the width of the web. The example below should refresh the student's memory on the use of the shear formulas.

EXAMPLE 6.1

Calculate the shear stresses at the neutral axis and at the midpoint of the flange in a W 16 × 77 if the shear force is 100 kips (444.8 KN). Use the classical shear stress equation for both locations, and use the AISC average shear stress formula to recalculate the shear stress at the neutral axis.

To calculate the shear stresses using the classical formula, the majority of the work involves calculation of the static moment of area $(Q,)$ since moment of inertia, I_x, and the width of the web and the flange can readily be taken from the appropriate section table in Appendix B. Remember that Q is simply the area outside the plane under consideration multiplied by the distance from the neutral axis to the centroid of that area.

For shear stress at the neutral axis (f_v @ N.A.) the Q can be calculated by breaking the area outside the neutral axis down into two rectangles. The Q can then be readily found by summing the areas multiplied by their respective distances from N.A. to their centroids, (See diagram below).

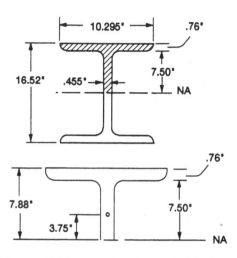

$Q_{@N.A.}$= (7.5 in. × .455 in.)(7.5 in./2) + (10.295 in. × .76 in.) (7.88 in.) = 74.45 in.^{3}

$Q_{@Mid\text{-}Flange}$= (10.295 in. × .38 in.)(8.07 in.) = 31.57 in.^{3}

Therefore, the shear stress can be calculated using the classical formula as follows:

$f_{v@N.A.}$ = 100 kips × 74.45 in.^{3}/1110 in.^{4} × .455 in. = 14.74 ksi

(= 4448N × 1.22 m^3/4.62 m^4 × (1.15 × 10^{-5} m) = 1.02 × 10^8 Pa)

$f_{v@mid\text{-}flange}$ = 100 kips × 31.57 in.^{3}/1110 in.^{4} × 10.295 in. = .27 ksi

As you can see, the shear stresses at the neutral axis are much greater than other parts of the section. It should be pointed out that the shear stress at the junction of the flange and web is much higher than at the midpoint of the flange. (Note that the "rounded corners" or fillets at the junction of the flange and web were excluded in order to simplify this example. If the student has access to the WT 8 × 38.5 section properties, the $Q_{@N.A.}$ can be calculated as 74.92 in.^{3} with the fillets included.)

To recalculate the average shear stress in the web using the AISC equation, we would simply find the depth and web thickness for the W 16 × 77 and calculate as follows:

$d = 16.52$ in.

$t_w = .455$ in.

therefore

$f_v = 100$ kips/(16.52 in.)(.455 in.)

$\quad = 13.30$ ksi

$\quad (= (4448N)/(.42 \text{ m})(.000011 \text{ m}) = 9.2 \times 10^8 \text{ Pa})$

As was previously mentioned, this average formula yields a somewhat smaller result than the classical formula.

FLEXURAL STRESS

The stress that the beam develops in response to applied bending moment is termed flexural stress or bending stress. The formula to calculate bending stress (f_b) is:

$$f_b = \frac{Mc}{I}$$

where

f_b = bending stress at location under consideration, ksi or psi

M = applied moment at point under consideration (usually the maximum moment along the beam), kip-ft. or kip-in.

c = distance from neutral axis to point on beam cross section desired (usually outer fiber for design), in.

I = moment of inertia about bending axis, in.^{4}

The student should be aware that because designers are typically concerned with maximum stress, the value c is usually ½ the beam depth. This will be the case on wide flange sections since they are symmetric sections with the neutral axis located at mid-depth. Bending stress is assumed to vary proportionally with the distance c in a homogeneous member and, therefore, reaches a maximum value at the extreme outside (top and bottom) of a section.

The stress distributions over a rectangular beam can be seen in Figure 6–3. Again, it should be reiterated that shear stress is maximum at the neutral axis, while the bending stress is zero at this point. Conversely, flexural stress is maximum at the outer fiber of the beam, while shear stress is zero.

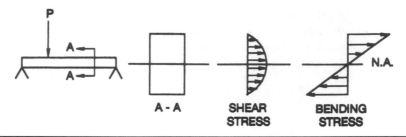

Figure 6–3   Stress Distribution over a Rectangular Beam Cross-Section.

A common revision of the flexural stress formula in beam design is the substitution of the elastic section modulus S for the ratio of I/c. The flexural formula can then be rewritten:

$$f_b = \frac{M}{S_x}$$

where

f_b = bending stress, ksi or psi

M = moment applied at point under consideration, kip-ft. or kip-in.

S_x = section modulus of the beam (equal to I/c) usually taken about the x-axis, in.[3]

The section modulus S is an elastic property of area that is useful only as stresses are kept in the elastic region of the material, i.e. under the proportional limit. In allowable stress design the section modulus is exclusively used since a potential strength limit state was the first yield of any fiber on the cross section. In the LRFD philosophy, the beam's ability to develop yield stresses over its entire cross section is recognized as the strength limit state. This ability to develop a higher capacity, while **all** fibers throughout the cross section are yielding, depends upon the individual elements of that beam remaining stable. A beam that has this stability is referred to as being "compact". The moment capacity attainable at this state of full yield is referred to as the **plastic moment** and a beam reaching this level is said to be exhibiting **plastic behavior**.

Through research[1] we know that rolled beams have a moment capacity of at least 10% greater than the moment at first yield. This conservative 10% increase of this plastic moment above the first yield moment is conveyed to us by a section's **shape factor**, ξ. The shape factor is a property of cross-sectional shape and is the ratio of a section's plastic capacity to its elastic capacity. Beacuse of a rolled beam's ability to attain this additional capacity before absolute failure, the LRFD method has changed (with respect to the ASD method) a beam's potential

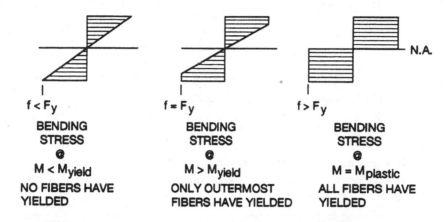

Figure 6–4 Varying Stresses over Beam Cross Section under Various Moments.

limit state from moment causing first yield to the moment causing full yield across the entire section.

Because we now acknowledge this plastic behavior, we can use a different section modulus in LRFD, called the **plastic section modulus**, Z_x. This plastic section modulus is larger than the elastic section modulus S_x because it relates yield stresses being reached over the entire cross section instead of just at the outermost fibers. When a beam reaches this plastic moment capacity, it has yielded every fiber along its cross section and is said to have developed a **plastic hinge** (Figure 6–4). The term *plastic hinge* essentially reflects the fact that the beam has no more rotational capacity at this point and will most probably collapse if no redistribution of moment occurs.

The following example illustrates the application of the bending stress formula and should be a helpful review.

EXAMPLE 6.2

Using the plastic section modulus (Z_x), determine the plastic moment capacity M_p for a W 12 × 79 using A36 steel.

The plastic section modulus (Z_x) for this section is listed in the section tables in Appendix B as 119 in.[3] and by rearranging the bending stress formula we can solve for the plastic moment as follows:

$F(Z_x) = M_p$

where

Z_x = plastic section modulus

F = stress level at plastic capacity which is equal to the yield stress, F_y

Realizing that the stress level under which the plastic moment can be achieved is the yield stress F_y, the plastic moment is as follows:

M_p = 36 ksi (119 in.³)/(12 in./ft.) = 357 kip-ft.

If a comparison to the yield moment, M_y, needed to be made, one would simply insert the elastic section modulus, S_x, into the equation and solve for M_y.

6.2 Potential Modes of Beam Failure

The behavior of a beam is a mixture of the two types of members that we have discussed up to this point—tension and compression members. Therefore, it only stands to reason that the types of failure that a beam can undergo are essentially a mixture of the failure modes that we have studied in previous chapters.

The tension side of a beam experiences tensile stresses that are highest at the extreme outside fiber. The mode of failure that we are concerned about on the tension side of the beam would involve excessive deformation, due to the reaching and exceeding of the yield stress F_y. Because the stresses and strains over the beam's cross section are assumed to vary linearly, the compression side of the beam would also be subject to the same stresses. However, the major concern on the compression side of the beam is its ability to remain stable under these stresses. A failure or limit state can occur due to instability on the compression side of the beam in two potential manners—local buckling and lateral torsional buckling.

Local buckling is an instability by which the individual elements of a beam (the flanges and the web) may fail under compressive stress before the beam is able to reach its plastic moment capacity. The ability of a steel shape to reach yield stress across its entire cross sectional area before failure is referred to as "compactness". If a beam is compact, its individual elements will remain stable and exhibit no local buckling until the section reaches its plastic moment capacity. This capacity is attained when all the fibers have yielded and is, on average, 10–12% greater than the moment needed to produce first yield[2] (Figure 6–5).

The AISC criteria for determining compactness is found in Table B5.1 of the LRFD manual and basically compares the width/thickness ratio of the compression elements to some limiting value. The applicable flange and web compactness criteria have been reproduced below in Table 6–1. Notice that there are two

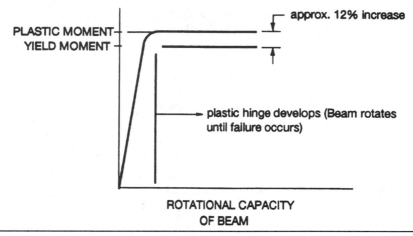

Figure 6–5   Rotational Behavior of a Steel Beam

levels in which the compactness of a beam can be measured—**compact** and **noncompact**. These criteria can simply be thought of as dividing lines that assure the beam of reaching its full plastic capacity (being compact and denoted by λ_p) or of at least behaving inelasticly (being noncompact and denoted by λ_r). It should be noted that most rolled-steel shapes meet the compactness criteria and therefore can achieve full plastic capacity.

The other potential limit state, affecting the development of a beam's resistance to bending stress, reflects the condition of lateral support along its com-

Table 6–1   AISC Compactness Criteria for Common Rolled Beam Elements.

Description of element	b/t Ratios	Limiting width/thickness ratios	
		Compact λ_p	Noncompact λ_r
Flanges of I-shaped rolled beams and channels in flexure	$b_f/2t_f$	$65/\sqrt{Fy}$	$141/\sqrt{Fy-10}$
Flanges of I-shaped sections in pure compression and plates projecting from compression elements	$b_f/2t_f$	NA	$95/\sqrt{Fy}$
All other uniformly compressed stiffened elements	h_c/t_w	NA	$253/\sqrt{Fy}$

pressive flange. This column-type instability in beams is referred to as **lateral torsional buckling** because as the slender compression flange begins to buckle out of plane, the beam undergoes a torsional component due to the downward forces along the top flange (Figure 6–6).

As discussed in the preceding chapter on columns, bracing of the buckling plane will make it more difficult for failure to occur by buckling. By bracing the compression flange, the beam's ability to resist load also increases.

A beam can have many conditions of lateral support along its compression flange. It could be fully supported (braced everywhere along its flange), partially supported (braced at intermittent points along its flange), or unsupported (having no external support along its flange). Some methods that achieve a degree of lateral support are listed below (Figure 6–7).

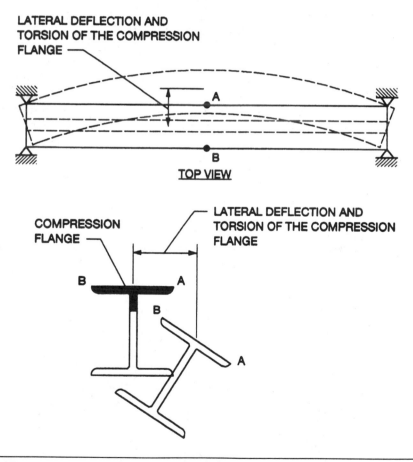

Figure 6–6   Illustration of Lateral Torsional Buckling Behavior.

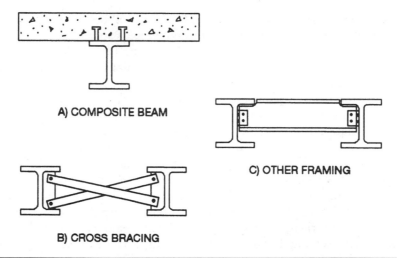

A) COMPOSITE BEAM

C) OTHER FRAMING

B) CROSS BRACING

Figure 6–7   Methods of Bracing the Compression Flange of a Steel Beam

- Non-Composite Flooring (at least by friction)
- Composite Flooring
- Cross Bracing
- Beams or struts which frame in a certain points

The assumption of what type of lateral support exists in a certain situation (unsupported, partial, full) is a judgment left up to the designer. It should be noted that rarely is a beam 100% unsupported along its compression flange since most beams would be subject to frictional restraint caused by the floor system's self weight.

6.3   Rolled-Beam Behavior

From our discussion in the previous section, it can be seen that beam behavior is largely a function of compactness and support of the compression flange. The following discussion will relate beam behavior as a function of these two criteria. Remember that most rolled-steel beams will meet all compactness requirements, therefore, the majority of our discussion will focus on the lateral bracing criteria concerning compact members. Some effort will also be spent on noncompact member behavior.

In a compact rolled beam being bent about the strong axis, the controlling criteria affecting capacity of the beam is the support of the compression flange. The more "fully" supported the compression flange is, the more likely that plastic hinge formation will be the limit state that occurs, and the less likely that a limit state of lateral torsional buckling will occur. Conversely, the farther apart the support along the compression flange is spaced, the more likely that the beam will fail due to lateral torsional buckling prior to reaching its full plastic capacity. Lateral torsional buckling is very similar to column behavior in the fact that there are two types of possible buckling—inelastic and elastic. Inelastic lateral torsional buckling takes place when the distance between braced points is short enough that it allows the beam to develop higher stresses that happen to be in the material's inelastic region. Elastic lateral torsional buckling occurs when the distance between lateral support of the compression flange becomes large so that the stresses developed in the beam at failure are relatively low—below the material's elastic limit. (Is the similarity between column behavior and lateral torsional buckling evident?) We can best understand this concept by imagining a beam of infinite length that is initially supported at every point along its compression flange. This fully supported beam cannot fail due to lateral torsional buckling, but if these points of support are taken away, one by one, at some point the beam will fail due to buckling. This beam would initially be able to reach its full plastic capacity but this capacity would be diminished as the lateral support slowly erodes away.

For compact sections, the AISC has developed equations defining the lengths of compression flange support that divide full plastic behavior from inelastic lateral torsional buckling (termed L_p) and from elastic lateral torsional buckling (termed L_r).

Noncompact rolled beams have their width/thickness ratios (λ) in excess of λ_p as listed in Table 6–1. The limit states of lateral torsional buckling (previously mentioned), flange buckling, and web buckling must all be checked and the smallest capacity chosen as critical. It should be noted that if a rolled wide flange section is noncompact, generally the flange buckling criteria will predominate over the web buckling criteria. If a member's flange or web has a width/thickness ratio in excess of λ_r, the member is classified as a slender compression member and treated as outlined in the AISC specifications. No rolled wide flange sections have slender elements, therefore they will not be covered in this text.

6.4   AISC Rolled-Beam Philosophy Using LRFD

The most basic beam design requirement in the LRFD method is that design moment capacity $\phi_b M_n$ must be greater than or equal to the required (factored) flexural strength M_u. The required flexural strength may be referred to by some as the "ultimate moment." This most basic requirement can be stated as follows:

$$\phi_b M_n \geq M_u$$

where

ϕ_b = .90 for bending
M_n = nominal moment capacity

M_u = required (factored) moment

As discussed earlier, bending strength is affected by unbraced length of the compression flange, the compactness of the member and the axis of bending. Since rolled shapes are primarily bent about the strong axis and compact, we will restrict our evaluation of the LRFD requirements to those which focus on unbraced length of the compression flange.

When considering the unbraced length of the compression flange l_b, there are two limiting lengths that were discussed in the previous section, L_p and L_r. The L_p limit is the dividing line at which a beam can actually reach the plastic moment M_p and is given as follows:

$$L_p = 300 r_y / \sqrt{F_{yf}} \qquad \text{(Eq. 6–1)}$$

where

r_y = radius of gyration, in.

F_y = specified yield stress of the flange, ksi

The L_r limit is the dividing line between elastic and inelastic buckling of the compression flange and is given in the LRFD manual as follows:

$$L_r = \frac{r_y X_1}{(F_{yf} - F_r)} \sqrt{1 + \sqrt{1 + X_2 (F_{yf} - F_r)^2}} \qquad \text{(Eq. 6–2)}$$

where

r_y = radius of gyration, in.

F_{yw} = specified yield stress of the flange steel, ksi

X_1, X_2 = beam buckling factors, found in section tables

F_r = compressive residual stress, generally taken as 10 ksi for rolled steel beams

The beam buckling factors, X_1 and X_2, are listed with the section properties in the AISC section tables (found in Appendix B) or they can be calculated from the equations as given in chapter F of the AISC manual or as listed below:

$$X_1 = \frac{\pi}{s_x} \sqrt{\frac{EGJA}{2}} \qquad \text{(Eq. 6–3)}$$

$$X_2 = 4 \frac{C_w}{I_y} \left(\frac{S_x}{GJ} \right)^2 \qquad \text{(Eq. 6–4)}$$

Although these terms seem to be somewhat hard to define, they can simply be thought of as terms that describe the bending efficiency of a member.[3] As the term X_1 decreases the bending efficiency of the member increases and as the term X_2 increases the efficiency increases. These terms can, in a simplified manner, be tied to the flange thickness and depth of a member. Therefore as depth and flange thickness increase the capacity of a section is likewise increased.

For compact rolled beams, the LRFD design philosophy for calculating nominal moment capacity M_n is illustrated in Figure 6–8. This curve can be explained by looking at the three separate items stated below that correspond to the three cases on the figure.

Case #1. Compact beams with $l_b < L_p$

Beams in this region can achieve full plastic moment capacity and therefore the nominal moment capacity in this region is the plastic moment M_p. As stated earlier in this chapter:

$$M_p = Z_x F_y.$$

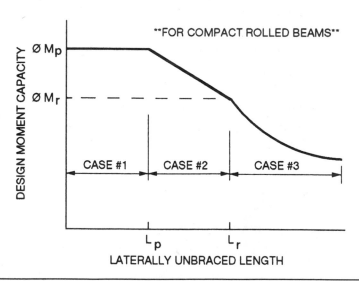

Figure 6–8   Effect of Laterally Unbraced Length on the Design Bending Capacity of a Compact Rolled Beam.

Case #2. Compact beams with $L_p < l_b < L_r$

Beams in this region exhibit inelastic lateral torsional buckling as the limit state before being able to achieve M_p. The LRFD manual gives the nominal moment capacity as follows:

$$M_n = C_b \left[M_p - (M_p - M_r) \left(\frac{l_b - L_p}{L_r - L_p} \right) \right] \leq M_p \qquad \text{(Eq. 6–5)}$$

This equation is simply a linear interpolation between M_p and M_r based on the unbraced length of beam. The moment capacity M_r requires some explanation at this point. M_r is the moment capacity of the beam as it reaches first yield, which in this case is due to lateral torsional buckling. As with columns, the consideration of residual stresses is important for members subject to compression and therefore M_r is the smaller of:

$$M_r = (F_{yf} - F_r) S_x \qquad \text{(Eq. 6–6)}$$

or

$$M_r = F_{yw} S_x$$

where

> F_r = compressive residual stress in flange considered to be 10 ksi for rolled beams
>
> F_y = specified yield stress
>
> S_x = elastic section modulus
>
> F_{yw} = yield stress of the web

The student should be advised that residual stresses affect only the value of M_r and not the value of M_p since plastic moment capacity considers yield over the entire area and residual stresses must be in equilibrium before loads are applied.

Case #3. Compact beams with $l_b > L_r$

This region contains beams that fail by exhibiting the behavior of elastic lateral torsional buckling. The beams in this region have long, slender unsupported lengths of the compression flange and failure occurs before the sections reach yield. The nominal moment capacity of a beam in this region is equal to the critical buckling moment M_{cr}. The LRFD formula for this is shown below:

$$M_{cr} = C_b \frac{\pi}{l_b} \sqrt{EI_y GJ + \left(\frac{\pi E}{l_b} \right)^2 I_y C_w} \leq M_p \qquad \text{(Eq. 6–7)}$$

or

$$M_{cr} = \frac{C_b \, S_x \, X_1 \, \sqrt{2}}{l_b/r_{xy}} \sqrt{1 + \frac{X_1^2 \, X_2}{2(l_b/r_y)^2}}$$

If a rolled section is noncompact, although as mentioned before this would be highly unlikely, the approach to calculating the design moment capacity, $\phi_b M_n$, is extremely similar to Case #2. The nominal moment capacity is calculated by checking the three potential modes of failure: lateral torsional buckling (LTB), flange buckling, and web buckling. The LTB calculation is handled exactly as it was in Case #2 and the nominal moment calculation for flange and web buckling is as shown below:

$$M_n = \left[M_p - (M_p - M_r)\left(\frac{\lambda - \lambda_p}{\lambda_r - \lambda_p}\right) \right] \qquad \text{(Eq. 6–8)}$$

The compactness parameters λ, λ_p and λ_r are the same as those found in Table 6–1. The nominal moment capacity in Case #2 can never be greater than the plastic moment capacity.

EXAMPLE 6.3

Determine the adequacy of the W 12 × 87 shown below if the compression flange is braced only at the ends. The load is shown 60% live, 40% dead, and unfactored. Assume load combination A4–2 (see section 2–6) controls. Steel is A36. Assume $C_b = 1.0$

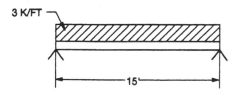

Load combination A4–2 controls, therefore the factored load is:

1.2(1.2) + 1.6(1.8) = 4.32 kips per ft.

Since it is a uniformly loaded, simply supported beam:

$M_u = 4.32(15)^2/8 = 121.5$ kip-ft. (164.8 KN–m)

Check to see if a W 12 × 87 is compact:

For the flanges, $b_f/2t_f = 7.5$ which is less than the $65/\sqrt{F_y}$ limit set in Table 6–1; therefore, flange is compact!

For the web, $h_c/t_w = 18.9$ which is less than the $640/\sqrt{F_y}$ limit set in Table 6–1; therefore, web is compact!

Check unbraced length criteria to determine what case it falls into:

Unbraced length, $l_b = 15'$ (4.57 m)
From section tables in Appendix B
$r_y = 3.07$ in.
$X_1 = 3880$ ksi
$X_2 = .000586$

Calculating L_p and L_r using Eq. 6–1 and 6–2:

$L_p = 300(3.07$ in.$)/\sqrt{36}$ ksi $= 153.5"$ or 12.8' (3.90 m)   (Eq. 6–1)

$L_r = (3.07(3880$ ksi$)/(36$ ksi $- 10$ ksi$) [\sqrt{I} + \sqrt{I} + .000586(36$ ksi $- 10$ ksi$)^2] = 676.6"$ or 56.4' (17.2 m) (Eq. 6–2)

Therefore since $L_p < l_b < L_r$, we can use Case #2 to determine nominal moment capacity. Calculate M_p and M_r which are then used in Eq. 6–5 as follows:

$M_p = Z_x F_y = 36$ ksi$(132$ in.$^3)/12$ in./ft. $= 396$ kip-ft. (537 KN – m)

$M_r = (F_y - F_r)S_x = (36 - 10$ ksi$)(118$ in.$^3)/12$ in./ft.
      $= 255.7$ kip-ft. (346.7 KN – m)

Calculate Eq. 6–5 for M_n:

$M_n = 1.0[396 - (396 - 255.7)(15 - 12.8/56.4 - 12.8)]$
      $= 388.9$ kip-ft. (527.3 KN – m) (Eq. 6–5)

Calculating design capacity:

$\phi_b M_n = .90(388.9$ kip-ft.$) = 350$ kip-ft. > 121.5 kip-ft.
  $(= .90(527.3$ KN – m$) = 474.6$ KN – m > 164.8 KN – m)

Therefore, the section is very adequate.

EXAMPLE 6.4

Recalculate the design moment capacity of the beam in the previous example if the W 12 × 87 has its compression flange braced at midspan.

In this case the unbraced length, l_b, is reduced to 7.5' which is less than L_p that was equal to 12.8' as calculated above. Therefore this case falls into Case #1 (a compact beam with $l_b < L_p$) and the nominal moment capacity is the plastic capacity.

$M_n = M_p = Z_x F_y$

$M_n = 132$ in.$^3 \times 36$ ksi $= 4752$ kip-in. or 396 kip-ft. (537KN – m)

$\phi_b M_n = .90 \times 396$ kip-ft. $= 356.4$ kip-ft. (483.3KN – m)

Therefore, the bracing increases the section's capacity is this example slightly because the beam is controlled by Case #1.

EXAMPLE 6.5

Calculate the adequacy of a W 10 × 33 that is 25 feet long and subject to a factored load of 1.2 kips per foot. The beam is unbraced and made from A242 steel ($F_y = 50$ ksi). Assume $C_b = 1.0$.

In this problem, first check to see if the beam is compact. Checking the flanges, we find that $b_f/2t_f = 9.1$ which is just less than the flange compactness criteria set forth in Table 6–1, $65/\sqrt{F_y}$. Therefore the flange is compact. Checking the web we see that $h_c/t_w = 27.1$ which again is less than the web compactness criteria set forth in Table 6–1, $640/\sqrt{F_y}$. Therefore the web is also compact. Next, let's check the unbraced length criteria.

$l_b = 25$ ft (7.62 m)

Calculating L_p and L_r from Eq. 6–1 and 6–2 as follows:

$r_y = 1.94$ in.

$X_1 = 2710$ ksi

$X_2 = .00251$

$L_p = 300(1.94)/\sqrt{50} = 82.3''$ or 6.85 ft. (2.09 m) (Eq. 6–1)

$L_r = (3.07(2710$ ksi$)/36$ ksi $- 10$ ksi$)[\sqrt{l} + \sqrt{l} + .00251(36 - 10)^2$

$\quad = 19.7'$ (6.0 m) (Eq. 6–2)

Since $l_b > L_r$, elastic lateral torsional buckling will predominate and the nominal moment is calculated as the critical moment M_{cr}, which is calculated by Eq. 6–7 and is shown as follows:

(To reduce the equation's length, the quantity l_b/r_y is precalculated as 25 ft. × 12 in./ft. ÷ 1.94 = 154.6)

$$M_{cr} = C_b \frac{\pi}{l_b} \sqrt{EI_y GJ + \left(\frac{\pi E}{l_b}\right)^2 I_y C_w} \qquad \text{(Eq. 6–7)}$$

or

$$M_{cr} = \frac{C_b S_x X_1 \sqrt{2}}{l_b / r_x} \sqrt{1 + \frac{X_1^2 X_2}{2(l_b / r_y)^2}}$$

$$\frac{1.0(35.0 \text{ in.}^3)(2710 \text{ ksi})(\sqrt{2})}{154.6} \sqrt{1 + \frac{(2710 \text{ ksi})^2(.00251)}{2(154.6)^2}} = 1021 \text{ kip-in.}$$

Therefore

$\phi_b M_n = .90 \times 85.1 \text{ kip-ft.} = 76.6 \text{ kip-ft.} (103.9 \text{KN} - \text{m})$

$M_u = 1.2 \times (25 \text{ ft.})^2 / 8 = 93.75 \text{ kip-ft.} (127.1 \text{KN} - \text{m})$

Since the required (factored) moment of 93.75 kip-ft. is greater than the design capacity of 76.6 kip-ft., the beam is no good. To make this beam adequate under the specified factored moment, lateral bracing would have to be added or possibly a higher strength steel could be used.

EXAMPLE 6.6

Calculate the nominal moment capacity of a W 12 × 65 that is 14 feet long and unbraced. The beam is made from A242 steel that has an $F_y = 50000$ psi.

First, check the compactness criteria. Looking at the flange we see that the ratio $b_f / 2t_f$ is 9.9 which is over the flange compactness criteria (as set forth in Table 6–1) of $65/\sqrt{F_y}$ but under the noncompactness limit of $141/\sqrt{F_y - 10}$. Therefore the flange is noncompact. The web compactness criteria meets the criteria specified in Table 6–1; therefore, the web is compact. The nominal moment capacity will be the smaller of the flange buckling calculation and the lateral torsional buckling (LTB) calculation. For the LTB we need to calculate the unbraced length criteria, L_p and L_r, which will determine whether lateral torsional buckling is a possible type of failure for our unbraced length, l_b. Through the calculation of Eq. 6–1 and Eq. 6–2 you will find the following for a W 12 × 65:

$$L_p = 300(3.02)/\sqrt{50} \qquad\qquad\qquad\qquad\qquad\text{(Eq. 6–1)}$$

$$L_p = 10.7 \text{ ft. } (3.25 \text{ m})$$

$$L_r = (3.02(2940 \text{ ksi})/50 \text{ ksi} - 10 \text{ ksi})[\sqrt{1} + \sqrt{1} + .00172(50 - 10)^2 =$$

$$L_r = 31.7 \text{ ft.} \qquad (9.67 \text{ m})$$

Therefore inelastic lateral torsional buckling controls (Case #2) and the nominal moment capacity can be calculated by Eq. 6–5 for lateral torsional buckling and by Eq. 6–8 for flange buckling as follows:

$$M_p = Z_x F_y = (50 \text{ ksi})(96.8 \text{ in.}^3)$$
$$= 4840 \text{ kip-in. or } 403.3 \text{ kip-ft.}$$

$$M_r = (F_y - F_r)S_x = (50 - 10 \text{ ksi})(87.9 \text{ in.}^3)$$
$$= 3516 \text{ kip-in. or } 293 \text{ kip-ft.}$$

For lateral torsional buckling per Eq. 6–5:

$$M_n = 403.3 \text{ k-ft.} - (403.3 \text{ k-ft.} - 293 \text{ k-ft.})[(14 \text{ ft.} - 10.7 \text{ ft.})/$$

$$31.7 \text{ ft.} - 10.7 \text{ ft.})] = 386 \text{ kip-ft. } (523.4 \text{ KN} - \text{m})$$

For flange buckling per Eq. 6–8 with $\delta_p = 9.2$ and $\delta_r = 22.2$:

$$M_n = 403.3 \text{ k-ft.} - (403.3 \text{ k-ft.} - 293 \text{ k-ft.})[(9.9 - 9.2)/(22.2 - 9.2)]$$

$$= 397.4 \text{ kip-ft. } (538.9 \text{ KN} - \text{m})$$

The smaller of the two nominal moment capacities is 386 kip-ft. (lateral torsional buckling controls) which is less than the plastic moment, M_p, of 403.3 kip-ft. Therefore the nominal moment capacity is 386 kip-ft.

6.5 The Bending Coefficient, C_b

Up to this point, you may have noticed the modifier, C_b, in the moment capacity equations that the AISC has presented. Why is this modifier needed, and what does it actually do to the equations we use in rolled-steel beam design?

In the development of its design equations, the AISC realized that the worst possible case for causing lateral torsional buckling would be to have the compression flange under constant uniform moment over its unbraced length. This worst case was therefore used as a conservative basis in the formulation of the moment capacity equations, Equations 6–5 and 6–7, that we presently use. But realizing that as the moment varied over the unbraced length, the failure mode of lateral torsional buckling was less likely to occur, the AISC introduced C_b as a modifier to account for this behavior. It might be better trying to understand this concept by envisioning a beam being broken up into individual unbraced segments. The segment that is most likely to undergo lateral torsional buckling (let's call this segment MAX) would be the segment under the highest applied moment over the beam length because this moment will induce the largest compressive forces into the flange. The segments adjacent to segment MAX may be less likely to undergo buckling since the total compressive force would be smaller if the applied moment is reduced. In fact, because these segments will be less likely to buckle laterally, they will actually provide a restraint on segment MAX as it tries to undergo lateral torsion buckling. This restraining effect can be viewed similarly to the effective length factor K, that we discussed in column buckling.

The value of C_b can be calculated from the following equation:

$$C_b = 12.5 \ M_{max}/(2.5M_{max} + 3M_a + 4M_b + 3M_c) \qquad \text{(Eq. 6–9)}$$

where

M_{max} = absolute value of the maximum moment in the unbraced segment

M_a = absolute value of moment at the quarter point of the unbraced segment

M_b = absolute value of moment at the center point of the unbraced segment

M_c = absolute value of moment at the three quarter point of the unbraced segment

The value of C_b may conservatively be taken as 1.0 in all instances. This formula has been found to give more accurate solutions for beams that have nonlinear moment diagrams across the unbraced segment. The previous formula that the AISC permitted in the first edition of the LRFD manual led to inaccuracies when the moment diagram within the unbraced segment was not straight. It is shown below, however, because of its long standing use in the design arena and the student may also be exposed to its use at some time.

$$C_b = 1.75 + 1.05(M_1/M_2) + 0.3(M_1/M_2)^2 \le 2.3$$

where M_1 = smaller end moment in unbraced segment

M_2 = larger end moment in unbraced segment

The ratio of M_1/M_2 in the aforementioned C_b equation is positive when the unbraced segment has reverse curvature and the ratio is negative when the unbraced segment is bent in single curvature. C_b can be taken as 1.0 for segments in which the moment within the unbraced length is larger than at its ends. Therefore, in an unbraced beam the value of C_b will always be equal to 1.0.

The effect of the modifier C_b as it becomes greater than 1.0 is to account for the increased resistance to lateral torsional buckling by increasing the moment capacity.

The following example will demonstrate the use of the bending coefficient C_b.

EXAMPLE 6.7

Calculate the adequacy of a W 12 × 96 that is 30 feet long and braced as shown below. The beam carries a total factored load of 5 kips per foot and is made from A36 steel.

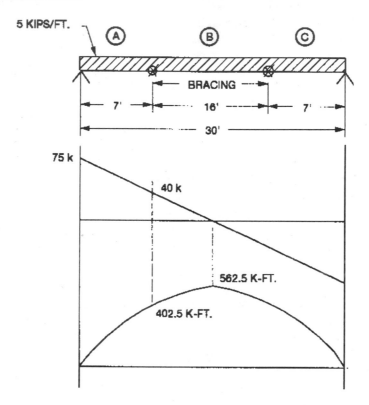

The moment the diagram has been drawn and from this it can be determined that segments A and C have a $C_b = 1.53$ by calculating out the C_b formula (since $M_a = 123.6$ kip-ft., $M_b = 231.9$ kip-ft., $M_c = 324.8$ kip-ft. and $M_{max} = 402.5$ kip-ft.). Segment 2 has a $C_b = 1.03$ from the formula (since $M_a = 522.5$ kip-ft., $M_b = 562.5$ kip-ft., $M_c = 522.5$ kip-ft. and $M_{max} = 562.5$ kip-ft.). However, since this is so close to 1.0, and since it is conservative to use 1.0, we will use 1.0. Therefore, segment 2 with an unbraced length, l_b, of 16 feet and a $C_b = 1.0$ is critical, since it is longer and has less resistance to lateral buckling due to the moment gradient.

Next, we must compare the critical unbraced length ($l_b = 16'$) to the values of L_p and L_r value to determine what case the nominal capacity will come from. Calculating the values of L_p and L_r for a W 12 × 96 using Eq. 6–1 and 6–2, we find the following:

$$L_p = 300(r_y)/\sqrt{F_y} \qquad \text{(Eq. 6–1)}$$
$$L_p = 300(3.09)/\sqrt{36} \text{ ksi} = 12.9 \text{ ft.} \quad (3.93 \text{ m})$$
$$L_r = (3.09(4250 \text{ ksi})/36 \text{ ksi} - 10 \text{ ksi})[\sqrt{1} + \sqrt{1} + .000405(36 - 10)^2$$
$$= 61.4 \text{ ft. } (18.7 \text{ m}) \qquad \text{(Eq. 6–2)}$$

Therefore, since our unbraced length is greater than the value of L_p but less than L_r, the moment nominal capacity is controlled by inelastic lateral torsional buckling and is calculated by Eq. 6–5 of Case #2.

Using the following information we can calculate the nominal moment capacity from Eq. 6–5:

$$l_b = 16 \text{ ft.} \qquad (4.88 \text{ m})$$
$$L_p = 12.9 \text{ ft.} \qquad (3.93 \text{ m})$$
$$L_r = 61.4 \text{ ft.} \qquad (18.7 \text{ m})$$
$$M_p = Z_x F_y = (147 \text{ in.}^3)(36 \text{ ksi})/12 = 441 \text{ kip-ft.} \qquad (598 \text{KN} - \text{m})$$
$$M_r = (F_y - F_r)S_x = (36 \text{ ksi} - 10 \text{ ksi})(131 \text{ in.}^3)/12 = 283.8 \text{ kip-ft.}$$
$$(384.2 \text{ KN} - \text{m})$$

Per Eq. 6–5:

$$M_n = 1.0[441 - (441 - 283.8)(3.1 \text{ ft.}/48.5 \text{ ft.})]$$
$$= 431 \text{ ft.-kip } (584.4 \text{KN-m})$$

The design moment capacity, $\phi_b M_n$, is then found to be:

$$\phi_b M_n = (.90)(431 \text{ kip-ft.}) = 387.9 \text{ kip-ft.}$$
$$(= (.90)(584.4 \text{ Kn-m}) = 526 \text{ KN-m})$$

This is less than the required moment capacity (562.5 kip-ft.), therefore the beam is no good. Since the beam's plastic capacity is well under the required capacity, it needs to be replaced by a much larger section.

6.6   AISC Rolled-Beam Design Using LRFD

There are numerous design tables and charts that are readily available to the experienced designer. However, until complete mastery of the fundamentals of beam mechanics and LRFD is achieved, the author recommends that the students hold off on the use of such charts. After some expertise has been achieved in the utilization of the LRFD beam formulas, the design charts will be introduced in the following section.

The following is a basic format that can be used to help the beginner in LRFD of rolled beams. As mentioned earlier in this chapter, beam design has to meet the following criteria:

$$M_u \le \phi_b M_n$$

or

$$M_u / \phi_b \le M_n$$

In this case, M_u and ϕ_b are known (or can be found) and the problem becomes finding a beam which equals or exceeds M_n.

From section 6.4, we know that compact rolled beams fall into one of three cases based on the unbraced length of the compression flange, l_b. Since l_b will be given or assumed in any problem, the task begins by looking at the dividing lines between plastic moment capacity and inelastic buckling, L_p, and inelastic and elastic buckling L_r. Should the sections under consideration fall into Case #1 (in which beams can reach their full plastic moment) then the section's unbraced length would have to be less than or equal to L_p. Using this strategy we can set $l_b = L_p$ and solve for a minimum value of r_y as shown below by rearranging Eq. 6–1:

$$r_{y\,min} = l_b \times \sqrt{F_y} / 300$$

If a majority of your beam sections meet the minimum requirement for r_y, you stand a very good chance of being in Case #1 and therefore

$$M_n = M_p = Z_x F_y$$

Solving for Z_x yields

$$Z_{x\,req'd} = M_n / F_y \qquad \qquad \text{(Eq. 6–10)}$$

The following example illustrates the design of a rolled beam section using the aforementioned logic.

EXAMPLE 6.8

Design a W 12 section to hold a factored moment of 400 kip-ft. Steel is A36 and beam is 12 feet long and unbraced ($C_b = 1.0$)

Using the logic stated above, the unbraced length can be set equal to the L_p value and a minimum value of r_y ($r_{y\,min}$) can be found that would place a section into Case #1.

$$l_b = 12' = 144''$$

Setting $l_b = L_p$ we can solve the following:

$$r_{y\,min} = 144 \times 6/300 = 2.88$$

Looking at the W 12 charts found in Appendix B, the majority of W 12 sections have r_y value in excess of the 2.88 minimum value (which would make the L_p value of a section equal to 12 feet). If our chosen section has an r_y above this value then it falls into Case #1 and the following is true:

$M_n = Z_x F_y$ (if Case 1)

$M_u = 400$ kip-ft.

$M_u / \phi_b \leq M_n$

$M_n = 400$ kip – ft./.90 = 444.4 kip-ft.   (602.6 KN-m)

$Z_{xreq'd} = 444.4$ kip-ft. × 12 in./ft./36 ksi = 148.1 in.³   (Eq. 6–10)

(= 602.6KN-m/248200KPa = .002427 m³ or 2427 mm³)

From the section tables in Appendix B, select W 12 × 106 (Z_x = 164 in.³ or 2670 mm³)

Since a W 12 × 106 has a r_y = 3.11 it does fall into Case# 1 because $l_b <$ L_p as shown below by Eq. 6–1 and it is also compact:

$L_p = 300(3.11)/\sqrt{36} = 155.5/12 = 12.9'$

Therefore the nominal moment capacity can be calculated as follows:

M_n = 164 in.³ × 36 ksi = 5904 kip-in. or 492 kip-ft. (667.2KN-m)

The design moment capacity is:

$\phi_b Mn = .90 × 492$ kip-ft. = 442.8 kip-ft.

(= .90 × 667.2 KN-m = 600.5 KN-m)

Since the design moment capacity is greater than the required capacity of 400 kip-ft., the beam is adequate.

The above example was nice in the fact that all assumptions were correct, but what happens if we did not fall into Case #1? The simple answer is that our design problem becomes more difficult, but if we remember the nominal moment capacity decreases as $l_b > L_p$ we can use logic to help us in our assumptions when our beam falls into Cases #2 and #3.

A beam is designed according to Case# 2 if $L_p < l_b < L_r$, and the nominal moment in Case #2 ranges from M_p (when the unbraced length is equal to L_p) to M_r (when the unbraced length is equal to L_r).

Therefore if the design fails to meet Case #1 requirements, a designer can try to gauge the upper and lower limits of Case #2 by solving the following (Figure 6–9):

$Z_{xreq'd} = M_n / F_y$ (Upper limit of Case# 2)

$S_{xreq'd} = M_n / (F_{yf} – F_r)$ (Lower limit of Case# 2)

Next, realizing that your first assumption of a beam to fall in Case #1 left you with a section's value of L_p and L_r, try to gauge where your section might

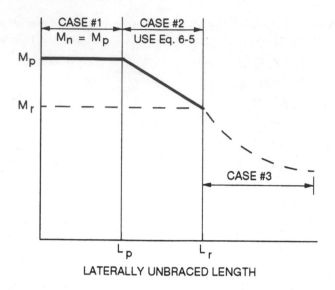

Figure 6–9   Illustration of Nominal Moment Capacities relative to the "Cases" or Categories of Beam.

fall. If your beam's unbraced length, l_b, is barely over L_p, then select a section using $Z_{xreq'd}$. If your l_b is barely greater than L_r, than choose a section using $S_{xreq'd}$. Example 6.9 illustrates this technique.

EXAMPLE 6.9

Design a W 12 section to hold a factored moment of 220 kip-ft. (298.3 KN-m). Steel is A36 and the beam is 12 feet long and unbraced ($C_b = 1.0$)

Using the logic stated above, the unbraced length can be set equal to the L_p value and a minimum value of r_y found that would place a section into Case #1. This can be performed as follows:

$$l_b = 144"$$

Setting $l_b = L_p$ we can solve the following:

$$r_{ymin} = 144 \times \sqrt{36}/300 = 2.88$$

If our sections have an r_y above this value then they fall into Case #1 and the following is true:

$M_n = Z_x F_y$ (if Case #1)

$M_u = 220$ kip-ft. (298.3KN-m)

$M_n = 220$ kip-ft./.90 = 244.4 kip-ft. (331.5KN-m)

If the assumption of Case #1 is correct, then $M_n = Z_x F_y$ and Eq. 6–10 can be used as follows:

$Z_{x\text{req'd}} = 244.4$ kip-ft. × 12/36 ksi = 81.4 in.^{3}

(= 331.5 KN-m/248200 KPa = .001335 m^3 or 1335 mm^3)

From tables choose W 12 × 58 ($Z_x = 86.4$ in.^{3} or 1420 mm^3)

Realizing that a W 12 × 58 has $r_y = 2.51$ in., which is less than $r_{y\text{min}}$, this section does not fall into Case #1. Using Eq 6–1 and 6–2 for a W 12 × 58 section, this can be verified:

$$L_p = 300(r_y)/\sqrt{F_y} \qquad \text{(Eq. 6–1)}$$

$L_p = 300(2.51)/\sqrt{36} = 125.5" = 10.4'$

$$Lr = \frac{r_y X_1}{(F_{yf} - F_r)} \sqrt{1 + \sqrt{1 + X_2 (F_{yf} - Fr)^2}} \qquad \text{(Eq. 6–2)}$$

$L_r = 38.4'$

Since this W 12 × 58's unbraced length falls between L_p and L_r (10.4 ft < 12 ft. < 38.4 ft.) the beam falls into Case #2 and our assumption is incorrect. However since the W 12 × 58 just barely falls into Case #2, this section may work since its plastic section modulus was a bit larger than necessary. Check to see if it does work anyway using Eq. 6–5.

$$M_n = C_b[M_p - (M_p - M_r)[(L_b - L_p/L_r - L_p)]] \qquad \text{(Eq. 6–5)}$$

$C_b = 1.0$

$M_p = Z_x F_y = 86.4$ in.^{3} × 36 ksi/12 = 259.2 kip-ft.

(= .00142 m^3 × 248200KPa = 352KN-m)

$M_r = (F_{yf} - F_r)S_x = (36$ ksi − 10 ksi$) 78$ in.^{3} /12 = 169 kip-ft.

((179270 KPa)(.00128 m^3) = 229.4KN-m)

$l_b = 12$ ft.

$L_p = 10.4$ ft.

$L_r = 38.4$ ft.

Calculating Eq. 6–5:

M_n = 1.0 (259.2 k-ft. – (259.2 k-ft. – 169 k-ft.)[12 ft. – 10.4 ft./

38.4 ft. – 10.4 ft.]) = 251.4 kip-ft. (340.9KN-m)

Since M_n = 251.4 kip-ft. > 244.4 kip-ft., a W 12 × 58 works. (It is also compact so flange buckling is not a consideration).

The logic continues by reasoning that if a W 12 × 58 failed we would try a larger section and if a W 12 × 58 was greatly overdesigned we would scale down.

EXAMPLE 6.10

Choose the most economical W 12 section to hold a uniform service load of 3 kips per foot over a 16 foot simple span braced at midspan. Steel is A36, DL/LL = 1.0, and load combination A4–2 from section 2.6 will control.

Calculate the required factored moment on the beam as follows. Realize that 50% of the service load is dead load and the other 50% is live load.

w_u = 1.2(1.5) + 1.6(1.5) = 4.2 kips per ft.

Calculating maximum moment:

M_u = 4.2(16)^2/8 = 134.4 kip-ft.   (182.2 KN-m)

Find the nominal moment capacity of a beam as follows:

$M_u / \phi_b \leq M_n$
$M_{nreq'd}$ = 134.4 kip-ft./.90 = 149.3 kip-ft. (202.4KN-m)

Since the unbraced length of 8 feet is small (l_b = 8 ft. or 96 in.) assume the section falls into Case #1. Calculate the minimum r_y value that will meet Case #1 criteria.

r_{ymin} = 96 × $\sqrt{36}$/300 = 1.92

Since many W 12 sections will meet this criteria, our assumption of Case #1 is reinforced. Calculate a plastic section modulus based on Eq. 6–10:

$Z_{xreq'd}$ = 149.33 kip-ft. × 12/36 ksi = 49.77 in.^{3}

(= 202.4 KN-m/248200 KPa = .000816 m^3 or 816 mm^3)

Choose W 12 × 35 (Z_x = 51.2 in.^{3} or 841 mm^3), but since its r_y = 1.54 this section will probably fall into Case #2. However upon comparing the unbraced length with the L_p and L_r values, again we see that the section is barely into Case #2.

l_b = 8 ft.   (2.44 m)

L_p = 6.4 ft.   (1.95 m)   (Eq. 6–1)

L_r = 20.6 ft.   (6.28 m)   (Eq. 6–2)

C_b = 1.30

(from equation 6–9 since M_a = 59 kip-ft., M_b = 101 kip-ft., M_c = 126 kip-ft. and M_{max} = 134.4 kip-ft.).

$M_p = Z_x F_y$ = 51.2 in.^{3} (36 ksi)/12 = 153.6 kip-ft.

  (= .000841 m^3 (248200KPa) = 208.7KN-m)

$M_r = (F_{yf} - F_r)S_x$ = (36 ksi – 10)(45.6 in.^{3})/12 = 98.8 kip-ft.

  (= (179270 KPa)(.000748 m^3) = 134.1KN-m)

Using the previous information calculate the nominal moment capacity of this section using Eq. 6–5 as follows:

M_n = 1.30(153.6 k-ft. – (153.6 k-ft. – 98.8 k-ft.)

  [8 ft. – 6.4 ft./20.6 ft. – 6.4 ft.])

  = 191.6 kip-ft.(260KN-m)

but you can never have $M_n > M_p$ therefore:

$M_n = M_p$ = 153.6 kip-ft. (208.7KN-m)

Since the section's M_n is greater than M_u/ϕ_b, (149.33 kip-ft. or 202.4 KN-m) the W 12 × 35 section is adequate. It is also compact so that flange buckling is not a consideration.

6.7   Preliminary Design Using the AISC Charts

As mentioned earlier, there are many charts and aids that are available to a steel designer. One of the most commonly used charts, to help in the design of rolled steel beams, is published in Part 2 of the LRFD manual. A sample of these charts is provided in Figure 6–10.

These charts have plotted the design moment ($\phi_b M_n$) that wide flange sections (and M sections) can carry based on their unbraced length, l_b. The charts given in the manual can be used for the aforementioned shapes made from steels with F_y = 36 ksi and F_y = 50 ksi. These charts are graphical representations utilizing the equations from the three cases mentioned earlier in this chapter and are to be used for cases when the bending coefficient, C_b, is equal to 1.0.

To use the AISC charts, a designer can simply enter the unbraced length, l_b, on the bottom scale and intersect that with the moment needed to be resisted on

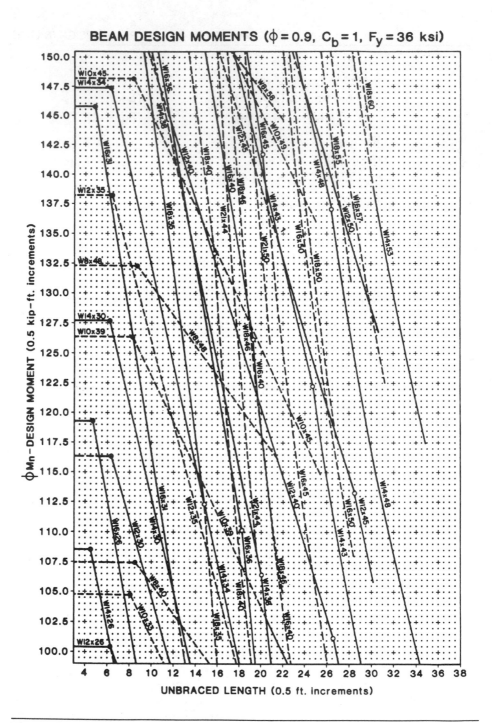

Figure 6–10 Beam Design Chart. (Courtesy of the American Institute of Steel Construction, Inc.)

the vertical scale. Any beam listed above and to the right of this intersection will satisfy the necessary requirements (considering that $C_b = 1.0$). Solid lines on the graph indicate the most economical section by weight in a given region, whereas the dashed line indicates that a lighter section will satisfy the strength requirement. The author encourages the readers to use this as a preliminary design step because the fundamentals of beam behavior must still be fully understood. Items such as compactness and the bending coefficient must still be checked, in order to ensure proper usage of these charts. The open circles that appear on the line for an individual section indicate the value of L_r, over which the beam begins elastic behavior. The closed circles that appear on the line for an individual section indicate that section's value of L_p.

The following example illustrates the use of the AISC beam charts.

EXAMPLE 6.11

Design the lightest W section to hold factored 5 kips per foot over a 15 foot unbraced simple span. The steel is A36 and beam weight is to be neglected.

To begin , let's calculate the factored moment that needs to be resisted by the beam to be selected.

$M_u = wl^2/8 = (5 \text{ kip/ft.})(15 \text{ ft.})^2/8 = 140.63 \text{ kip-ft.}$

Also, realize that we have steel with $F_y = 36$ ksi and can conservatively assume a $C_b = 1.0$ since the beam was simply supported and unbraced. Entering the charts with an unbraced length of 15 feet and a moment of 140.63 kip-ft (which happens to be the same one as shown in Figure 6–10), the first solid line that lies above this intersection is for a W 16 × 40. At this unbraced length this section can hold approximately 150 kip-ft. of moment and the section is compact (although it does not matter since it falls into Case #3).

6.8   AISC Requirements for Shear

Shear can be thought of as the sum of the loads on a beam up to the point under consideration. Therefore, shear forces will generally be the largest near the supports. From our discussion about beam behavior earlier in this chapter, we know that the maximum shear stress over a beam's cross-section occurs at the neutral axis. Consequently, the focus of shear forces on rolled-steel sections concentrates itself on the beam's web and near the beam's supports.

Generally, the design of rolled-steel beams is not controlled by shear. Only when you have short, very heavily loaded beams or where coping occurs, shear criteria might become a controlling factor.

The LRFD criteria for shear over a rolled-beam cross-section follows the same logic as with other behaviors, namely that the design shear strength ($\phi_v V_n$) has to equal or exceed the required shear (V_u). This is given by the following equation:

$$\phi_v \, V_n \geq V_u$$

where

$\phi_v = .90$ for shear

V_n = nominal shear capacity of the beam

V_u = required (factored) shear applied to the beam

There are three categories that may govern the type of shear behavior that a beam may experience. These categories are basically a function of web slenderness and are outlined as follows:

1. Web Yielding (when $h/t_w \leq 418/\sqrt{F_{yw}}$)

In this category, the nominal shear strength, V_n, is as follows:

$$V_n = (0.6 F_{yw})(A_w) \qquad \text{(Eq. 6–11)}$$

where

A_w = web thickness multiplied by beam depth
F_{yw} = specified web yield stress

2. Inelastic Web Buckling (when $418/\sqrt{F_{yw}} < h/t_w \leq 523/\sqrt{F_{yw}}$)

In this category, the nominal shear strength, V_n is:

$$V_n = (0.6 \, F_{yw})(A_w)(418/\sqrt{F_{yw}}/h/t_w) \qquad \text{(Eq. 6–12)}$$

where

h = distance between the flanges

t_w = web thickness

3. Elastic Web Buckling (when $h/t_w > 523/\sqrt{F_{yw}}$)
In this category, the nominal shear strength is as follows:

$$V_n = (132{,}000 A_w/(h/t_w)^2) \qquad \text{(Eq. 6–13)}$$

The reader should be aware that practically all rolled beams will be controlled by the web yielding case and are typically adequate with regard to shear. If plate girders are used, the student should realize stiffeners might be needed and this will be discussed in Chapter 11 and Chapter G in the LRFD specifications. The following example illustrates the usage of the LRFD shear requirements.

EXAMPLE 6.12

Calculate the design shear capacity $\phi_v V_n$ of a W 12 × 58 beam made from A36 steel. If the beam is 12 feet long, calculate the factored uniform load needed to make the factored shear equal the design capacity.

In this example, we can start by finding which case for shear controls in this instance. Calculate h/t_w as follows:

For a W 12 × 58

h = depth − 2(t_f) = 12.19 in. − 2(.64 in.) = 10.91 in.

t_w = .36 in.

h/t_w = 10.91 in./.36 in. = 30.3

Compare this to the limit for web yielding as follows:

$418/\sqrt{F_{y\,w}}$ = $418/\sqrt{36}$ ksi = 69.7

Since 30.3 is less than 69.7, Case #1 controls, and the nominal shear strength can be calculated by Eq. 6–11 as follows:

$$V_n = (0.6F_{yw})(A_w)$$
$$= (0.6)(36\text{ ksi})(12.19\text{ in.} \times .36\text{ in.})$$
$$= 94.8\text{ kips}$$

Therefore the design shear capacity is

$\phi_v V_n$ = .90(94.8 kips) = 85.3 kips

The factored uniform load that would produce this amount of shear over a 12 foot long, simply supported beam can be calculated as:

85.3 kips = w_u(12 ft.)²/8

w_u = 4.74 kips/ft.

6.9   Weak Axis Bending

Earlier in this chapter, when discussing the factors that affect the nominal moment capacity of a rolled section, the two main factors given were compactness and lateral support of the compression flange. Actually, during this discussion we assumed that bending would occur about the shape's strong axis, but there is a possibility, that bending may occur about a shape's weak axis (especially in beam-columns).

If bending occurs about the weak axis, which has a higher shape factor, the specification recognizes that failure due to lateral torsional buckling will not occur in a doubly symmetrical section. Therefore the two applicable limit states are development of the section's plastic capacity and local buckling of the flanges that was discussed in section 5.8. Although this absence of the lateral torsional limit state may seem advantageous, members are rarely bent about the weak axis since the other properties are so much lower than those about the strong axis.

6.10 Open Web Steel Joists

Open-web steel joists, also referred to as bar joists, are small parallel chord, truss-type beams whose members are often composed of small angles, round bars, or other steel shapes. The first open-web steel joist was manufactured as a Warren truss-type structure in 1923. Since then, open-web steel joists have become a very common structural steel beam member, used in both floor and roof construction of small to medium sized buildings (Figure 6–11).

Open-web joists have been standardized to fall into a number of "series" that define certain purposes. The *K-Series* of open web steel joists are made for typical loads, spanning lengths of approximately 60 feet. These joist are typically 8" to 30" in depth and have chords made from steel with a F_y = 50,000 psi. The *J-Series* joists are similar to the K-series but are made from steels having a F_y = 36000 psi, thereby reducing the span length which they can handle under a given load. The J-Series have essentially been replaced with the advent of higher strength steel joists (namely the K-Series). Another short-span open web steel joist series that has been used frequently in the past is the *H-series*. H-Series joists were designed with steels having a minimum F_y = 50000 psi, but were replaced in 1986 by the K-series to meet the demands for roofs with lighter loads, especially in the 18" to 30" depth range. Also available are *LH-* and *DLH-Series* that are made from steels with a F_y = 50000 psi and are manufactured for longer span lengths. The LH-Series (Longspan-series) has joists with standardized depths up to 48 inches and can span over 90 feet. The DLH-Series (Deep Longspan-series) has joists that are 52" to 72" in depth and can span up to 144 feet. This makes them ideal for roof framing in warehouses, offices, and other mid-size structures.

In designating the K-series of open-web steel joists, the following format is typically used:

20 *K* 7

where

20 = the approximate depth of the joist, in.

K = the Series designation

7 = chord size with sizes increasing as the number gets larger

In designating the LH-Series of steel joists, the following format is used:

32 *LH* 14

where

32 = the depth of the joist in inches

LH = the Series designation

14 = the chord size, larger with increasing number

The designation for the DLH-series is also similar to the LH series with DLH

Figure 6–11   Open Web Steel Joist Construction. (Courtesy of the Steel Joist Institute.)

replacing the LH.

The Steel Joist Institute (as well as practically all manufacturers of open web steel joists) publish load tables[4] that tabulate the safe uniform load that certain joists can support at certain span lengths. Safe loads are also typically given so as to maintain a deflection of no more than 1/360 of the span. At the present time, the load tables that exist are based on the allowable stress philosophy although the Steel Joist Institute will be publishing a specification based on the LRFD philosophy in the very near future. Although the tables shown in this text are based on allowable stress design methods, the conversion of these into LRFD tables is handled very easily as discussed below.

A standard type of load table is shown below in Figure 6–12 and in Appendix D. The design of open-web joists has become standardized and has become the responsibility of the joist manufacturers. Because of this standardization, a designer in a typical situation does not design the open web steel joist but rather utilizes a standard load table and chooses an applicable member. Such tables are superb for selection of joists under uniform load only, but further analysis must be given if other load cases are to be considered. The conversion of these allowable stress load tables into LRFD load tables is handled by calculating the ultimate joist capacity, w_u, from the black (or top) load values found in each block of the allowable stress load tables such as the one shown in Figure 6–12. This is done as follows:

$$w_u = 1.65 W_{sji}$$

where

w_u = ultimate joist capacity, pounds per foot
w_{sji} = safe load in pounds per foot from the allowable stress table (the top number)

The design capacity of a steel joist is then found by taking the ultimate capacity and applying a reduction value of 0.90. therefore the design capacity ø w_u of an open web steel joist is as follows:

$$\phi w_u = 0.90(1.65 W_{sji})$$

Once again, this conversion procedure for LRFD using the load tables is only for uniform gravity loads and other loading situations must be appropriately analyzed by the designer.

Other factors must be remembered in the design of open web steel joists. For instance, when designing a K-series joist, the span must never exceed 24 times its depth and the chords of these K-series joists must be adequately braced against buckling. Typically this bracing is accomplished by **bridging**, which is typically a horizontal member attached to the top and bottom chord that runs perpendicular to the span length (Figure 6–13). The specification for K-series joists will specify the number of rows of bridging to be used with regard to a specific span

STANDARD LOAD TABLE
Based on a Maximum Allowable Tensile Stress of 30,000 psi

OPEN WEB STEEL JOISTS, K-SERIES

Adopted by the Steel Joist Institute November 4, 1985; Revised to May 19, 1987.

The black figures in the following table give the TOTAL safe uniformly distributed load-carrying capacities, in pounds per linear foot, of K- Series Steel Joists. The weight of DEAD loads, including the joists, must be deducted to determine the LIVE load-carrying capacities of the joists. The load table may be used for parallel chord joists installed to a maximum slope of 1/2 inch per foot.

The figures shown in RED in this load table are the LIVE loads per linear foot of joist which will produce an approximate deflection of 1/360 of the span. LIVE loads which will produce a deflection of 1/240 of the span may be obtained by multiplying the figures in RED by 1.5. In no case shall the TOTAL load capacity of the joists be exceeded.

The approximate joist weights per linear foot shown in these tables do not include accessories.

The approximate moment of inertia of the joist, in inches^4 is: $I_J = 26.767 (W_{LL}) (L') (10^4)$, where W_{LL} = RED figure in the Load Table; L = (Span - 0.33), in feet.

For the proper handling of concentrated and/or varying loads, see Section 5.5 in the Recommended Code of Standard Practice (page 65).

Joist Designation	8K1	10K1	12K1	12K3	12K5	14K1	14K3	14K4	14K6	16K2	16K3	16K4	16K5	16K6	16K7	16K9
Depth (In.)	8	10	12	12	12	14	14	14	14	16	16	16	16	16	16	16
Approx. Wt. (lbs./ft.)	5.1	5.0	5.0	5.7	7.1	5.2	6.0	6.7	7.7	5.5	6.3	7.0	7.5	8.1	8.6	10.0
Span (ft.) ↓																
8	550 / 550															
9	550 / 550															
10	550 / 480	550 / 550														
11	532 / 377	550 / 542														
12	444 / 288	550 / 455	550 / 550	550 / 550	550 / 550											
13	377 / 225	479 / 363	550 / 510	550 / 510	550 / 510											
14	324 / 179	412 / 289	500 / 425	550 / 463	550 / 463	550 / 550	550 / 550	550 / 550	550 / 550							
15	281 / 145	358 / 234	434 / 344	543 / 428	550 / 434	511 / 475	550 / 507	550 / 507	550 / 507							
16	246 / 119	313 / 192	380 / 282	476 / 351	550 / 396	448 / 390	550 / 467	550 / 467	550 / 467	550 / 550	550 / 550	550 / 550	550 / 550	550 / 550	550 / 550	550 / 550
17		277 / 159	336 / 234	420 / 291	550 / 366	395 / 324	495 / 404	550 / 443	550 / 443	512 / 488	550 / 526	550 / 526	550 / 526	550 / 526	550 / 526	550 / 526
18		246 / 134	299 / 197	374 / 245	507 / 317	352 / 272	441 / 339	530 / 397	550 / 408	456 / 409	508 / 456	550 / 490	550 / 490	550 / 490	550 / 490	550 / 490
19		221 / 113	268 / 167	335 / 207	454 / 269	315 / 230	395 / 287	475 / 336	550 / 383	408 / 347	455 / 386	547 / 452	550 / 455	550 / 455	550 / 455	550 / 455
20		199 / 97	241 / 142	302 / 177	409 / 230	284 / 197	356 / 246	428 / 287	525 / 347	368 / 297	410 / 330	493 / 386	550 / 426	550 / 426	550 / 426	550 / 426
21			218 / 123	273 / 153	370 / 198	257 / 170	322 / 212	388 / 248	475 / 299	333 / 255	371 / 285	447 / 333	503 / 373	548 / 405	550 / 406	550 / 406
22			199 / 106	249 / 132	337 / 172	234 / 147	293 / 184	353 / 215	432 / 259	303 / 222	337 / 247	406 / 289	458 / 323	498 / 351	550 / 385	550 / 385
23			181 / 93	227 / 116	308 / 150	214 / 128	268 / 160	322 / 188	395 / 226	277 / 194	308 / 216	371 / 252	418 / 282	455 / 307	507 / 339	550 / 363
24			166 / 81	208 / 101	282 / 132	196 / 113	245 / 141	295 / 165	362 / 199	254 / 170	283 / 189	340 / 221	384 / 248	418 / 269	465 / 298	550 / 346
25						180 / 100	226 / 124	272 / 145	334 / 175	234 / 150	260 / 167	313 / 195	353 / 219	384 / 238	428 / 263	514 / 311
26						166 / 88	209 / 110	251 / 129	308 / 156	216 / 133	240 / 148	289 / 173	326 / 194	355 / 211	395 / 233	474 / 276
27						154 / 79	193 / 98	233 / 115	285 / 139	200 / 119	223 / 132	268 / 155	302 / 173	329 / 188	366 / 208	439 / 246
28						143 / 70	180 / 88	216 / 103	265 / 124	186 / 106	207 / 118	249 / 138	281 / 155	306 / 168	340 / 186	408 / 220
29										173 / 95	193 / 106	232 / 124	261 / 139	285 / 151	317 / 167	380 / 198
30										161 / 86	180 / 96	216 / 112	244 / 126	266 / 137	296 / 151	355 / 178
31										151 / 78	168 / 87	203 / 101	228 / 114	249 / 124	277 / 137	332 / 161
32										142 / 71	158 / 79	190 / 92	214 / 103	233 / 112	259 / 124	311 / 147

Figure 6–12 Standard Load Table for K-series Joists. (Courtesy of the Steel Joist Institute.)

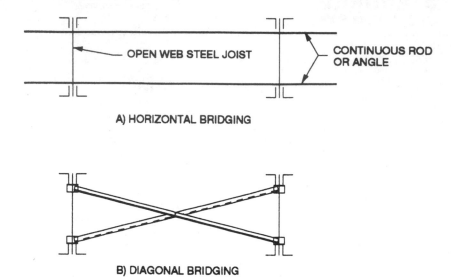

Figure 6–13   Illustration of Bridging Techniques in Open Web Steel Joists.

length of the joist. This horizontal bridging must be capable of resisting a horizontal force of not less than 700 pounds and can be attached by welding or mechanical attachments. Bridging may also be accomplished through diagonal cross-bracing, if the slenderness ratio of the bracing member is not less than 200. The quantity of bridging is specified in the steel joint institute standards[4] as well as other pertinent information concerning the proper use of a K-series open web steel joist.

Specifications covering the DLH and LH-series of open web steel joists are also found in the above standards[4]. While similar in some aspects to the specifications of the K-series joists, the requirements for bridging specify the maximum spacing of rows relative to the type of joist used. The use of welded bridging on span lengths over 60 feet is prohibited.

The following example illustrates the use of the load tables when selecting a K-series open web steel joist.

EXAMPLE 6.13

Select the proper K-series open web steel joist that is used as part of the roof framing of a warehouse to carry a service dead load of 40 psf and a service live load of 60 psf. The span length is 22 feet and the joists are to be spaced at 4 feet on center. Assume proper bridging requirements and other criteria is met.

Also calculate the design capacity of the selected joist based on the LRFD conversion.

To begin this problem, the designer should calculate the load per foot that the K-series joist will have to safely carry. In this case the distributive area on the joist is 4 feet and the total roof load is 100 psf.

Therefore total load per foot of joist length to be carried is:

4 feet × 100 psf = 400 lbs./ft.

Searching the K-series load table for a 22 foot span length, the joist that can safely handle this is a 14K6. You will notice that there are two numbers that are listed under this joist. In the actual load table found in the SJI specification, the top number is in black and the bottom number is in red. The top number (432) reflects the total safe load (in lbs. per ft.) that this joist can carry. Since it can safely carry 432 lbs./ft. and our total load is only 400 lbs./ft., the joist is adequate. The bottom number (259) reflects the live load in pounds per foot that would cause an approximate deflection of 1/360 of the span length. The deflection (1/360 of span) is the typical value of allowable deflection that most building codes specify as the maximum permissible deflection for beams supporting plastered ceilings. More on this topic will be discussed in Chapter 7. Because the live load per foot on this beam is only 240 lbs./ft. which is less than 259 lbs./ft., the deflection would also be adequate under the 1/360 of span length criteria.

To calculate the design capacity, ϕw_u using the LRFD conversion of the 14K6 is found as follows:

$$\phi w_u = 0.90(1.65 W_{sji})$$
$$= 0.90(1.65 \times 432 \text{ lbs./ft.}) = 641.5 \text{ lbs./ft.}$$

Therefore the design capacity of this joist would be compared to the factored load per foot from the applicable load combination in an LRFD design.

6.11 Summary

Rolled-beams are one of the basic building blocks for steel construction. In LRFD a failure is referred to as a limit state. Steel beam limit states may initiate in several different manners, depending on the stability or buckling of the compression flange. This instability is referred to as lateral torsional buckling and is associated with the unbraced length, l_b, of the compression flange. If a beam is prevented (usually by lateral bracing) from this instability, it will typically be able to reach its plastic moment.

Design of steel beams can involve trial-and-error procedures and may be supplemented by using some of the many design aids that are available. Shear failure on steel beams is typically not a controlling feature of steel design, unless the beams are very short, heavily loaded, or have coped sections. Open web steel joists are another subset of steel beam design, and are commonly used in light, industrial and commercial projects.

EXERCISES

1. Explain the differences between local buckling and lateral torsional buckling. Discuss the factors relating to each type of behavior.
2. Explain the concept of plastic behavior in beams and how does this limit state differ from those typically associated with Allowable Stress Design?
3. Explain how the bending coefficient, C_b, effects the AISC allowable bending stress equations. Is a higher value of C_b good or bad as far as beam behavior is concerned?
4. A W 12 × 120 is used as a beam that is 20 feet long braced along its compression flange at 5 foot intervals. If the maximum factored moment is 400 kip-ft. (occurring at the beam's midpoint) and the steel is A36, will the beam be adequate per AISC criteria? Assume $C_b = 1.0$.
5. A W 310 × 86 is used as a beam to span 5 meters and is unbraced. If the beam holds a factored load of 10 Kn/m, is it adequate per LRFD criteria. The steel is A36. Assume $C_b = 1.0$.
6. If the beam in problem 5 is braced at its midpoint, how does this affect its design capacity.
7. Same information as in problem 4, but calculate the maximum uniform load that the beam can safely carry.
8. Check the adequacy of a W 24 × 84 to hold a service DL of 1 kip/ft. and a service live load of 2 kips/ft. if the beam is 20 feet long and unbraced along its compression flange. The beam is made from A36 steel. Assume $C_b = 1.0$.
9. Recheck the beam in problem 8, if the beam is braced at its midpoint.
10. Calculate the adequacy per LRFD specifications of a W 12 × 79 beam that carries a factored uniform load of 5 kips per foot over a span length of 25 feet. The beam is made from A36 steel and is braced at points located 5 feet from each end. Check bending and shear requirements.
11. Calculate the adequacy per LRFD specifications of a W 310 × 143 beam that carries a factored uniform load of 25 KN/m over a span length of 9 meters. The beam is made from A36 steel and is braced at points located 1.5 meters from each end. Check bending and shear requirements.
12. Design an economical W section to carry a service dead load of 2 kips per foot and a service live load of 10 kips located at midspan. The beam is 20 feet long and is braced at midspan. The steel is A36, also check shear requirements. Depth of the beam is limited to 18 inches.

13. For the beam shown below, design the lightest W 10 section, if it is:
a. unbraced (Assume $C_b = 1.0$)
b. braced at mid-span
c. braced at quarter points
Steel is A36 and the loads are service loads with 50% live load and 50% dead load.

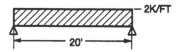

14. Design the steel support beam in the basement of the small building that is outlined below. The floor system consists of 2 × 10's @ 16" o.c. with 3/4" plywood. Floor live loads are 40 psf (service) and steel is A36. Consider self weight of all components and consider the beam unbraced. Assume $C_b = 1.0$.

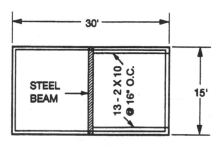

PLAN OF FOUNDATION

15. Design an economical W-section to hold a total factored load of 20 KN/m over a span of 9 meters. The beam is braced laterally at midspan and the steel is A36. Due to clearance restrictions the beam depth cannot exceed 500 mm. Check shear capacity for adequacy per LRFD requirements.

16. A W 12 × 58 spans 8 feet and is fully braced. Determine the magnitude of factored uniform load that would produce a shear equal to the beam's design shear capacity. The steel is A36.

17. For the beam discussed in problem 16, calculate the magnitude of factored uniform load that the beam can resist in bending. What behavior controls?

18. For the beam shown below, design an economical W-section made from A36 steel. The beam is braced only at the supports and the loads shown are factored. Consider moment requirements and shear requirements in the design. Assume $C_b = 1.0$.

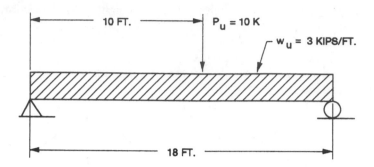

19. For the beam shown below, design an economical W-section made from A36 steel. The beam is braced only at its supports and the loads shown are factored. Consider moment requirements and shear requirements in the design. Assume $C_b = 1.0$.

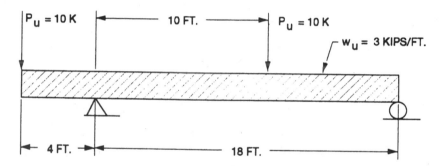

20. Using the open web steel joists load tables found in Appendix D, select an open web steel joist to span 20 feet if the distributive area to that joist is 2 feet. The uniform dead load is 100 psf and the uniform live load is 150 psf.
21. Calculate the total floor load (psf) that a 16K6 can safely support over a span of 20 feet. The distributive area to this joist is 4 feet.

REFERENCES

1. Mrazih, Augustin, *Plastic Design of Steel Structures*, Ellis Horwood Limited, London, 1987, p. 94–95.
2. Disque, Robert, *Applied Plastic Design in Steel*, Van Nostrand Reinhold Co., New York, 1971, p. 10.
3. Hoadley, Peter, "Practical Signifcance of LRFD Beam Buckling Factors," *Journal of Structural Engineering*, ASCE, March 1991, p. 988–996.
4. "Standard Specifications, Load Tables and Weight Tables for Steel Joists and Joists Girders," Steel Joist Institute, Myrtle Beach, SC, 1992.

7

SERVICEABILITY AND DEFLECTION REQUIREMENTS

7. 1   Introduction to Serviceability

The AISC specification defines **serviceability** as "a state in which the function of a building, its appearance, maintainability, durability, and comfort of its occupants are preserved under normal usage."[1] A building or member must function as its occupants wish or it will fail to perform its function adequately. A serviceability failure can be as much of a problem as a strength-based failure, because the structure may not be used in the manner intended. Serviceability items, such as limiting the maximum beam deflection, may control the design of a member rather than the standard strength criteria. The concept of designing in LRFD is usually to prevent some certain limit state from occurring under factored loads, however, the LRFD specification states that serviceability be checked using "realistic loads". This means that the designer will typically check serviceability limit states using service loads.

The topic of serviceability is given secondary status by some in the design profession, because it does not involve absolute quantities but rather deals with *quality* of acceptable behavior. While strength criteria is rather straight forward (design capacity ≥ required capacity), serviceability criteria usually relies heavily on the designer's personal judgment (how much floor vibration is acceptable?). A serviceability decision that works well on one particular project, may not work well on another.

Common items that fall under the realm of serviceability include deflection, vibration, lateral drift, and overall appearance. The relationship with serviceability of each is briefly discussed below.

Deflection

As members are loaded, they will deflect. If these deflections become excessive, it can lead to problems associated with appearance such as cracking or bulging in ceilings and walls. Other problems caused by excessive defections may include improper functioning of other building components such as doors and windows. Excessive deflections may also lead to strength failures (as in the case of ponding which will be discussed later in this chapter). Deflection is the most common serviceability-based design item and will be the focus of the next section.

Vibration

Members subjected to certain live loads (such as wind gusts, earthquakes, moving vehicles, and aerobic classes) will tend to vibrate under such load. As long as the vibration does not become excessive, it is usually of little concern. However, when the frequency of the live load approaches that of the structure's natural frequency, vibration can reach unacceptable levels. One such case was a restaurant/dance club located in Flushing, New York, where floor vibrations caused by the dancing greatly alarmed the dining patrons.[2] This problem, although it did not constitute a strength-based structural defect, caused the building to be unacceptable for use in its intended function. The function of a building also directly affects the acceptability (or unacceptability) of a particular amount of vibration. For instance, a hospital would have a lower threshold for acceptable vibration than would an industrial machine shop. Excessive vibration may also cause serviceability problems in industrial applications where precisely-tuned mechanical systems cannot tolerate movements over some limiting amount.

Lateral Drift

This item generally refers to the swaying of multistory buildings under wind loads. Large buildings, such as the World Trade Center in New York City, will sway laterally by as much as three feet in a storm with high winds. During such storms, lateral drifting must not be perceptible to the occupants of the building to minimize any anxiety regarding the structure's integrity. Excessive drifting might also damage other building components such as doors and windows.

Overall Appearance

Excessive cracking in walls or ceilings, bulges or gaps in exterior facades, and damage due to improper drainage, all project a poor appearance to the casual observer. Such an appearance does nothing to instill confidence in the structural integrity of the building and, therefore, should be considered a serviceability aspect in any design.

7. 2   Deflection Calculations and Requirements

The computation of beam deflection is necessary to ensure the serviceability of the structure as was discussed in the previous section. Usually, in civil engineering structures, the deflections are known to be relatively small compared to the overall dimensions of the section and its span length. However, since deflection criterion may control in some instances, the structural designer needs to be able to calculate the anticipated deflection in order to compare this value to the limiting values as set forth in the applicable building code.

As a beam is subjected to load, it will deflect. Deflection (δ) can simply be thought of as the distance that the beam displaces from its original horizontal position. This displacement is the result of the change of rotation or slope (θ) that occurs between different points along a beam (Figure 7–1). In fact, deflection can be defined as the *sum of incremental changes in rotation* along a beam. The amount of slope change that a beam undergoes between two points is a function of the moment (at that point) and the beam's flexural stiffness (*EI*). This slope relationship is typically stated as follows:

$$\Delta\theta = \Sigma(M/EI)\,\Delta x \qquad\qquad \text{(Eq. 7–1)}$$

where

$\Delta\theta$ = incremental change of slope between two points
Δx = incremental "x" distance under consideration

Using this information, how is beam deflection calculated? Actually, there are many methods that are available based on the relationships that exist between the bending moment on a beam of known rigidity and the correspond-

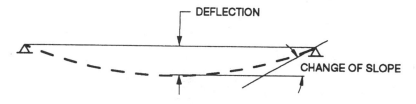

Figure 7–1   Deflection as a Function of Change of Slope

ing rotation (slope) and deflection that this moment causes. Such methods of deflection calculation include the *moment-area* method, the *conjugate beam* method, and the *double integration* method. Possibly, the easiest of these techniques is the moment-area method. This method is fully covered in any strength-of-materials text and, therefore, only a limited explanation of this technique will follow. Students interested only in maximum deflections for typical load cases can proceed to the explanation of tabular deflection values described after Example 7.1.

Moment-Area Method

The moment-area method for calculating deflection is based on the principle that the change of slope between any two points on a deflection curve is equal to the area between those two points on the M/EI diagram, which for illustrative purposes are points A and B in Figure 7–2. (It should be noted that for a beam made of one material and constant cross section, the M/EI diagram is the same shape as the beam's moment diagram.) From Equation 7–1 it was shown that the total change of slope between points A and B is the basis for finding deflection,

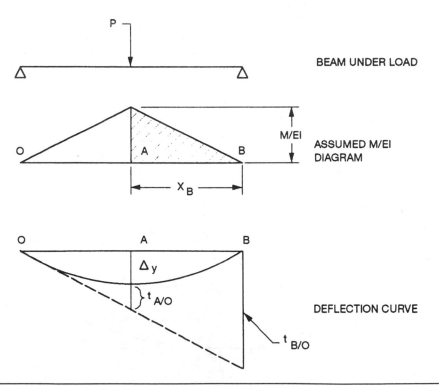

Figure 7–2 Application of the Moment-Area Method for Deflection.

and now the shaded area between those points on the M/EI diagram must be found. This area for small increments of the M/EI diagram is approximately rectangular and, therefore, the change in slope ($\Delta\theta$) is simply value of M/EI multiplied by the incremental x distance (Δx).

The deflection (δ) of the beam at point A can be looked at as the elevation difference (tangent deviation) at various points relative to one another along the beam. This tangent deviation of one point relative to another (let's assume B relative to O) is found by intersecting a vertical line through B with a tangent line from O. Due to bending, the tangent deviation of the B relative to O is shown in Figure 7–2 and is calculated as follows:

$$t_{B/O} = x_B(\Delta\theta) \qquad\qquad \text{(Eq. 7–2)}$$

where

x_B = the centroidal distance from B to the area bounded by B-O under the M/EI diagram

In Eq. 7–2 a substitution for $\Delta\theta$ (Eq. 7–1) can be made and the resulting formula may be written as follows:

$$t_{B/O} = \Sigma(M/EI\,\Delta x)\,x_B \qquad\qquad \text{(Eq. 7–3)}$$

The deflection at some point (such as A) may then be found by taking the tangent deviation from A to O ($t_{A/O}$) and subtracting that from the weighted value of tangent deviation from B to O ($t_{B/O}$).

The following example demonstrates the use of this method in calculating deflection.

EXAMPLE 7.1

Using the moment-area method, derive the formula for deflection at the center of a simply-supported beam with a concentrated load at its midpoint.

The first order of business is to construct the M/EI diagram for such a case as shown below. Notice the M/EI diagram is simply the moment diagram divided by the flexural stiffness.

The deflection at the beam's center, the maximum deflection, is desired. Consider the amount of deflection to be equal to 1/2 $t_{B/A}$ minus $t_{O/A}$. Working with the two triangular areas under the M/EI diagram ($\Delta\theta$) lists these areas (between these points B and A) as follows:

Area 1 = $(1/2) \times (L/2) \times (PL/4EI)$

        = $PL^2/16EI$

Area 2 = Same

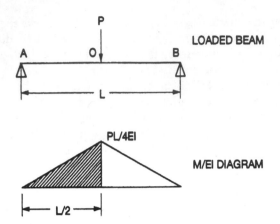

Considering the distance from the centroid of these areas to the points from which the vertical lines are drawn (from O and from point B). In this case that distance would be as follows:

Distance 1 = $(2/3) \times (L/2) = 2L/6 = L/3$
Distance 2 = $2L/3$
Distance 3 = $L/6$

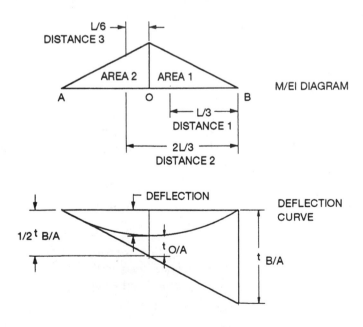

Therefore, the deflection can be calculated as follows:

$$\delta = (1/2)t_{B/A} - t_{O/A}$$

where

$$t_{B/A} = (\text{Area 1} \times \text{Dist. 1}) + (\text{Area 2} \times \text{Dist. 2})$$

$$t_{O/A} = (\text{Area 2} \times \text{Dist. 3})$$

or $\quad \delta = 3PL^3/96\text{EI} - PL^3/96\text{EI} = PL^3/48\text{EI}$

Although this method can be used easily in many beam deflection cases, for typical beam loadings, there already exists deflection formulas (derived from these aforementioned methods).

Standard Deflection Formulas

Many formulas exist for the calculation of beam deflection under standard load cases. Formulas may be written to calculate the maximum deflection of a beam or the deflection at a required point. Most of the time, designers are concerned with the maximum beam deflection. Such formulas are found in many references such as the AISC Manual of Steel Construction. For a quick reference, a partial list of beam deflection formulas for some of the more common beam loadings is shown in Figure 7–3.

The following examples illustrate how some of these deflection formulas are used. The most important reminder when using these formulas—*keep consistent units!!* Remember that deflection is usually measured in inches or meters. Therefore it is imperative that all units are expressed in dimensionally correct forms. Make sure all uniform loads are in units of pounds per inch, kips per inch, kilonewtons per meter or other (depending on what units that the modulus of elasticity is expressed). All span lengths are also typically listed in units of inches or millimeters.

EXAMPLE 7.2

Calculate the live load deflection of the 20 foot long W 12 × 50 under a uniform live load of 3 kips per foot over its entire length.

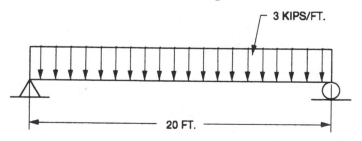

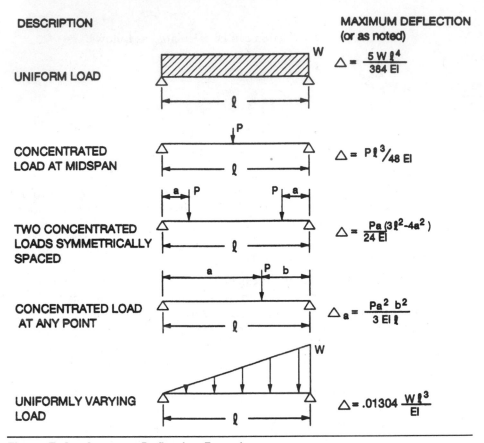

Figure 7–3   Common Deflection Formulas

In this problem, the deflection is calculated from the formula found in Figure 7–2. The variables needed for this calculation are as follows:

w = 3 kips/foot = 3 kips/ft. ÷ (12 in./ft.) or .25 kips/in.

(w = 43.78 KN/m)

$\qquad l$ = 20 ft = 240 in.   (6.1 m)

$\qquad E$ = 29000 ksi   (2×10^8 KPa)

I = 394. in.^{4} (W 12 × 50 about its strong axis)

$\qquad$ (164 × 10^6 mm^4 or .000164 m^4)

Calculating deflection from the formula given in Figure 7–3:

$\delta = 5wl^4/384EI$

$\delta = 5 \times (.25 \text{ kips/in.}) \times (240 \text{ in.})^4/384(29000 \text{ ksi})(394 \text{in.}^4)$

= .945 in.

$\delta = 5 \times (43.78 \text{ KN/m})(6.1 \text{ m})^4/384(2 \times 10^8 \text{KPa})(.000164 \text{ m}^4)$

= .024 m or 24 mm)

(Note: To include dead load deflection caused by the beam's self weight, one would simply consider an additional 50 pounds per foot of loading (or 4.17 lb./in.). This selfweight would cause an additional .015 in. of deflection).

EXAMPLE 7.3

Calculate the live load deflection on the same beam as in Example 7.2 under a concentrated live load of 60 kips located at midspan.

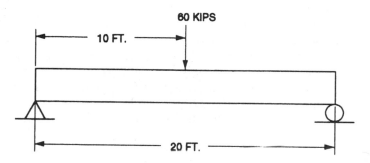

Use the appropriate formula from Figure 7–3. The variables needed to calculate the formula are as follows:

l = 20 ft. = 240 in.	(6.1 m)
P = 60 kips	(266.9 KN)
I = 394 in.^{4}	(.000164 m^4)
E = 29000 ksi	(2 × 10^8 KPa)

Using the formula:

$\delta = Pl^3/48\,EI$

$\delta = (60 \text{ kips})(240 \text{ in.})^3/48(29000 \text{ ksi})(394 \text{ in.}^4)$

= 1.51 in.

$(\delta = (266.9 \text{ KN})(6.1 \text{ m})^3/48(2 \times 10^8 \text{ KPa})(.000164 \text{ m}^4)$

= .0384 m or 38.4 mm)

EXAMPLE 7.4

Calculate the live load deflection at midspan on the beam shown below. The beam is the same beam as used in Examples 7.2 and 7.3 although the loading are now combined.

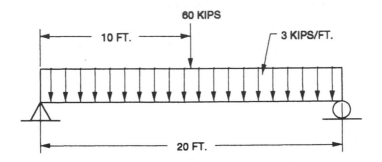

Looking at the formulas in Figure 7–3, notice that there is no formula for this exact case. However because both the uniform load case and the concentrated load case produced maximum deflections at the beam's midspan, it is accurate to simply sum the deflections from each individual load case to get the combined deflection. This procedure is known as **superpositioning**, where the effects of the combined deflection are accurately viewed as the sum of their parts. The variables needed to calculate the formula are as follows:

l = 20 ft. = 240 in.   (6.1 m)

w = 3 kips/ft. = .25 kips/in.   (w = 43.78 KN/m)

P = 60 kips   (266.9 KN)

I = 394 in.^{4} (.000164 m^4)

E = 29000 ksi   (2×10^8 KPa)

Using the individual formulas taken from Figure 7–3, a "superimposed" formula is created as follows:

$\delta_{total} = 5wl^4/384EI + Pl^3/48\ EI$

δ = .945 in. + 1.51 in. = 2.455 in.

(δ = 24 mm + 38.4 mm = 62.4 mm)

Previously, discussion has focused on possible methods to calculate deflections, but what are the limiting values of deflections that are used in standard practice?

Usually, building codes and specifications will limit deflections to a fraction of a beam's span length. Most building codes, as well as the LRFD specification in Chapter L, limit the live load deflection on beams under **service load conditions** to 1/360th of the span length (or $l/360$) in plastered construction. When dealing with beams that are a part of unplastered construction this requirement is relaxed to 1/180th of the span length (or $l/180$) in roof assemblies and to 1/240th of the span length in floor assemblies. In comparison, the AASHTO specification[3] limits the live load deflection on steel bridge girders to 1/800th of the span length (or $l/800$) to maintain clearance height under typically heavy live loads.

The student should remember that the above deflection limits are recommended maximums, which are meant to provide guidance (not a guarantee) in achieving a serviceable design. A designer must always use his or her personal judgment, taking into account the goals of a specific project. These values may be adjusted, either upward or downward, should that individual project warrant such a decision.

7.3   Deflection Strength Failure: Ponding

Up to now, we have discussed beam deflection solely as a serviceability concern. Usually, this is indeed the case. There is, however, one notable exception where deflection problems can actually be the catalyst behind a destructive strength-based failure. This one exception is a phenomena referred to as ponding, the results of which can be devastating.

Ponding refers to the retention of water on a flat or semi-flat roof during periods of heavy rainfall or snow melt. As the water accumulates on the roof faster than it can drain off, the roof deflects under the weight of the water, forming a bowl-shaped profile that enables the roof to retain even more water (Figure 7–4). The roof will keep deflecting, thereby holding more water, until it finally collapses.

Ponding has become more of a problem with the advent of flexible or "light" roof framing systems. With the roof beams and girders being more flexible, there is a greater chance that ponding may occur in a severe rainstorm. Therefore, the AISC requires that ponding criteria (which is found in section K2 of the AISC specification) be met to ensure adequate stiffness for primary and secondary roof members. This criteria calculates the approximate stiffness of the primary roof framing (C_p) and the secondary roof framing (C_s) and compares them to the appropriate limits as shown below. If the stiffness of the framing members meets this criteria, the specification considers the framing system to be stable and

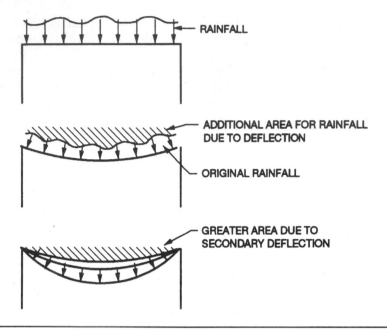

Figure 7–4 Progression of Ponding Failure

probably not a ponding concern. However, if these equations are not satisfied, the specification requires further study and appropriate action.

$$C_p + .9C_s \leq .25 \qquad \text{(Eq. 7–4)}$$

where

$$C_p = 32 L_s L_p^4 / 10^7 I_p \qquad \text{(Eq. 7–6)}$$
$$C_s = 32 S L_s^4 / 10^7 I_s \qquad \text{(Eq. 7–7)}$$

L_p, L_s = column spacing in the primary and secondary framing direction respectively, ft.

When metal roof decking spans between secondary framing, it should also be checked regarding adequate stiffness. The AISC criteria for metal roof decking is as follows:

$$I_d \geq 25(S^4)10^{-6} \qquad \text{(Eq. 7–5)}$$

where

S = spacing of secondary members, ft.

I_p, I_s, I_d = moment of inertia for the primary, secondary, and metal decking respectively, in.⁴ (or in.⁴ per foot for the decking)

If metal roof decking is used as the secondary framing, then it should be checked according to Eq. 7–4.

Other specification criteria stipulate that moment of inertia for steel joists and trusses used as secondary framing should be decreased by 15% and that steel decking be considered as a secondary member when supported by primary framing. The following example illustrates the use of the AISC ponding criteria.

EXAMPLE 7.5

Determine the adequacy of the roof framing system shown below with regard to the AISC ponding criteria. Also calculate the minimum moment of inertia required for metal roof decking to satisfy the AISC criteria.

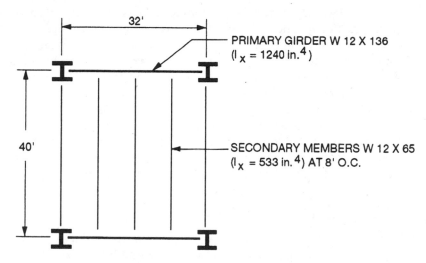

For the primary framing members (W 12 × 136's), calculate the primary ponding flexibility coefficient C_p as follows:

$$C_p = 32L_s L_p^4/10^7 I_p \qquad\qquad \text{(Eq. 7–6)}$$
$$C_p = 32(40 \text{ ft.})(32 \text{ ft.})^4/(10^7)(1240 \text{ in.}^4) = .108$$

For the secondary framing members (W 12 × 65's), calculate the secondary ponding flexibility coefficient as follows:

$$C_s = 32S L_s^4/10^7 I_s \qquad\qquad \text{(Eq. 7–7)}$$
$$C_s = 32(8 \text{ ft.})(40 \text{ ft.})^4/(10^7)(533 \text{ in.}^4) = .122$$

Therefore, calculating the requirements of Eq. 7–4 we find

$$C_p + .9C_s \leq .25 \qquad \text{(Eq. 7–4)}$$
$$C_p + .9C_s = .108 + .9(.122) = .219 \leq .25$$

meets AISC criteria.

The roof decking spans between the secondary framing, which is at 8 feet on center. Therefore, the minimum moment of interia for this decking can be calculated from Eq. 7–5 as follows:

$$I_d \geq 25(S^4)10^{-6} \qquad \text{(Eq. 7–5)}$$
$$I_d = 25(8 \text{ ft.})^4 10^{-6} = .102 \text{ in.}^4/\text{ft.}$$

Some lessons learned from ponding failures are more subtle in nature and more practically oriented than the above stiffness specifications. The easiest solution to ponding is simply to have the roof sloping at an adequate pitch, typically a minimum of 1/4 in. per foot. Other solutions can be equally as simple. When a 12,000 square foot roof section of an Internal Revenue Service warehouse collapsed in Philadelphia, one of the seemingly simple lessons to be learned was to locate roof drains away from column lines. This is because the columns do not deflect nearly as much as the roof framing and, therefore, the areas adjacent to columns remain "high" in regards to roof profile. Ponding will take place between columns and, therefore, the optimum location for roof drains would be at midspan between columns (if feasible). [4]

7.4   Vibration as a Serviceability Concern

With society placing an increasingly high value on entertainment and fitness in the last twenty years, vibration problems caused by human movement in structures is not a rare occurrence anymore. Numerous gymnasiums, sporting arenas, and concert halls have experienced excessive vibration due to the rhythmic motions caused by either the participants or the spectators.[5] Aerobic classes, rock concerts, and periodic motions (such as the "wave") all impart a vibrational behavior to a structure. Vibrations are also caused due to running machinery and vehicles within a building's proximity. Although these vibrations are primarily a serviceability concern, strength aspects such as fatigue stresses must also be considered.

Excessive vibration can rattle windows and doors, generally making a person uncomfortable in occupying a structure. As the human motion (jumping, running, clapping of hands) or mechanical vibration becomes rhythmic, it begins to occur at a certain sustained frequency. These motions set the structure into vibration at its own particular frequency, called its natural frequency. If the periodic human or mechanical motion has a frequency close to the structure's natural frequency, vibrational behavior tends to be amplified. This amplification is the behavior that greatly disturbs a casual observer.

Generally, there are a couple of different ways to alleviate vibrational problems should they occur in existing structures. The first is to stiffen the existing structural framing system.[6] This may be accomplished by adding inter-mediate beams, columns, or other bracing members. This stiffening tends to increase the structure's natural frequency, thereby avoiding the above amplification behavior. Another technique being used successfully in treating vibrational problems is the use of *tuned-mass dampers (TMD's)*. Tuned-mass dampers are mechanical vibration control systems that work similarly to the shock absorber of an automobile. The system typically involves fastening a counter weight to the vibrating member using a spring and damper. As the member reaches its critical frequency, it produces a corresponding movement in the TMD (Figure 7–5). This movement in the TMD produces a "damping effect" on the vibrating member, reducing the vibrational behavior. This would be analogous to a person pushing on a swing before it reached the apex of its arc.

Other damping systems are presently being researched and show signs of being effective in controlling excessive vibrations. One notable method uses viscoelastic dampers, in which a viscous material converts mechanical energy, induced from the vibration, into heat. For vibrations caused by mechanical equipment or construction, it has generally been suggested that a possible solu-

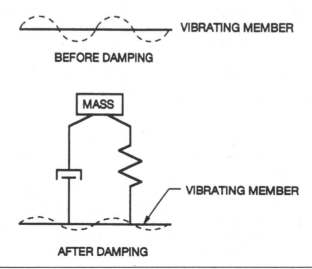

Figure 7–5 Schematic Illustration of a Tuned Mass Damper

tion is to isolate the source. This concept of isolation involves placing a neoprene pad or other viscoelastic material between the source and the surrounding structure. This has reduced unwanted vibrations in a variety of industrial and construction retrofitting projects.[7]

At the present, most building codes and specifications will only discuss virations in qualitative terms. Most research tends to express acceptable vibrations in terms of specified frequency. The Canadian National Building Code (CNBC) incorporates quantitative guidelines requiring that vibrations be kept below specified acceleration levels. For instance, this code sets a target level for vibration in office floors to 0.5% of gravity or 0.005 grams. The specifying of such target accelerations may become more widespread as structure use and function expand and change.

7. 5   Summary

Serviceability can be thought of as the functioning of a structure in the manner for which it was designed. Some of the more typical problems of serviceability stem from excessive deflection, vibration, or lateral drift. In the worst case scenario, serviceability problems may lead to catastrophic failure such as a structure's collapse due to ponding.

The designer must be aware of the serviceability aspects of his or her particular structure and adjust specification requirements accordingly.

EXERCISES

1. Explain why serviceability should be very important for a structural designer. Why, then, is it sometimes overlooked?
2. Calculate the live load deflection caused by two 50 kip live loads, each located at 5 feet in from their respective supports on a 25 foot simply supported beam. The beam is a W 12 × 120 and the self weight is neglected. Would this deflection be acceptable under service floor load conditions using plastered construction?
3. Calculate the live load deflection for a W 310 × 97 that is 10 meters long and has a 20 KN force located at midspan.
4. Calculate the total deflection for the beam in problem 2 if dead load from the beam's self weight is to be included.
5. Using the moment-area method calculate the deflection at the quarter point for the beam described and loaded in problem 3.
6. Calculate the uniform live load that would cause a live load deflection of 1" in a W 12 × 106 that is 15 feet long. Recalculate for a beam that is 20 feet long.
7. Calculate the concentrated live load P, which when applied to midspan of a W 250 × 101 causes a deflection of 65 mm. The beam is 7.5 meters long.

8. Calculate the concentrated live load to cause a 0.50" live load deflection in a W 12 × 14 that is 22 feet long. This is a typical beam in some areas for residential framing. Is there anything in your house that may cause such a deflection?

9. Calculate the deflection caused by a uniform load of 2KN/m over a W 250 × 101 that is 9 meters long. The beam also has a 10KN load applied at midspan.

10. Refer back to problem 6.6 in Chapter 6. Calculate the live load deflection for the W 12 × 96 used if the service load over the span is 3 kips per foot. Would this meet the plastered construction deflection criteria?

11. Calculate the deflection caused by a 8KN load applied at the third point on a W 310 × 179 that is 9 meters long.

12. Design a W 12 section to hold a uniform service live load of 4.5 kips per foot over a simple span of 17 feet. The beam is braced at midspan and is made from A36 steel. Consider live load deflection criteria for unplastered floor load construction. Neglect selfweight.

13. Design a W310 section to hold a uniform load of 5KN/m over a simple span of 8 meters. The beam is fully braced and is made from A36 steel. Consider the live load deflection criteria for plastered floor construction.

14. Design a W 12 section to hold a concentrated service live load of 30 kips at the center of a 20 foot long, simply-supported beam. The beam is to be made from A36 steel and is unbraced except for the ends. In addition, the live load deflection must be limited to 1/1000th of the span.

15. Using the moment-area method, derive the deflection formula at the 1/4 point for a beam with a concentrated load at its center.

16. For the roof framing system shown below, check its adequacy with regard to the AISC ponding specifications.

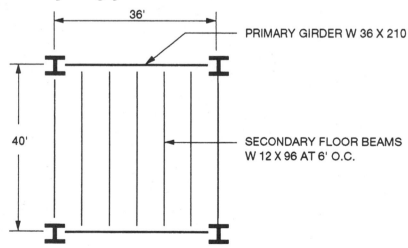

REFERENCES

1. *Manual of Steel Construction*, Ninth Edition, American Institute of Steel Construction, Chicago, IL, 1989.
2. Anthony C. Webster and Matthys P. Levy, "A Case of the Shakes," *Civil Engineering*, February, 1992, p. 58.
3. *Standard Specifications for Highway Bridges*, 14th Edition, American Association of State Highway and Transportation Officials, Washington, DC, 1989.
4. Dov Kaminetsky, *Design and Construction Failures, Lessons Learned from Forensic Investigations*, McGraw-Hill Publishing, New York, NY, 1991, p. 249.
5. H. Bachman, "Case studies of Structures with Man-Induced Vibrations," *Journal of Structural Engineering*, ASCE, Vol. 118, No. 3, March 1992.
6. T. M. Murray, "Controlling Floor Movement," *Modern Steel Construction*, AISC, June 1991, pp. 17–19.
7. AISC, "Special Design Isolates Vibration," *Modern Steel Construction*, AISC, January 1992, pp. 20–25.

C H A P T E R

8

COMBINED BENDING AND AXIAL MEMBERS: BEAM-COLUMNS

8.1 Introduction

Up to this point, we have discussed structural steel members that are subjected to either direct axial stress (tension or compression members) or flexural stress (beams). We have considered these stresses to act on these members to the exclusion of all others. But, in reality, will members be subjected to just one type of stress?

The simple answer is no. Structural members encounter many different combinations of stress under normal loading conditions. Many times the student has probably assumed that these combinations are nonexistent in order to simplify the analysis and calculations. The most common combination of stresses occurs when a member is subjected to axial and bending stresses simultaneously. This situation occurs frequently in cases such as eccentrically loaded axial members (tension or compression), beams and columns subjected to lateral forces, or even truss members bending due to their own self weight.

The most common case of combined axial and bending stress (and probably the most important) is the case of an axially loaded compression member subjected to appreciable amounts of bending moment. Such members are referred to as **beam-columns**. Beam-columns are a serious concern because the moment applied to this member will cause a deflection, thereby creating more moment due to the effect of the axial load and the lateral displacement. This additional moment is referred to as **secondary moment** and can lead to further lateral displacement, which leads to more moment, etc. Remembering the tendency of a column to laterally buckle under the application of compressive stress, the concern over beam-columns can be readily accepted.

Members subjected to combined axial compression and bending stresses will be the focus of this chapter. The concern over members subjected to axial tension and bending is not as great because the tension stress tends to "straighten out" the member, limiting lateral deflections and thereby reducing the secondary moment effect. Therefore, the following sections will primarily attempt to enlighten the student to only on fundamentals of beam-column behavior and design.

8.2 Potential Modes of Failure and Beam-Column Behavior

Since a beam-column is actually a mixture of two separate types of behaviors, it only stands to reason that the potential failure mechanisms may also reflect the aforementioned behaviors of these two member types. As the axial load becomes ever-increasingly large on an individual beam-column, the failure mode will gravitate towards that of a true column. Likewise, as the bending moment grows increasingly larger, the failure mode will more closely resemble that of a true beam. The failure mechanisms of both a beam and column have previously been discussed at some length (and will not be fully reiterated here); the student is urged to review these as needed. Because the most common failure mechanism in both beams and columns revolves around buckling of the compression elements, the lateral stability of the beam-column is the primary concern in the design and analysis of this member.

This concern over the lateral stability of the beam-column is heightened due to the fact that as bending moment is applied the member will deflect laterally. This lateral displacement actually causes additional moment (called secondary moment or second-order moment) due to the eccentricity of the load with column's longitudinal axis (Figure 8–1). As this secondary moment appears, the beam-column is further deflected and the secondary moment increases until it reaches equilibrium.

Because of the potential increase in moment, the LRFD specification requires that these second-order moments be included in the design of beam-columns. To account for the secondary effects, the designer can perform a second order elastic analysis (which can be rather tedious) or perform a simplified method that the AISC presents in lieu of the more rigorous analysis. This simplified alternative is as follows:

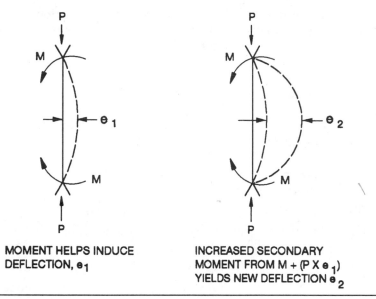

MOMENT HELPS INDUCE
DEFLECTION, e_1

INCREASED SECONDARY
MOMENT FROM M + (P X e_1)
YIELDS NEW DEFLECTION e_2

Figure 8–1   The Development of Secondary Moment

$$M_u = B_1 M_{nt} + B_2 M_{lt} \qquad\qquad \text{(Eq. 8–1)}$$

where

M_u = required moment capacity, kip-ft.

M_{nt} = required moment capacity of the member assuming no lateral translation of the frame, kip-ft.

M_{lt} = required moment capacity of the member as a result of the lateral translation of the frame only, kip-ft.

B_1, B_2 = amplification factors to be discussed further

This alternative method allows the designer to easily consider the magnifying effects of member deflection in a braced frame (no sidesway), as well as magnifying effects of lateral forces or unsymmetrical loadings on an unbraced frame that will again amplify the total moment on the member. In general, the portion of required moment referred to as M_{nt} (no translation) includes the first order moments produced by vertical gravity loads. The portion of required moment referred to as M_{lt} (lateral translation) occurs only in unbraced frames and includes the moments caused by lateral loads. This moment can also include *induced* lateral loads from vertical loads that are unsymmetrical as well as from loads placed on unsymmetrical frames. More will be discussed on this topic in the upcoming sections.

The AISC specification introduces a pair of amplification factors, B_1 and B_2, for use in the alternative method to calculate the required moment capacity. These amplification factors are as follows:

$$B_1 = C_m/(1 - P_u/P_e) \geq 1 \qquad\qquad\qquad (\text{Eq. } 8\text{–}2)$$

$$B_2 = 1/(1 - \Sigma P_u(\delta_{oh}/\Sigma HL)) \qquad\qquad (\text{Eq. } 8\text{–}3)$$

or

$$B_2 = 1/(1 - \Sigma P_u/\Sigma P_e) \qquad\qquad\qquad (\text{Eq. } 8\text{–}5)$$

where

C_m = modification factor discussed below

ΣP_u = Summation of required axial load of all columns in a story, kips

P_u = required axial load on a particular column, kips

ΣP_e = Euler buckling load for all columns in a story where P_e is defined by the following, $P_e = A_g F_y/\Omega_c^2$. Where Ω_c is as defined in Chapter 5.

P_e = Euler buckling load for a particular column, kips as defined previously.

δ_{oh} = translation deflection for the story under consideration, in.

ΣH = Sum of all horizontal forces producing the aforementioned deflection, kips

L = story height, in.

These amplification factors will be larger than 1.0 and will be multiplied to the bending moment for each specific effect (no translation and lateral translation) to effectively show an increase in the magnitude of applied moment. The AISC specification will incorporate this amplification factor into its formulas and this will be the focus of the Section 8.4.

In the braced frame scenario, the B_1 amplification factor overestimates the effect of the secondary moment. To counteract this possible overestimation, the AISC also introduces a modification factor, C_m, into this formula. This modification factor will be 1.0 or less depending on items such as presence of transverse loading and member end restraint conditions. The general values of C_m are broken down into the following categories:

a. For columns that are braced against sidesway and are not subjected to transverse loadings between their ends.

    $C_m = .6 - .4(M_1/M_2)$; The ratio M_1/M_2 is the ratio of smaller end moment to larger end moment. This ratio is negative if bent in single curvature and positive if bent in reverse curvature.

b. For columns that are braced against sidesway and subject to transverse loadings:

$C_m = 1.0$ for members subjected to transverse loadings between unrestrained ends.

$C_m = .85$ for members subjected to transverse loadings between restrained ends.

Although there are more refined methods to obtain modification factors for members subjected to transverse loadings (as discussed in the LRFD Commentary), the above expressions are considered suitable for most applications.

8.3   Development of the Interaction Formulas

When studying a course in strength of materials, the student no doubt remembers the subject of combined stresses. Under the topic of combined stresses, the principle of superpositioning was advanced where it was learned that stresses of the same type could be added and subtracted numerically (See Figure 8–2).

When discussing combined bending and axial stresses, this principle led to the derivation of the combined stress formula which is shown as:

$$f = P/A \pm Mc/I$$

where

P/A = axial stress
Mc/I = bending stress

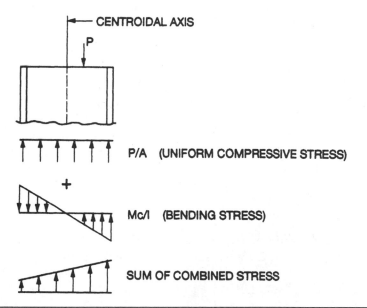

Figure 8–2   The Combined Stress Principle in an Eccentrically Loaded Column

Although approximate in nature (because it does not include the effects of secondary moments), this formula is widely accepted for the calculation of combined bending and axial effects. Since we can roughly calculate these combined effects, how might the use of interaction formulas be applied in LRFD to beam-column design and behavior?

The answer is: calculate the ratio of the required (factored) strength, with the aforementioned magnifiers included, to the member's design capacity. These interaction formulas calculate ratios or percentages of required capacity to design capacity for both axial and bending behaviors, and then add these ratios. If the ratio is less than 1.0, the combined effect is considered to be acceptable. This general format for the use of interaction formulas in LRFD can be seen as follows:

$$P_u/\phi_c P_n + M_u/\phi_b M_n \leq 1.0 \qquad \text{(Eq. 8–6)}$$

where

P_u, M_u = required axial and bending capacity

P_n, M_n = nominal axial and bending capacity

ϕ_c, ϕ_b = appropriate resistance factors (ϕ_c = .85 for compression behavior, ϕ_b = .90 for bending behavior

A good way to view this interaction formula is to consider the percent of design capacity used in any given type of behavior. For instance, if the required (factored) axial effect was only 20% of its design value, then it would follow that the safe amount of required (factored) moment would be 80% of the design value.

8.4   AISC Specifications for Beam-Columns

The LRFD specification[1] discusses the handling of members subjected to combined axial and bending stresses. Two interaction formulas regarding this behavior are presented in this chapter for use with beam-columns. When appreciable axial compressive loads are applied to a beam-column (where the ratio of $P_u/\phi_c P_n \geq .20$) the LRFD specification checks the following formula:

$$\frac{P_u}{\phi_c P_n} + \frac{8}{9}\left(\frac{M_{ux}}{\phi_b M_{nx}} + \frac{M_{uy}}{\phi_b M_{ny}}\right) \leq 1.0 \qquad \text{(Eq. 8–7)}$$

When the ratio of required axial load to design axial capacity decreases ($P_u/\phi_c P_n < .20$), the designer is required to use the following:

$$\frac{P_u}{2\phi_c P_n} + \left(\frac{M_{ux}}{\phi_b M_{nx}} + \frac{M_{uy}}{\phi_b M_{ny}}\right) \leq 1.0 \qquad \text{(Eq. 8–8)}$$

The first equation checks both stability near the midpoint of the beam-column as well as strength requirements near the ends of the beam-column. The second equation primarily checks the stability-related aspects of the member as it more closely represents the behavior of a true beam. The use of these formulas is illustrated in Figure 8–3. The aforementioned equations also display terms for bending about both the strong and weak axis, although if bending occurs about one axis only, the other bending term would be eliminated.

In these interaction equations, the expressions for required axial and bending strength (P_u, M_u), and design axial and bending capacity $(\phi_c P_n, \phi_b M_n)$ are the same values that have been mentioned previously in this chapter and throughout the book. It should be noted that P_n is based on the largest effective slenderness ratio regardless of the plane of bending, while the value of P_e is based on the slenderness ratio in the plane of bending.

The following examples demonstrate the use of these interaction formulas and clarify the evaluation procedure for beam-columns.

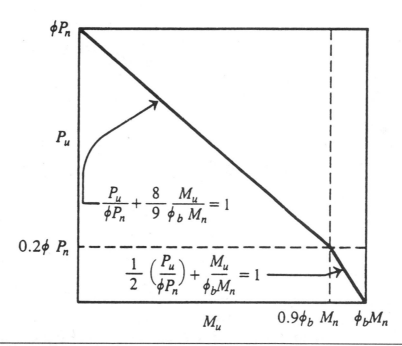

Figure 8–3 Use of LRFD Interaction Equations on Beam-Columns. (Courtesy of the American Institute of Steel Construction, Inc.)

EXAMPLE 8.1

A W 12 × 120 is used to support the loads and moments as shown below, and is not subjected to sidesway. Determine if the member is adequate and if the factored bending moment occurs about the weak axis. The column is assumed to be perfectly pinned ($K = 1.0$) in both the strong and weak directions and no bracing is supplied. Steel is A36 and assume $C_b = 1.0$.

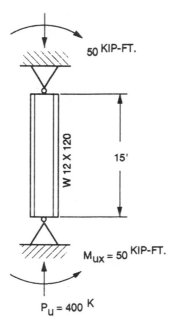

Initially, we should calculate the slenderness ratios in both the weak and strong directions (even though when unbraced in both directions, the weak axis will of course be critical).

$Kl_x/r_x = 1.0(15 \text{ ft.} \times 12 \text{ in./ft.})/5.51 \text{ in.} = 32.67$

$Kl_y/r_y = 1.0(15 \text{ ft.} \times 12 \text{ in./ft.})/3.13 \text{ in.} = 57.50$ (controls)

Using Table 5–1 from Chapter 5 , we can find the design axial stress ($\phi_c F_{cr}$) as 25.71 ksi. And, multiplying that with the area of the section, we can find the design axial capacity ($\phi_c P_n$) as follows:

$\phi_c P_n = \phi_c F_{cr} \times A_g$
$= 25.71 \text{ ksi} \times 35.3 \text{ in.}^2 = 907.6 \text{ kips}$
$(= 177.3 \text{ MPa} \times .0228 \text{ m}^2 = 4.042 \text{ MN or } 4042 \text{ KN})$

Since the factored axial load is 400 kips, the ratio of $P_u/\phi_c P_n$ is as follows:

400 kips / 907.6 kips = .44 > .20

therefore the designer is required to use Eq. 8–7 as the beam-column analysis.

$$\frac{P_u}{\phi_c P_n} + \frac{8}{9}\left(\frac{M_{ux}}{\phi_b M_{nx}} + \frac{M_{uy}}{\phi_b M_{ny}}\right) \le 1.0 \qquad \text{(Eq. 8–7)}$$

To start, calculate the design moment capacity $(\phi_b M_n)$ of the W 12×120. This will required knowledge of some of the concepts previously discussed in Chapter 6. The beam is compact and the unbraced length, l_b, is 15 feet. This value of unbraced length is then compared to limits referred to as L_p and L_r to determine whether plastic behavior can be developed or whether buckling behavior controls the bending behavior. The values for L_p and L_r can be calculated using Eq. 6–1 and 6–2 respectively or they can be found in the beam section of the LRFD manual. In either case these values for a W 12×120 are:

$L_p = 13$ ft. (3.96 m)

$L_r = 75.5$ ft. (23 m)

Since our unbraced length falls between these two values, the beam will be controlled by inelastic buckling (we referred to this as Case #2 in Chapter 6), and the nominal moment capacity M_n can be calculated from Eq. 6–5. Using this equation we must first calculate the plastic and elastic moment capacity values, M_p and M_r.

$M_p = F_y Z_x = 36$ ksi (186 in.³)/12 in./ft. = 558 kip-ft.

$\qquad$ (= 248200KPa (.00305 m³) = 758.7N-m)

$M_r = (F_{yw} - 10 \text{ ksi})S_x$

$\qquad$ (36 ksi – 10 ksi)163 in.³ = 353.2 kip-ft.

$\qquad$ (= 179250KPa (.00267 m³) = 478.8N-m)

Using Eq. 6-5 (assuming C_b is equal to 1.0) we find:

$M_n = C_b[M_p - (M_p - M_r)][(l_b - L_p)/(L_r - L_p)]$ $\qquad$ (Eq. 6–5)

$M_n = 1.0[558 \text{ kip-ft.} - (204.8)][(15 \text{ ft.} - 13 \text{ ft.})/(75.5 \text{ ft.} - 15 \text{ ft.})]$

$\qquad = 551.4$ kip-ft.(747.5N-m)

Therefore the design moment capacity is as follows:

$\phi_b M_n = 0.90(551.4 \text{ kip-ft.}) = 496.3$ kip-ft.

$\qquad$ (= 0.90(747.5N-m) = 672.7 N-m)

Now consider the effects of moment magnification on this section. Based on the alternative method and since the member is not subjected to sidesway $(M_{lt} = 0)$

$$M_u = B_1 M_{nt}$$

Calculating B_1

$$B_1 = C_m/(1 - P_u/P_e)$$

where

$C_m = .60 - .4(M_1/M_2)$

$C_m = .60 - .4(-50/50) = 1.0$

$P_u = 400$ kips

$P_e = \pi^2 E A_g/(Kl/r)^2$ (Euler's Buckling Load Equation)

  $= \pi^2(29000$ ksi$)(35.3$ in.$^2)/(32.67)^2 = 9456$ kips

The reader will notice that in the prior calculation the value for slenderness ratio was taken relative to the x-axis. This is due to the fact that, in this example, the bending moment is about the x-axis and the magnifier is to amplify the bending moment. Therefore, calculating the B_1 magnifier we find:

$$B_1 = 1/(1 - 400 \text{ kips}/9456 \text{ kips}) = 1.044$$

Calculating the amplified momemt as follows:

$M_u = B_1 M_{nt}$

$M_u = 1.044(50$ kip-ft.$) = 52.2$ kip-ft.

  $(= 1.044 (67.8$ N-m$) = 70.8$ N-m$)$

Therefore the adequacy of the section is calculated from Eq. 8–7 as follows:

$P_u/\phi_c P_n + 8/9(M_u x/\phi_b M_n x) \leq 1.0$

  400 kips/907.6 kips + 8/9(52.2 kip-ft./496.3 kip-ft.)

  (1779N/4037N + 8/9(70.8N-m/672.7N-m)

  $= .53 < 1.0$ — the section is adequate.

When dealing with unbraced frames, the procedure gets more involved since the calculation of sidesway effects (sidesway moments and sidesway axial loads) is required to utilize the alternate method that we perform to estimate the secondary effects. This generally means that a single load case on an unbraced frame that causes sidesway must be analyzed as if it were two separate load cases—one that would have a negligible sidesway effect (typically the vertical gravity loads) and one that would cause sidesway (typically the lateral loads). This is illustrated in Figure 8–4.

As the forces and moments for each of these "broken-down" load cases are calculated for a member, the same basic procedure is then followed as it was in the first example. The analysis of frames and frames subject to sidesway is not

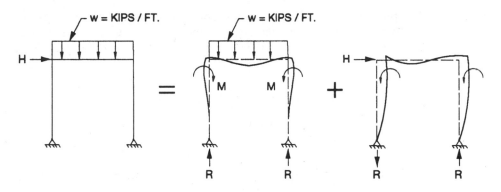

Figure 8-4   Illustration of Analysis for Rigid Frames Subjected to Lateral Loadings.

within the scope of this text, although an abbreviated explanation is given in Appendix C. The student should be aware that as unbraced members are encountered, the B_2 magnifier will become active as the frame exhibits sidesway behavior. The following example illustrates this situation.

EXAMPLE 8.2

In the unbraced frame shown below, determine the adequacy of either W 14 × 90 columns under the factored loads given. The steel is A36 and assume that the columns have a $K_y = 1.0$ and $K_x = 1.5$. The lateral load is causing bending to occur about the x-axis.

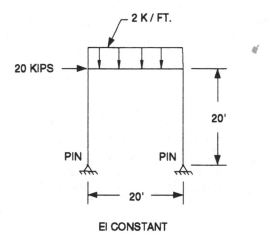

Typically, we would start this problem by separating the loads into those that cause sidesway effects (the lateral load) and those that have little influence on such effects (the vertical loads). As shown below, the effects on the columns from the lateral load and the vertical load can be computed separately by various standard techniques of analysis such as moment distribution. This method is discussed in Appendix A.

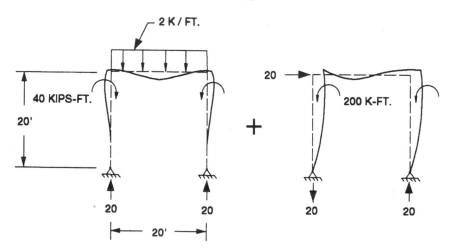

From these techniques, we find that each column is under approximately 20 kips of factored axial load and a moment of 40 kip-feet in no sidesway case. And, they are under 20 kips of factored axial load (different directions) and a moment of 200 kip-feet (assuming pinned supports) in the sidesway case. The reactions are found through equilibrium equations, and the moments on the members are found through standard techniques such as moment distribution. This is discussed further in Appendix A.

To begin the evaluation, calculate the column section's design axial capacity $\phi_c P_n$. Calculating the slenderness ratios about both axis (although the weak axis will control in this case):

$Kl/r_y = 1.0(240 \text{ in.})/3.70 \text{ in.} = 64.8$

$Kl/r_x = 1.5(240 \text{ in.})/6.14 \text{ in.} = 58.6$

Since the weak axis controls, find the design axial stress $\phi_c F_{cr}$ that can be taken from Table 5–1 in Chapter 5. In this case the design axial stress corresponding to the critical slenderness ratio is 24.54 ksi. This would make the design axial capacity of this section as follows:

$\phi_c P_n = \phi_c F_{cr} \times A_g$

$\phi_c P_n = 24.54$ ksi (26.5 in.^{2}) = 650.3 kips

(= 169.2 MPa (.0171 m^2) = 2.89 MN or 2893 KN)

$P_u = 20$ kips (no sidesway) + 20 kips (sidesway) = 40 kips

Since $P_u/\phi_c P_n = 40$ kips/650.3 kips = .061 < .20, Eq. 8–8 controls and should be used to check the adequacy of the section. Next calculate the design bending capacity of these sections about the strong axis. The unbraced length of this column is assumed to be 20 feet and the nominal moment capacity depends on what bending behavior controls in this case. Compare the unbraced length (20 ft.) to the L_p and L_r limits that were discussed in Chapter 6. These values can be calculated from Equations 6–1 and 6–2 or taken from the LRFD manual. Since the L_p value for a W 14 × 90 is 15.4 feet and the L_r value is 54.1 feet, the section's capacity is controlled by Case 2 (compact beams exhibiting inelastic lateral torsional buckling). The capacity of this section is found by calculating Eq. 6–5 (see Chapter 6) as follows and notice that C_b is equal to 1.67 using $M_{max} = 40$, $M_a = 10$, $M_b = 20$, and $M_c = 30$. Before calculating the nominal moment capacity from Eq. 6–5, first calculate the plastic and elastic moment capacity M_p and M_r.

$M_p = F_y Z_x = 36$ ksi (157 in.^{3})/12 in./ft. = 471 kip-ft.

(= 248200 KPa (.00256 m^3) = 635.4 KN-m)

$M_r = (F_{yw} - 10$ ksi)S_x

(36 ksi – 10 ksi) 143 in.^{3} = 309.8 kip-ft.

(= 179250 KPa (.00233 m^3) = 417.6 N-m)

Calculating Eq. 6–5:

$M_n = 1.67[471$ kip-ft. – [(471 kip-ft. – 309.8 kip-ft.)((20 ft. – 15.4 ft.)/ (54.1 ft. – 15.4 ft.))] = 791.5 kip-ft.

However because the nominal moment capacity cannot be greater than the plastic moment capacity, use 471 ft.-kips which is the plastic moment capacity. The design moment capacity is:

$\phi_b M_n = 0.90(471$ kip-ft.) = 423.9 kip-ft.

(= 0.90(635.4 KN-m) = 571.9 KN-m)

After this we can calculate the magnification factors B_1 and B_2, remembering that B_1 is used for the nonsway effects and B_2 for the sway effects. In this case, the axis of bending has been stated to be the x-axis and the effective length factor K was given as 1.5.

Therefore for B_1;

$$B_1 = C_m/(1 - P_u/P_e)$$

where

$C_m = .60 - .4(M_1/M_2)$

$C_m = .6$ since M_1/M_2 equals zero

$P_e = \pi^2 EA_g/(Kl/r)^2 = \pi^2 E(26.5 \text{ in.}^2)/(58.6)^2$
   $= 2206 \text{ kips} (9812.3 KN)$

$P_u = 40 \text{ kips} (177.9 KN)$

Therefore, $B_1 = .6/(1 - (40 \text{ kips}/2206 \text{ kips}) = .61$— use 1.0

Calculating B_2 from Eq. 8–5:

$$B_2 = 1/(1 - \Sigma P_u/\Sigma P_e) \qquad\qquad \text{(Eq. 8–5)}$$

$\Sigma P_u = 2(20 \text{ kips}) = 40 \text{ kips}$ (for both columns in the story)

$\Sigma P_e = 2206 \text{ kips} \times 2 \text{ columns} = 4412 \text{ kips}$

$B_2 = 1/1 - (40/4412) = 1.01$

Calculating the nominal moment capacity about the x-axis, M_{ux}, from Equation 8–1 as follows:

$$M_u = B_1 M_{nt} + B_2 M_{lt} \qquad\qquad \text{(Eq. 8–1)}$$

$M_{ux} = 1.0(40 \text{ kip-ft.}) + 1.01(200 \text{ kip-ft.}) = 242 \text{ kip-ft.}$
   $(= 1.0(54.2 KN\text{-}m) + 1.01(271.2 KN\text{-}m) = 328.1 KN\text{-}m)$

Calculating the adequacy per Eq. 8–8:

$$P_u/2\phi_c P_n + (M_{ux}/\phi_b M_{nx}) \qquad\qquad \text{(Eq. 8–8)}$$

$40 \text{ kips}/(2)(650.3 \text{ kips}) + (242 \text{ kip-ft.}/423.9 \text{ kip-ft.}) = .60 < 1.0$

$(177.9 KN/(2)(2892.5 KN) + (328.1 KN\text{-}m/571.9 KN\text{-}m) = .60 < 1.0)$

Therefore the section is good. Notice that the calculation of P_e for the B_1 and B_2 magnifiers is always taken about the axis of bending, in this case the strong axis.

8.5   Design of Beam-Columns Using LRFD

The design of beam-columns is truly a trial and error procedure and depends a great deal on the designer's experience. If the designer can select a good trial section at the very beginning, the work in obtaining a safe and economical member is greatly simplified although, in any case, the process will ultimately converge on a solution. The most popular method of selecting a beam-column is the *equivalent axial load method.* This method replaces the factored axial load and moment that are applied to the column with a fictitious concentric axial load. This fictitious concentric axial load will be larger than the factored axial load but will produce approximately the same maximum effect.

The following equation is used to convert the factored bending moment into an estimated axial load, P'. The actual factored axial load P_u, is added to P' resulting in a fictitious axial load called the equivalent factored axial load P_{uequiv}. This idea is shown below:

$$P_u + P' = P_{uequiv} \qquad \text{(Eq. 8–9)}$$

where P_u = actual factored axial load

P' = estimated axial load caused by moment

P_{uequiv} = Equivalent factored axial load

Although there are equations that would estimate the equivalent factored axial load based on the assumptions used by the interaction formulas separately (Eq. 8–7 and 8–8), it is much faster to use the following combined approximation developed from these formulas. This approximation is as follows:

$$P_{uequiv} = P_u + M_{ux}m + M_{uy}mU \qquad \text{(Eq. 8–9)}$$

In this formula, P_u is again the actual factored load expressed in kips and M_{ux} and M_{uy} are the bending moments expressed in kip-feet. If bending should occur about one axis only, the corresponding term regarding the other axis will then drop out. The value of m is taken from Table 8–1 as shown below. The value of U, which is the bending moment conversion factor, is taken from the column load tables that are shown in Appendix C. (A full set of the column load tables can be found in the column section of the LRFD manual as well).

The procedure using this approximate formula is an iterative process that begins by assuming the value of m from Table 8–1 and a typical value of U (usually about 2.0). After a section is selected, the section is checked against the applicable AISC interactions formulas (Eq. 8–7 and 8–8). With successive trials the values of m and U can be refined to a point where their values begin to stabilize.

The following example utilizes this procedure in the design of a beam-column.

EXAMPLE 8.3

Design the most economical W 12 section subjected to the loads and moments shown below. The value of $K = 1.0$ in both strong and weak directions and steel is A36. Assume this member to be part of a frame that is not subjected to sidesway.

Table 8–1 Values of "m" for use in Beam-Column Design Equation

Preliminary Beam-Column Design $F_y = 36$ ksi, $F_y = 50$ ksi													
Values of m													
Fy	36ksi							50 ksi						
KL(ft)	10	12	14	16	18	20	22 and over	10	12	14	16	18	20	22 and over
1st Approximation													
All Shapes	2.0	1.9	1.8	1.7	1.6	1.5	1.3	1.9	1.8	1.7	1.6	1.4	1.3	1.2
Subsequent Approximation													
W4	3.1	2.3	1.7	1.4	1.1	1.0	0.8	2.4	1.8	1.4	1.1	1.0	0.9	0.8
W6	3.2	2.7	2.1	1.7	1.4	1.2	1.0	2.8	2.2	1.7	1.4	1.1	1.0	0.9
W8	2.8	2.5	2.1	1.8	1.5	1.3	1.1	2.5	2.2	1.8	1.5	1.3	1.2	1.1
W8	2.5	2.3	2.2	2.0	1.8	1.6	1.4	2.4	2.2	2.0	1.7	1.5	1.3	1.2
W10	2.1	2.0	1.9	1.8	1.7	1.6	1.4	2.0	1.9	1.8	1.7	1.5	1.4	1.3
W12	1.7	1.7	1.6	1.5	1.5	1.4	1.3	1.7	1.6	1.5	1.5	1.4	1.3	1.2
W14	1.5	1.5	1.4	1.4	1.3	1.3	1.2	1.5	1.4	1.4	1.3	1.3	1.2	1.2

This Table is from a paper in AISC Engineering Journal by Uang, Wattar, and Leet (1990).

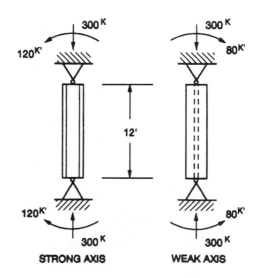

Using the equivalent load formula and choosing the first trial values of $m = 1.9$ as suggested in Table 8–1 and $U = 2.0$ (approximate), the equivalent load is as follows:

$$P_{uequiv} = P_u + M_{ux}m + M_{uy}mU \qquad \text{(Eq. 8–9)}$$

$$P_{uequiv} = 300 \text{ kips} + 120 \text{ kip-ft.}(1.9) + 80 \text{ kip-ft.}(1.9)(2.0)$$

$$= 832 \text{ kips}(3700KN)$$

From Column Load tables found in Appendix C for $Kl = 12$ ft. try a W 12×106 (with an axial design strength of 853 kips)

Checking this section with the interaction formulas we find the following:

Since $P_u/\phi P_n = 300 \text{ kips}/853 \text{ kips} = .352 > .20$, the Eq. 8–7 will control.

Calculating the design moment capacity about each axis we find the following:

$$L_p = 13.0 \text{ ft.}$$

Since this value is greater than 12 ft. which is this W 12×106's unbraced length, the section is able to develop as plastic capacity. Therefore,

$$\phi_b M_{nx} = 0.90(36 \text{ ksi})(164 \text{ in.}^3)/12 \text{ in./ft.} = 442.8 \text{ kip-ft.}$$

$$(= 0.90(248.2 \text{ MPa})(.00267 \text{ m}^3) = .596 \text{MN-m or } 596 \text{ KN-m})$$

$$\phi_b M_{ny} = .90(36 \text{ ksi})(75.1 \text{ in.}^3)/12 \text{ in./ft.} = 202.8 \text{ kip-ft.}$$

$$(= 0.90(248.2 \text{ MPa})(.00122 \text{ m}^3) = .273 \text{MN-m or } 273 \text{ KN-m})$$

Calculating the magnifier, B_1, similar to what was done previously, we would find the following:

$$C_{mx} = .6 - .4(-120/120) = 1.0$$

$$C_{my} = 1.0 \text{ (similarly)}$$

$$Kl/r_x = 26.3 (\lambda_c = .295)$$

$$Kl/r_y = 46.3 (\lambda_c = .519)$$

Calculating the Euler buckling load as follows:

$$P_e = A_g F_y / \lambda_c^2$$

$$P_{ex} = (31.2 \text{ in.}^2)(36 \text{ ksi})/(.295)^2$$

$$P_{ex} = 12,907 \text{ kips (based on } \lambda_c = .295)$$

$$(P_{ex} = (.0201 \text{ m}^2)(248200KPa)/(.295)^2 = 57,326KN)$$

$$P_{ey} = (31.2 \text{ in.}^2)(36 \text{ ksi})/(.519)^2$$

$$P_{ey} = 4,162 \text{ kips (based on } \lambda_c = .519)$$

$$(P_{ey} = (.0201 \text{ m}^2)(248200 \text{ KPa})/(.519)^2 = 18,250 \text{ KN})$$

$$B_{1x} = 1/1 - (300/12,907) = 1.023$$

$$B_{1y} = 1/1 - (300/4,162) = 1.078$$

This would make the magnified factored as shown below:

$M_u = B_1 M_{nt}$

$M_{ux} = 120$ kip-ft.$(1.023) = 122.76$ kip-ft.

$M_{uy} = 80$ kip-ft.$(1.078) = 86.24$ kip-ft.

Applying AISC Eq. 8–7 to the above information:

(300 kips/853 kips) + 8/9[(122.76 kip-ft./442.8 kip-ft.) + 86.24 kip-ft./202.8 kip-ft.)] = .976 < 1.0 which works well and therefore is a very good choice!

8.6 Summary

Beam-columns are members under axial load that are also subjected to appreciable bending moments. In a compression member, the deflection caused by the bending moment can be further exaggerated due to the axial load effects. This is referred to as secondary moment. The evaluation and design of beam-columns are handled through the use of interaction equations that assume a member to be adequate if the sum of the ratios of required capacities to design capacities are less than or equal to 1.0.

EXERCISES

1. Explain what is meant by "moment amplification" in a beam-column. Why would a member under axial tension and bending not have this effect?
2. Why are beam-columns more prevalent throughout construction than a simple column? What assumptions are made many times with the design of columns?
3. Using the combined stress formula, calculate the combined stress on the outside of each flange for the eccentrically loaded W 12 × 72 column shown below.

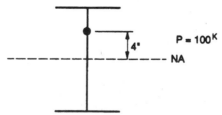

4. Calculate the adequacy of a W 14 × 53 that is 16 feet long with K = 1.0. The member is supporting a factored axial load of 200 kips, a factored moment about the strong axis of 160 kip-ft., and a factored moment about the weak axis of 20 kip-ft. The steel is A36 and the member is part of a frame not

subjected to sidesway. Assume $C_b = 1.0$ and column bends in single curvature.

5. Calculate the adequacy of a W 360 × 110 that is 6 meters long with pinned ends. The member supports a factored axial load of 1100 KN, and a factored moment about the strong axis of 350 KN-m. The steel is A36 and the member is part of a frame not subjected to sidesway. Assume $C_b = 1.0$ and column bends in single curvature.

6. Using the same information as given in problem 4, calculate what reduction in factored moment about the strong axis would make the interaction formulas approximately equal to 1.0. Assume weak axis moment to be eliminated.

7. Calculate the adequacy of a W 360 × 79 that is 5 meters long with pinned ends. The member supports a factored axial load of 600 KN, and a factored moment about the strong axis of 150 KN-m, and a factored moment about the weak axis of 100 KN-m. The steel is A36 and the member is part of a frame not subjected to sidesway. Assume $C_b = 1.0$.

8. A pin-connected W 12 × 120 made of A36 steel is subjected to factored axial load of 280 kips and a moment, $M_{ux} = 195$ kip-ft. If $C_{mx} = 1.0$ and the column is 14 feet long will it be adequate per AISC specifications? No sidesway can occur and steel is A36.

9. For the member shown below calculate the adequacy per AISC specifications. The column is braced against sidesway and the steel is A242 ($F_y = 50000$ psi).

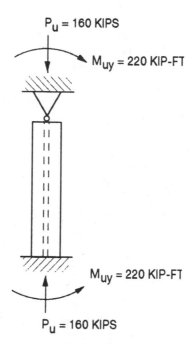

$P_u = 160$ KIPS

$M_{uy} = 220$ KIP-FT

$M_{uy} = 220$ KIP-FT

$P_u = 160$ KIPS

10. Select the most economical W 14 section for the beam-column shown below. Assume that the column ends are pinned and that no sidesway can occur. The steel is A36.

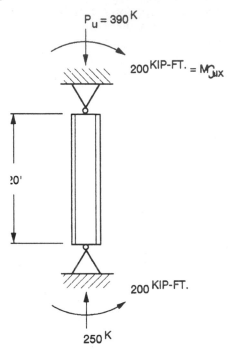

$P_u = 390^K$

$200^{KIP\text{-}FT.} = M_{ux}$

20'

$200^{KIP\text{-}FT.}$

250^K

11. Select an economical W 360 section to hold a factored axial load of 600 KN and a factored moment of 250 KN-m about its strong axis. The beam-column is 6 meter long and is assumed to be braced against sidesway. Steel is A36 and $K = 1.0$.

12. Select the most economical section using the same information as given in problem 10, except the column is braced at its midpoint in the weak direction.

13. Select an economical W360 under the exact same conditions as discussed in problem 11, except that it is now braced at midpoint in the weak direction.

14. Select the most economical W 12 section for the beam-column shown below. Assume that the column ends are fixed supports and are restrained against rotation. The end moments are assumed equal to PL/8 and the column is part of a braced frame. The steel is A36. Assume the unbraced length for bending is 18 feet and $C_b = 1.0$.

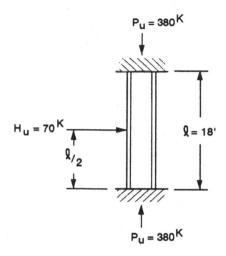

15. Rework problem 14 if the column length, *l*, was changed to 22 feet and the ends of the column were unrestrained.

16. The members shown in the unbraced frame below are W 14 x 53 sections made from A36 steel. The vertical and horizontal loads are factored loads. Determine their adequacy as beam-columns per the LRFD specifications. Break down the frame load shown into the nonsway portion (vertical load) and the sway portion (lateral load) and determine the force and moment effects for each. Refer to Appendix A if necessary. Assume K = 1.5.

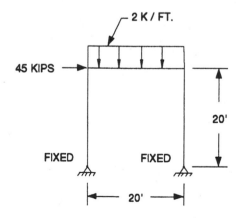

9

BOLTED AND RIVETED CONNECTIONS

9.1 Introduction and Historical Perspective

The need to join steel members together has existed since the introduction of steel as a building material in the latter half of the nineteenth century. Steel structures of every type require the fastening of individual members to achieve their ultimate structural form (Figure 9–1). Two of the most common methods of connecting steel structures—high strength bolting and riveting—will be discussed in this chapter and welding will be the topic of Chapter 10.

An early method of connecting steel members that was widely accepted was riveting. Riveting consisted of heating a "slug" of steel to approximately 1800°F and inserting this slug into holes that joined the members together. Once in the hole, the ends of the soft slug were formed by using a pneumatic hammer that would shape the ends of the rivet while also filling up more of the original hole. Many end shapes for rivets were utilized as shown in Figure 9–2, but by far the most common was the "buttonhead" shape.

Rivets have virtually been replaced in today's world with the advent of high strength bolting due primarily to economic considerations. Riveting is a labor intensive operation requiring a crew of approximately four to five skilled people and is a slower process in terms of installation. High strength bolting is much quicker requiring a much smaller two-person crew that does not have to be as

Figure 9–1   Use of Fasteners in Structural Steel Building Frames. Sheraton Hotel, Philadelphia. (Courtesy Bethlehem Steel Corporation.)

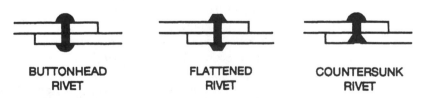

BUTTONHEAD RIVET   FLATTENED RIVET   COUNTERSUNK RIVET

Figure 9–2   Types of Rivets

skilled. Although riveting is rarely used anymore, many existing structures (approximately pre-1960) are made with rivets and therefore they should still be considered because of the many rehabilitation and retrofitting projects that are untaken with such structures.

High strength bolting is one of the most common procedures used today in the connection of structural steel members. High strength bolts are made from medium carbon or alloy steel and have very large tensile strengths. The use of high strength bolting began in earnest during the 1950s and by the early 1960s had virtually replaced riveting altogether. Besides the economic advantages that bolting enjoys, it also has other important advantages such as higher fatigue strength and easier retrofitting ability.

The two most common high strength bolts are the A325 bolt and the A490 bolt. The A325 bolt is the most common high strength bolt used today and is made from heat-treated medium carbon steel, while the A490 bolt is a higher strength bolt manufactured from an alloy steel and is used in situations requiring its improved properties.

The proper installation of bolts in some connections requires that the bolts be "fully tensioned", while in other connections the bolts need only be "snug-tight". The snug-tight condition brings the plates being joined into firm contact, and is achieved by a few impacts of an impact wrench or the complete effort of a worker using a spud wrench. A fully tensioned connection is based on achieving adequate clamping forces between the members being joined. This clamping force is provided by attaining the proper tension in the bolts, which is required to prevent slippage of the plates being connected and to prevent the bolts from becoming loose. This is especially critical in structures that are subject to repeated stresses or stress reversals. Minimum bolt tensions for fully tensioned A325 and A490 bolts are shown in Table 9–1 and are accomplished by using one of the four accepted methods that are outlined by the AISC's *Specification for Structural Joints Using ASTM A325 or A490 Bolts*. These methods are briefly outlined below.

Turn-of-the Nut Method

This method installs bolts by placing them in a snug-tight condition and then turning the nut by the rotation listed in Table 9–2. During this operation there must be no rotation of the part not being turned by the wrench.

Calibrated Wrench Method

This method utilizes an automatic wrench calibrated to "stall" at a torque that produces the required tension. Proper calibration must occur on a daily basis and maintenance of the wrench is critical in achieving the desired results. Tightening should proceed from the most rigid part of the connection to the free edges in a systematic fashion. The initial bolts in the tightening sequence maybe "touched

Table 9–1 Installation Requirements for Minimum Tension on Slip-Critical Bolts. (Courtesy of the American Institute of Steel Construction, Inc.)

Nominal Bolt Size, Inches	Minimum Tension[a] in 1000's of pounds (kips)	
	A325 Bolts	A490 Bolts
½	12	15
⅝	19	24
¾	28	35
⅞	39	49
1	51	64
1⅛	56	80
1¼	71	102
1⅜	85	121
1½	103	148

*Equal to 70 percent of specified minimum tensile strengths of bolts (as specified in ASTM Specifications for tests of full size A325 and A490 bolts with UNC threads loaded in axial tension) rounded to the nearest kip.

up" with the wrench later, since some relaxation may occur as adjacent bolts are tightened.

Direct Tension Indicators (DTI's)

This method installs bolts using a hardened washer with arched protrusions placed on its bottom surface. This washer is typically placed between the bolt head and the edge of a connection plate. These protrusions form a gap and as the bolt is tightened, these protrusions become flattened. By measuring the gap between the bolt head and the washer (or between the plate and the washer) one can assess the correct tension placed on the bolt (Figure 9–3). Research[1] has shown that DTI's are very reliable in achieving proper bolt tension and effectively inhibit the loss of pretension that may occur over extended periods of time.[2]

Table 9–2 Requirements for "Snug-Tight" Condition. (Courtesy of the American Institute of Steel Construction, Inc.)

Disposition of Outer Fact of Bolted Parts			
Bolt length (Under side of head to end of bolt)	Both faces normal to bolt axis	One face normal to bolt axis and other sloped not more than 1:20 (beveled washer not used)	Both faces sloped not more than 1:20 from normal to the bolt axis (beveled washer not used)
Up to and including 4 diameters.	$1/_3$ turn	$1/_2$ turn	$2/_3$ turn
Over 4 diameters but not exceeding 8 dia.	$1/_2$ turn	$2/_3$ turn	$5/_6$ turn
Over 8 diameters but not exceeding 12 dia.^{c}	$2/_3$ turn	$5/_6$ turn	1 turn

^{a}Nut rotation is relative to bolt regardless of the element (nut or bolt) being turned. For bolts installed by 1/2 turn and less, the tolerance should be plus or minus 30 degrees; for bolts installed by 2/3 turn and more, the tolerance should be plus or minus 45 degrees.

^{b}Applicable only to connections in which all material within the grip of the bolt is steel.

^{c}No research has been performed by the Council to establish the turn-of-nut procedure for bolt lengths exceeding 12 diameters. Therefore, the required rotation must be determined by actual test in a suitable tension measuring device which simulates conditions of solidly fitted steel.

Calibrated Bolt Assemblies

This method utilizes a specially calibrated assembly of bolts, nuts, and washers used to estimate the proper tension in the bolt. In this method, bolts having splined ends that extend beyond the threaded portion are tightened with a special wrench. This tightening causes the tip of the bolt to shear off once the proper tension has been achieved. (Figure 9–4)

A) Direct Tension Indicator (DTI).

B) DTI before tensioning.

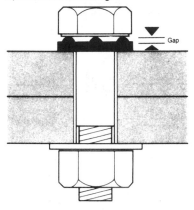

C) DTI after tensioning.

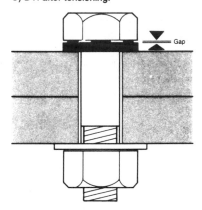

Figure 9–3   Direct Tension Indicators. (Courtesy of J & M Turner, Inc.)

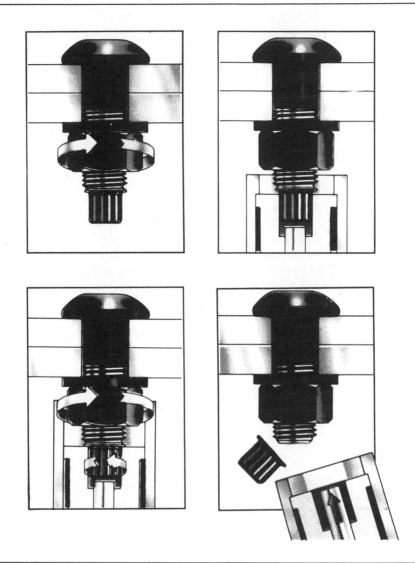

Figure 9–4 Typical Installation Procedure of Calibrated Bolt Assemblage. Rapid Tension Bolting System. (Courtesy of NSS Industries.)

9.2   Types of Connections

No matter what types of steel shapes are utilized, the connection of steel members almost always boils down to a "plate-to-plate" configuration. Therefore, the two most common configurations for connections are the "two-plate" and "three-plate", sometimes referred to as the lap joint and butt joint (See Figure 9–5).

Although two-plate and three-plate systems might seem simplistic, their use is wide spread throughout steel construction. In the typical beam-to-column connection shown in Figure 9–6 the student will notice that the angle-to-column flange connection is a two plate system and the angle-to-beam web connection is a three-plate system.

One of the most important distinctions in any connection system is the number of shear planes that pass through a single bolt. In the two plate system, the student will notice that as the plates are pulled, movement of the connection plates will attempt to rip the bolts apart along one shear plane should slippage occur. This phenomena is referred to as *single shear*. Consequently, in the three plate system, the bolts are trying to be ripped apart along two shear planes. This phenomena is referred to as *double shear*. The most important difference between single and double shear is the number of areas per bolt that are resisting stress. This will be a major focus when analyzing and designing bolted connections later in this chapter.

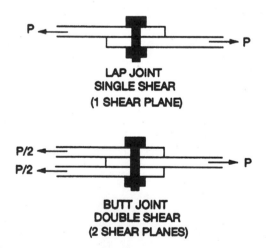

Figure 9–5   Common Types of Bolted and Riveted Connections.

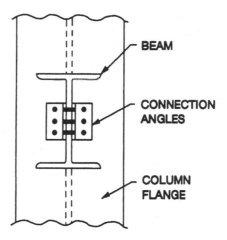

Figure 9–6   Typical Beam-Column Connection

Another category under the heading of connection types revolves around the performance of the connection under loading. A connection can be designed as a *bearing type* connection or a *slip-critical type* connection. The basic difference between the two types is an assumption of slippage under service load that results in the use of different nominal strength values.

The slip critical-type connection is assumed to be slip-free under all service load conditions and is to transfer load through the joint by the clamping forces generated between the connected plates. Therefore, the AISC specification requires that slip-critical connection be fully tensioned using one of the aforementioned procedures. This type of connection is primarily used for structures that have high impact load cases or where slippage in the joint is considered undesirable by the designer.

The bearing-type connection is assumed to slip only under very high load conditions. If this slippage occurred, the joint would transfer load through shear on the bolts and plate bearing. This type of connection is used when the designer feels the structure is less susceptible to impact, stress-reversals, or vibration. The installation of bearing type connections requires only that they be tightened to the snug-tight condition.

The difference in the nominal shear strength for these two types of connections can be found in Tables 9–3 and 9–4 that are Table J3.2 and Table J3.6 respectively in the LRFD specification. The reader will notice that the nominal strengths for bearing-type connections are substantially higher than those for the slip critical-type connection. These higher strength values translate into fewer

TABLE 9–3 Design Strength of Bolts and Rivets (Courtesy of the American Institute of Steel Construction, Inc.)

Description of Fasteners	Tensile Strength		Shear Strength in Bearing-type Connections	
	Resistance Factor	Nominal Strength, ksi	Resistance Factor	Nominal Strength, ksi
A307 bolts	0.75	45.0[a]	0.60	27.0[b,e]
A325 bolts, when threads are *not* excluded from shear planes		90.0[d]	0.65	54.0[e]
A325 bolts, when threads *are* excluded from shear planes		90.0[d]		72.0[e]
A490 bolts, when threads are *not* excluded from shear planes		112.5[d]		67.5[e]
A490 bolts, when threads *are* excluded from the shear planes		112.5[d]		90.0[e]
Threaded parts meeting the requirements of Sect. A3, when threads are *not* excluded from the shear planes		$0.75F_u$[a,c]		$0.45F^u$
Threaded parts meeting the requirements of Sect. A3, when threads *are* excluded from the shear planes		$0.75F_u$[a,c]		$0.60F^u$
A502, Gr. 1, hot-driven rivets		45.0[a]		36.0[e]
A502, Gr. 2 & 3, hot-driven rivets.		60.0[a]		48.0[e]

[a] Static loading only.
[b] Threads permitted in shear planes.
[c] The nominal tensile strength of the threaded portion of an upset rod, based upon the cross-sectional area at its major thread diameter, A_b, shall be larger than the nominal body area of the rod before upsetting times F_y.
[d] For A325 and A490 bolts subject to tensile fatigue loading, see Appendix K4.
  When bearing-type connections used to splice tension members have a fastener pattern whose length, measured parallel to the line of force, exceeds 50 in., tabulated values shall be reduced by 20%.

TABLE 9–4 Nominal Shear Strength for Slip Critical Bolts. (Courtesy of the American Institute of Steel Construction, Inc.)

Type of Bolt	Nominal Shear Strength		
	Standard Size Holes	Oversized and Shortslotted Holes	Long-slotted Holes[b]
A325	17	15	12
A490	21	18	15

[a] Class A (slip coefficient 0.33). Clean mill scale and blast cleaned surfaces with class A coatings. For design strengths with other coatings see RCSC "Load and Resistence Factor Design Specification for Structural Joints Using ASTM A325 or A490 Bolts."
[b] Tabulated values are for the case of load application transverse to the slot. When the load is parallel to the slot multiply tabulated values by 0.85.

bolts needed per connection when designing with a bearing type of joint. This bearing type of connection would be used for structures that are not likely to be loaded in a sudden, high stress manner. And, the friction between the plates will remain as the load transfer mechanism until slippage occurs. In structures subjected to high impact stresses, the lower nominal strength translates into more bolts per connection. This increased number of fasteners per connection provides a safeguard against slippage.

Before closing this section, it should again be stressed that slip-critical connections and bearing connections should be installed differently. Specifications[3] require that slip-critical connections should be "fully tensioned" to 70% of the bolt's minimum tensile strength while bearing type connections need to be only installed in a "snug-tight" condition. The slip-critical connections must be inspected to ensure that the minimum tension force was correctly applied. The reality of steel construction is that some high strength bolted connections are installed identically whether they are friction-type or bearing-type. Therefore the reader must realize that it is very difficult and time-consuming to distinguish between correct and incorrect tensioning after installation unless a tension indicating system is utilized. This underscores the importance of proper installation techniques and shows that proper bolt tensioning is paramount to the structure's economic, as well as structural, well-being.

9.3   Modes of Failure In Bolts

The possible modes of failure in the vicinity of bolted or riveted connections are shown in Figure 9–7 and are listed as follows:

- *Shearing of bolts.* Bolts break due to excessive shear forces along predetermined shearing planes. Typical number of shearing planes is either one

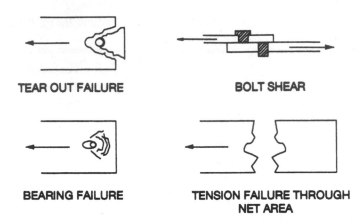

Figure 9–7 Common Potential Failures in Bolted Connections

(single shear) or two (double shear), although in special configurations there could be more.

- *Plate crushing by bolt.* Commonly referred to as bearing failure where the bolt comes into contact with the edge of the bolt hole and causes a crushing type of failure of the plate material. Becomes more common as the connecting plates are thin relative to the bolt size. Typically does not contol the connection design.
- *Tear out failure of plate.* Ripping failure in the plate due to excessive shear forces, can be common if the plate is thin or bolts are close to the edge of the plate. This failure can easily be avoided by following minimum edge and center-to-center spacing requirements that will be discussed later.
- *Plate failure across net area.* Fracture failure across a tension member's net area was discussed in Chapter 4. This failure involves the cracking or fracture of the tension member through the bolt holes and will not be discussed further here, although the student is referred back to section 4.3.

Of the potential failure modes listed previously, the primary mode of failure in bolted connections (and therefore, the usual controlling feature of connection design) is bolt shear. The shear resistance in this case are assumed split evenly among all bolts in the connection, because we assume the plate to be rigid and nondeforming. This is the standard assumption by the average designer, although the approach is oversimplified, because the typical connection is flexible enough to allow unequal deformations resulting in lower stresses on the bolts in the center of the connection area.[4]

The shear stress on a bolt can be calculated using the direct stress formula $S = P/A$. From rearranging this formula, the nominal capacity (referred to as R_n) of a bolt in shear is simply the design stress multiplied by the bolt's cross-sectional area. The design strength (ϕR_n) is the nominal capacity multiplied by the applicable reduction factor. This may be seen as follows:

$$S = P/A$$
$$P = S \times A$$

$\phi(\text{Nominal Strength}) = \text{Reduction Factor} \times (\text{Design strength} \times \text{Area})$

or

$$\phi R_n = \phi \text{ (Design strength} \times A) \tag{Eq. 9–1}$$

where

R_n = nominal strength

Design strength = value from Table 9–3 or 9–4

A = unthreaded bolt area

ϕ = .75 for all bolts in bearing type connections

ϕ = 1.0 for all bolts in slip-critical connections (except when long-slotted holes are used where ϕ = .85)

It should be noted that slip-critical type connections are checked against service loads, since the onset of slippage may induce some type of serviceability limit state. Slippage of a slip-critical connection would most likely indicate overall poor performance and could possibly introduce second order effects that again could lead to a variety of negative behaviors. Although the maximum strength capacity of the connection may be higher, the serviceability concerns warrant the use of the service loads to ensure adequate functioning of a slip-critical connection.

Again the student should be reminded of the single and double shear cases because in the double shear case, the bolt has twice as much area resisting the load.

The second mode of failure is the crushing of the plate by the bolt bearing on it. This failure mechanism is relatively rare unless very thin plates are used. Still, it must be checked as part of any analysis or design. The bearing stress of a bolt on a plate are given can again be rearranged from the direct stress formula $S = P/A$. The only difference being that the resisting area is the projection of the contact area of the bolt on the plate. This area is simply the thickness of the plate multiplied by the diameter of the bolt. (See Figure 9–8)

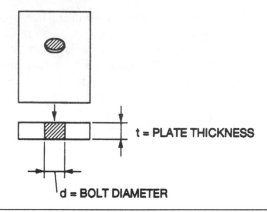

Figure 9–8 Bearing Area of Bolt in Bolt Hole.

The design bearing strength ($\phi \times$ nominal capacity) of a bolt if deformation is not a consideration and adequate bolt spacing and edge distance requirements are met (if both 3d or greater), is as follows:

$$\phi R_n = \phi(3.0)(d)(t)F_u \qquad \text{(Eq. 9–2)}$$

where

F_u = minimum tensile strength of the plate

d = diameter of the bolt

t = thickness of the plate

ϕ = .75 (reduction factor for plate, not bolt)

When deformation is to be considered, (adequate spacing criteria are met), and where there are more than two bolts in the line of stress, the design capacity is given as follows:

For standard or short-slotted holes:

$$\phi R_n = \phi(2.4)(d)(t)F_u \qquad \text{(Eq. 9–3)}$$

For long-slotted holes perpendicular to the load:

$$\phi R_n = \phi(2.0)(d)(t)F_u \qquad \text{(Eq. 9–4)}$$

where

F_u = minimum tensile strength of the plate

d = diameter of the bolt

t = thickness of the plate

ϕ = .75 (reduction factor for plate, not bolt)

For other cases regarding bearing, the nominal strength requirements can be found in section J3 of the LRFD specification.

The last mode of failure is plate tearing or shearing, which is only probable when bolt spacings and edge distances become very small. To effectively eliminate this behavior the AISC lists minimum spacing and edge distance requirements in the LRFD specification. Generally, if at all possible, the minimum bolt spacing (center-to-center of bolts) should be taken as $3d$ (where d is the bolt diameter) and the minimum edge spacing should be taken as $1.5d$. When the edge distance and center-to-center spacing falls under these general criteria specification shall be consulted.

9.4   AISC Specifications for Bolted and Riveted Connections

The Load and Resistance Factor Design philosophy of steel design strives to keep the design capacity of a connection greater than the required (factored) strength. The design capacity is typically the design strength (stress) multiplied by the resisting area and the appropriate reduction factor. The design strength for a behavior such as shear is specified in Table 9–3 and listed in Chapter J3 in the AISC *Manual of Steel Construction*. The primary considerations that designers should be concerned for in the adequacy of a connection are typically those for *bolt shear and bearing* on the members being fastened. Although typically not a great concern, minimum bolt spacing and edge distance might also be checked so that a failure due to plate tearing does not occur. The tension failure mechanism (previously discussed in Chapter 4) across the net area should be checked in the tensile capacity calculations during some part of the total design.

The design strength values for bolt shear were previously listed in Tables 9–3 and 9–4. The student should remember that the area resisting this shear force is the cross sectional area of the bolt and that a bolt may have more than one area resisting (as in the case of double shear).

The design capacity calculations for plate bearing were discussed in the previous section. The area that resists this bearing force is the projected area of the bolt on the plate that it bears. This projected area is conveniently taken as the bolt diameter multiplied by the thickness of the plate. The adequacy of both the shear and the bearing parameters should be verified in every simple connection design, since it would be futile to design a connection able to withstand one behavior while not the other.

9.5   Design of Bolted and Riveted Connections

As discussed previously, there are basically two types of problems that are encountered by the designer. The first is the "evaluation" problem where you have an existing connection and you need to determine its capacity for new load conditions. The known entities in this problem are typically area and design strength of the fastener being used. As we have seen previously, by using the direct stress equation the designer will be able to calculate the design capacity (ø × nominal strength) for a given type of behavior. The required capacity, which is calculated from the factored loads and applicable load combinations, would then be compared to the design capacity. If the design capacity is greater than or equal to the required capacity, the connection will work. Of course, the designer should always keep in mind that a design is an allocation of resources. And in the event that a connection's design capacity is much larger than the required capacity, the optimization of materials is paramount.

The second type of problem is the "design" problem where you find the minimum area of bolts and plate bearing area needed to make your connection work. This type of problem is more open-ended, since there are a number of solutions that may be possible. The known quantities in this problem are typically the factored load and the type of fastener to be used. Again we rearrange the direct stress equation to solve for area required. The designer must keep in mind that his or her determination of area required in connections will also impact other parts of the total design, namely net area and bolt layout. All factors must be considered in the complete design.

Below are some examples presenting solution techniques for the aforementioned problem types.

EXAMPLE 9.1

Determine the adequacy of the connection shown below. The bolts are A325 with threads not excluded from the shear plane and the steel plates are A36. The factored load is 75 kips and connection is bearing-type.

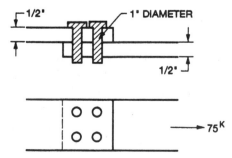

Remember the two items necessary to check, as far as the connection is concerned, are shear and bearing as long as the bolt spacing and edge layout are adequate. (In our problems we will assume that this is so.) This an evaluation type of problem and will evaluate by comparing required strength (factored load) to the connection's design capacity in both shear and bearing.

Shear

Since this is a two-plate system, single shear exists and therefore there is only one shear plane in each bolt. Therefore:

$A = \pi/4(1 \text{ in.})^2 \times 4 \text{ bolts} = 3.14 \text{ in.}^2 \ (.00203 \text{ m}^2)$

From Table 9–3, for A325 bolts in a bearing-type connection, with the threads not excluded from the shear plane, we find that the nominal strength of such a bolt is 48.0 ksi. This makes the design capacity in shear using Eq. 9–1 for this connection as follows:

$\phi R_n = \phi \text{ (Design strength} \times A)$ \hfill (Eq. 9–1)

$\phi Rn = (0.75)(48.0 \text{ ksi})(3.14 \text{in.}^2) = 113 \text{ kips}$

$(= 0.75(330960\text{KPa})(.00203 \text{ m}^2) = 503.9 \text{ KN}$

Compare this to the factored load:

113 kips > 75 kips — this is OK

Now we should check bearing (always) to make sure that this connection is also adequate for this type of behavior.

Area of bearing surface:

$A = d \times t$ (for one bolt)

$A = 1/2" \times 1" \times 4 \text{ bolts} = 2\text{in.}^2 \ (.00129 \text{ m}^2)$

Calculate the design capacity in bearing (considering no deformation and spacings are adequate) by using Eq. 9–2 as follows:

$\phi R_n = \phi(3.0)(d)(t)F_u$ \hfill (Eq. 9–2)

$\phi R_n = (.75)(3.0)(2\text{in.}^2)(58 \text{ ksi}) = 261 \text{ kips}$

$(\phi R_n = (.75)(3.0)(.00129\text{m}^2)(399910\text{KPa}) = 1161 \text{ KN})$

Since 261 kips is greater than 75 kips, the connection works in bearing as well. Please remember that as part of a complete evaluation we would also check the plate tension over the net and gross area for their adequacy. This check will be demonstrated in the following example to refresh the reader on the points that were covered in Chapter 4.

EXAMPLE 9.2

Check the adequacy of the tension member used in Example 9.1 across its gross and effective net areas if the width of the plate is 8 inches.

From Chapter 4, the adequacy of a tension member typically started with checking the gross area and then evaluating the effective net area. The tension member is a plate; therefore, calculate the gross and effective net areas as follows:

$$A_g = 8" \times 1/2" = 4 \text{ in.}^2 \ (2581 \text{ mm}^2 \text{ or } .00258 \text{ m}^2)$$
$$A_n = 4 \text{ in.}^2 - 2(1 \text{ in.} + 1/8 \text{ in.})(1/2 \text{ in.}) = 2.875 \text{ in.}^2 \ (1855 \text{ mm}^2)$$

Now, using the requirements from the LRFD specification, calculate the design capacity across the gross and net areas using Equations 4–1 and 4–2 and compare these values to the required capacity of 75 kips.

Gross Area

$$\phi_t P_n = \phi_t (F_y \times A_g) \qquad \text{(Eq. 4–1)}$$
$$= .90 (36 \text{ ksi} \times 4 \text{ in.}^2) = 129.6 \text{ kips} > 75 \text{ kips} \text{ — O.K.}$$
$$(= .90 (248.2 \text{MPa} \times .00258 \text{ m}^2) = .576 \text{MN or } 576 \text{KN} > 333.6 \text{KN})$$

Net Area

$$\phi_t P_n = \phi_t (F_u \times A_e) \qquad \text{(Eq. 4–2)}$$
$$= .75 (58 \text{ ksi} \times 2.875 \text{ in.}^2) = 125.1 \text{ kips} > 75 \text{ kips} \text{ — O.K.}$$
$$(= .75 (399.9 \text{MPa} \times .001855 \text{ m}^2) = .556 \text{MN or } 556 \text{KN} > 333.6 \text{KN})$$

Since the member is adequate at both gross and net areas , as well as in bolt shear and plate bearing (as determined from Example 9.1) the member will work per LRFD specification.

EXAMPLE 9.3

The connection to be made in the lap-joint shown below is to withstand a service tensile force of 100 kips assumed to be 50% dead load and 50% live load. The connection is a slip-critical type, the steel is A36, and bolts are A325–X (threads not in the shear plane). Design the bolt size and number of bolts to be used.

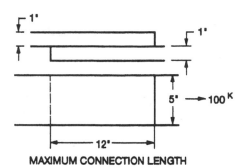

MAXIMUM CONNECTION LENGTH

Using the proper load combimations, we must establish the required strength for this connection. With only dead and live load applied to this connection, load combination A4–2 controls (refer to Chapter 2). The required strength is as follows:

R_u = 1.2(50 kips) + 1.6(50 kips) = 140 kips

Next, calculate bolt area needed based on shear requirements, but remember that the shear behavior of slip-critical connections is checked against *service conditions*:

R = 100 kips

Nominal shear strength = 17.0 ksi (from Table 9–4). Rearranging Eq. 9–1 to solve for area required under service loads, we would find:

$\phi R_n = \phi$ (Design strength × A)   (Eq. 9–1)

$R_u = \phi\, R_n$

$A_{req'd}$ = R/Slip-critical Design strength

$A_{req'd}$ = 100 kips/17.0 ksi = 5.71 in.^{2} (Try 1" diameter bolts)

Using 1" diam. bolts (A = .785 in.^{2}) you would need 5.71 in.^{2}/(.785 in.^{2} per bolt) = 7.27; therefore 8 bolts. This is probably a wise choice because you could lay out the bolts in four rows of two each (see figure below), a smaller diameter of bolt would lead to a larger number and a minimum spacing of bolts might be in jeopardy.

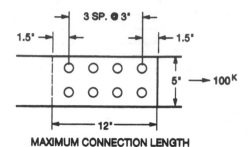

MAXIMUM CONNECTION LENGTH

Check bearing area using 1" bolts to ensure its adequacy R_u = 140 kips (using the factored load because the bolts have already slipped under this scenario).

Bearing area with eight 1" bolts:
= 8 bolts × 1" diameter × 1" thickness = 8 in.² (.00516 m²)

The design capacity of this connection assuming no deformation and proper edge distances and spacings from Eq. 9–2 is as follows:

$$\phi Rn = \phi(3.0)(d)(t)F_u \qquad \text{(Eq. 9–2)}$$

$$\phi R_n = (.75)(3.0)(8.0 \text{ in.}^2)(58 \text{ ksi}) = 1044 \text{ kips}$$

$$(\phi R_n = (.75)(3.0)(.00516 \text{ m}^2)(399910 \text{ KPa}) = 4643 \text{ KN})$$

Since 1044 kips is greater than 140 kips the connection is adequate in bearing. Remember that in total design we need to check a tension member's net area and gross area capacities. This tension member check will again be demonstrated in the following example.

EXAMPLE 9.4

Determine if the member used in Example 9.3 is adequate in tension across its gross and effective net areas, based on the bolt design as previously calculated. The member width is 5 inches.

The tension member is a plate; therefore, calculate the gross and effective net areas as follows:

$A_g = 5" \times 1" = 5$ in.^{2} (3226 mm^2 or .003226 m^2)

$A_n = 5$ in.$^2 - 2(1$ in. $+ 1/8$ in.$)(1$ in.$) = 2.75$ in^2 (1774 mm^2)

Now, using the requirements from the LRFD specification, calculate the design capacity across the gross and net areas using Equations 4–1 and 4–2 and compare these values to the required capacity of 140 kips.

Gross Area

$$\phi_t P_n = \phi_t(F_y \times A_g) \qquad\qquad\qquad \text{(Eq. 4–1)}$$

$\qquad = .90\ (36$ ksi $\times 5$ in.$^2) = 162$ kips > 140 kips — Good

$\qquad (= .90\ (248.2$MPa $\times .003226$ m$^2) = .721$MN or 721KN > 623KN$)$

Net Area

$$\phi_t P_n = \phi_t(F_u \times A_e) \qquad\qquad\qquad \text{(Eq. 4–2)}$$

$\qquad = .75\ (58$ ksi $\times 2.75$ in.$^2) = 119.6$ kips < 140 kips — No Good

$\qquad (= .75\ (399.9$MPa $\times .001774$ m$^2) = .532$MN or 532KN < 623KN$)$

The member fails over net area, therefore although it is adequate in bolt shear and plate bearing (as determined from Example 9.3), the member will not work per LRFD specification. One possibility to produce a member that would be adequate in tension is to increase the plate width.

EXAMPLE 9.5

Calculate the adequacy of the butt joint shown below if the bolts are 5/8" diameter A490s with the threads not in the shear plane. The steel is A36 and the connection is a bearing type. The load is factored.

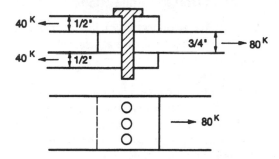

Check bolt shear adequacy by calculating bolt shear stress:

$A = \pi/4(5/8 \text{ in.})^2 = .306 \text{ in.}^2$ per bolt × 3 bolts = .92 in.^{2}

Remember that you have double shear, therefore

$A = .92 \times 2 = 1.84 \text{ in.}^2$ (.001187 m^2)

The bolts have a design stress of 75 ksi from Table 9–3, therefore calclate the shear capacity of the connection as follows:

$$\phi R_n = \phi \text{ (Design strength} \times A) \qquad \text{(Eq. 9–1)}$$
$$\phi R_n = (.75)(75 \text{ ksi})(1.84 \text{ in.}^2) = 103.5 \text{ kips}$$
$$(\phi R_n = (.75)(517125 KPa)(.001187 \text{ m}^2) = 460.3KN)$$

Since 103.5 kips is greater than 80 kips the connection is adequate in shear. Check bearing (as usual):

Bearing area = 3 bolts × 5/8" diameter × 3/4" thick = 1.41 in.^{2}. Calculate the bearing design capacity as follows assuming deformation could be a consideration from Eq. 9–3.

$$\phi R_n = \phi(2.4)(d)(t)F_u \qquad \text{(Eq. 9–3)}$$
$$\phi R_n = (.75)(2.4)(1.41 \text{ in.}^2)(58 \text{ ksi}) = 147.2 \text{ kips}$$
$$(\phi R_n = (.75)(2.4)(.0009 \text{ m}^2)(399910KPa) = 655KN)$$

Therefore, since 147.2 kips is greater than 80 kips, bearing is also adequate. (Notice in the bearing calculation that we used the 3/4" plate. This is because in a butt joint the critical bearing area will be smallest area subjected to the full load. Therefore the 3/4" plate under a load of 80 kips was more critical than two 1/2" plates under the full 80 kip load.)

9.6   Eccentric Shear on Bolted Connections

Many times the load on a connection group does not act through the centroid of the bolt group, thus causing a rotational effect that must somehow be accounted. A typical example of such a situation is shown in Figure 9–9 where an eccentric load is applied to a bracket connection. The load being applied at an eccentricity is statically equivalent to a concentric load plus a moment ($P \times e$). The addition of this rotational effect will cause the individual bolts in the group to have different forces based on their distance from the centroid of the bolt group.

There are two commonly used methods to calculate the forces that are placed on fastener groups under eccentric shear. The first is the **elastic vector method** that views the bolts as elastic entities and assumes that no friction exists between the plates. This method will be discussed in this section although the results are usually quite conservative since the service loads on such a connection are always carried by the friction that is conveniently neglected. In spite of this

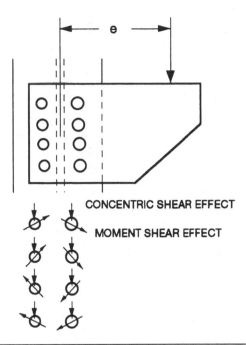

CONCENTRIC SHEAR EFFECT

MOMENT SHEAR EFFECT

Figure 9–9   Resultant Shear Force associated with Eccentric Loads on Bolt Groups.

shortcoming, the simplicity of this method makes it a widely accepted choice. The other method that can be used is called the **ultimate strength method**. In this method the rotation of the bolt group is considered about a point known as the *instantaneous center of rotation*. The ultimate strength of a fastener group is based on an equation utilizing the load-deformation relationship of a single bolt. The maximum shear force for a bolt can then be computed by using a maximum deformation for the bolt most remote from the instantaneous center. Since we strive to illustrate and understand the fundamentals, the ultimate strength procedure will not be further expanded on in this text. However, should the student wish to study this method further, the AISC has developed a number of tables which simplify this procedure and which are found in the LRFD manual.

The elastic vector method will resolve an eccentric load on a fastener group two separate effects. The first is a concentric load acting through the bolt group's centroid and the second is a torsional moment causing rotation about the bolt group's centroid. The concentric factored load will cause a shear force that is assumed to be divided equally among all bolts in the group. This effect will be termed R_{uv} and is shown as follows:

$$R_{uv} = P_u/n \qquad\qquad\qquad\qquad \text{(Eq. 9–5)}$$

where

R_{uv} = factored shear on an individual bolt, kips

P_u = total factored load, kips

n = number of bolts in the group

The effect of the moment that acts upon the group is based on the deformation in each bolt that is assumed to be proportional to its distance from the group's centroid. Reviewing the torsional stress formula which was developed in the student's strength of materials course, we would find the following:

$$\tau = Mr/J \qquad\qquad\qquad\qquad \text{(Eq. 9–6)}$$

where

τ = torsional shear stress, Ksi

M = torsional moment, $P \times e$, kip-in.

r = radial distance from group centroid, in.

J = polar moment of inertia, in.^{4}

The polar moment of inertia can be expressed by the term ΣAr^2 and it is typically convenient to substitute the horizontal and vertical distances in lieu of r^2. The aforementioned formula could then be rearranged as follows:

$$\tau = Mr \,/\, A \,(\Sigma x^2 + \Sigma y^2) \qquad\qquad\qquad \text{(Eq. 9–7)}$$

where

A = the area of the bolt

$(\Sigma x^2 + \Sigma y^2)$ = sum of $\times$ and y of distances from the center of the group

Finally, by placing the area term on the opposite side, we can see that the factored shear effect due to the torsional moment (R_{um}) can be expressed as follows:

$$R_{um} = Mr/(\Sigma x^2 + \Sigma y^2) \qquad\qquad\qquad \text{(Eq. 9–8)}$$

Usually this effect will be broken down into its horizontal and vertical components so it can easily be added to the concentric shear effect R_{uv} to obtain a resultant shear effect. The components can be accomplished by substituting the $\times$ and y coordinates as for r in a given bolt calculation. The resultant shear calculation can be performed as follows:

$$R_u = \sqrt{(R_{um})_x{}^2 + [(R_{uv}) + (R_{um})_y]^2}$$

The following example illustrates the use of the elastic vector method.

EXAMPLE 9.6

The factored load of 80 kips is placed eccentricity as shown on the bracket connection. Determine the resultant shear effects on all the bolts and establish whether they are adequate per AISC shear requirements. The bolts are 3/4" diameter, A325–N bolts in single shear and the connection is a bearing-type.

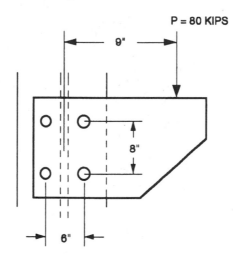

The factored load on the fastener group is 80 kips at an eccentricity of 9 inches. This would yield a torsional moment on the bolt group of:

80 kips × 9 in. = 720 kip-in.

Next we can calculate the ($\Sigma x^2 + \Sigma y^2$) of the bolt group as follows:

$$(\Sigma x^2 + \Sigma y^2) = 4 \text{ bolts}(3 \text{ in.})^2 + 4 \text{ bolts}(4 \text{ in.})^2$$
$$= 100 \text{ bolt-in.}^2$$

The shear effect (in its horizontal and vertical components) from the torsional moment can then be calculated as follows. Notice that the numerical values for this effect are equal for all the bolts in this example since the x and y distance for all are the same. However, the direction of the shear effect must be in the direction of the moment and perpendicular to the radial line from the group's centroid (see figure on next page).

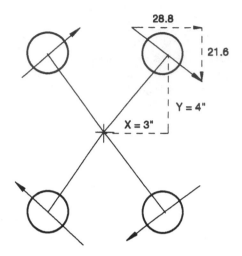

Shear effect from moment using:

$$\tau = Mr/A \; (\Sigma x^2 + \Sigma y^2) \tag{Eq. 9–7}$$

$(R_{um})_x$ = 720 kip-in. (4 in.)/100 bolt-in.^{2} = 28.8 kips/bolt

$(R_{um})_y$ = 720 kip-in. (3 in.)/100 bolt-in.^{2} = 21.6 kips/bolt

Realizing that the concentric shear effect on an individual bolt is simply 20 kips in a downward direction:

$$R_{uv} = P_u/n \tag{Eq. 9–5}$$

= 80 kips/4 bolts = 20 kips

The resultant effect can be calculated as follows:
Upper righthand bolt:

$$R_u = \sqrt{(28.8 \text{ kips})^2 + (20 \text{ kips} + 21.6 \text{ kips})^2} = 50.6 \text{ kips}$$

Lower righthand bolt:

$$R_u = \sqrt{(28.8)^2 + (20 + 21.6)^2} = 50.6 \text{ kips}$$

Lower lefthand bolt:

$$R_u = \sqrt{(28.8)^2 + (20 - 21.6)^2} = 28.84 \text{ kips}$$

Upper lefthand bolt:

$$R_u = \sqrt{(28.8)^2 + (20 - 21.6)^2} = 28.84 \text{ kips}$$

The design capacity (ϕR_n) of a 3/4" diameter, A325–N bolt in single shear is found by Eq. 9–1 as follows:

$$\phi R_n = \phi \text{ (Design strength} \times A) \tag{Eq. 9-1}$$
$$= 0.75(48 \text{ ksi})(.44 \text{ in.}^2) = 15.8 \text{ kips}$$

Since 15.8 kips is less than all the factored and previously calculated shear forces, all bolts in this group would fail.

9.7   Summary

High strength bolting is the most common method of connecting steel members used in construction today. It is very important that proper bolt tension be achieved during the installation process, for which a number of different methods that strive to ensure this outcome.

Analysis and design of bolted connections focuses primarily on preventing bolt shear and plate bearing failures, although other mechanisms (such as tensile modes of failure) must always be checked. The good designer will realize that changes to the connection will most probably be reflected in other parts of the member design, such as the tensile capacity. Eccentricity loaded connections will induce effects other than just pure shear into a bolt group and therefore the designer must be able to account for these additional effects by some method.

EXERCISES

1. Discuss the significance of a slip-critcal type versus a bearing type of connection. Where would you expect to see each of these used? Are they both installed in similar fashions?
2. Discuss the direct tension indicators used in the tensioning of bolts. Do you think this is a reliable method of obtaining the proper tension? Do you believe imperfections such as burrs or rust may affect this method?
3. Compare the calibrated bolt assemblage method of bolt tensioning to the method discussed in problem 2. How does this method compare?
4. Determine the maximum factored load on the bearing connection shown below if the bolts are A325–N, 7/8" diameter. Steel is A36, check plate tension also.

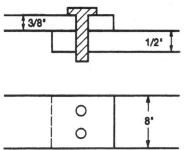

5. Check the adequacy of the slip-critical connection shown below if the bolts are A490–X, 3/4" diameter. Steel is A36, check plate tension also. The load shown is factored with the service portion being 60 KIPS.

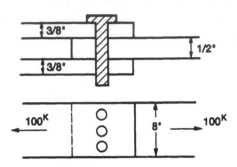

6. Determine the maximum factored load on a bearing type, lap joint that is connected by six 25.4 mm diameter, A490–X bolts arranged in three rows of two bolts each. The plates are 200 mm wide by 20 mm thick and the steel is A36.

7. Design the size and number of A325–X bolts required in the bearing connection shown under a 150 KIP factored load. Check shear and bearing, assume required edge distance is 1 1/2" to bolt center and minimum spacing between centers of bolts is 3d. Steel is A36.

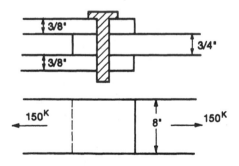

8. Design the size and number of A325–N bolts required in the bearing-type connection shown below. Check shear and bearing, and assume that deformation is not a consideration. Steel is A36.

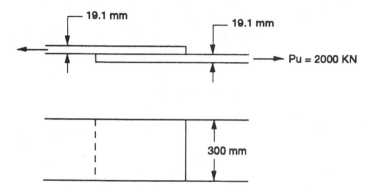

9. Redesign the connection in problem 7 if the two outside plates are 1/4" thick and consider deformation around the holes.

10. Redesign the connection shown in problem 8 if the connection is now a slip-critical type of connection. Also consider the tension requirements in the member as well. Service load is 1500 KN.

11. Recalculate the adequacy of the connection shown in problem 5 if the connection is now a bearing type. How does this change your answer?

12. Why are the shear strengths given in Table 9–3 so much lower for bolts with threads included in the shear plane? Why are these stresses even lower when a slip-critical type of connection is considered?

13. Design the proper diameter for the bearing-type lap joint shown below under a factored load of 40 KIPS. The bolts are A490s with the threads not in the shear plane and the steel is A36. Assume proper spacing and edge distance and that deformation is not a concern.

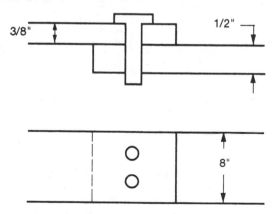

14. Calculate the adequacy of the bearing-type connection shown below. All the bolts are A325–X, 25.4 mm diameter and deformation is not a consideration. Steel is A36

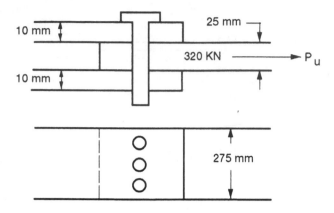

15. If the connection in problem 14, has the outside plates changed to a 6.3mm thickness, how does this affect the result?

16. Calculate the adequacy of all the bolts in shear for the connection shown below. The bolts are 7/8" diameter, A325–X, under single shear. The connection is bearing type. What is the design capacity for such bolts? Eccentricity is 8 inches.

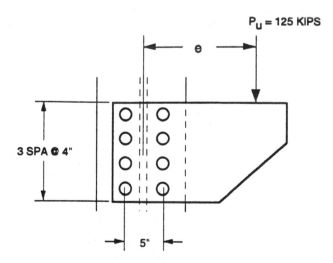

17. If the connection in problem 16 uses 1 1/8" diameter bolts, how does this affect your answer?

REFERENCES

1. John A. Struik, Abayomi O. Oyeledun, and John W. Fisher, "Bolt Tension Control with a Direct Tension Indicator," *Engineering Journal*, AISC, 1973
2. J. O. Surtees and M. E. Ibrahi, "Load Indicating Washers," *Civil Engineering*, ASCE, April 1982
3. *Specifications for Structural Joints Using ASTM A325 or A490 Bolts*, Research Council on Structural Connections of the Engineering Foundation, June 8, 1988.
4. Jack C. McCormac, *Structural Steel Design: ASD Method* 4th ed. Harper Collins Publishers, New York, 1992, p. 308.

CHAPTER

10

WELDED CONNECTION DESIGN IN LRFD

10.1 Introduction

Welding can be thought of as the fusing of two pieces of metal together to form a continuous, rigid plate. The earliest welding was probably accomplished by craftsman and artists in ancient times. There are many modern day welding techniques, although the two basic catagories are gas and arc welding. These modern techniques can trace their roots back to the late nineteenth century when arc welding was first patented and used on a limited scale.

Generally, all welding processes will have the following common elements:

- Base metals
- Heat source
- Electrode or Welding Rod
- Shielding Mechanism

The base metals are simply the pieces to be joined together. They are joined together using some type of heat source. In structural steel welding this heat source is most frequently generated through an electric arc that creates a confined temperature in excess of 6000°F. In gas welding the heat source is generated through the burning of gas (typically acetylene and oxygen) at the end of a welder's "torch". In both cases, the heat source melts not only the base metal, but also an electrode or welding rod. As the electrode or welding rod is melted, it is deposited as additional steel into the area of the weld. The electrode or welding rod may be thought of as the "weld metal".

The weld must also be protected from coming in contact with the surrounding air during its cooling period. This is usually accomplished through some type of shielding mechanism. This shielding can be accomplished by a gaseous cloud or by immersion of the electrode into a material generally referred to as flux. Flux is a material that will help prevent the intrusion of undesirable contaminants into the pool of molten weld. A common contaminant, which hopefully is minimized by good welding techniques, is air or other gases. If air is allowed to penetrate the weld during its cooling period, it can greatly reduce the strength and quality of the weld due to pitting or high porosity. Flux can be either a loose, granular material through which the electrode is moved—or it can be contained on a coating that shrouds the electrode. Such a coating would then melt as the electrode is consumed thereby creating a gaseous cloud.

The use of welding is very popular in steel construction because it has a number of advantages. Among them are a savings produced by the reduction of splicing plates, the ease of welding odd shapes (i.e. pipes), and the ease of implementing field changes. Disadvantages of welding include their fatigue behavior and quality assurance. The former of these disadvantages has led to the development of fatigue criteria and special details in practically all welded structures. These criteria will be discussed later in this chapter.

As mentioned earlier, the most common method of welding structural steel is arc welding. This chapter will consider the two most basic types of arc welding: the shielded metal arc welding (SMAW) process and the submerged arc welding (SAW) process (Figure 10–1).

The shielded metal arc welding (SMAW) process is the traditional type of welding that is manually produced. The generation of heat is from an electric arc and the electrode, usually designated by a term such as E70XX, is melted into the weld area to fuse together with the base metal. In the electrode designation, E70XX, the 70 represents the ultimate tensile strength (ksi) of the electrode. The subscript symbols (xx) may reflect a variety of things such as coating, positions, and other characteristics. In general, A36 steel can be used successfully with either E60XX or E70XX electrodes. Further designations can be found in the American Welding Society's *Structural Welding Code*[1].

The submerged arc welding (SAW) process also uses an electric arc for its heat source. This method is used most often in a fabrication shop and is accomplished by a automated welding machine. The machine will lay down a coating of granular flux through a feeding tube that advances in front of an uncoated electrode. This covering of loose flux provides a shielding mechanism to protect the weld from contaminant intrusion while cooling. This type of weld is very advantageous when welding long lengths (such as web to flange connections on plate girders) and is considered to be superior because of the uniform

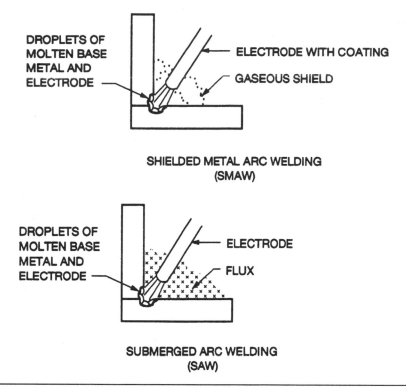

Figure 10–1   Illustration of Common Welding Techniques

quality characteristics, mechanical properties, and speed of production. The designation for submerged arc welding (SAW) is somewhat different than that for the SMAW method; a standard designation includes the combination of the flux and electrode. A SAW weld might be F7X-E7XX, where the first part stands for its flux and its tensile strength and the latter part represents the electrode and its corresponding properties.

10.2   Common Types of Welds

There are many different ways to classify welds based on the type of weld, the welding position, and the type of end treatment in which a plate may be fabricated to better adapt to the welding procedure. The standard welding symbols given by the AISC are shown in Figure 10–2. In this section we will be concerned with identifying the characteristics and terminology for the common weld types.

BASIC WELD SYMBOLS

BACK	FILLET	PLUG OR SLOT	Groove or Butt						
			SQUARE	V	BEVEL	U	J	FLARE V	FLARE BEVEL

SUPPLEMENTARY WELD SYMBOLS

BACKING	SPACER	WELD ALL AROUND	FIELD WELD	CONTOUR		For other basic and supplementary weld symbols, see AWS A2.4-86
				FLUSH	CONVEX	

STANDARD LOCATION OF ELEMENTS OF A WELDING SYMBOL

Finish symbol

Contour symbol

Root opening, depth of filling for plug and slot welds

Effective throat

Depth of preparation; size or strength for certain welds

Reference line

Specification, process or other reference

Tail (omitted when reference is not used)

Basic weld symbol or detail reference

Groove angle or included angle of countersink for plug welds

Length of weld

Pitch (c. to c. spacing) of welds

Field weld symbol

Weld-all-around symbol

Arrow connecting reference line to arrow side member of joint or arrow side of joint

F A R S(E) T (Other sides) (Both Arrow side) L @ P

Note:

Size, weld symbol, length of weld and spacing must read in that order from left to right along the reference line. Neither orientation of reference line nor location of the arrow alters this rule.

The perpendicular leg of ⊿, V, Ⴒ, ⊾ weld symbols must be at left.

Arrow and Other Side welds are of the same size unless otherwise shown. Dimensions of fillet welds must be shown on both the Arrow Side and the Other Side Symbol.

Flag of field-weld symbol shall be placed above and at right angle to reference line of junction with the arrow.

Symbols apply between abrupt changes in direction of welding unless governed by the "all around" symbol or otherwise dimensioned.

These symbols do not explicitly provide for the case that frequently occurs in structural work, where duplicate material (such as stiffeners) occurs on the far side of a web or gusset plate. The fabricating industry has adopted this convention: that when the billing of the detail material discloses the existence of a member on the far side as well as on the near side, the welding shown for the near side shall be duplicated on the far side.

Figure 10–2 Standard Welding Symbols. (Courtesy of the American Institute of Steel Construction, Inc.)

The most common type of weld is the *fillet weld,* comprising probably 85% of all welds that are produced. These welds are used to join two pieces of steel that form a perpendicular corner where the weld is placed and can be used in many different types of connections (Figure 10–3). The abundance of fillet welds is due in part to their ease of production because of the "pocket" formed by the perpendicular edges. This pocket serves as a holder of the molten steel and eliminates the requirement for additional backup plates. Fillet welds also require less precise alignment of the members to be connected, in contrast to the stringent alignment required for groove-welded members.

The most common fillet weld is the *equal leg fillet weld,* where the leg dimensions are the same length. The different parts of the fillet weld are shown in Figure 10–4. The most important part of the fillet weld, as far as design is concerned, is the throat dimension. The throat dimension is the shortest length from the root of the weld to its face. This distance is critical because, although fillet welds have a generally rounded face, the throat distance is the probable line of failure through the weld. In an equal leg fillet weld this throat distance will be

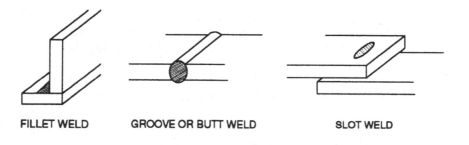

FILLET WELD   GROOVE OR BUTT WELD   SLOT WELD

Figure 10–3 Schematic Illustration of Fillet, Groove, and Slot Welds

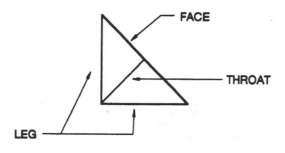

Figure 10–4 Standard Fillet Weld Terminology

.707 × *the leg*. If a fillet weld should be asymmetrical (having unequal legs), the throat distance should be calculated as the perpendicular distance from the face of the weld to its root using trigonometric principles. Fillet welds are called out by their leg size in equal leg welds (i.e. a 3/8" fillet weld has a leg 3/8" long).

The other common type of weld is a *groove* or *butt weld*. This weld is used when connecting two plates that lie in the same plane and is meant to transfer the load in that plane from one member to the other. (Figure 10–3) A groove weld is referred to as a **full penetration groove weld** if the weld extends the full thickness of the plate being joined and it is referred to as a **partial penetration groove weld** if the weld does not extend the full thickness. The partial penetration groove welds may occur in a situation where access to the welding area is restricted and can only be accomplished from one side. A groove weld has many other variations based on the depth of the weld, the edge fabrication of the plates, and the configuration of the plates to be welded. Such configurations may include single and double U, V, or J welds as illustrated in Figure 10–5. In any case, groove welds are more difficult to produce and should be avoided if possible because of the cost associated with additional plate fabrication and weld production. The additional cost is incurred because the weld is not confined in a pre-made "pocket" such as the fillet weld.

The critical throat distance in a full penetration groove weld is defined by the AISC to be the thickness of·the thinnest plate joined. That is to say, if a 1/4" thick plate was to be groove welded to a 1/2" thick plate, the throat distance of the groove weld would be 1/4".

The last type of weld shown in Figure 10–3, is the *slot* or *plug weld*. These welds are typically used in a lap connections where weld material is placed in standard or slotted holes that have been prepunched in the steel members. These welds increase the shear resistance of the connected parts and inhibits potential buckling of the members along their interface.

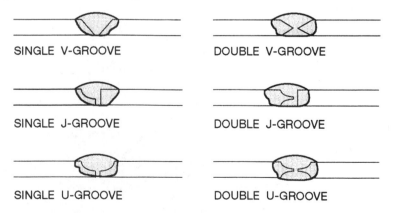

Figure 10–5 Types of Common Groove Welds

10.3   Potential Modes of Failure in Welded Connections

There are basically two manners in which a welded connection can fail: either the weld itself cracks under some type of stress or the base material being joined actually cracks with the weld intact. Both of these mechanisms are induced due to the stresses that act along some plane, either a plane in the weld itself or a plane in the base metal. This plane of failure in the weld is referred to as the **effective weld area.**

The effective weld area is the area that is most susceptible to cracking, assuming the weld to be of uniform quality. In general, this area would be the smallest area resisting the loads placed upon the weld, and therefore the most likely to fail. Whether these loads are placing the weld in tension, compression, or shear, the weld will tend towards resisting a stress with this effective weld area. The student may best picture this area as the surface area that would be remaining *after* the weld had failed. The effective weld area is simply the critical throat distance (sometimes referred to as the *effective throat*) multiplied by the length of the weld (Figure 10–6).

With fillet welds, the weld can be loaded along the length of the weld (parallel to the weld axis) or across the length of the weld (perpendicular to the weld axis). Such loadings would cause tension or compression on a weld stressed parallel to its length and shear on a weld stressed perpendicular to its length. Although testing has indicated a substantial increase in strength for fillet welds stressed in shear, the AISC considers both cases as equivalent.

The effective weld area for a fillet weld is that area that resists the stresses applied to the weld. As stated earlier, the critical throat distance is theoretically the shortest distance from the root of the weld to its face, which would be

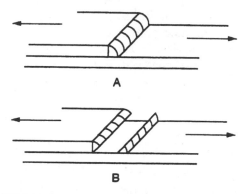

Figure 10–6   Typical Failure Plane in a Welded Connection Exposing the Effective Area. (A) Weld Intact (B) Weld Broken

.707 × leg for an equal leg fillet weld. This makes the effective weld area for an equal leg fillet weld simply the inclined projection of a rectangular area, .707 × leg × length of weld.

The effective areas as stated above are to be used when welding by the shielded metal arc welding (SMAW) process, but since the submerged arc welding (SAW) process leads to an inherently better fillet weld because of the deeper penetration, the AISC specification permits a modified critical throat distance. For a fillet weld made by the SAW process, the following effective weld areas are established by the AISC.

For fillet welds 3/8" and smaller:

Effective Area = Leg × Length of weld

For fillet welds larger than 3/8":

Effective Area = (Leg + .11") × Length of weld

The effective weld area for a complete penetration groove weld is typically another rectangular area. For a groove weld (with a critical throat distance equal to the thickness of the thinner part) this rectangular projection makes the effective weld area simply the critical throat × the weld length.

To gain a further insight to the requirements of the LRFD specification regarding welding, students should familiarize themselves with the weld requirements in the LRFD specification. These requirements are especially important with regard to the maximum and minimum welds sizes used in proper connection design that will be discussed in the next section.

10.4   AISC Requirements in Welded Connections Using LRFD

The requirements established for welded connections in the LRFD specification are very straight forward. The student should remember both the weld itself and the connecting members must be designed and/or checked in order to completely determine the connection's capacity. The planes of failure in a typical welded connection are summarized in Figure 10–7 and include shear failure of the weld, shear failure of the base material, and a tensile failure of the base material.

The LRFD philosophy for welded connections can be summarized as follows:

$$\phi R_n \geq R_u$$

where

ϕR_n = design capacity of the welded component

R_u = factored load or required capacity of that component

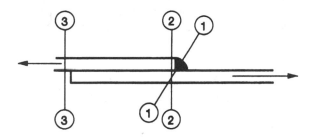

Figure 10–7   Potential Failure Zones in a Welded Connection. 1-1) Shear through Weld 2-2) Shear through Plate 3-3) Tension in Plate

In fillet welds, the transfer of stress through the welds is assumed to be shear over the effective weld area, and failure is assumed to occur in plane 1–1, as shown in Figure 10–6. When subjected to a force perpendicular to the axis of the weld, the design strength for a fillet weld is given in Table J2.5 of LRFD specification as $0.75(0.60F_{Exx})$ for the weld where 0.75 is the reduction factor and $0.60F_{Exx}$ is the nominal strength of the weld. This design capacity can then be illustrated as follows:

$$\phi R_n = .75(A \times (0.60F_{Exx})) \tag{Eq. 10–1}$$

where

A = effective weld area

The term $0.60F_{Exx}$ represents 60% of the ultimate tensile strength of the electrode since this is approximately the relationship between ultimate shear capacity and ultimate tensile capacity in steel. This design capacity must not be less than the shear capacity of the base material which can be seen as follows:

$$\phi R_n = .75(A \times (0.60F_u)) \tag{Eq. 10–2}$$

where

A = shear area of the base material

Also when a fillet weld is subjected to tension or compression parallel to the weld's longitudinal axis, the design capacity must be checked against a yielding mechanism over the base material, with the reduction factor being 0.90 and the nominal capacity being the yield strength of the base material, F_y.

When dealing with complete penetration groove welds the designer should recognize that the stress is transferred exactly in the same manner as it is carried in the plates. Therefore when a groove welded member is subjected to tension or compressive stresses, either parallel or perpendicular to the weld axis, the design capacities of the base material and weld are as follows:

For the base material:

$$\phi R_n = .90(A \times F_y) \qquad \text{(Eq. 10–3)}$$

For the weld material:

$$\phi R_n = .90(A_w \times F_{yw}) \qquad \text{(Eq. 10–4)}$$

where

A and A_w = area of the base material resisting said stress and the effective weld area respectively

F_y and F_{yw} = tensile yield strength of the base metal and weld metal respectively

However, when tension stress is applied normal to the weld's effective area the AISC specification recommends that "matching" weld metal shall be used. Matching weld metal refers to using the yield strength of the weakest base material in lieu of the electrode yield strength. A complete table outlining the matching weld metal can be found in the American Welding Society's *Welding Handbook*.[1]

When a groove weld is subjected to shear on the effective area, the design capacity for the base material and the weld are as follows:

For the base material:

$$\phi R_n = .90(A \times .60F_y) \qquad \text{(Eq. 10–5)}$$

For the weld material:

$$\phi R_n = .80(A \times 0.60F_{EXX}) \qquad \text{(Eq. 10–6)}$$

The terminology in the aforementioned equations are the same as previously mentioned. The following section demonstrates the use of these formulas in the solution of welded connection problems.

10.5 Design of Welded Connections

Welds are used to transfer forces from one piece of steel to another. This transfer of force produces stress on the welds and this stress can be quantified in terms of the direct stress equation that we have repeatedly used, $f = P/A$. The area is now the effective weld area that was discussed in a previous section.

Weld analysis or design can be viewed in terms of one inch segments of the weld under consideration. This is because a one inch segment of a weld has a particular load capacity based on the strength of the electrode used and the size of the weld. To double this load capacity, the designer merely needs to double the weld length. When designing side or end fillet welds, it should be noted that these welds do not typically terminate at the corner of a connected part, but are "wrapped around" the corner. The "wrap-around" is referred to as an **end return** and this return should be at least two times the nominal weld size. The end return does not considerably increase the strength of the weld but does delay the initial tearing of the weld.

Again there are two basic problems that are commonly encountered: evaluation and design. The following examples illustrate the use of the LRFD requirements in the solutions of these common problems.

EXAMPLE 10.1

Determine the design capacity of the connection shown below. The welds are 5/16" fillet with E70XX electrodes using the SMAW process. Plates are made of A36 steel.

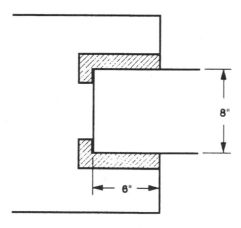

NOTE:
BOTH PLATES ARE 1/2" THICK

Since the problem is to determine the design capacity of the connection, it is an evaluation type of problem. Therefore, we should determine the effective weld area and calculate capacity from the appropriate equation.

Effective weld area = $(5/16)(.707) \times 12" = 2.65$ in.^{2}

Weld Nominal Strength = $0.60F_{EXX} = 0.60(70 \text{ ksi}) = 42 \text{ ksi}$

Reduction Factor = .75

Design capacity based on weld from Eq. 10–1 is:

$$\phi R_n = .75(A \times (0.60F_{EXX})) \qquad \text{(Eq. 10–1)}$$
$$= .75(2.65 \text{ in.}^2 \times 42 \text{ ksi}) = 83.5 \text{ kips}$$
$$(= .75(.0017 \text{ m}^2 \times 289.6 \text{ MPa}) = .37 \text{MN or } 370 \text{KN})$$

Also check tension and/or shear on base material to make sure they are not weaker than the weld itself.

Plate Tension

A_{gross} = 8 in. × 1/2 in. = 4 in.^{2}

Nominal tensile strength of plate = 36 ksi

Calculating design capacity from Eq. 4–1:

$\phi_t P_n = \phi_t(F_y A_g)$ (Eq. 4–1)

Design capacity = 0.90(4 in.^{2} × 36 ksi) = 129.6 kips

(= 0.90(.00258 m^2)(248.2MPa) = .576MN or 576KN)

Plate Shear (around weld area)

Area = 12" × 1/2" = 6 in.^{2}

Nominal shear strength of plate = .60(F_u) = 34.8 ksi

Calculating the shear design capacity from Eq. 10–2:

$\phi R_n = .75(A \times (0.60F_u))$ (Eq. 10–2)

Design capacity = .75(6 in.^{2} × 34.8 ksi) = 156.6 kips

(= .75(.003871 m^2)(239.9MPa) = .696MN or 696KN)

Therefore, the weld's design capacity, ϕR_n is 83.5 kips. The weld strength controls the connection's strength.

In actual weld design, the weld size that is chosen should be checked against the minimum and maximum weld sizes that are allowed per the LRFD specification. For fillet welds, the maximum weld size is 1/16" less than the thickness of the plate for plate thickness over 1/4", and the thickness of the plate for plates 1/4" or smaller. In this example, the maximum fillet weld size would be 7/16" (1/2" − 1/16"). The minimum fillet weld size is given in Table 10–1 and is based on the thickness of the *thicker* part being joined. According to Table 10–1, the minimum weld size is 3/16" for a 1/2" plate. Since our weld is 5/16", it fits between the minimum and maximum specified weld sizes and therefore, is adequate. This weld is also good because it can be produced manually with a single pass of the welding rod. Larger welds require multiple passes and therefore are more difficult and costly to produce. This minimum requirement is to assure that enough heat is generated to provide a decent penetration of the weld into a thick piece of base material. The student is urged to become familiar with these requirements as their familiarity with steel design advances.

Table 10-1 AISC Requirements for Minimum Fillet Weld Size. (Courtesy of the American Institute of Steel Construction, Inc.)

Material Thickness of Thicker Part Joined (in.)	Minimum size of fillet weld[a] (in.)
To ¼ inclusive	$1/8$
Over ¼ to ½	$3/16$
Over ½ to ¾	¼
Over ¾	$5/16$

[a]Leg dimension of fillet welds.

EXAMPLE 10.2

Design the welds for the connection shown below using two equal length side fillets welds. Use E70XX electrodes with SMAW process and A36 steel. The load shown is a service load with 50% live load and 50% dead load.

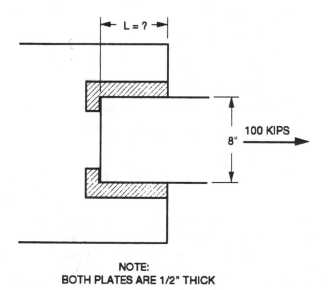

NOTE:
BOTH PLATES ARE 1/2" THICK

This is the design type problem where we are left to design the size and the length of weld to be used. Because the student may not be familiar with maximum weld sizes, please refer to the appropriate section of the LRFD specification for the logic used below.

Since the plates are each 1/2" thick, the maximum size weld per the LRFD specification is 7/16"; but use 3/8" because it may be easier in some cases to produce.

Effective weld area = (.707 × 3/8) × length = .265 × Length

Since the service load is given at 100 kips, we must calculate the required strength using the standard load combinations. Since only dead load and live load are involved, the combination A4–2 controls (see section 2.5) and the required strength is as follows:

R_u = 1.2(50 kips) + 1.6(50 kips) = 140 kips (622.7KN)

Since the design capacity (ϕR_n) must equal or exceed 140 kips the length can be found as follows:

Area = 140 kips/0.75(.60 × 70 ksi) = 4.44 in.² (.00286 mm²)

4.44 in.² = .265 × Length

Length = 16.77 in.

Therefore use 2 welds that are each 8.5 inches long, with an end return of at least two times the nominal weld size. In this case the end returns would be a minimum of 3/4 in.

Remember to check tension and shear on plates.

Plate Tension

A_g = 8 in. × 1/2 in. = 4 in.²

Nominal tensile strength = 36 ksi

Calculating design capacity from Eq. 4–1:

$\phi_t P_n = \phi_t(F_y A_g)$ (Eq. 4–1)

Design capacity = 0.90(36 ksi × 4 in.²) = 129.6 kips

(= 0.90(.00258 m²)(248.2MPa) = .576MN or 576KN)

Since the design tensile capacity is less than the required capacity of 140 kips the member would have to be redesigned appropriately. This redesign will be accomplished in the next example. However, check shear for adequacy.

Plate Shear (using 8.5" side welds, but neglecting the end returns)

A = 1/2 in. × (17 in.) = 8.5 in.² (plate area susceptible to shear)

Nominal shear strength of plate = .60(F_u) = 34.8 ksi

Calculating the shear design capacity from Eq. 10–2:

$$\phi R_n = .75(A \times (0.60F_u)) \qquad \text{(Eq. 10-2)}$$

Design capacity = $.75(8.5 \text{ in.}^2 \times 34.8 \text{ ksi}) = 221.8 \text{ kips}$

$(= .75(.005484 \text{ m}^2)(239.9\text{MPa}) = .987\text{MN or } 987\text{KN})$

Since the design shear capacity is greater the required strength of 140 kips, the plate shear is adequate.

EXAMPLE 10.3

Redesign the member in Example 10.2 to be adequate for tensile capacity. The steel is A36.

Since the member was adequate in weld capacity and plate shear capacity, redesign based on the tension strength. From Chapter 4, the minimum gross area required can be found by the following:

$A_{gmin} = P_u/\phi_t F_y$

$\quad = 140 \text{ kips}/(0.90)(36 \text{ ksi}) = 4.32 \text{ in.}^2$

Since the plate thickness is 1/2 in., the width of the plate is:

$4.32 \text{ in.}^2 = b(1/2 \text{ in.})$

$b = 8.64 \text{ in.}$

Therefore the plate width should be at least 8.64 inches and most designers would probably make this width 9 inches. Adequacy over net area can be checked in accordance with chapter B requirements.

EXAMPLE 10.4

Calculate the required strength of the connection shown below. The full penetration groove weld uses E70XX electrodes with the SMAW process and connects the plates made from A36 steel.

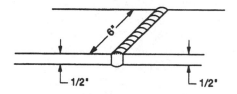

Since the plates are both 1/2" thick, the critical throat distance is 1/2". The effective weld area is :

$$A = 1/2 \text{ in.} \times 6 \text{ in.} = 3 \text{ in.}^2 \ (.00193 \text{ m}^2)$$

The nominal strength for tension perpendicular to the weld's longitudinal axis is controlled by nominal strength relative to the base material, which is the yield strength F_y of the material. The reduction factor to be used is 0.90.

The design strength based on the weld capacity is calculated using Eq. 10–3:

$$\phi R_n = .90(A \times F_y) \tag{Eq. 10–3}$$

$\phi R_n = .90(3 \text{ in.}^2 \times 36 \text{ ksi}) = 97.2 \text{ kips}$ (Matching weld metal must be used)

$(.90(.00193 \text{ m}^2)(248.2 \text{ MPa}) = .432 \text{ MN or } 432 \text{ KN})$

Checking plate tension is not necessary since the weld strength was controlled by this limit state. Also checking plate shear does not need to be done in this case since the plane of tension excludes the possibility of shear failure. Therefore the design capacity is 97.2 kips.

10.6 Fatigue Considerations in Welded Connections

Fatigue in structural members can be defined as the tendency to fail at a lower stress when subjected to cyclical loading than when subjected to a static loading.[2] Although these loadings may cause stresses that are greatly under a material's threshold stress, a member can exhibit cracking due to the large number of repetitions.

Welded structures are extremely sensitive to fatigue cracking because of the discontinuous and flawed nature of welded connections in general. A weld can be thought of as the boundary between two discontinuous plates that bind these plates into a rigid body. Some welded details, such as the cover plate shown in Figure 10–8, are prone to cracking because of the varying rigidity on each side of the weld. In this particular case, the weld is solely responsible for transferring the stress from one part of the flange to another over a short distance. This essentially places the weld in a position of extremely high stress.

Besides being located in positions of high stress, welds by their very nature may be the cause of high stress due to the flawed nature of their production. Welds are susceptible to flaws such as the possible inclusion of slag, incomplete fusion, air pockets, improper starts and stops, or arc strikes. Flaws, such as these, cause **stress risers** or areas where the stress concentrates at a much higher rate. The most critical condition for a fatigue crack to initiate is that which combines

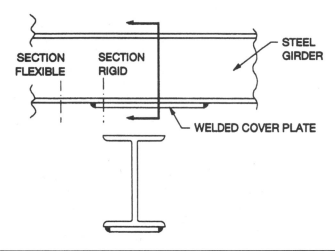

Figure 10–8   Potential Fatigue-Prone Area.

a flaw with a detail of high stress.[3] These flaws are particularly critical when they are oriented perpendicular to the applied stress.[4] Fatigue crack initiation will be much more likely to occur with a flaw oriented in this manner coupled with a high stress detail. When a crack finally initiates, it will grow at a rate depending on the number and intensity of stress cycles. Finally, the member will fracture as the crack size becomes critical. Some member fractures, such as the one shown in Figure 10–9, have been caused by seemingly trivial details such as filling misplaced holes with weld material.

Figure 10–9   Crack Caused by Weld-Filled Rivet Hole in a Bridge Girder. (Courtesy of ATLSS Engineering Research Center, Lehigh University.)

For welded structures that are subjected to repetitive or cyclical loads, specifications dictate how fatigue prone details shall be designed. In Chapter K, the AISC specification lists different stress categories when dealing with welds on cyclically loaded members. These categories are determined by the type of weld detail and the number of service cycles that a member is expected to incur over its lifetime as shown in Tables 10–2 and 10–3. As the weld detail becomes more

Table 10–2 AISC Fatigue Loading Cycle Criteria. (Courtesy of the American Institute of Steel construction, Inc.)

Loading Condition	Form	To
1	20.000[a]	100,000[b]
2	100,000	500,000[c]
3	500,000	2,000,000[d]
4	Over 2,000,000	

Source: Courtesy of the American Insitiute of Steel Construction, Inc.
[a]Approximately equivalentto two applications every day for 25years.
[b]Approximately equivalent to 10 applications every day for 25 years.
[c]Approximately equivalent to 50 applications every day for 25 years.
[d]Approximately equivalent to 200 applications every day for 25 years.

Table 10–3 AISC Allowable Stress Ranges for various fatigue Conditions. (Courtesy of the American Institute of Steel construction, Inc.)

Category (from Table A-K4.2)	Loading Condition 1	Loading Condition 2	Loading Condition 3	Loading Condition 4
A	63	37	24	24
B	49	29	18	16
B'	39	23	15	12
C	35	21	13	10[a]
D	28	16	10	7
E	22	13	8	5
E'	16	9	6	3
F	15	12	9	8

Source: Courtesy of the American Institute of Steel Construction, Inc.
[a]Flexural stress range of 12 ksi permitted at toe of stiffener welds on flanges.

prone to fatigue behavior and as the number of expected cycles in a member's lifetime increases, the AISC specification will reduce the allowable stress on that connection. For a complete description of each fatigue category listed in these Tables, the student is referred to the Appendix of the LRFD specification.

Fatigue behavior in welded connection is a complex and thought-provoking topic where much of today's research will be reflected in tomorrow's specifications. New methods and new details are constantly being tried and evaluated to try to reduce the problems associated with this behavior. The beginning designer should be made aware of the potential for problems related to fatigue cracking in these details and seek experienced help when involved in this matter.

10.7   Eccentrically Loaded Weld Groups

As discussed in Chapter 9, connections are often loaded in a manner such that the resultant load does not pass through the centroid of the connection group thereby causing an eccentricity. Such eccentricity will cause a rotational component that has to be accounted for in the connection design. A common type of connection that causes this eccentricity is the welded bracket connection shown in Figure 10–10. In this case, the welds shown are subject to a direct shear force and a torsional moment which occurs due to the eccentric load, $P_u \times e$.

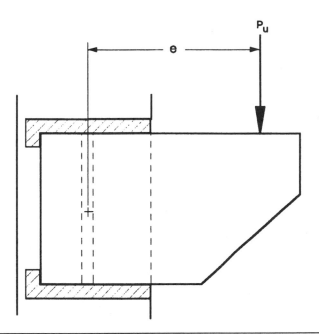

Figure 10–10   Weld Group subjected to Eccentric Load.

In Chapter 9, using the elastic vector method of analysis, this eccentrically loaded connection was considered as being acted on by a concentric shear force R_{uv} and a torsional moment acting about the centroid of the connection group, R_{um}. In this section we will use the same method when analyzing eccentrically loaded welds groups realizing, as discussed in the previous chapter, that such a method is inherently conservative. With welds it is assumed that each segment of weld length resists its portion of the concentric load R_{uv} (much in the same manner that the load was equally distributed to all bolts in Chapter 9). The torsional moment R_{um} which occurs about a weld segment is assumed to vary with the distance r from the centroid of the weld group to that particular segment (Figure 10–11). The moment will be assumed to act in a direction normal to the distance r which stretches between the centroid of the weld group and that segment. The components of forces due to the concentric shear load and those from the torsional moment can then be vectorially added.

As was discussed in the earlier chapter, the torsional moment can be calculated using the formula:

$$\tau = Mr/J \qquad\qquad\qquad \text{(Eq. 10–7)}$$

where

τ = shearing stress
M = torsional moment $(P_u \times e)$
r = distance from the centroid of the group to the segment
J = polar moment of inertia for the weld

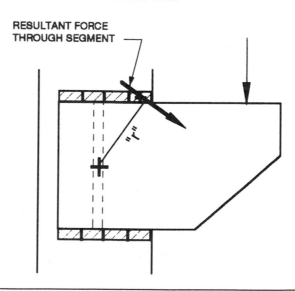

**RESULTANT FORCE
THROUGH SEGMENT**

Figure 10–11   Resultant Shear acting on a Portion of the Weld Group

Since the throat dimensions of the welds are relatively small, it is common to define the weld as a line segment that has only a location and no area. This allows the designer to calculate a force-per-unit length of weld rather than a stress-per-unit area. For the polar moment of inertia in the aforementioned formula, it is generally convenient to view the weld segments as a rectangular area and to calculate them as follows:

$$J = I_x + I_y \qquad\qquad\qquad\qquad \text{(Eq. 10–8)}$$
$$= (1/12 \; l^3 + ly^2)_x + (1/12 \; l^3 + lx^2)_y$$

where

l = length of weld in a particular segment

x,y = the x and y distances from the group centroid to the segment

This formula is simply converted from the classic parallel axis theorem representing moment of inertia $I_x + Ad^2$ except that the area units have been replaced by length since the weld is viewed in terms of length only. The following example illustrates the use of this method on a typical welded connection under eccentric shear.

EXAMPLE 10.5

Determine the maximum factored load effect on the weld group shown in the bracket connection below. The factored load is 50 kips. If the weld is a 3/8" fillet weld, using E70 electrodes and the SMAW process, will it be adequate per AISC specifications?

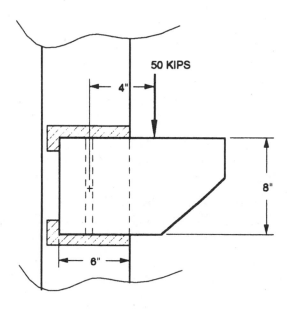

The maximum effect will occur at points *A* and *B,* at the ends of the weld "lines". With the centroid of the weld group very obvious, we can compute the polar moment of inertia as follows from Eq. 10–8:

$$J = I_x + I_y \qquad \text{(Eq. 10–8)}$$
$$= (1/12 \; l^3 + ly^2)_x + (1/12 \; l^3 + lx^2)_y$$
$$(0 + 2 \text{ welds}(6 \text{ in.})(4 \text{ in.})^2)_x + ((2 \text{ welds})1/12(6 \text{ in.})^3 + 0)_y$$
$$= 228 \text{ in.}^3$$

(The first zero was approximate because the "length" value of these welds with respect to the x axis is very small. The second zero is due to the fact that the centroidal axis of the weld and the weld group coincide.)

Using the same logic that was developed for eccentrically loaded bolt groups in Chapter 9 the calculation of the shear and moment effects are as follows:

Using Eq. 9–5 calculate the shear due to the factored load:

$$R_{uv} = P_u/n \qquad \text{(Eq. 9–5)}$$

where

R_{uv} = factored shear on an individual bolt, kips

P_u = total factored load, kips

n = length of weld used, inches

R_{uv} = 50 kips/12 in. = 4.17 kips/in.

Using Eq. 10–7 to calculate the shear effect in the x and y direction (R_{um}) due to the torsional moment:

$$\tau = Mr/J \qquad \text{(Eq. 10–7)}$$

where

τ = shearing stress

M = torsional moment ($P_u \times e$)

r = distance from the centroid of the group to the segment expressed in x and y distances

$(R_{um})_x$ = 200 kip-in.(4 in.) / 228 in.^{3} = 3.51 kips /in.

$(R_{um})_y$ = 200 kip-in.(3 in.) / 228 in.^{3} = 2.63 kips / in.

Notice that the x and y distances have been substituted for the *r* value in order to break the torsional effect down into the corresponding x and *y* components. This is done in order to accommodate the addition of vector components.

The vector sum would yield:

$$R_u = \sqrt{(R_{um})_x{}^2 + [(R_{uv}) + (R_{um})_y]^2}$$

$$R_u = \sqrt{(3.51)^2 + (4.17 + 2.63)^2} = 7.65 \text{ kips/in.}$$

Since the welds have to support a required capacity of 7.65 kips per inch, now let's calculate the design capacity of this weld.

Effective weld area per inch = (.707)(.375 in.)(1") = .265 in.^{2}

Calculating design capacity of the weld from Eq. 10–1:

$$\phi R_n = .75(A \times (0.60F_{Exx})) \qquad \text{(Eq. 10–1)}$$
$$= .75(.265 \text{ in.}^2 \times (.60 \times 70 \text{ ksi})) = 8.35 \text{ kip/inch}$$

Since the design capacity (8.35 kips/in) is greater than the required capacity (7.65 kips/inch), the weld group is adequate.

10.7 Summary

Welding is the fusing of steel plates into a single, rigid member using a heat source, which is typically an electric arc. An electrode or welding rod is melted by the electric arc along with the base metal to form the weld. The most common weld is a fillet weld.

Analysis and design of welded connections utilizes the direct stress formula and nominal stresses as set forth in the AISC specification. The critical area over which the weld is most likely to break is termed the effective weld area. An eccentric loading on a weld group exerts a force that can be represented by a concentric shear force and a torsional moment. This causes the resultant shear to be much higher and needs to be accounted for in design. Fatigue behavior in welded connections is a concern in design and the specifications should be consulted to determine how this behavior is handled.

EXERCISES

1. Discuss the differences between shielded metal arc welding (SMAW) and submerged arc welding (SAW). How does the AISC specification differentiate these two?
2. Why do welds need to be protected from air intrusion while they are being fused? How do we protect these welds from air?
3. Explain what fatigue is and how it can affect welded structural members. How do specifications such as the AISC handle fatigue related details as far as allowable stresses are concerned?

4. Calculate the design capacity on the welded connection shown below. The weld is a 3/8" fillet weld made from E70XX electrodes. The base steel is A36 and the weld is made from the SMAW process.

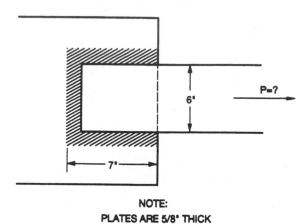

NOTE:
PLATES ARE 5/8" THICK

5. Calculate the adequacy of the welded connection shown below. The weld is a 9.5 mm fillet weld made from E70XX electrodes using the SAW process. The base steel is A36.

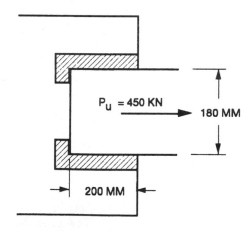

BOTH PLATES ARE 18 MM THICK

6. Calculate the adequacy of the welded connection shown below. The weld is a 1/4" fillet weld made from E60XX electrodes and using the SAW process. The steel is A36.

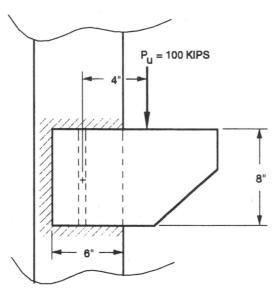

7. If the connection used in problem 5 changes to a 13mm fillet weld, how does this change the capacity?

8. Calculate the length of the full penetration groove weld shown below if the connection is to hold a factored load of 80 kips. The electrode is an E60XX and the base steel is A36. The SMAW process is used.

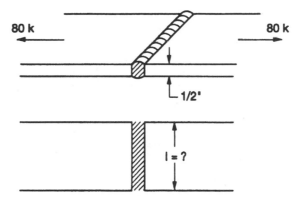

9. If the welded connection shown below is made from a 1/4" fillet weld around the total plate perimeter using the SMAW process, will the connection work? The load is factored, the steel is A36 and electrodes are E70XX.

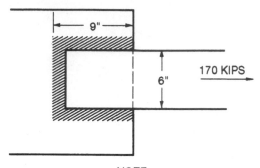

NOTE:
PLATES ARE 5/8" THICK

10. If the welded connection is made from a 6mm fillet weld around the total plate perimeter (which is 300mm long) using the SMAW process, will the connction work? The factored load is 200KN, the steel is A36 and electrodes are E70XX.

11. If the connection in problem 9 used the SAW process, would the connection's capacity be improved? Explain.

12. Design a fillet weld (size and length) to hold a 200 kip service tensile force in the connection shown below. The electrodes are E80XX and the steel is A36. Use the SAW process. The load is assumed to be 40% dead load and 60% live load.

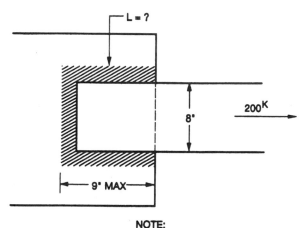

NOTE:
ALL PLATES 1/2" THICK

13. Design a fillet weld (size and length) to hold a 500 KN factored tensile force in the connection shown below. The electrodes are E80XX and the steel is A36. Use the SAW process.

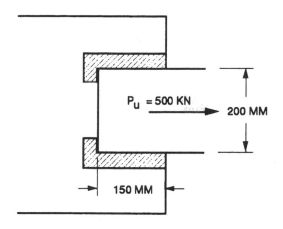

BOTH PLATES ARE 20 MM THICK

14. If the connection in problem 12 used only an end weld and a weld underneath the 8" plate, could the connection be adequately designed?

15. Determine the weld size required for the bracket connection shown below. The weld is to be a fillet weld, using E60 electrodes and the SMAW process. Assume shear on the base material does not control.

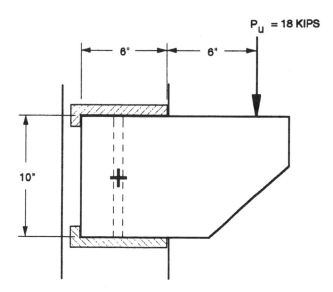

16. Determine the weld size required for the bracket connection shown below. The weld is to be a fillet weld, using E70 electrodes and the SMAW process. Assume shear on the base material does not control.

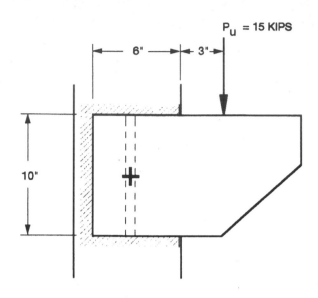

REFERENCES

1. American Welding Society, *Structural Welding Code–Steel (D1.1–88)*, 11th ed., Miami, FL, 1988.
2. U.S. Department of Transportation, Federal Highway Administration, *Bridge Inspector's Training Manual 70*, Washington, DC, 1979.
3. U.S. Department of Transportation, Federal Highway Administration, *Inspection of Fracture Critical Bridge Members*, Report No. FHWA–IP–86–26, 1986, p. 55.
4. John Fisher, Hans Hausammann, Michael Sullivan, Alan Pense, Transportation Research Board's National Cooperative Highway Research Program Report No. 206 "Detection and Repair of Fatigue Damage in Highway Bridges", Washington, DC, June 1979, p. 50.

11

PLATE GIRDERS

11.1 Introduction

In instances where a beam-type member spans long distances, the standard rolled beam shapes, which we have discussed exclusively up to this point, may not have sufficient strength to resist the applied loadings. Therefore it becomes necessary for the designer to create other alternate methods that will carry the desired loads over a particular span. Some alternate methods include trusses, arches, suspended systems, and plate girders. In this chapter we will focus on the discussion of plate girders.

A **plate girder** is a large beam that is typically made up from three plates being placed together in the standard I-shape that is typical of beams in general (Figure 11–1, 11–2). Today, plate girders are welded longitudinally, connecting their flange plates to the web plate. The typical plate girder will have a greater depth than their rolled-beam counterparts because the greater distance between flanges will create an increased resistance to bending. Recall from Chapter 6, that a beam's resistance to moment is accomplished by the creation of an internal (T–C) moment couple. By creating a beam with a greater depth, the designer can give a beam more capacity by spreading out the distance between the tension and compression forces. Such is the case with the plate girder.

There are other types of plate girders that can be fabricated such as the box plate girder and the built-up plate girder (Figure 11–3). The built-up plate girder was frequently used before welding became the standard method of connecting the flange plates to the web plate. The built-up plate girder typically uses angles

Figure 11-1 Plate Girder Construction, Mohawk River Bridge, New York Thruway. (Courtesy Bethlehem Steel Corporation.)

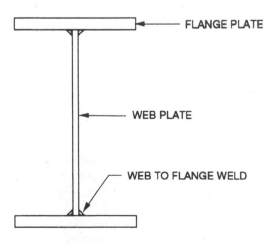

Figure 11-2 Typical Elements of a I-shaped Plate Girder.

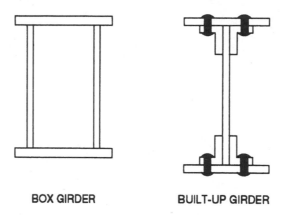

BOX GIRDER   BUILT-UP GIRDER

Figure 11–3   Other types of Plate Girders.

that connect the flange plates to the web plate with the connection made by riveting. This again was typically accomplished before the days of welding, but none the less, many existing structures are constructed using this arrangement.

The following sections discuss the fundamental behavior of a plate girder and the design criteria that is set forth in the LRFD specification.

11.2 Potential Plate Girder Failure Modes

Being a beam, the plate girder will exhibit many of the same failure modes that were discussed with beams in Chapter 6. However, because plate girders are typically much deeper than rolled-steel beams, other failure behaviors will tend to become more dominant.

The basic limit states that plate girders have in common with rolled steel beams are: yielding of the tension flange, buckling of the compression flange in a localized manner, and lateral torsional buckling (LTB) of the compression flange. These behaviors were discussed in Chapter 6 and will only be expanded on here as they pertain specifically to plate girders. The major difference in limit states will revolve around the behavior of a plate girder's web. Since the web of a plate girder is deepened to accommodate increased bending resistance, it is usually a very thin plate and therefore is susceptible to various shear type of behaviors not normally considered in rolled beams.

The limit state that can occur in the web of a plate girder is referred to as web buckling and is due to the thinness or the slenderness of the web plate. In regions of high shear, the principle stresses felt by a web element are diagonal tension and compression (Figure 11–4). The diagonal compression force in the web can lead to a buckling type of failure if not properly accounted for. To

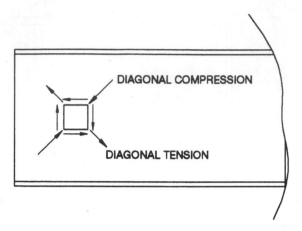

Figure 11–4   Resultant Forces from Shear Stress in Web.

handle this diagonal compression the web can be made less slender by decreasing its depth to thickness ratio or, more commonly, by the use of **intermediate web stiffeners** (Figure 11–5).

Intermediate web stiffeners are steel plates that are spaced at particular distances along the length of the plate girder and are meant to provide stability to the web with respect to buckling. The use of intermediate stiffeners in plate girders will provide additional capacity to the girder by accepting the vertical component of the diagonal compression force that was previously mentioned. As

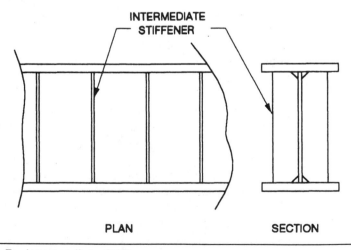

Figure 11–5   Intermediate Stiffeners.

the web of the plate girder can no longer accept any more compression force, the compression force is shifted to the intermediate stiffeners and the flanges. This behavior is known as **tension-field action** because the web will only accept the tensile forces while the compressive forces are shifted to the stiffeners and flanges. The behavior of the plate girder under this condition is very similar to that of a Pratt truss, with the stiffeners acting as compression struts (Figure 11–6). This tension field behavior is very important to the shear capacity of the plate girder and its contribution is referred to as **post buckling capacity**. This will be discussed further in section 11.4. The buckling of the web is such an important possibility that the LRFD specification will classify bending members as plate girders based on the member's web height to web thickness ratio (h/t_w). If this ratio is greater than $970/\sqrt{F_{yf}}$, then the provisions of Appendix G in the LRFD specification apply. The term F_{yf} refers to the yield strength of the girder flange since it has been determined that this will directly affect the web buckling potential.

The intermediate stiffeners typically can be placed on each side of the web, or may be located on one side only. Usually these stiffeners will extend from flange to flange or from compression flange to just above the tension flange. The latter is sometimes done to accomodate fatigue criteria on some structures. The stiffener plates are welded to the web and the flanges, although a portion of the stiffener may be "clipped" to prevent the intersection of a stiffener weld with the main longitudinal plate girder weld (Figure 11–7). Such an intersection of welds would be a very poor detail for fatigue considerations. Another type of stiffener, **bearing stiffeners** are placed in locations of large concentrated loads to help distribute the loads and to prevent the failures known as local web yielding, web crippling, or sidesway web buckling. The use and criteria concerning stiffeners will be discussed at length later in the chapter.

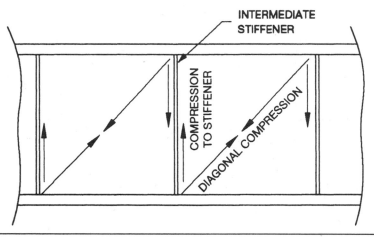

Figure 11–6   Tension-Field Action.

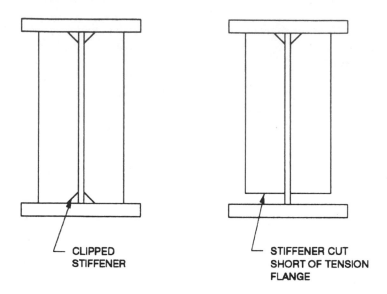

Figure 11–7 Other Intermediate Stiffener Configurations.

11.3 Plate Girder Design for Bending Moment

The design of plate girder for bending moment follows the same logic that was presented in Chapter 6 for rolled beam design. The design moment capacity of the plate girder must be greater than or equal to the required moment capacity placed on a member. This can be expressed as follows:

$$\phi_b M_n \geq M_u$$

where

$\phi_b = 0.90$, reduction factor

M_n = nominal moment capacity

M_u = required (factored) moment

The nominal moment capacity M_n of a plate girder is based on the lowest value obtained when considering three potential limit states. The three limit states are: **tension flange yielding, local buckling of the compression flange,** and **lateral torsional buckling.**

Tension flange yielding occurs when stresses in the tension flange begin to exceed the yield strength of the flange material. The nominal moment capacity for this limit state is:

$$M_n = (S_{xt})(R_e)(F_{yt}) \tag{Eq. 11–1}$$

where

S_{xt} = tension flange section modulus about the x-axis

R_e = hybrid girder factor (equal to 1.0 for a non-hybrid girder)

F_{yf} = yield strength of the flange material

The plate girder bending reduction factor R_{pg} is used to account for the decreased ability of the slender web to carry its share of the applied moment. This is due to the creation of compressive forces in the plane of the web that will cause buckling. This reduction factor can be calculated as:

$$R_{pg} = 1 - \frac{a_r}{1200 + 300a_r} \left(\frac{h}{t_w} - \frac{970}{\sqrt{F_{cr}}} \right) \leq 1.0 \qquad \text{(Eq.11–2)}$$

where

a_r = ratio of web area to compression flange area

h_c = twice the distance from the centroid to the nearest line of fasteners at the compression flange or the inside face of the compression flange when welds are used

t_w = web thickness

F_{cr} = critical compression flange stress

The critical compression flange stress, F_{cr} is the lowest value from the local buckling or lateral torsional buckling limit states.

The compression flange buckling limit states involve local buckling of the flange or lateral torsional buckling of the girder. The nominal moment capacity for the buckling limit states can be shown as:

$$M_n = (S_{xc})(R_{pg})(R_e)(F_{cr}) \qquad \text{(Eq. 11–3)}$$

where

S_{xc} = compression flange section modulus about the x axis

R_e = as previously defined

R_{pg} = plate girder bending reduction factor

F_{cr} = critical compression flange stress

To determine the value of F_{cr}, the designer must calculate the controlling mechanism of failure involving the buckling of the compression flange. This can be accomplished as follows.

The local buckling limit state is a failure mechanism in which the compression flange buckles in an isolated area due to high compressive stresses. In Chapter 6, beams that had the ability to develop their full capacity before any local buckling occurred were said to be compact. The flange compactness criteria of a plate girder is based on the flange width to thickness ratio ($b_f/2t_f$) and is referred to by the parameter λ. The flange width to thickness parameter λ, is then compared to a limit for compact behavior and a limit for noncompact behavior. The compact limit is referred to by the term λ_p and the noncompact limit is referred to by the term λ_r. The expressions that define these compactness limits are:

$$\lambda = b_f/2t_f$$

$$\lambda_p = 65/\sqrt{F_{yf}}$$

$$\lambda_r = 230/\sqrt{F_{yf}/k_c}$$

where

F_{yf} = yield strength of the flange material

$k_c = 4\sqrt{h/t_w}$ and $0.35 \leq k_c \leq 0.763$

Should a plate girder's flange width to thickness parameter, λ, be less than the compactness limit, λ_p, then flange yielding will control the bending mechanism.

In this case the critical compression flange stress, F_{cr} is defined as:

$$F_{cr} = F_{yf} \tag{Eq.11-4}$$

Should a plate girder's flange width to thickness parameter, λ, fall between the compact (λ_p) and the noncompact (λ_r) limits, then failure will occur by inelastic flange buckling. In this case the critical compression flange stress F_{cr} is defined as:

$$F_{cr} = C_b F_{yf} \left[1 - \frac{1}{2} \left(\frac{\lambda - \lambda_p}{\lambda_r - \lambda_p} \right) \right] \leq F_{yf} \tag{Eq.11-5}$$

where

$C_b = 1.0$
$\lambda, \lambda_p, \lambda_r$ = previously defined

Should a plate girder's flange width to thickness parameter λ, fall above the noncompact limit λ_r, the flange then behaves as a slender element and failure occurs by elastic buckling. In this case the critical compression flange stress F_{cr}, is defined as:

$$F_{cr} = C_{pg}/\lambda^2 \tag{Eq. 11-6}$$

where

$C_{pg} = 26,200k_c$

The other possibility of failure related to compression flange buckling is lateral torsional buckling. This limit state involves the slender flange element buckling laterally out of plane and is accompanied by a torsional component. This behavior is dependent on a girder's unbraced length of the compression flange l_b and can be alleviated by providing more lateral bracing. The critical compression flange stress F_{cr} is again based on a slenderness parameter, λ. However this parameter accounts for buckling of the full compression flange and 1/6 of the web. The slenderness parameter for lateral torsional buckling is:

$$\lambda = l_b/r_T$$

where

l_b = unbraced length of the compression flange

r_T = radius of gyration of the compression flange

This slenderness parameter of the beam under consideration is then compared with the limits to determine whether failure will occur by yielding, inelastic lateral torsional buckling, or elastic lateral torsional buckling. The slenderness parameter that divides the yielding limit state from the inelastic buckling limit state is termed λ_p while the parameter that divides the inelastic buckling limit state from the elastic limit state is termed λ_r. These two parameters are defined below:

$$\lambda_p = 300/\sqrt{F_{yf}}$$

$$\lambda_r = 756/\sqrt{F_{yf}}$$

Should a plate girder's compression flange slenderness parameter λ be less than the slenderness limit λ_p, then flange yielding will control the bending mechanism. In this case the critical compression flange stress F_{cr} is defined as:

$$F_{cr} = F_{yf} \qquad \text{(Eq.11–7)}$$

Should a plate girder's compression flange slenderness parameter λ fall between the inelastic (λ_p) and the elastic (λ_r) limits, then failure will occur by inelastic lateral torsional buckling. In this case the critical compression flange stress F_{cr}, is defined by Eq. 11–8 (which is equivalent to Eq. 11–5):

$$F_{cr} = C_b F_{yf} \left[1 - \frac{1}{2} \left(\frac{\lambda - \lambda_p}{\lambda_r - \lambda_p} \right) \right] \leq F_{yf} \quad \text{(Eq.11–8)}$$

where

C_b = as defined in Chapter 6

$\lambda, \lambda_p, \lambda_r$ = previously defined

Should a plate girder's compression flange slenderness parameter λ fall above the elastic buckling limit λ_r, the flange then behaves as a slender element and failure occurs by elastic lateral torsional buckling. In this case the critical compression flange stress, F_{cr}, is defined as:

$$F_{cr} = C_{pg}/\lambda^2 \qquad\qquad\qquad \text{(Eq. 11–9)}$$

where

$C_{pg} = 286,000\ C_b$

C_b = bending coefficient discussed in Chapter 6

In summary, the design moment capacity of a plate girder is the smaller value obtained by tension flange yielding (Eq. 11–1) or compression flange failure (Eq. 11–3). The compression flange has three possible limit states: yielding, local buckling of the compression flange and lateral torsionl buckling. The controlling compression flange limit state is the smallest of all calculated possibilities. The following example illustrates the determination of design moment capacity of a plate girder using the LRFD cirteria.

EXAMPLE 11.1

Determine the nominal moment capacity of the plate girder shown below. All elements of the girder are made from A36 steel and the unbraced length of the girder is assumed to be 30 feet. Assume $C_b = 1.0$.

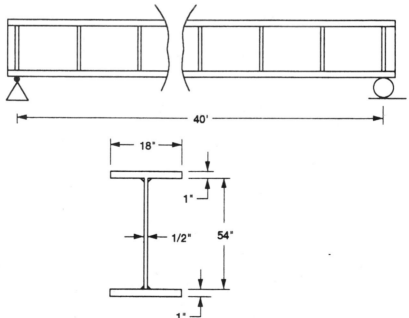

To begin, the cross-sectional properties of the plate girder should be found. These can be summarized as:

Flange area = 18 in. × 1 in. = 18 in.² (.0116 m²)

Web area = 54 in. × 1/2 in. = 27 in.²   (.0174 m²)

$I_x = (1/12bh^3)_{web} + 2(Ad^2)_{flange}$

$\quad = (1/12)(.5 \text{ in.})(54 \text{ in.})^3 + 2(18 \text{ in.}^2)(27.5 \text{ in.})^2$

$\quad = 33,786 \text{ in.}^4 \ (.014 \text{ m}^4)$

$S_{xc} = S_{xt} = 33,786 \text{ in.}^4/28 \text{ in.} = 1206.6 \text{ in.}^3 \ (.0197 \text{ m}^3)$

To find the radius of gyration of the compression flange (r_T) we must first calculate the moment of inertia about the compression flange's weak axis I_y. This moment of inertia is to be calculated for the compression flange plus 1/6 the depth of the web. The value of r_T can then be found as:

$I_y = (1/12bh^3)_{flange} + (1/12bh^3)1/6_{web}$

$\quad = 1/12(1 \text{ in.})(18 \text{ in.})^3 + 1/12(9 \text{ in.})(.5 \text{ in.})^3 = 486.1 \text{ in.}^4 \quad (.0002 \text{ m}^4)$

Area of the compression flange (A_{cf}) for r_T calculation would be as follows:

$A_{cf} = 18 \text{ in.}^2 + 1/6(54 \text{ in.})(.5 \text{ in.}) = 22.5 \text{ in.}^2 \ (.0145 \text{ m}^2)$

$r_T = \sqrt{I_y/A_{cf}} = \sqrt{486.1/22.5} = 4.64 \text{ in. } (.1178 \text{ m})$

Checking the lateral torsional buckling criteria we find:

$\lambda = l_b/r_T = 30 \text{ ft.} \times 12 \text{ in./ft.}/4.64 \text{ in.}$

$\quad = 77.6$

$\lambda_p = 300/\sqrt{F_{yf}} = 300/\sqrt{36} \text{ ksi} = 50$

$\lambda_r = 756/\sqrt{F_{yf}} = 756/\sqrt{36} \text{ ksi} = 126$

Since the girder's compression flange slenderness parameter falls between λ_p and λ_r, the critical compression flange stress is controlled by inelastic lateral torsional buckling and calculated as:

$$F_{cr} = 1.0(36 \text{ ksi}) \left[1 - \frac{1}{2} \left(\frac{77.6 - 50}{126 - 50} \right) \right] = 29.46 \text{ ksi} \qquad (\text{Eq.11–8})$$

$$(1.0(248.2\text{MPa}) \left[1 - \frac{1}{2} \left(\frac{77.6 - 50}{126 - 50} \right) \right] = 203.1 \text{ MPa})$$

Checking the criteria for local flange buckling we first calculate the girder's flange width to thickness parameter and then compare that to the appropriate limits. This can be done as follows:

$$\lambda = b_f/2t_f = 18 \text{ in.}/2(.5 \text{ in.}) = 18$$

$$\lambda_p = 65/\sqrt{F_{yf}} = 65/\sqrt{36} = 10.83$$

$$\lambda_r = 230/\sqrt{36/.385} = 23.78$$

Since the girder's parameter falls between the λ_p and λ_r limits, the critical compression flange stress for local flange buckling is calculated from Eq. 11–5 as follows:

$$F_{cr} = 1.0(36 \text{ ksi}) \left[1 - \frac{1}{2} \left(\frac{18 - 10.83}{23.78 - 10.83} \right) \right] = 26.1 \text{ ksi} \qquad \text{(Eq.11–5)}$$

$$(1.0(248.2\text{Mpa}) \left[1 - \frac{1}{2} \left(\frac{18 - 10.83}{23.78 - 10.83} \right) \right] = 180 \text{ MPa})$$

Therefore the controlling compression flange stress is 26.1 ksi for local flange buckling since this is smaller than the stress for lateral torsional buckling. Before calculating either the moment capacity based on the tension flange yield or the compression flange buckling, we must first calculate the plate girder reduction factor from Eq. 11–2 as follows:

$$A_r = 27 \text{ in.}^2/22.5 \text{ in.}^2 = 1.2$$

$$R_{pg} = 1 - \frac{a_r}{1200 + 300a_r} \left(\frac{h}{t_w} - \frac{970}{\sqrt{F_{cr}}} \right) \le 1.0 \qquad \text{(Eq.11–2)}$$

$$R_{pg} = 1 - \frac{1.2}{1200 + 300(1.2)} \left(108 - \frac{970}{\sqrt{26.1}} \right) = 1.06$$

but this must always be less than or equal to 1.0, therefore use 1.0.

Now calculating the nominal moment capacity of the plate girder based on tension flange yield from Eq. 11–1 we find:

$$M_n = (S_{xt})(R_e)(F_{yt}) \qquad \text{(Eq. 11–1)}$$

$$= (1206.6 \text{ in.}^3)(1.0)(36 \text{ ksi})/12 \text{ in./ft.} = 3619.8 \text{ kip-ft.}$$

$$(= (.0197 \text{ m}^3)(1.0)(248.2\text{MPa}) = 4.89\text{MN or } 4890\text{KN-m})$$

Calculating the nominal moment capacity of the plate girder based on compression flange buckling from Eq. 11–3 we find:

$$M_n = (S_{xc})(R_{pg})(R_c)(F_{cr}) \qquad\qquad \text{(Eq. 11–3)}$$
$$= (1206.6 \text{ in.}^3)(1.0)(1.0)(26.1 \text{ ksi})/12 \text{ in./ft.} = 2624 \text{ kip-ft.}$$
$$(= .0197 \text{ m}^3)(1.0)(180\text{MPa}) = 3.55\text{MN or } 3550\text{KN-m})$$

Since the compression flange buckling nominal strength is smaller, it controls and therefore the nominal moment capacity for this plate girder is 2624 kip-ft.

11.4 Plate Girder Design for Shear

The shear strength of plate girders is a very important item to consider in their design. The web of the plate girder is usually long and thin, thereby increasing the possibility of failure for this element by buckling before it has a chance to yield. The shear strength of the plate girder must again follow the methodology as was found with moment capacity, namely that its design shear strength must equal or exceed the ultimate factored shear. This can be expressed as follows:

$$\phi_v V_n \geq V_u$$

where

$\phi_v = 0.90$, reduction factor
V_n = nominal shear capacity
V_u = required (factored) shear

The limit states, regarding the behavior of the web, are yielding of the web and buckling of the web. The web buckling behavior may include the capacity added by the plate girder's post-buckling strength. This post-buckling strength occurs if the girder is able to develop tension field action that was discussed earlier in the chapter. Tension field action is the redistribution of diagonal compressive stresses in the web to the intermediate stiffeners and the flange. This can only be accomplished if the stiffeners are spaced close enough together.

The LRFD specification provides two equations for calculating the nominal shear capacity of a plate girder. The first equation is based on the limit state of web yielding that would occur if the web was prevented from buckling. The equation for the nominal shear capacity for the web yielding scenario is used only when the slenderness of the web is small enough to preclude buckling. This occurs when

$$h/t_w \leq 187\sqrt{k/F_{yw}}$$

where

$$k = 5 + (5/(a/h)^2)$$

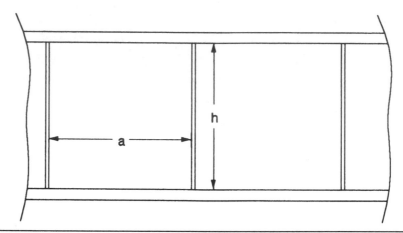

Figure 11–8   a/h Ratio

F_{yw} = specified minimum web yield stress

The value k is a web buckling coefficient and is based on the **aspect ratio** (a/h) which is ratio of clear distance between the stiffeners (a) to the clear height of the web (h) (Figure 11–8). If the aspect ratio of a plate girder exceeds 3.0, the value of k shall be taken as 5.0.

When the h/t_w ratio meets the aforementioned criteria the nominal shear capacity of a plate girder is:

$$V_n = 0.6A_w F_{yw} \qquad \text{(Eq. 11–9)}$$

where

A_w = area of the web

F_{yw} = specified minimum web yield stress

The web buckling limit state calculates a nominal shear capacity based on the element's buckling and post-buckling strength. Post-buckling strength is attained through tension-field action, which can only occur if the stiffeners are properly spaced. The nominal shear strength for the web buckling limit state is used only when

$$h/t_w > 187\sqrt{k/F_{yw}}$$

and the nominal shear capacity is given as:

$$V_n = 0.6(A_w)F_{yw}\left(C_v + \frac{1 - C_v}{1.15\sqrt{1 + (a/h)^2}}\right) \qquad \text{(Eq. 11–10)}$$

$$C_v = \frac{187\sqrt{k/F_{yw}}}{h/t_w} \text{ when } 187\sqrt{\frac{k}{F_{yw}}} \le h/t_w \le 234\sqrt{\frac{k}{F_{yw}}}$$

$$C_v = \frac{44000k}{(h/t_w)^2 F_{yw}} \text{ when } h/t_w > 234\sqrt{\frac{k}{F_{yw}}}$$

The C_v term is the ratio of critical web stress to shear yield stress of the web steel. It is used in the nominal shear stress equations because the stress level where shear buckling occurs is easier to express as a function of the web yield stress F_{yw}. The web yield stress F_{yw} is multiplied by the C_v factor to, in effect, express the critical buckling stress due to shear.

The end panel (which is the last web panel defined by the stiffeners at the girder end) cannot develop tension-field action due to the fact that the forces that need to be transferred to the flange are unbalanced. Tension-field action also cannot be developed when the a/h ratio exceeds 3.0. In these cases the nominal shear capacity is given as:

$$V_n = (0.6)(A_w)(F_{yw})C_v \tag{Eq. 11–11}$$

where all terms are as previously defined.

Therefore shear strength of a plate girder can have two potential limit states, web yielding and web buckling. The limit state that controls is based on the h/t_w ratio of the plate girder that is compared to the appropriate LRFD limit. Should buckling be the controlling limit state, a determination must be made concerning the ability of the girder to develop post-buckling strength due to tension-field action. Equation 11–10 will be used if post-buckling strength can be developed, while equation 11–11 will be used when post-buckling strength cannot be developed, such as in the case of end panels.

The following example illustrates the use of the LRFD criteria regarding shear for plate girders.

EXAMPLE 11.2

Determine the nominal shear capacity of the plate girder that was used in Example 1 and is shown below. All elements of the girder are made from A36 steel and the unbraced length of the girder is assumed to be 20 feet.

A determination should be made as to the appropriate limit state that controls: either web yield or web buckling. Calculating the h/t_w ratio we find the following:

h/t_w = 54 in./.5 in. = 108

This ratio must be compared to the following limit:

$187\sqrt{k/F_{yw}}$

where

$k = 5 + (5/(a/h)^2)$
a = clear distance between stiffener = 47 in.
h = clear web height = 54 in.

Therefore

$k = 5 + 5/(47/54)^2 = 11.6$

and

$187\sqrt{k/F_{yw}} = 187\sqrt{11.6/36 \text{ ksi}} = 106.1$

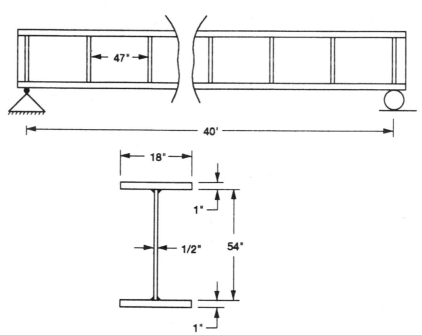

Since the plate girder's h/t_w ratio is 108, which is greater than the limit dividing web yielding from web buckling, the limit state will be web buckling. Therefore, the nominal shear capacity will be calculated from Eq. 11–10 as follows:

$$V_n = 0.6(A_w)F_{yw}\left(C_v + \frac{1 - C_v}{1.15\sqrt{1 + (a/h)^2}}\right) \qquad \text{(Eq. 11–10)}$$

$$C_v = \frac{187\sqrt{k/F_{yw}}}{h/t_w} \text{ when } 187\sqrt{\frac{k}{F_{yw}}} \leq h/t_w \leq 234\sqrt{\frac{k}{F_{yw}}}$$

$$C_v = \frac{44000k}{(h/t_w)^2 F_{yw}} \text{ when } h/t_w > 234\sqrt{\frac{k}{F_{yw}}}$$

where

$A_w = 27 \text{ in.}^2 \qquad (.0174 \text{ m}^2)$
$F_{yw} = 36 \text{ ksi} \qquad (248.2 \text{ MPa})$
$C_v = (187\sqrt{k/F_{yw}})/(h/t_w)$
$\quad = (187\sqrt{11.6/36 \text{ ksi}})/(108) = .983$
$a/h = 47/54 = .87$

Therefore calculating Eq. 11–10 yields:

$$V_n = 0.6(27 \text{ in.}^2)(36 \text{ ksi})\left(.983 + \frac{1 - .983}{1.15\sqrt{1 + (.87)^2}}\right)$$

$$= 0.6(27 \text{ in.}^2)(36 \text{ ksi})(.994) = 579.8 \text{ kips}$$

$$(= 0.6(.0174 \text{ m}^2)(248.2 \text{ MPa})(.994) = 2.576 \text{ MN or } 2576 \text{ KN})$$

The end panels cannot develop the post-buckling strength and the nominal strength for these is calculated from Eq. 11–11:

$$V_n = (0.6)(A_w)(F_{yw})C_v \qquad \text{(Eq. 11–11)}$$

$$= 0.6(27 \text{ in.2})(36 \text{ ksi})(.983) = 573.3 \text{ kips}$$

$$(= 0.6(.0174 \text{ m}^2)(248.2 \text{MPa})(.983) = 2.547 \text{MN or } 2547 \text{KN})$$

Therefore if this is a simply supported beam with the stiffeners as shown, the nominal shear capacity is controlled by the end panels and is 573.3 kips. The design shear capacity is attained by multiplying this value by 0.90 as follows:

$$\phi_v V_n = (0.90)(573.3 \text{ kips}) = 516 \text{ kips}$$

$$(= 0.90(2547 \text{KN}) = 2292 \text{KN})$$

11.5   Intermediate and Bearing Stiffeners

There are two types of stiffeners used in plate girders. Those used to increase the shear capacity of the girder by allowing the girder to develop tension-field action are referred to as **intermediate stiffeners**. These intermediate stiffeners are spaced along the beam at a spacing necessary to achieve the tension-field behavior. Stiffeners used to distribute the load from concentrated loads or reactions are referred to as **bearing stiffeners**. These are typically placed in pairs and are directly in line with the concentrated load or reaction.

Intermediate stiffeners are typically designed so that buckling due to the shear stresses will not occur. The stability of the girder's web are related by the parameters h/t_w and a/h (previously discussed). When these two parameters are kept low enough, the intermediate stiffeners can actively accept the vertical compression component of the diagonal shear force and therefore achieve additional strength called post-buckling strength.

Intermediate stiffeners are not needed when the girder's web height to thickness ratio, h/t_w, is less than or equal to the following:

$$187 \sqrt{k/F_{yw}}$$

Since $k = 5$ when no stiffeners are used, the above equation can be rearranged and h/t_w ratio needs to be less than or equal to the following for no stiffeners to be used:

$$418/\sqrt{F_{yw}}$$

When the h/t_w ratio for the plate girder exceeds this limit, intermediate stiffeners will be needed. The minimum moment of inertia for an intermediate stiffener about its face, that is in contact with the web, can be given as:

$$I_{st} = at_w^3 j \qquad\qquad \text{(Eq. 11–12)}$$

where

I_{st} = stiffener moment of inertia

a = clear spacing between stiffeners

t_w = web thickness

$j = (2.5/(a/h)^2) - 2 \geq 0.5$

The minimum area of intermediate stiffener to be used is based on the ability of the stiffener to handle the compressive forces that need to be developed under tension-field action. This is given by the LRFD specification as:

$$A_{st} = \frac{F_{yw}}{F_{yst}} \left[.15 D h t_w (1 - C_v) \frac{V_u}{\phi_v V_n} - 18 t_w^2 \right] \geq 0 \qquad\qquad \text{(Eq. 11–13)}$$

where

A_{st} = minimum stiffener area

F_{yw} = specified web yield strength

F_{yst} = specified stiffener yield strength

C_v = coefficient defined in previous section

D = 1 for stiffeners placed in pairs and 2.4 for single plate stiffeners

V_u = required (factored) shear force

$\phi_v V_n$ = design shear capacity

Intermediate stiffeners, when required, are typically spaced so as to achieve an increase in shear capacity of the web. The improved behavior will depend to an extent on the a/h ratio of the girder web. As these stiffeners are spaced more closely, the girder is able to achieve its upper limit state of web buckling; however, in many cases we would only want to provide a design shear capacity $\phi_v V_n$ greater than the required shear capacity V_u. Therefore the AISC provides design charts as listed in Table 11–1. These charts express nominal shear capacity (relative to web area) as a function of different a/h ratios and h/t_w ratios. Proper spacing (or proper a/h ratio) can then be seen relative to the needed design shear capacity. Example 11.3 illustrates the use of this particular chart.

Bearing stiffeners are typically placed in pairs, one on each side of the web, to help reinforce the web in regions of concentrated loads or reactions. This reinforcement is needed so that the web will not experience **local yielding, web crippling,** or **buckling due to sidesway** of the web. Bearing stiffeners must be used when the required bearing force R_u is greater than the design bearing capacity of the girder ϕR_n. The design bearing capacity of the girder is based on the smallest of the three aforementioned limit states. However, if bearing stiffeners are used, the limit states regarding web yielding, web crippling, and sidesway buckling do not need to be checked.

For local web buckling, the reduction factor ϕ is taken as 1.0 the nominal bearing capacity is given by Eq. 11–14 when the concentrated load is greater than the depth of the girder from its end:

$$R_n = (5k + N)F_{yw}t_w \qquad \text{(Eq. 11–14)}$$

When the load is applied near the end of the member the nominal bearing capacity is given by Eq. 11–15:

$$R_n = (2.5k + N)F_{yw}t_w \qquad \text{(Eq. 11–15)}$$

where

F_{yw} = specified yield stress

N = length of bearing

Table 11–1   Plate Girder Nominal Shear Capacity Design Chart

(*Italic* values indicate gross area, as percent of ($h \times t_w$) required for pairs of intermediate stiffeners of 36 ksi yield stress steel with $V_u/\phi V_n = 1.0$.)[a]

$\dfrac{h}{t_w}$	Aspect Ratio a/h: Stiffener Spacing to Web Depth													
	0.5	0.6	0.7	0.8	0.9	1.0	1.2	1.4	1.6	1.8	2.0	2.5	3.0	Over 3.0[c]
60	19.4	19.4	19.4	19.4	19.4	19.4	19.4	19.4	19.4	19.4	19.4	19.4	19.4	19.4
70	19.4	19.4	19.4	19.4	19.4	19.4	19.4	19.4	19.4	19.4	19.4	19.4	19.4	19.4
80	19.4	19.4	19.4	19.4	19.4	19.4	19.4	19.4	19.4	19.4	19.1	18.6	18.3	16.9
90	19.4	19.4	19.4	19.4	19.4	19.4	19.4	19.0	18.5	18.2	17.8	17.3	16.8	14.7
100	19.4	19.4	19.4	19.4	19.4	19.3	18.6	18.1	17.6	17.2	16.6	15.6	14.9	11.9
110	19.4	19.4	19.4	19.4	19.1	18.7	17.9	17.2	16.3	15.6	15.1	14.0	13.3	9.8
120	19.4	19.4	19.4	19.0	18.5	18.1	17.0	16.0	15.1	14.4	13.9	12.8	12.0	8.3
130	19.4	19.4	19.1	18.6	18.1	17.4	16.1	15.1	14.2	13.5	12.9	11.8	11.0	7.0
140	19.4	19.3	18.7	18.2	17.4	16.6	15.4	14.4	13.5	12.8	12.2	11.0	10.2	6.1
150	19.4	19.0	18.4	17.5	16.7	16.0	14.8	13.8	12.9	12.2	11.6	10.4	9.6	5.3
160	19.3	18.7	17.9	17.0	16.2	15.5	14.3	13.3	12.4	11.7	11.1	9.9		4.6
170	19.1	18.4	17.4	16.6	15.8	15.1	13.9	12.9	12.0	11.3 *0.3*	10.7 *0.4*			4.1
180	18.9	18.0	17.1	16.2	15.5	14.8	13.6 *0.2*	12.6 *0.7*	11.7 *1.1*	11.0 *1.3*	10.4 *1.5*			3.7
200	18.4	17.3	16.4	15.6 *0.1*	14.9 *0.9*	14.2 *1.4*	13.1 *2.1*	12.0 *2.5*	11.2 *2.8*					3.0
220	17.8	16.9	16.0 *1.1*	15.2 *2.0*	14.5 *2.6*	13.8 *3.0*	12.7 *3.6*							2.5
240	17.4	16.5 *1.5*	15.7 *2.7*	14.9 *3.4*	14.2 *3.9*	13.5 *4.3*								2.1
260	17.1 *1.3*	16.2 *3.0*	15.4 *4.0*	14.6 *4.6*	14.0 *5.0*	13.3 *5.4*								1.8
280	16.8 *2.7*	16.0 *4.2*	15.2 *5.0*	14.4 *5.6*										
300	16.6 *3.9*	15.8 *5.2*	15.0 *5.9*											
320	16.4 *4.9*	15.6 *6.0*												

[a]For area of single-angle and single-plate stiffeners, or when $V_u/\phi V_n < 1.0$, see Formula A-G4-2.
[b]For end-panels and all panels in hybrid and web-tapered plate girders use Table 10-36.
[c]Same as for Table 10-36.
Note: Girders so proportioned that the computed shear is less than that given in right-hand column do not require intermediate stiffeners.

k = distance from outer flange face to web toe of fillet

t_w = web thickness

For the web crippling limit state, the reduction factor ø is equal to 0.75 and the nominal bearing capacity is equal to the following.

When the load is applied at a distance greater than or equal to $d/2$ from the member end:

$$R_n = 135t_w^2 \left[1 + 3\left(\frac{N}{d}\right)\left(\frac{t_w}{t_f}\right)^{1.5}\right]\sqrt{F_{yw}t_f/t_w} \qquad \text{(Eq. 11–16)}$$

When the load is applied within this $d/2$ distance, the nominal capacity is equal to:

$$R_n = 68t_w^2 \left[1 + 3\left(\frac{N}{d}\right)\left(\frac{t_w}{t_f}\right)^{1.5}\right]\sqrt{F_{yw}t_f/t_w} \quad \text{when } N/d \leq 0.2 \qquad \text{(Eq. 11–17)}$$

where

d = girder depth

t_f = flange thickness

$$R_n = 68t_w^2 \left[1 + \left(\frac{4N}{d} - 0.2\right)\left(\frac{t_w}{t_f}\right)^{1.5}\right]\sqrt{F_{yw}t_f/t_w} \quad \text{when } N/d > 0.2 \quad \text{(Eq. 11–17a)}$$

For the limit state of sidesway web buckling, the reduction factor ø is taken as 0.85 and the nominal bearing capacity is calculated as follows:

When the loaded flange is restrained from rotation and $(h/t_w)/(l/b_f)$ is less than 2.3:

$$R_n = \frac{C_r t_w^3 t_f}{h_2}\left[1 + 0.4\left(\frac{h/t_w}{l/b_f}\right)^3\right] \qquad \text{(Eq. 11–18)}$$

When the loaded flange is not restrained against rotation and $(h/t_w)/(l/b_f)$ is less than 1.7:

$$R_n = \frac{C_r t_w^3 t_f}{h_2}\left[0.4\left(\frac{h/t_w}{l/b_f}\right)^3\right] \qquad \text{(Eq. 11–19)}$$

where

l = largest laterally unbraced length along a flange

b_f = flange width

t_w = web thickness

h = clear web depth

C_r = 960,000 when $M_u < M_y$ at location of force

= 480,00 when $M_u \geq M_y$ at location of force

If the ratio of $(h_c/t_w)/(l/b_f)$ exceeds either 2.3 or 1.7 in Eq. 11–18 and 11–19 the equation need not be checked.

Upon ascertaining that bearing stiffeners should be used or when checking the feasibility of a bearing stiffener, the stiffener should meet the following width to thickness ratio as specified in the LRFD specification:

$b/t < 95/\sqrt{F_y}$

Upon meeting this criteria, the bearing stiffeners should also meet a bearing criterion and a column stability criterion to ensure proper behavior. The design bearing strength of a stiffener is calculated from Eq. 11–20

$$\phi R_n = 2.0 F_y A_{pb} \qquad\qquad\qquad (Eq. 11\text{–}20)$$

where

$\phi = 0.75$

A_{pb} = contact area of the bearing stiffener (Figure 11–9)

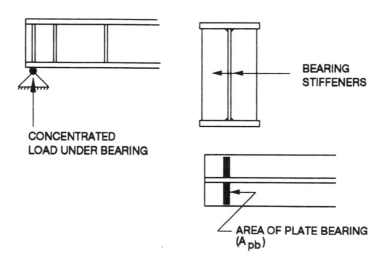

CONCENTRATED
LOAD UNDER BEARING

BEARING
STIFFENERS

AREA OF PLATE BEARING
(A_{pb})

Figure 11–9 Use of Bearing Stiffeners in a Plate Girder.

The column stability criterion accesses the ability of the bearing stiffeners to transmit loads as if they were columns. The effective length of the stiffeners is taken as:

$$Kl = 0.75h$$

where

h = the clear web height

and the slenderness ratio of the stiffeners is then calculated using the radius of gyration as approximately:

$$r = 0.25b$$

where

b = the combined stiffener width, generally taken as the flange width minus an inch or so. This is because bearing stiffener usually cover almost the complete flange width.

The column stability limit state can then be assessed in the same manner as in Chapter 5, by calculating a design column capacity $\phi_c P_n$ and comparing that to the factored concentrated load P_u. Remember from Chapter 5 that the following is true:

$$\phi_c P_n \geq P_u$$

where

ϕ_c = .85, column reduction factor

$P_n = A_g F_{cr}$, nominal column strength

P_u = maximum factored column load

Also remember that the column design stress $\phi_c F_{cr}$ can quickly be calculated from using the AISC chart listed in Table 5–1.

Bearing stiffeners should also meet the LRFD guidelines concerning the ability of the stiffener welds to transfer shear stresses to the web. The LRFD specification should be consulted regarding these guidelines and other guidelines regarding the interaction of shear and moment as they are beyond the scope of this text. The following example illustrates the application of the intermediate and bearing stiffener requirements.

EXAMPLE 11.3

For the girder shown below, check the intermediate and bearing stiffeners per requirements by the LRFD specification. All steel is A36. Assume the bearing stiffeners will extend to within 1 inch of the edge of the flange.

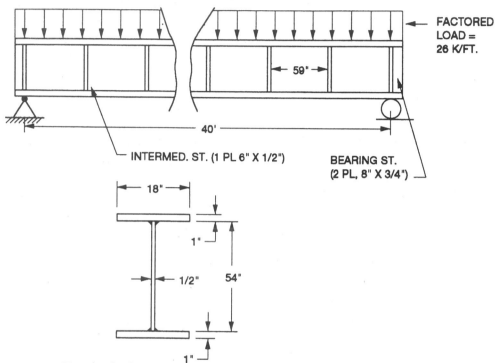

To check the intermediate stiffeners we must first calculate the required shear capacity V_u and the design shear capacity of the beam, $\phi_v V_n$. The required or factored shear capacity V_u is conservatively taken as the maximum shear at the reaction which is 520 kips. Before this, the designer can check to make sure stiffeners are needed by comparing the h/t_w ratio to the following:

$h/t_w > 418/\sqrt{F_{yw}}$ — stiffeners needed

$108 > 418/\sqrt{36}$

$108 > 69.6$ — therefore need stiffeners

Next, a determination should be made as to the appropriate limit state that controls the nominal shear strength of the web: web yield or web buckling. Calculating the h/t_w ratio we find the following:

$h/t_w = 54$ in./.5 in. = 108

This ratio must be compared to the following limit:

$187\sqrt{k/F_{yw}}$

where

$k = 5/5 + (a/h)^2$

a = clear distance between stiffener = 59 in.

h = clear web height = 54 in.

Therefore

$k = 5 + 5/(59/54)^2 = 9.2$ and

$187\sqrt{k/F_{yw}} = 187\sqrt{9.2/36 \text{ ksi}} = 94.5$

Since the plate girder's h/t_w ratio is 108, which is greater than the limit dividing web yielding from web buckling, the limit state will be web buckling. Therefore, the nominal shear capacity will be calculated from Eq. 11–10 as follows:

$$V_n = 0.6(A_w)F_{yw}\left(C_v + \frac{1 - C_v}{1.15\sqrt{1 + (a/h)^2}}\right) \qquad \text{(Eq. 11–10)}$$

$$C_v = \frac{187\sqrt{k/F_{yw}}}{h/t_w} \text{ when } 187\sqrt{\frac{k}{F_{yw}}} \le h/t_w \le 234\sqrt{\frac{k}{F_{yw}}}$$

$$C_v = \frac{44000k}{(h/t_w)^2 F_{yw}} \text{ when } h/t_w > 234\sqrt{\frac{k}{F_{yw}}}$$

where

$A_w = 27$ in.^{2} (.0174 m^2)
$F_{yw} = 36$ ksi (248.2 MPa)
$C_v = (187\sqrt{k/F_{yw}})/(h/t_w)$
$\quad = (187\sqrt{9.2/36 \text{ ksi}})/(108) = .875$

$a/h = 59/54 = 1.09$

Therefore calculating Eq. 11–10 yields:

$$V_n = 0.6(27 \text{ in.}^2)(36 \text{ ksi}).875 + \frac{1 - .875}{1.15\sqrt{1 + (1.09)^2}}$$

$$= 0.6(27 \text{ in.}^2)(36 \text{ ksi})(.95) = 553 \text{ kips}$$
$$(= 0.6(.0174 \text{ m}^2)(248.2 \text{MPa})(.95) = 2.46\text{MN or } 2462\text{KN})$$

The end panels cannot develop the post-buckling strength and the nominal strength for these is calculated from Eq. 11–11:

$$V_n = (0.6)(A_w)(F_{yw})C_v \qquad\qquad \text{(Eq. 11–11)}$$
$$= 0.6(27 \text{ in.}^2)(36 \text{ ksi})(.875) = 510.3 \text{ kips}$$
$$(= 0.6(.0174 \text{ m}^2)(248.2 \text{ MPa})(.875) = 2.26 \text{ MN or } 2267 \text{ KN})$$

Therefore the design shear capacity $\phi_v V_n$ can be conservatively taken as that for the end panel:

$$\phi_v V_n = (.90)(510.3 \text{ kips}) = 459 \text{ kips}$$
$$(= .90(2267 \text{ KN}) = 2040 \text{ KN})$$

Because the factored shear, 520 kips, exceeds the design shear strength, 459 kips, the stiffener spacing must be decreased. By entering Table 11–1 we can see that for a h/t_w ratio of 110 (our girder has $h/t_w = 108$), the design shear stress can increase to a maximum at a a/h_w ratio of 0.80. The design shear stress can be calculated by taking the tabular value of $\phi_v V_n/A_w$ equal to 19.4 ksi (133.7 MPa) and multiplying it by the area of this girder's web. This yields the following:

$$\phi_v V_n = (19.4 \text{ ksi})(27 \text{ in.}^2) = 523.8 \text{ kips}$$
$$(= (133.7\text{MPa})(.0174 \text{ m}^2) = 2.32\text{MN or } 2327\text{KN})$$

Since this exceeds the required shear capacity (520 kips), the stiffeners should be spaced at an a/h ratio of approximately 0.80. The spacing would then be:

$$(a/h)(\text{height of web}) = 0.80(54 \text{ in.}) = 43.2" \ (1.09 \text{ m})$$

It would be adequate to then space at roughly 43 inch center to center spacing of the stiffeners for the first two panels. After this point the required shear has been reduced to the point of having stiffeners at the original spacing. The area of the intermediate stiffeners is calculated as:

$$A_{st} = \frac{F_{yw}}{F_{yst}}\left[.15Dht_w(1 - C_v)\frac{V_u}{\phi_v V_n} - 18t_w^2\right] \geq 0 \qquad\qquad \text{(Eq. 11–13)}$$

where

A_{st} = minimum stiffener area

F_{yw} = 36 ksi

F_{yst} = 36 ksi

C_v = coefficient defined in previous section = .875

D = 2.4 (the stiffener is single)

$$A_{st} = \frac{36 \text{ ksi}}{36 \text{ ksi}} \left[.15(2.4)(54 \text{ in.})(.5 \text{ in.})(1 - .875)\frac{520}{532.8} - 18(.5 \text{ in.})^2 \right]$$

$$= -3.28 \text{ in.}^2$$

Since the required area of the stiffener is negative, it indicates that the area of the stiffener is not critical. Therefore the size of stiffeners as originally shown will be adequate.

Since bearing stiffeners are already provided at each reaction, the limit states of web yielding, web crippling, and sidesway buckling do not have to be checked. The bearing stiffeners should be checked for column stability and bearing capacity using the maximum factored reaction that is 520 kips. Checking the column stability requirement, we would first calculate the effective length of the bearing stiffener as:

$$Kl = (0.75(54 \text{ in.}) = 40.5 \text{ in.}(1.03 \text{ m})$$

The bearing stiffeners extend to within one inch of the edge of the flange therefore the bearing stiffener width can be taken as 16 inches. Calculating the approximate radius of gyration of the bearing stiffeners we find:

$$r = 0.25(16 \text{ in.}) = 4 \text{ in.}(.10 \text{ m})$$

The slenderness ratio is calculated as:

$$Kl/r = 40.5 \text{ in.}/4 \text{ in.} = 10.125$$

From Table 5–1, the design axial stress, $\phi c \, F_{cr}$, is 30.43 ksi and the design axial capacity is:

$$\phi_c P_n = A_g \phi_c F_{cr}$$

where

A_g = stiffener area = (16 in.)(.75) = 12 in.^{2}

Therefore

$$\phi_c P_n = (30.43 \text{ ksi})(12 \text{ in.}^2) = 365 \text{ kips}$$
$$(= (209.8 \text{ MPa})(.0077 \text{ m}^2) = 1.624 \text{ MN or } 1624 \text{ KN})$$

Since this is less than the factored axial reaction of 520 kips, the stiffener size must be increased. A thickness of 1.125 in. is one possibility that will work adequately.

If the stiffeners are now 1.125 inches thick, check the bearing criterion by Eq. 11–20:

$$\phi R_n = 0.75(2.0F_y A_{pb}) \qquad\qquad \text{(Eq.11–20)}$$

where

$A_{pb} = (16 \text{ in.} - 1 \text{ in.})(1.125 \text{ in.}) = 16.87 \text{ in.}^2$

$\phi R_n = 0.75(2.0)(36 \text{ ksi})(16.87 \text{ in.}^2) = 910 \text{ kips}$

$(= 0.75(2.0)(248.2\text{MPa})(.011 \text{ m}^2) = 4.05\text{MN})$

This is greater than the factored reaction of 520 kips, therefore it is adequate. The 1 inch subtraction in the above equation for A_{pb} is to conservatively account for the welds along the web.

Finally, checking the stiffeners width to thickness criteria, we find the following:

$b = 7.75$ in. (for single stiffener)

$t = 1.125$ in.

$b/t = 6.88 < 95/\sqrt{F_y}$ —*good.*

Summarizing, the spacing of the intermediate stiffeners should be decreased in the end regions to approximately 43 inches. Space the first two panels at 43 inches. The remaining intermediate stiffeners can be spaced at approximately the original spacing of 59 inches. Calculating the overall girder dimensions, we find that these stiffeners can be placed at a spacing of 60.5 inches which will work out fine. The bearing stiffeners should be placed on each side of the web, over the reactions as shown, and be increased to 1.125 inches thick.

Design Considerations for Plate Girders

As one can see by the last example, the design of plate girders can be quite an involved project. Although it is beyond the scope of this book to design a plate girder "from scratch", the concepts involved in preliminary sizing of the web and flange plates will be addressed in this section.

The overall depth of a plate girder can be estimated to approximately be 1/10 the span length for most applications. The web size can be estimated by comparing the h/t_w ratio that will prevent vertical flange buckling into the web. This limit state will depend on the a/h ratios as follows:

When $a/h \leq 1.5$:

$h/t_w \leq 2000/\sqrt{F_{yf}}$

When $a/h > 1.5$

$$h/t_w \leq 14{,}000/\sqrt{F_{yf}(F_{yf} + 16.5)}$$

where

h = clear web height
t_w = web thickness
F_{yf} = flange yield stress

Using the approximate 1/10 of span guideline, the designer can estimate a total depth of plate girder and then after subtracting out an estimated flange thickness, the designer can arrive at a preliminary web thickness using the above limits.

The flanges can be estimated by calculating the section modulus of the girder about its x axis, which can be expressed approximately as:

$$S_x = (t_w h^2/6) + A_f h \qquad \text{(Eq. 11–21)}$$

where

t_w = web thickness

h = web height

A_f = flange area

Recognizing that the nominal moment capacity, which the plate girder must achieve, can be expressed as:

$$M_n = M_u/\phi$$

and that nominal moment capacity was expressed as:

$$M_n = (S_{xc})(R_{pg})(R_e)(F_{cr}) \qquad \text{(Eq. 11–3)}$$

The section modulus required can be found by:

$$(S_x)(R_{pg})(F_{cr}) = M_u/\phi$$

or

$$S_x = M_u/(\phi)(R_{pg})(F_{cr})$$

(We are, of course, assuming a symmetrical cross-section where $S_{xc} = S_{xt} = S_x$ and $R_e = 1.0$)

Equating the section modulus required with the formula found in Eq. 11–21 to yield the area of flange required:

$$A_f = M_u/\phi h (R_{pg})(F_{cr}) - [(t_w)(h)/6] \qquad \text{(Eq. 11–22)}$$

For preliminary operations the value of R_{pg} can be assumed to be 1.0 and the value of F_{cr} can be assumed as F_y. The following example demonstrates this technique of preliminary sizing.

EXAMPLE 11.4

For the plate girder used in Example 3, use the preliminary sizing techniques to determine whether the girder may need to be resized. All steel is A36.

The approximate depth of a 40 foot long girder can be estimated to be approximately 1/10 (which in this case is 4 feet or 48 inches).

Checking the h/t_w ratio for a girder having an $a/h \leq 1.5$, we find the following:

$$h/t_w \leq 2000/\sqrt{F_{yf}}$$

$$h/t_w \leq 2000/\sqrt{36} = 333$$

Assuming the web height is two inches less than the overall depth and solving for web thickness we find:

$$t_w = h/333 = 46/333 = .14 \text{ in.}$$

Therefore a 1/4 in. × 46 in. web plate may be a possibility. Checking the required flange area by Eq. 11–22 we find the following:

Assume $R_{pg} = 1.0$ and $F_{cr} = F_y$

$$A_f = M_u/\phi h(R_{pg})(F_{cr}) - (t_w)(h)/6 \qquad \text{(Eq. 11–22)}$$

$$A_f = 5200 \text{ kip-ft.}(12)/(0.90)(46 \text{ in.})(1)(36 \text{ ksi}) - [(1/4)(46)/6] = 39.95 \text{ in.}^2$$

Each flange should be approximately 39.95 in.². Our flanges presently have 18 in.², therefore the girder definetely has to be resized.

It must be realized that if these changes are initiated, the girder would have to be redesigned per moment, shear, and stiffener guidelines.

11.6 Summary

Plate girders are beams that are formed by the welding of plates into an I-shape, a box shape, or other built-up shapes. They are used in long span situations where a rolled shape will no longer be sufficient. Typical plate girders will be deeper than the standard rolled sections, although the fabrication of such girders also has to considered when estimating overall cost. Because plate girders are typically deeper than rolled sections, many buckling types of behavior, which were not critical for rolled beams, effect both the bending and shear capacity of this member. Stiffeners can be classified as either intermediate or bearing and will be needed in many situations to help the web reach its full strength before a buckling type of failure occurs.

EXERCISES

1. For the plate girder shown below, calculate the nominal moment capacity M_n. Also calculate the design moment capacity $\phi_b M_n$. The steel is A36. Unbraced length = 20 ft. and C_b and R_{pg} equal 1.0.

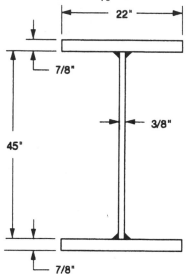

22"

7/8"

3/8"

45"

7/8"

2. For the plate girder shown below, calculate the nominal moment capacity M_n and also calculate the design moment capacity $\phi_b M_n$. All steel is A36. Unbraced length = 10 meters and $C_b = 1.0$ $R_{pg} = 1.0$.

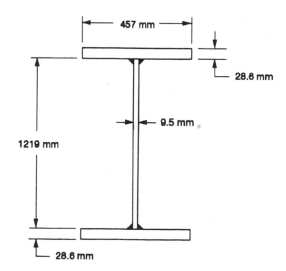

457 mm

28.6 mm

9.5 mm

1219 mm

28.6 mm

3. If the plate girder in problem 1 had a web plate of 58 inches, how would the nominal moment capacity change? Also calculate the design moment capacity $\phi_b M_n$.

4. If the plate girder in problem 2 had flange plates that were 457 mm × 25.4 mm, how would the nominal moment capacity change?

5. For the plate girder shown below, calculate the nominal shear capacity, V_n. The stiffener spacing is as shown and all steel is A36.

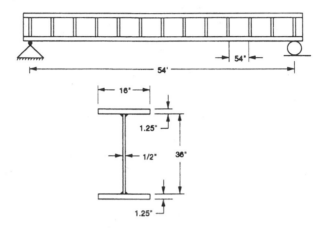

6. If the girder shown in problem 5 was uniformly loaded, what would be the maximum factored uniform load that the girder could support while still being adequate in shear? Would the moment capacity be adequate under this uniform load? Consider $C_b = 1.0$ and the unbraced length to be 27 feet.

7. For the plate girder shown below, determine if the intermediate stiffeners are necessary and if they are spaced properly? Are the intermediate stiffeners sized correctly if they occur on both sides of the web? All steel is A36 and the factored shear is 225 Kips occurring at the supports.

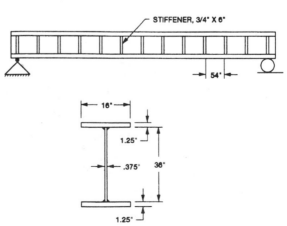

8. For the girder in problem 7, check local web yielding, web crippling, and sidesway buckling to determine if bearing stiffeners are needed over the supports. If so, what size would they be? Assume length of bearing is 9", K = 1.5 inches, C_r = 960,000, unbraced length is 20 feet, and the compression flange is restrained against rotation.

9. For the girder shown in problem 7, determine if it is adequate in moment capacity. Consider C_b = 1.0 and the unbraced length to be 30 feet.

10. For the plate girder shown below, calculate its adequacy for moment, shear, and stiffener requirements. The steel is A36 and stiffeners are on one side only. Consider C_b = 1.0 and the unbraced length to be 40 feet.

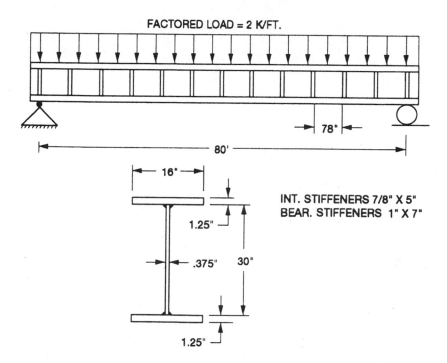

CHAPTER

12

CAPSTONE DESIGN

12.1 Introduction to the Structural Design Process

This chapter outlines the fundamentals of steel design as the working elements that comprise a larger structure. Although there is a tendency in the classroom to "isolate" different members according to their particular behavior, the designer must remember that individual building elements are part of a larger structural form (Figure 12–1). This chapter illustrates the design sequence that may occur by examining the different individual components that comprise the full design process. While the example may be somewhat limited in scope, the author believes it will enhance the reader's understanding of the complexities of the design process.

Although this chapter focuses only on the structural design of building elements, many other factors are involved in the actual decision of which element or structural form is ultimately chosen. Complete building design will incorporate architectural considerations and building code requirements such as power systems, ventilation systems, plumbing, lighting, and transportation of its occupants. Decisions on these considerations must be made according to the building's intended usage or its function. A building is constructed to serve a particular function as designated by its owners. The function of a building and the structural form that will best achieve this function is dictated by a number of items—such as safety, cost, and integration with the building's environment.

Safety is, of course, the primary concern of the structural designer. Local and model building codes, as well as various material specifications will set the

Figure 12–1 High-rise Steel Framed Construction, Chase Manhattan Bank Building, New York. (Courtesy Bethlehem Steel Corporation.)

parameters to be addressed when designing the structure. This text has attempted to introduce the reader to the fundamentals regarding the design of various elements to meet such requirements. The cost of a building involves more than strictly the structural framing system, although since the structural portion of the building is indeed costly, all good designers must strive to economize their particular portion. Finally, the building and its structural elements must be fully integrated with each other as well as the surrounding environment to achieve the full potential of its intended function. The structural elements must fit together with the other aforementioned physical systems, and the designer must realize how changes in the structural system will impact the other physical systems. Changes in the other building systems are very likely to influence the design and any redesign of the structural framing system. The structural framing system must also meet possible requirements imposed by certain environmental conditions. Such cases are typically addressed in local building codes and may include excessive snow, wind, or seismic loads.

11.2   Building Design Example

The design of a total structure involves many separate pieces that the author has attempted to discuss in the previous chapters. Generally before a design begins, the designer must have a general concept of the many constraints that are placed on the project. Such constraints may involve the availability of steel types, member shapes, equipment, and craftsmanship. Other constraints may be imposed by the site, such as a building that is being built in close proximity to another structure. These constraints are typically apparent during a visit to the site prior to the preliminary design phase.

In general, the structural design process may be viewed as consisting of several phases after the general form of the structure has been decided upon. These phases are analysis, preliminary design, and final design. Each phase is discussed briefly below. Such analysis may consist of manual analysis, computer-generated analysis, or a combination of both.

Analysis

The first phase of a building's structural design consists of the analysis of the preliminary structure to determine the approximate forces and their effects that are applied to the members. This preliminary analysis will take into account all applicable load effects and combinations. During this phase, an estimation of the member's selfweight will have to be estimated since this may have a significant impact on the analyzed forces.

Preliminary Design

In this phase, the designer utilizes the forces and moments that were found in the structural analysis and begins a process to determine a safe and cost-effective member to be used for all the structural elements. This phase is typically deemed preliminary because the members selected in this phase may vary from the sizes that were assumed for the purpose of analysis. This variation will cause the forces and moments found in the initial analysis to change somewhat, but hopefully not too much. The preliminary design phase will possibly contain several iterations of the design process to converge upon the proper members to be used. As the process converges on the proper members to be selected, the final analysis should be performed which will then lead to the final design phase.

Final Design

After an analysis is performed using what the designer feels may be very close to the proper member sizes, the designer can begin the final design phase. In this phase the members that were used in the final analysis should be checked for adequacy under the applied forces and moments. Also the connection details and other criteria should be addressed as to their impact on the members that they will connect. Remember for certain behavior (such as tension) the location of bolts holes in the connected parts is critical. Final design should also address any serviceability criteria (such as deflection, drift, etc.) to which the building may be sensitive.

    The following example demonstrates the design process as it may be used on a small building frame. The example utilizes many of the design principles and methods that have been used throughout the text. Of course, some simplifying assumptions will be made to show the major portions of the design more clearly.

EXAMPLE 12.1

Analyze and design the building frame shown below. Assumed that all steel is to be A36 and the effective length factor is to be conservatively taken as 1.0. The beam to column connections are to be designed as bearing-type connections, simple shear connections using A325–X bolts and the frame is considered to be braced. Bending of all members is assumed to take place about the strong axis and all loads shown are service loads.

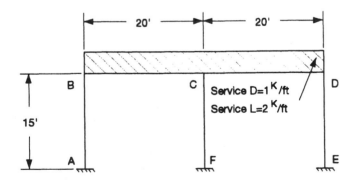

Loads

To begin the process, a calculation of the factored loads must be made since the LRFD method will be utilized. Since the problem was given with only dead and live loads applied to the frame, the load combination that will control would be A4-2 (from section 2.5) and the applied service dead and live loads on the beams are multiplied by the appropriate load factors as:

D = 1 kip/ft. × 1.4 = 1.4 kips/ft.
L = 2 kips/ft. × 1.7 = 3.4 kips/ft.

A total factored load of 4.8 kips per foot of beam length is then applied. Remembering to include the factored effect from the beams selfweight, an estimation of beam weight may be viewed as:

Selfweight = 50 lbs/ft. × 1.4 = 70 lbs/ft. or .07 kips/ft.

This would make the total factored load with member selfweight 4.87 kips per foot.

Next, using this applied factored load, the frame would have to be analyzed using rigid frame or computer analysis. A common method of rigid frame analysis is the moment distribution method covered in Appendix A and will be utilized in this example. The following section will only be useful for those who have studied moment distribution or rigid frames analysis. Those who are only interested in the design methodology may skip to the preliminary design section.

Analysis

We will assume all members at this point to have equal moments of inertias (I) to facilitate the computation of distribution factors. The distribution factors should be calculated for joints B, C and D since those joints have at least two members framing into them. The distribution factors for joints A, E, and F can be assumed as 1.0, since there are no other members to receive a distributed moment at these locations.

At Joint B:

DF_{BA} = (1I/15 ft.)/(1I/15 ft. + 1I/20 ft.) = .57
DF_{BC} = (1I/20 ft.)/(1I/15 ft. + 1I/20 ft.) = .43

Similarly at Joint C:

DF_{CB} = (1I/20 ft.)/(2(1I/20 ft.) + 1I/15 ft.) = .30
DF_{CD} = same as above = .30
DF_{CF} = (1I/15 ft.)/(2(1I/20 ft.) + 1I/15 ft.) = .40

Similarly at Joint D:

$$DF_{DC} = .43$$
$$DF_{DE} = .57$$

Next, calculate the fixed end moments. Only members BC and CD have applied loads, therefore the fixed end moments will be applied at the B end of member BC (termed BC) and the C end of member BC (termed CB), as well as at CD and DC. From table A–1 in Appendix A, the fixed end moments for a uniformly loaded beam are:

$FEM = wl^2/12 = (4.87 \text{ kips/ft.})(20 \text{ ft.})^2/12$

$FEM = 162.3$ kip-ft. (CCW at BC and CD, CW at CB and DC)

$(FEM = 220.7 \text{KN-m})$

From here the moment distributions proceeds by balancing the FEM's at each joint at a time, redistributing those carry-over moments, and balancing again. A tabular format is typically the most convenient method for performing and clearly demonstrating this procedure and the iteration process.

	A	B		C			D		E	F
		BA	BC	CB	CF	CD	DC	DE		
D.F.	1	.57	.43	.30	.40	.30	.43	.57	1	1
FEM			−162.3	+162.3		−162.3	+162.3			
BAL		92.5	69.8				69.8	−92.5		
CO	46.3			34.9		−34.9			46.2	
SUM	46.3	92.5	−92.5	197.2	0	−197.2	92.5	−92.5	−46.2	0

Preliminary Design

From the end moments produced by the moment distribution, the shear at each end of a member can be calculated by summing moments at one end of each member. Once the shear force at each member end has been calculated, the shear and moment diagrams can be drawn for each member as shown below.

Using the maximum forces and moments for each member, the preliminary member size can be started. In this problem we have two beams and two columns (the exterior) that are identical: therefore, the design needs to only be performed for a beam, an exterior column, and the interior column.

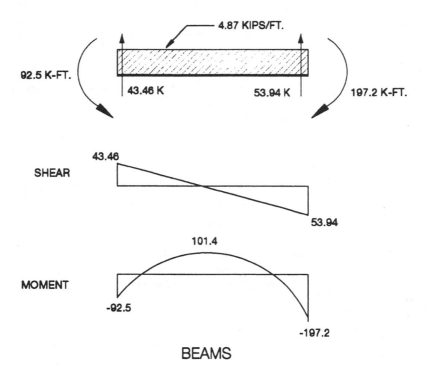

4.87 KIPS/FT.

92.5 K-FT.

43.46 K   53.94 K

197.2 K-FT.

SHEAR

43.46

53.94

MOMENT

101.4

-92.5

-197.2

BEAMS

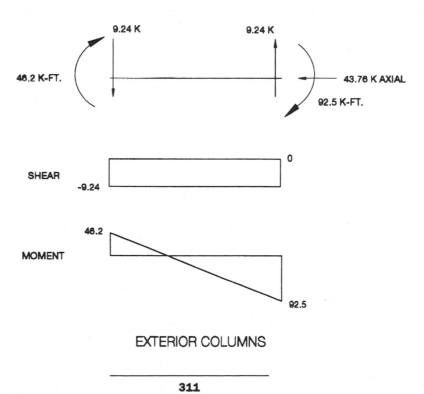

9.24 K   9.24 K

46.2 K-FT.

43.76 K AXIAL

92.5 K-FT.

SHEAR

0

-9.24

MOMENT

46.2

92.5

EXTERIOR COLUMNS

311

Beams

For the beam design, we will use the principles that were established in Chapter 6. Rolled-beams are typically selected based on their moment carrying capability. The maximum factored moment effect on our beam is 197.2 kip-ft. (267.4 KN-m). Therefore in LRFD terminology, 197.2 kip-ft. is the required moment M_u.

From Chapter 6, we know that rolled beams will fall into different "categories" based on their behavior, which in many cases depends on the unbraced length of its compression flange l_b. By setting the beam's unbraced length equal to the value of L_p (which divides beam's capable of reaching their plastic moment from other limit states), the designer can solve for a minimum value of r_y. Using this logic, the unbraced length can be set equal to the L_p value and a minimum value of r_y ($r_{y\,min}$) can be found that would place a section into Case #1. For the beams in our example:

$$l_b = 20' = 240"$$
$$L_p = 300r_y/\sqrt{F_y} \tag{Eq. 6–1}$$

Setting $l_b = L_p$ we can solve the following:

$$r_{y\,min} = 240 \text{ in. } (\sqrt{36})/300 = 4.8$$

Looking at the wide flange tables found in Appendix B, the majority of W 12 sections do not have r_y values close to this minimum. Therefore, our section almost has to be controlled by Case #2 (inelastic lateral torsional buckling) or Case #3 (elastic lateral torsional buckling). Since a 20 foot long unbraced length is not extremely large, it seems reasonable that Case #2 may control. The nominal moment equation for this limit state of inelastic lateral torsional buckling is:

$$M_n = C_b \left[M_p - (M_p - M_r)\right]\left[(l_b - L_p)/(L_r - L_p)\right] \tag{Eq. 6–5}$$

The student should remember from Chapter 6 that Case #2 is bounded by nominal moment capacities that range from the plastic moment capacity M_p to the elastic moment capacity M_r. The equations for each are:

$$M_p = Z_x F_y$$
$$M_r = (F_{yf} - F_r)S_x$$

Realizing that the beam's nominal moment capacity will fall between these limits, the nominal moment capacity can be set equal to:

$M_n = Z_x F_y$ (upper limit)

$M_n = S_x(F_{yf} - F_r)$ (lower limit)

$M_u = 197.2$ kip-ft. (267.4 KN-m)

$M_u/\phi_b \leq M_n$

M_n = 197.2 kip-ft./.90 = 219.1 kip-ft. (297.1KN-m)

Solving for the upper and lower limit:

$Z_{xreq'd}$ = 219.1 kip-ft. × 12 in./ft./36 ksi = 73 in.^{3} $\qquad$ (Eq. 6–9)

$\qquad$ (= 297.1KN-m/248200 KPa = .001197 m^3 or 1197 mm^3)

$S_{xreq'd}$ = 219.1 kip-ft. × 12 in./ft./26 ksi = 101 in.^{3}

$\qquad$ (= 297.1KN-m/179250KPa = .001657 m^3 or 1657 mm^3)

From the section tables in Appendix B, we would look for a section that would tend to meet both of these as a first trial. Select W 18 × 60 (Z_x = 123 in.^{3} and S_x = 108 in.^{3})

Trying a W 18 × 60 we would find by calculating Eq. 6–1 and Eq. 6–2 the following:

L_p = 7 ft.

L_r = 22.4 ft.

Since the actual unbraced length, l_b, is 20 feet, this beam does fall into Case #2, which has a nominal moment capacity calculated by Eq. 6–5, however, we must first find the value of the bending coefficient C_b.

The value of C_b will be calculated from the equation below and using the values of M_{max} = 197.2, M_a = 63.9, M_b = 98.6 and M_c = 11.4. C_b is then calculated as

$$C_b = \frac{12.5M_{max}}{2.5M_{max} + 3M_a + 4M_b + 3M_c}$$

$$C_b = \frac{12.5 (197.2)}{2.5(197.2) + 3(63.9) + 4(98.6) + 3(11.4)} = 2.21$$

Calculating the plastic and elastic moment capacity for the W 18 × 60 section as follows:

M_p = Z_xF_y = 123 in.^{3}(36 ksi) = 4428 kip-in. or 369 kip-ft.

(M_p = Z_xF_y = .00201 mm^3(248200 KPa) = 498.9KN-m)

M_r = (F_y – F_r)S_x = 26 ksi(108 in.^{3}) = 2808 kip-in. or 234 kip-ft.

(M_r = (F_y – F_r)S_x = 179250KPa(.00177 in.^{3}) = 317.3KN-m)

Therefore

M_n = 2.21[369 – (135)(13 ft./15.4)] = 563.6 kip-ft.

however this can never be more than the plastic moment capacity. Therefore, in this case, the nominal moment capacity is the plastic capacity M_p.

Calculating design capacity:

$\phi_b M_n = .90(369 \text{ kip-ft.}) = 332.1 \text{ kip-ft.} > 197.2 \text{ kip-ft.}$

$(\phi_b M_n = .90(498.9 \text{KN-m}) = 449 \text{KN-m} > 267.4 \text{KN-m})$

This works but is much too large and a redesign is in order. Since the C_b ratio is large (2.21), the selected beam will probably be somewhat smaller. Still using a W 18 section, let's drop down to a W 18 × 40 and see how this works. Calculating L_p and L_r from Eq. 6–1 and 6–2 for a W 18 × 40 we find:

$L_p = 5.3 \text{ ft.}$

$L_r = 15.7 \text{ ft.}$

Therefore since our unbraced length (20 ft.) exceeds L_r this beam falls into Case #3. The nominal moment capacity in Case #3 is calculated from Eq. 6–7 as follows:

$$M_n = M_{cr} = \frac{C_b X_1 S_x \sqrt{2}}{l_b/r_y} \sqrt{1 + \frac{X_1^2 X_2}{2(l_b/r_y)^2}}$$

$M_n = 228 \text{ kip-ft.} (309 \text{ KN-m})$

Calculating design capacity:

$\phi_b M_n = .90(228 \text{ kip-ft.}) = 205 \text{ kip-ft.} > 197.2 \text{ kip-ft.}$

$(\phi_b M_n = .90(309 \text{ KN-m}) = 278 \text{ KN-m} > 267.4 \text{ KN-m})$

So this barely works. A W 18 × 50 may be a likely choice as we start into final design. Also remember that the beam has a small compressive force that comes from the column shear, which we neglected in this example. Therefore a beam with additional capacity may be a wise choice.

Interior Column

From the moment distribution, we found the shears on the beams at the interior column to be approximately 53.94 kips each. Therefore, the axial load imparted to the column would be twice that value or simply 108 kips when rounded. From the analysis there is no moment applied to the interior column, so the design will consider only axial load. (The designer should be careful of a situation such as this because under different load cases a moment could be applied causing beam-column action).

For this column, let's conservatively assume an effective length value of 1.0, since it is part of a braced frame. (If the designer so chooses, the alignment chart method could be used to get a more accurate K value.) The buckling in this frame was also stated to occur about the x axis since the weak axis is continuously braced. The required axial capacity is approximately 108 kips plus selfweight, although selfweight of a 15 foot long column will be minimal. Let's assume a factored selfweight of 1000 pounds. Therefore, P_u is equal to 109 kips.

Using the logic presented in Chapter 5, assume a design stress $\phi_c F_{cr}$ equal to about 25 ksi. Therefore the column area needed would be:

$A_{g\ trial}$ = 109 kips/25 ksi = 4.36 in.^{2}

Try a W 12 × 22

Kl/r_x = 1.0(15 ft. × 12 in./ft.)/4.91 = 36.6

From Table 5–1, the critical stress $\phi_c F_{cr}$ for such a slenderness ratio is 28.5 ksi. Therefore the design capacity of this section is:

$\phi_c P_n = \phi_c F_{cr} A_g$ = 28.5 ksi (6.48 in.^{2})
       = 184.7 kips > 109 kips. (821.5 KN > 484.8 KN)

This works but there is probably a more economical member. Retry with a W 10 × 17:

Kl/r_x = 1.0(15 ft. × 12 in./ft.)/4.05 = 44.4

From Table 5–1, the critical stress, $\phi_c F_{cr}$ for such a slenderness ratio is 27.58 ksi. Therefore the design capacity of this section is:

$\phi_c P_n = \phi_c F_{cr} A_g$ = 27.58 ksi (4.99 in.^{2})
       = 137 kips > 109 kips. (609.4KN > 484.8KN)

This works and is a bit lighter. A W 10 × 17 seems adequate in the preliminary section for the interior column. Please realize that this section was only designed for pure axial load since the analysis showed no applied moment. Moment on this column could occur if the loadings were different or if the structure was not symmetrical. A beam-column analysis would then be necessary.

Exterior Columns

From the preliminary moment distribution, the exterior columns are subjected to an axial load of about 43.76 kips (from the beam shear) and a moment about the strong axis of 92.5 kip-feet. Therefore this member should be designed as a beam-column. Applying selfweight to the column would make the factored axial a bit higher let's assume 44.5 kips.

From Chapter 8, the design of beam-columns was found to be based on calculating an equivalent axial load from the following equation:

$$P_{u\text{equiv}} = P_u + M_{ux}m + M_{uy}mU \qquad \text{(Eq. 8–9)}$$

The values of m are found in Table 8–1 and U is taken from the column load tables. After calculating the equivalent axial load, the design then checks the member for adequacy based on the following two equations:

when $\dfrac{P_u}{\phi_c P_n} \geq 0.2$

$$\frac{P_u}{\phi_c P_n} + \frac{8}{9}\left(\frac{M_{ux}}{\phi_b M_{nx}} + \frac{M_{uy}}{\phi_b M_{ny}}\right) \leq 1.0 \qquad \text{(Eq. 8-7)}$$

when $\dfrac{P_u}{\phi_c P_n} < 0.2$

$$\frac{P_u}{2\phi_c P_n} + \left(\frac{M_{ux}}{\phi_b M_{nx}} + \frac{M_{uy}}{\phi_b M_{ny}}\right) \leq 1.0 \qquad \text{(Eq. 8-8)}$$

In this problem, a W 10 will be designed since a W 10 is tentatively being used for the interior column. This may be advantageous for interior finish purposes. The factored axial load is 44.5 kips and the moment about the strong axis is 92.5 kip-ft. From the problem statement the effective length factor is 1.0. Calculating the equivalent factored load by Eq. 8–9, we need to start with a value of m approximately equal to 1.9 (from Table 8–1). The equivalent axial load is then:

P_{uequiv} = 44.5 kips + 92.5 kip-ft.(1.9) = 220.3 kips (980KN)

Based on our knowledge of the interior column (W 10 × 17) having a design capacity of 137 kips, we would choose a section somewhat heavier. Let's investigate a W 10 × 33.

Kl/r_x = 1.0(15 ft. × 12 in./ft.)/4.19 = 42.95

From Table 5–1, the critical stress, $\phi_c F_{cr}$, for such a slenderness ratio is 27.78 ksi. Therefore the design capacity of this section is:

$\phi_c P_n = \phi_c F_{cr} A_g$ = 27.78 ksi (9.71 in.^{2}) = 269.7 kips (1200KN)

Checking this section with the interaction formulas we find the following:

Since $P_u/\phi P_n$ = 44.5 kips/269.7 kips = .165 < .20 the aforementioned Eq. 8–8 will control.

Calculating the design moment capacity about the strong axis we find the following regarding the W 10 × 33.

From Equation 6–1 and 6–2:

L_p = 8.1 ft.
L_r = 27.4 ft.

Since the column's unbraced length, 15 ft, lies between these two limits, the section's nominal moment capacity is calculated based on Eq. 6–5 as follows:

$$M_n = C_b[M_p - (M_p - M_r)][(l_b - L_p)/(L_r - L_p)] \qquad \text{(Eq. 6–5)}$$

The value of C_b will be calculated from the equation listed below using the values of M_{max} = 97.2, M_a = 11.5, M_b = 23.1, and M_c = 57.7. This yields the following:

$$C_b = \frac{12.5(97.2)}{2.5(97.2) + 3(11.5) + 4(23.1) + 3(57.7)} = 2.23$$

Calculating the plastic and elastic moment capacity as follows:

$M_p = Z_xF_y$ = 38.8 in.^{3} (36 ksi) = 1397 kip-in. or 116.4 kip-ft.
($M_p = Z_xF_y$ = .000633m^3 (248200KPa) = 157.1KN-m)
$M_r = (F_{yf} - F_r)S_x$ = 26 ksi (35 in.^{3}) = 910 kip-in. or 75.8 kip-ft.
($M_r = (F_{yl} - F_r)S_x$ = 179250KPa (.000572 m^3) = 102.5KN-m)

Therefore

M_n = 2.23[116.4 – 40.6)(6.9 ft./19.3)] = 227 kip-ft. (307KN-m)

This nominal moment capacity is greater than the plastic moment capacity M_p, therefore use the plastic moment capacity (116.4 kip-ft.) as the nominal strength. Calculating the design moment capacity we find:

$\phi_b\,M_n$ = .90(116.4 kip-ft.) = 104.7 kip-ft.
($\phi_b M_n$ = .90(157.1KN-m) = 141.4KN-m)

The design moment capacity is greater than the maximum factored moment about the strong axis M_{ux} which is 97.2 kip-ft. This factored moment should be magnified by the braced frame magnifier, B_1. Calculating the magnifier B_1 find the following:

$$B_1 = C_m/(1 - P_u/P_e)$$

where

C_m = .60 – .4(M_1/M_2)
C_{mx} = .6 – .4(46.2/92.5) = .4
P_u = 44.5 kips

To calculate the Euler buckling load for this section, the slenderness ratios and corresponding slenderness parameter (Ω_c) about the strong axis must be calculated;

$Kl/r_x = 42.95 \ (\lambda_c = .482)$

Calculating the Euler buckling load as follows:

$P_e = A_g F_y / \lambda_c^2$

$P_{ex} = (9.71 \text{ in.}^2)(36 \text{ ksi})/(.482)^2$

$P_{ex} = 1504 \text{ kips (based on } \lambda_c = .482)$

$(=(.00626 \text{ m}^2)(248200 \text{KPa})/(.482)^2 = 6688 \text{KN})$

$B_{1x} = .4/1 - (44.5 \text{ kips}/1504 \text{ kips}) = .41$— can not be less than 1.0, use 1.0.

This would make the magnified factored as shown below:

$M_{ux} = B_1 M_{ux}$

$M_{ux} = (1.0)97.2 \text{ kip-ft.} = 97.2 \text{ kip-ft.}$

$(M_{ux} = 131.8 \text{KN-m}(1.0) = 131.8 \text{KN-m})$

Applying Eq. 8–8 to the above information:

$(44.5 \text{ kips}/(2)269.7 \text{ kips}) + (97.2 \text{ kip-ft.}/104.7 \text{ kip-ft.}) = 1.01 \approx 1.0$

therefore this works very well. Therefore, use a W 10×33 for the exterior columns in this prelimainary stage.

Since we have performed the preliminary design for the beams, interior and exterior columns, it is now wise to reanalyze the structure using the preliminary selfweight and stiffnesses of the chosen members. This is performed to ensure that the moments and shears of the member forces do not appreciably change.

Final Design

To begin, we will perform a moment distribution using the exact moment of inertias for the trial members. The selfweight of the beams (50 lb./ft.) multiplied by the dead load factor of 1.4 will be added to the service loads to bring the total factored load to 4.87 kips per foot of beam. This is the same load we had at the start. The moment distribution will then be performed as follows. Notice that the fixed end moments kept the same because the load is the same while the distribution factors have changed significantly because the actual moment of inertias for the members are now used.

	A	B		C			D		E	F
D.F	1	BA .22	BC .78	CB .47	CF .06	CD .47	DC .78	DE .22	1	1
FEM BAL CO	17.9	35.7	−162.3 126.6	+162.3 63.3	0	−162.3 −63.3	+162.3 −126.6	−35.7	17.9	0
SUM	17.9	35.7	−35.7	225.6	0	−225.6	35.7	−35.7	−17.9	0

This analysis changes the shears and moments on the members by a bit so the designer should check the adequacy of the selected members under this more precise analysis. The shears and moments on the different members are shown below.

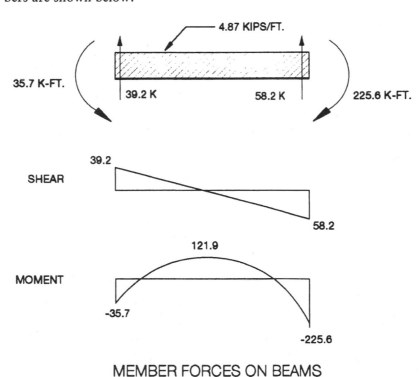

MEMBER FORCES ON BEAMS

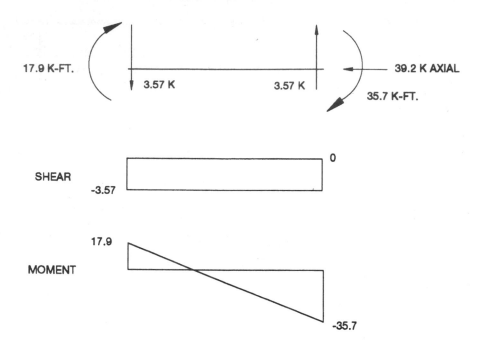

MEMBER FORCES ON EXTERIOR COLUMNS

The beams are subjected to a slightly higher factored moment of 225.6 kip-ft. (306 KN-m). When calculating the design moment capacity $\phi b\, M_n$ of the W 18 × 50 we should remember that the bending coefficient C_b will change due to the change in moments at the end of its unbraced length.

Calculating C_b using M_{MAX} = 225.6, M_a = 9.94 M_b = 112.6, and M_c = 4.3. as follows:

$$C_b = \frac{12.5(225.6)}{2.5(225.6) + 3(99.4) + 4(112.6) + 3(43)} = 2.13$$

Calculating the plastic and elastic moment capacity as follows:

$M_p = Z_x F_y = 101$ in.^{3} (36 ksi) = 3636 kip-in. or 303 kip-ft.

($M_p = Z_x F_y = .00165$ m^3 (248200KPa) = 409.5KN-m)

$M_r = (F_y - F_r)S_x = 26$ ksi (88.9 in.^{3}) = 2311 kip-in. or 192.6 kip-ft.

($M_r = (F_{yf} - F_r)S_x = 179250$KPa (.00146 m^3) = 261.7KN)

Therefore

$M_n = 2.13[303 - (110.4)(13.1\text{ ft.}/13.6)] = 419$ kip-ft.

however this can never be more than the plastic moment capacity. Therefore, in this case, the nominal moment capacity is the plastic capacity M_p. Calculating design capacity:

$\phi_b M_n$ = .90(303 kip-ft.) = 272.7 kip-ft. > 225.6 kip-ft.

($\phi_b M_n$ = .90(409.5KN-m) = 368.6KN-m > 300.4KN-m)

This seems to work well, and considering that there is also a compressive force on the beams (as mentioned earlier) it may be prudent to leave our beams with a little more capacity.

In this new analysis the interior column has approximately 117 kips of factored axial load applied to it and no appreciable moment. The W 10 × 17 as designed previously, had a design capacity of 137 kips. Since the factored load in the reanalysis is still under this member's design capacity, the W 10 × 17 is still adequate.

The exterior columns under the reanalysis have an applied factored axial load of approximately 39.2 kips and with selfweight of the column we can round this to 40 kips (177.9 KN). The maximum factored moment on this member is 35.7 kip-ft (48.4 KN-m). Both of these values are smaller than the values of axial load and moment that were used to design the preliminary section. Therefore the W 10 × 33 is adequate but could possibly be down-sized. Let's investigate a W 10 × 26.

Kl/r_x = 1.0(15 ft. × 12 in./ft.)/4.35 = 41.8

From Table 5–1, the critical stress $\phi c\ F_{cr}$ for such a slenderness ratio is 27.9 ksi. Therefore the design capacity of this section is:

$\phi_c P_n = \phi_c F_{cr} A_g$ = 27.9 ksi (7.61 in.²) = 212.3 kips

Checking this section with the interaction formulas we find the following:

Since $P_u/\phi P_n$ = 40 kips/212.3 kips = .188 < .20. the aforementioned Eq. 8–8 will control.

Calculating the design moment capacity about the strong axis we find the nominal moment capacity of the W 10 × 26 is based on Eq. 6–5 as follows:

$$M_n = C_b[M_p - (M_p - M_r)][(l_b - L_p)/(L_r - L_p)] \qquad \text{(Eq. 6–5)}$$

The value of C_b will be 2.18 and the plastic and elastic moment capacity as follows:

$M_p = Z_x F_y$ = 31.3 in.³ (36 ksi) = 1127 kip-in. or 93.9 kip-ft.

($M_p = Z_x F_y$ = .000514 m³ (248200KPa) = 127.6KN-m)

$M_r = (F_y - F_r)S_x$ = 26 ksi (27.9 in.³) = 725 kip-in. or 60.5 kip-ft.

($M_r = (F_y - F_r)S_x$ = 179250KPa (.000459 m³) = 82.3KN-m)

Therefore by Eq. 6–5;

$M_n = 2.18[93.9 - (33.5)(9.3 \text{ ft.}/12.8)] = 151.6$ kip-ft.

This nominal moment capacity is greater than the plastic moment capacity M_p, therefore use the plastic moment capacity (93.9 kip-ft) as the nominal strength. Calculating the design moment capacity we find:

$\phi_b M_n = .90(93.9 \text{ kip-ft.}) = 84.5$ kip-ft.

The design moment capacity is greater than the maximum factored moment about the strong axis M_{ux} which is 35.7 kip-ft. This factored moment should be magnified by the braced frame magnifier B_1. Calculating the magnifier B_1 as before we find the following:

$C_{mx} = .6 - .4(17.9/35.7) = .4$

$P_u = 40$ kips

To calculate the Euler buckling load for this section, the slenderness ratios and corresponding slenderness parameter (λ_c) about the strong axis must be calculated;

$Kl/r_x = 41.4$ ($\lambda_c = .464$)

Calculating the Euler buckling load as follows:

$P_e = A_g F_y/\lambda_c^2$

$P_{ex} = (7.61 \text{ in.}^2)(36 \text{ ksi})/(.464)^2$

$P_{ex} = 1272$ kips (based on $\lambda_c = .464$)

$\quad (= (.00491 \text{ m}^2)(248200 \text{KPa})/(.464)^2 = 5658\text{KN})$

$B_{1x} = .4/1 - (40 \text{ kips}/1272 \text{ kips}) = .41$ — can not be less than 1.0, use 1.0.

This would make the magnified factored as shown below:

$M_{ux} = B_1 M_{ux}$

$M_{ux} = (1.0)35.7 \text{ kip-ft.} = 35.7$ kip-ft.

$(M_{ux} = 48.4 \text{KN-m}(1.0) = 48.4 \text{KN-m})$

Applying Eq. 8–8 to the above information:

$(40 \text{ kips}/(2)212.3 \text{ kips}) + (35.7 \text{ kip-ft.}/84.5 \text{ kip-ft.}) = .52 < 1.0$ — therefore this works well.

Now rework one final analysis using W 18×50s for the beams, a W 10×17 for the interior column, and a W 10×26 for the exterior columns to make sure that the forces and moments do not change appreciably. This can be done as follows:

	A	B		C			D		E	F
		BA	BC	CB	CF	CD	DC	DE		
D.F	1	.2	.8	.47	.06	.47	.8	.2	1	1
FEM			−162.3	+162.3		−162.3	+162.3			
BAL		32.5	129.8				−129.8	−32.5		
CO	16.2			64.9		−64.9			16.2	0
SUM	16.2	32.5	−32.5	227.2	0	−227.2	32.5	−32.5	−16.2	0

Since the moments out of the moment distribution are relatively close to the previous analysis, the members can be considered adequate.

Connections

The beam-to-column connections in the example are assumed to be simple shear connections, allowing some rotation under loading. In reality, a moment connection would be designed if the frame was truly rigid so that the moment would transfer across the connection. This type of connection is beyond the scope of this text and is thoroughly covered in reference[1]. The following design will only consider the shear effect under the gravity loads and the use of a seated connection will be employed in this case because we are attaching the beams into the column webs. Framing angles on the beam web (which is more typical) probably would not be used when connecting to the column web because the column flanges would interfere with the tightening of the bolts in the beam web. The connection is assumed to be bearing-type and the maximum factor shear at the column will be considered for all the connections (V_u = 58.9 kips × 2 beams = 117.8 kips).

From Chapter 9, the design shear capacity was found to be:

$$\phi R_n = \phi \,(\text{Design strength} \times A) \qquad \text{(Eq. 9–1)}$$

where

Design strength = nominal strength from Table 9–3 or 9–4

A = unthreaded bolt area

ϕ = .75 for all bolts in bearing type connections

ϕ = 1.0 for all bolts in slip-critical connections

Since the design shear capacity ϕR_n needs to be a minimum of 117.8 kips, the aforementioned equation can be rearranged to solve for area as follows for A325–X bolts:

$A = 117.8$ kips/0.75(60 ksi) = 2.61 in.^{2}

At the center column there would be a double shear condition, so the real minimum area required for shear would be one-half that amount or 1.30 in.^{2}. (Single shear exists at the exterior column although this location is not critical since only 39.2 kips of shear exists). If we chose a 3/4" diameter bolt ($A = .44$ in.^{2}), the number of bolts needed would be:

bolts = 1.30 in.^{2}/.44 in.^{2} per bolt = 2.95 bolts

We will use six bolts (4 bottom, 2 top) in the seated connection (this will be discussed below). A typical seated connection would have a top and bottom angle; therefore, the connection may look as shown in the following diagram.

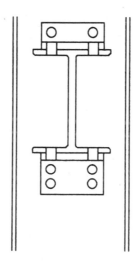

The bearing capacity of the W 10 × 17 column should be checked since it has a relatively thin web ($t_w = .24$ in). From Chapter 9, we found the design bearing capacity of a connected part based on no deformation was:

$$\phi Rn = \phi(3.0)(d)(t)F_u \qquad \text{(Eq. 9–3)}$$

Checking bearing:
Bearing area = 6 bolts × 3/4" diameter × .24 in. thick = 1.08 in.^{2}. Calculate the bearing design capacity as follows assuming deformation could be a consideration from Eq. 9–3.

$$\phi R_n = \phi(3.0)(d)(t)F_u \qquad \text{(Eq. 9–3)}$$
$$\phi R_n = (.75)(3.0)(1.08 \text{ in.}^2)(58 \text{ ksi}) = 140.9 \text{ kips}$$
$$(\phi R_n = (.75)(2.4)(.0007\text{m}^2)(399910\text{KPa}) = 630\text{KN})$$

This is a greater than the required capacity of 117.8 kips, and therefore adequate.

Although the above example contained some simplifications, the student can gain a decent understanding of the design process.

12.3 Summary

A complete building design project has many different pieces associated with its construction. This text has focused on the structural aspects of steel design. The process of structural design also contains many parts and is an iterative and highly individual process. The designer must always understand the impact that a particular design component may have on the other design components. A change to a beam or a connection will have an impact on the other members, through a change in dead load or maybe even a change in the analysis output.

All designs should start with an analysis in which preliminary forces are determined. After this is accomplished an iterative design procedure begins and progresses through a preliminary and final design stage.

EXERCISES

1. For the frame shown below, design the members and connections if under the service loads as shown. Steel is to be A36, frame is to be considered braced with bending about the weak axis, and all connections are bearing-type, simple shear seated connections using A325–N bolts.

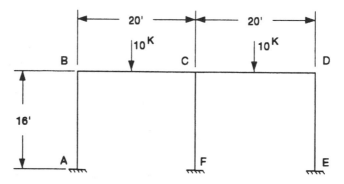

2. The section shown below is part of a roof truss framing system that is to be designed using W sections. Assume the truss to behave as a true truss, and perform the analysis based on roof dead loads of 45 psf and roof live loads of 60 psf (both service). Design members using A36 steel and connections to be simple shear, bearing type connections into gusset plates. The fasteners

are to be A325–X, 3/4" diameter. Assume $K = 1.0$ for all compression members and the selfweight causes no appreciable bending moment.

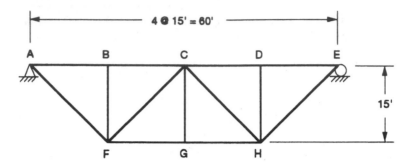

3. Design the continuous beam shown below for maximum bending moment. Use the moment distribution method to analyze the member and steel used is A36. Also include selfweight of the beam and check shear. Will the beam designed be adequate if the deflection is limited to 1/360 of the span length.

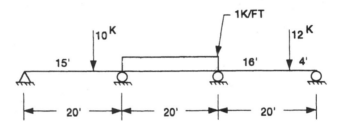

4. Design the continuous beam shown below for maximum bending moment. Use the moment distribution method to analyze the member and steel used is A242. Also include selfweight of the beam and check shear. Will the beam designed be adequate if the deflection is limited to 1/360 of the span length.

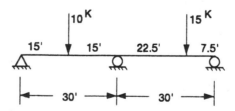

REFERENCES

1. AISC. *Manual of Steel Construction, Volume II Connections ASD/LRFD,* Chicago, American Institute of Steel Construction, 1992.

A

SIMPLIFIED FRAME ANALYSIS

A.1 Introduction

Rigid framed structures are widely used in construction today because of their increased load carrying capability. The frame's increased strength is due to the moment resistance of the joints that cause moments at the member's midspan to be reduced. Although this increased capacity is a definite advantage, a rigid frame is more complicated to analyze because it is indeterminate. This indeterminancy requires the designer to be familiar with techniques of calculating the moments and forces on the members of a rigid frame. These forces and moments must first be determined so that the member design can be performed. Therefore, rigid frame analysis is an extremely important skill that the structural designer will utilize frequently.

Although this book only strives to cover the fundamentals of steel design, a brief summarization of a very common frame analysis technique will be illustrated in the following paragraphs.

As was mentioned in Chapter 8, frames can generally be broken down into two broad categories: braced and unbraced. Braced frames are those having some element or elements that restrict lateral movement or sidesway. Unbraced frames are those having insufficient structural elements to restrict lateral movement and therefore, are free to exhibit sidesway. As we will see in the upcoming sections, the handling of frames subjected to sidesway involves somewhat more complicated analysis procedure. One of the most common, manual frame analysis techniques is the moment distribution method.

A.2   Moment Distribution

The **moment distribution method** was pioneered by Hardy Cross in the 1920s and is the predominant method of analyzing the forces in indeterminate structures. This method is based on redistributing moments to the ends of a member in a series of successive iterations. The method is based on calculating the sum of moments in an indeterminate structure by first considering the moments at the member ends assuming that all the joints were fixed, and then successively redistributing the moments as one joint (at a time) becomes free to rotate. This procedure may go through a number of iterations, depending on the precision required.

The procedure begins by assuming all joints in the structure are fixed. The loads on the structure would then impart **fixed end moments (FEM's)** to the ends of the member. Typical fixed-end moments are shown in Table A-1.

The procedure continues by unlocking one joint at a time, thus allowing the unbalanced moment at that joint to cause a moment in the opposite, fixed end of the member. This moment, which is transferred to the opposite end, is referred to as the **carry-over moment**. The carry-over moment to the opposite end of a member will be one-half of the moment at the unlocked end and of the same sign convention (clockwise or counterclockwise). This 1/2 carry-over moment holds true if the member is prismatic (of constant cross-section) and is illustrated in Figure A–1. The examples shown in this text always consider the members to be of constant cross-section since this is typically the case.

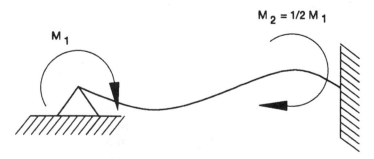

Figure A–1   Carryover Effect of Moment from a Pinned End to the Fixed End

Table A–1 Typical Fixed End Moment Cases

FIXED END MOMENT @ A	LOAD CASE	FIXED END MOMENT @ B
$-P\ell/8$	$\ell/2$ ↓P $\ell/2$ — A, B — beam, fixed ends	$+P\ell/8$
$\dfrac{-Pab^2}{\ell^2}$	↓P — a — b — ℓ — A, B	$\dfrac{+Pa^2b}{\ell^2}$
$\dfrac{-w\ell^2}{12}$	$w=$ LOAD / UNIT LENGTH — ℓ	$\dfrac{+w\ell^2}{12}$
$\dfrac{-Pa}{\ell}(\ell-a)$	↓ a ↓ a — ℓ	$\dfrac{+Pa}{\ell}(\ell-a)$

Throughout this structure, this sequence of locking and unlocking will continue, one joint at a time. There must be an accounting for any variation of rotational stiffnesses in the members that frame into a particular joint. An applied moment will split itself among the members framing into that joint based upon the relative rotational stiffness of each member. For instance, if two members frame into a joint, each having the same rotational stiffness, a moment applied to that joint will split equally among the two members. A **distribution factor (DF)** can be calculated for each member at a joint, realizing that the sum of all distribution factors should equal 1. The distribution factor can be calculated as follows:

$$DF_{AB} = (I/L)_{AB}/\Sigma I/L$$

where DF_{AB} = distribution factor for member AB at joint A

$(I/L)_{AB}$ = stiffness of member AB
$\Sigma I/L$ = sum of all stiffnesses framing into a particular joint, joint A

It should be noted that for simple (pinned) supports, the final moment must always be balanced to zero. To consolidate the moment distribution procedure, it is convenient to modify the distribution factor for a pinned member by 3/4. This is because the stiffness of a pinned end has only 3/4 the stiffness of a fixed end. In a similar manner, it is sometimes convenient to modify the distribution factor of a symmetrical member by 1/2, again to consolidate the procedure. It should be remembered that neither of the modifications has to be performed in a moment distribution and that such modifications are only done in order to shorten the procedure. In the following examples, neither modification will be used in order to fully concentrate on the procedure.

The procedure for moment distribution can be outlined as follows:

1. Calculate distribution factors at the joints.
2. Lock all joints, calculate fixed end moments.
3. Unlock a joint, calculate the carry-over moment.
4. Calculate new moment at each joint.
5. Distribution of new moment at each joint using distribution factors.
6. Repeat steps 3 through 6.

The procedure as outlined will typically converge on a solution after three or four iterations, although good approximate solutions may be calculated after one or two iterations. The following example will illustrate this technique.

EXAMPLE A.1

Analyze the braced frame shown below using moment distribution. The length of all members is 10 feet. The moment of inertia of the beam is 1/2 that of the columns (or $I_{col} = 2I$ while $I_{beam} = 1I$).

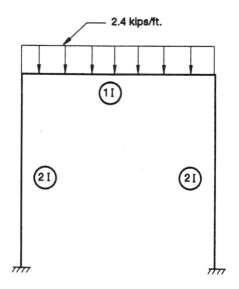

To begin with the distribution factors should be calculated for joints B and C since those joints have two members framing into them. The distribution factors for joints A and D can be assumed as 1.0, since there are no other members to receive a distributed moment at these locations.

At joint B:

$$DF_{BA} = (2I/10 \text{ ft.})/(2I/10 \text{ ft.} + 1I/10 \text{ ft.}) = .67$$
$$DF_{BC} = (1I/10 \text{ ft.})/(2I/10 \text{ ft.} + 1I/10 \text{ ft.}) = .33$$

Similarly at joint C;

$$DF_{CB} = (1I/10 \text{ ft.})/(2I/10 \text{ ft.} + 1I/10 \text{ ft.}) = .33$$
$$DF_{CD} = (2I/10 \text{ ft.})/(2I/10 \text{ ft.} + 1I/10 \text{ ft.}) = .67$$

Next, calculate the fixed end moments. Only member BC has a load on it, therefore the fixed end moments will be applied at the B end of member BC (termed BC) and the C end of member BC (termed CB). From table A–1, the fixed end moments are:

$$FEM = wl^2/12 = (2.4 \text{ kips/ft.})(10 \text{ ft.})^2/12$$
$$FEM = 20 \text{ kip-ft. (CCW at BC, CW at CB)}$$

From here the moment distributions proceeds by balancing the FEM's at each joint at a time, redistributing those carry-over moments, and balancing

	JT. A	JT. B		JT. C		JT. D
	AB	BA	BC	CB	CD	DC
DF	1	.67	.33	.33	.67	1
FEM			−20	+20		
BAL		+13.3	+6.67	−6.67	−13.33	
CO	+6.67		−3.33	+3.33		−6.67
BAL		+2.23	+1.1	−1.1	−2.23	
CO	+1.11		−0.55	+0.55		−1.11
BAL		+0.37	+0.18	−0.18	−0.37	
SUM	+7.78	+15.93	−15.93	+15.93	−15.93	−7.78

again. A tabular format is typically the most convenient method for performing and clearly demonstrating this procedure and the iteration process.

From the moments that were found in the technique, the designer can create shear and moment diagrams for each member in the frame. Thus, the maximum shears and moment could be found and the design process initiated.

The next section describes the moment distribution process when unbraced frames are utilized and sidesway can occur.

A.3   Moment Distribution for Frames Subjected to Sidesway

Frames may be subjected to sidesway due to lateral loads, unsymmetrical loadings, or even different member stiffnesses. Because of the deflection that may occur in unbraced frames, the value of moments produced by the moment distribution method as previously outlined is affected. When using the moment distribution method, the sum of the horizontal forces will not be equal to zero when sidesway is involved. This, of course, cannot be the case since it violates the laws of equilibrium. Because the standard moment distribution procedure will yield erroneous results, it will need to be modified. A common modification of the moment distribution procedure is to perform two separate moment distributions. The first involves supplying a imaginary reaction that balances the discrepancy of horizontal forces. The second distribution is performed as the imaginary reaction is removed and the frame is allowed to sway. This swaying will produce fixed end moments in the tops and bottoms of the columns that will have an assumed value. This assumption will not affect the final result because the horizontal forces at the column bases will be compared to the imaginary reaction needed to stabilize the first distribution and the final sway moments adjusted so that these forces equalize. It is typical convention to apply the fixed end sway moments as counterclockwise if the frame sways to the right and clockwise should it sway to the left (Figure A–2).

This moment distribution procedure for unbraced frames is outlined in the following example. The reader will notice that this is the same problem as in Example A.1 except that the frame is now considered unbraced and there has been a 5 kip load supplied at joint B acting to the right.

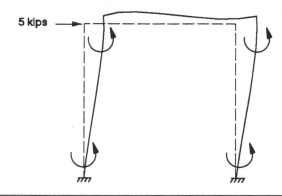

Figure A–2   Fixed End Moments caused by Sidesway

EXAMPLE A.2

Analyze the unbraced frame shown below using moment distribution. The length of all members is 10 feet. The moment of inertia of the beam is 1/2 that of the columns (or $I_{col} = 2I$ while $I_{beam} = 1I$).

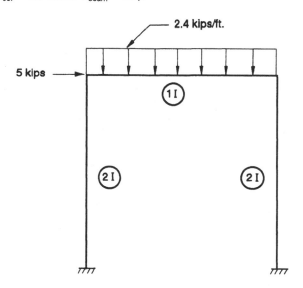

Since the 5 kip load is applied at a joint it will cause no fixed end moments in the frame, but it will cause the frame to sway to the right. The moment distribution procedure would then be broken down into a distribution having an imaginary support preventing sidesway and a second distribution considering the sidesway effects. The first distribution would be identical to that of Example A.1 since the 5 kip load being applied at a joint does not influence that moment distribution. From these moments, it can be found that the reaction at the column bases is about 2.34 kips as shown in the figure below. This still leaves an unbalanced horizontal force of 5 kips on the frame that obviously has to be resisted. This is why the assumption of a imaginary reaction is made.

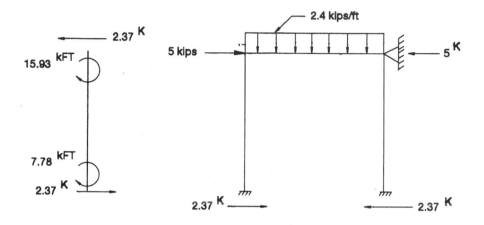

When this imaginary reaction is removed the frame sways to the right causing moments to be applied in a counterclockwise direction at the top and bottom of each column. Let's assume this sidesway moment to be 15 kip-feet as shown below. Since the column lengths and moments of inertia are identical, the moments on each column are identical. (If the length or moment of inertias would be different, we would ratio the moments based on the *I/L* ratio of the columns). The moment distribution for the sway case would be as follows.

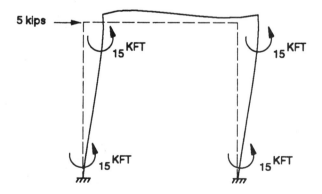

	JT. A	JT. B		JT. C		JT. D
	AB	BA	BC	CB	CD	DC
DF	1	.67	.33	.33	.67	1
FEM	−15	−15			−15	−15
BAL		+10	+5	+5	+10	
CO	+5		+2.5	+2.5		+5
BAL		−1.67	−.83	−.83	−1.67	
CO	−.83		−.41	−.41		−.83
BAL		+.27	+.14	+.14	+.27	
CO	+.13		+.07	+.07		+.13
BAL		−.05	−.02	−.02	−.05	
SUM	−10.7	−6.45	+6.45	+6.45	−6.45	−10.7

From this distribution, we can find the moments produced at the column ends from the assumed 15 ft.-kip sway moment. By summing moments on a free body diagram of a column, we can find that the column base reactions are 1.72 kips at each column (to the left) as shown. To balance the 5 kips horizontal load to the right, we must multiply all moments in this distribution by 5 kips/3.44 kips, or 1.45. This would bring the horizontal forces into equilibrium and yield adjusted sway moments as follows:

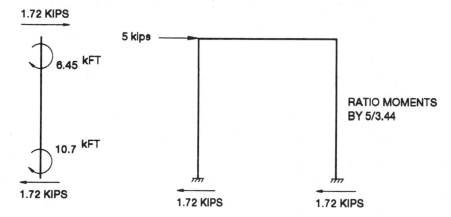

AB = DC = –10.7 × 1.45 = –15.55 kip-ft.
BA = CD = –6.45 × 1.45 = –9.38 kip-ft.
BC = CB = +6.45 × 1.45 = +9.38 kip-ft.

Many times the moments from the initial distribution and those from the sway distribution would be added together to give the final total moment. However, it may also be convenient to keep the moments separated, since the designer may want to apply separate modifiers such as the B_1 and B_2 modifiers that were used in the design and analysis of beam-columns (Chapter 8).

B

SIMPLIFIED FRAME ANALYSIS

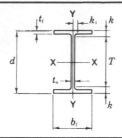

W SHAPES
Dimensions

Desig- nation	Area A	Depth d		Web			Flange				Distance		
				Thickness t_w		$\dfrac{t_w}{2}$	Width b_f		Thickness t_f		T	k	k_1
	In.²	In.		In.		In.	In.		In.		In.	In.	In.
W 24x117	34.4	24.26	24¼	0.550	9/16	5/16	12.800	12¾	0.850	7/8	21	1⅝	1
x104	30.6	24.06	24	0.500	½	¼	12.750	12¾	0.750	¾	21	1½	1
W 24x103ᵇ	30.3	24.53	24½	0.550	9/16	5/16	9.000	9	0.980	1	21	1¾	13/16
x 94	27.7	24.31	24¼	0.515	½	¼	9.065	9⅛	0.875	7/8	21	1⅝	1
x 84	24.7	24.10	24⅛	0.470	½	¼	9.020	9	0.770	¾	21	1 9/16	15/16
x 76	22.4	23.92	23⅞	0.440	7/16	¼	8.990	9	0.680	11/16	21	1 7/16	15/16
x 68	20.1	23.73	23¾	0.415	7/16	¼	8.965	9	0.585	9/16	21	1⅜	15/16
W 24x 62	18.2	23.74	23¾	0.430	7/16	¼	7.040	7	0.590	9/16	21	1⅜	15/16
x 55	16.2	23.57	23⅝	0.395	⅜	3/16	7.005	7	0.505	½	21	1 5/16	15/16
W 21x402ᵃ	118.0	26.02	26	1.730	1¾	7/8	13.405	13⅜	3.130	3⅛	18¼	3⅞	1 7/16
x364ᵃ	107.0	25.47	25½	1.590	1 9/16	13/16	13.265	13¼	2.850	2⅞	18¼	3⅝	1⅜
x333ᵃ	97.9	25.00	25	1.460	1 7/16	¾	13.130	13⅛	2.620	2⅝	18¼	3⅜	1 5/16
x300ᵃ	88.2	24.53	24½	1.320	1 5/16	11/16	12.990	13	2.380	2⅜	18¼	3⅛	1¼
x275ᵃ	80.8	24.13	24⅛	1.220	1¼	⅝	12.890	12⅞	2.190	2 3/16	18¼	3	1 3/16
x248ᵃ	72.8	23.74	23¾	1.100	1⅛	9/16	12.775	12¾	1.990	2	18¼	2¾	1⅛
x223	65.4	23.35	23⅜	1.000	1	½	12.675	12⅝	1.790	1 13/16	18¼	2 9/16	1 1/16
x201	59.2	23.03	23	0.910	15/16	½	12.575	12⅝	1.630	1⅝	18¼	2⅜	1
x182	53.6	22.72	22¾	0.830	13/16	7/16	12.500	12½	1.480	1½	18¼	2¼	1
x166	48.8	22.48	22½	0.750	¾	⅜	12.420	12⅜	1.360	1⅜	18¼	2⅛	15/16
x147	43.2	22.06	22	0.720	¾	⅜	12.510	12½	1.150	1⅛	18¼	1⅞	1 1/16
x132	38.8	21.83	21⅞	0.650	⅝	5/16	12.440	12½	1.035	1 1/16	18¼	1 13/16	1
x122	35.9	21.68	21⅝	0.600	⅝	5/16	12.390	12⅜	0.960	15/16	18¼	1 11/16	1
x111	32.7	21.51	21½	0.550	9/16	5/16	12.340	12⅜	0.875	7/8	18¼	1⅝	15/16
x101	29.8	21.36	21⅜	0.500	½	¼	12.290	12¼	0.800	13/16	18¼	1 9/16	15/16
W 21x 93	27.3	21.62	21⅝	0.580	9/16	5/16	8.420	8⅜	0.930	15/16	18¼	1 11/16	1
x 83	24.3	21.43	21⅜	0.515	½	¼	8.355	8⅜	0.835	13/16	18¼	1 9/16	15/16
x 73	21.5	21.24	21¼	0.455	7/16	¼	8.295	8¼	0.740	¾	18¼	1½	15/16
x 68	20.0	21.13	21⅛	0.430	7/16	¼	8.270	8¼	0.685	11/16	18¼	1 7/16	7/8
x 62	18.3	20.99	21	0.400	⅜	3/16	8.240	8¼	0.615	⅝	18¼	1⅜	7/8
W 21x 57	16.7	21.06	21	0.405	⅜	3/16	6.555	6½	0.650	⅝	18¼	1⅜	7/8
x 50	14.7	20.83	20⅞	0.380	⅜	3/16	6.530	6½	0.535	9/16	18¼	1 5/16	7/8
x 44	13.0	20.66	20⅝	0.350	⅜	3/16	6.500	6½	0.450	7/16	18¼	1 3/16	7/8

ᵃFor application refer to Notes in Table 2.
ᵇHeavier shapes in this series are available from some producers.

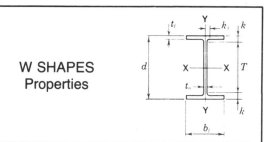

W SHAPES
Properties

Nominal Wt. per Ft	Compact Section Criteria		F_y'''	X_1	$X_2 \times 10^6$	Elastic Properties						Plastic Modulus	
	$\frac{b_f}{2t_f}$	$\frac{h_c}{t_w}$				Axis X-X			Axis Y-Y			Z_x	Z_y
						I	S	r	I	S	r		
Lb.			Ksi	Ksi	(1/Ksi)²	In.⁴	In.³	In.	In.⁴	In.³	In.	In.³	In.³
117	7.5	39.2	42	2090	8190	3540	291	10.1	297	46.5	2.94	327	71.4
104	8.5	43.1	34	1860	12900	3100	258	10.1	259	40.7	2.91	289	62.4
103	4.6	39.2	42	2400	5280	3000	245	9.96	119	26.5	1.99	280	41.5
94	5.2	41.9	37	2180	7800	2700	222	9.87	109	24.0	1.98	254	37.5
84	5.9	45.9	30	1950	12200	2370	196	9.79	94.4	20.9	1.95	224	32.6
76	6.6	49.0	27	1760	18600	2100	176	9.69	82.5	18.4	1.92	200	28.6
68	7.7	52.0	24	1590	29000	1830	154	9.55	70.4	15.7	1.87	177	24.5
62	6.0	50.1	25	1700	25100	1550	131	9.23	34.5	9.80	1.38	153	15.7
55	6.9	54.6	21	1540	39600	1350	114	9.11	29.1	8.30	1.34	134	13.3
402	2.1	10.8	—	8000	41	12200	937	10.2	1270	189	3.27	1130	296
364	2.3	11.8	—	7340	57	10800	846	10.0	1120	168	3.23	1010	263
333	2.5	12.8	—	6790	78	9610	769	9.91	994	151	3.19	915	237
300	2.7	14.2	—	6200	111	8480	692	9.81	873	134	3.15	816	210
275	2.9	15.4	—	5720	150	7620	632	9.71	785	122	3.12	741	189
248	3.2	17.1	—	5210	215	6760	569	9.63	694	109	3.09	663	169
223	3.5	18.8	—	4700	319	5950	510	9.54	609	96.1	3.05	589	149
201	3.9	20.6	—	4290	453	5310	461	9.47	542	86.1	3.02	530	133
182	4.2	22.6	—	3910	649	4730	417	9.40	483	77.2	3.00	476	119
166	4.6	25.0	—	3590	904	4280	380	9.36	435	70.1	2.98	432	108
147	5.4	26.1	—	3140	1590	3630	329	9.17	376	60.1	2.95	373	92.6
132	6.0	28.9	—	2840	2350	3220	295	9.12	333	53.5	2.93	333	82.3
122	6.5	31.3	—	2630	3160	2960	273	9.09	305	49.2	2.92	307	75.6
111	7.1	34.1	55	2400	4510	2670	249	9.05	274	44.5	2.90	279	68.2
101	7.7	37.5	45	2200	6400	2420	227	9.02	248	40.3	2.89	253	61.7
93	4.5	32.3	61	2680	3460	2070	192	8.70	92.9	22.1	1.84	221	34.7
83	5.0	36.4	48	2400	5250	1830	171	8.67	81.4	19.5	1.83	196	30.5
73	5.6	41.2	38	2140	8380	1600	151	8.64	70.6	17.0	1.81	172	26.6
68	6.0	43.6	34	2000	10900	1480	140	8.60	64.7	15.7	1.80	160	24.4
62	6.7	46.9	29	1820	15900	1330	127	8.54	57.5	13.9	1.77	144	21.7
57	5.0	46.3	30	1960	13100	1170	111	8.36	30.6	9.35	1.35	129	14.8
50	6.1	49.4	26	1730	22600	984	94.5	8.18	24.9	7.64	1.30	110	12.2
44	7.2	53.6	22	1550	36600	843	81.6	8.06	20.7	6.36	1.26	95.4	10.2

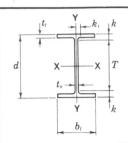

W SHAPES
Dimensions

Desig-nation	Area A	Depth d		Web Thickness t_w		$\frac{t_w}{2}$	Flange Width b_f		Thickness t_f		Distance T	k	k_1
	In.^{2}	In.		In.		In.	In.		In.		In.	In.	In.
W 18x311[a]	91.5	22.32	22⅜	1.520	1½	¾	12.005	12	2.740	2¾	15½	3⁷⁄₁₆	1³⁄₁₆
x283[a]	83.2	21.85	21⅞	1.400	1⅜	¹¹⁄₁₆	11.890	11⅞	2.500	2½	15½	3³⁄₁₆	1³⁄₁₆
x258[a]	75.9	21.46	21½	1.280	1¼	⅝	11.770	11¾	2.300	2⁵⁄₁₆	15½	3	1⅛
x234[a]	68.8	21.06	21	1.160	1³⁄₁₆	⅝	11.650	11⅝	2.110	2⅛	15½	2¾	1
x211[a]	62.1	20.67	20⅝	1.060	1¹⁄₁₆	⁹⁄₁₆	11.555	11½	1.910	1¹⁵⁄₁₆	15½	2⁹⁄₁₆	1
x192	56.4	20.35	20⅜	0.960	1	½	11.455	11½	1.750	1¾	15½	2⁷⁄₁₆	¹⁵⁄₁₆
x175	51.3	20.04	20	0.890	⅞	⁷⁄₁₆	11.375	11⅜	1.590	1⁹⁄₁₆	15½	2¼	⅞
x158	46.3	19.72	19¾	0.810	¹³⁄₁₆	⁷⁄₁₆	11.300	11¼	1.440	1⁷⁄₁₆	15½	2⅛	⅞
x143	42.1	19.49	19½	0.730	¾	⅜	11.220	11¼	1.320	1⁵⁄₁₆	15½	2	¹³⁄₁₆
x130	38.2	19.25	19¼	0.670	¹¹⁄₁₆	⅜	11.160	11⅛	1.200	1³⁄₁₆	15½	1⅞	¹³⁄₁₆
x119	35.1	18.97	19	0.655	⅝	⁵⁄₁₆	11.265	11¼	1.060	1¹⁄₁₆	15½	1¾	¹⁵⁄₁₆
x106	31.1	18.73	18¾	0.590	⁹⁄₁₆	⁵⁄₁₆	11.200	11¼	0.940	¹⁵⁄₁₆	15½	1⅝	¹⁵⁄₁₆
x 97	28.5	18.59	18⅝	0.535	⁹⁄₁₆	⁵⁄₁₆	11.145	11⅛	0.870	⅞	15½	1⁹⁄₁₆	⅞
x 86	25.3	18.39	18⅜	0.480	½	¼	11.090	11⅛	0.770	¾	15½	1⁷⁄₁₆	⅞
x 76	22.3	18.21	18¼	0.425	⁷⁄₁₆	¼	11.035	11	0.680	¹¹⁄₁₆	15½	1⅜	¹³⁄₁₆
W 18x 71	20.8	18.47	18½	0.495	½	¼	7.635	7⅝	0.810	¹³⁄₁₆	15½	1½	⅞
x 65	19.1	18.35	18⅜	0.450	⁷⁄₁₆	¼	7.590	7⅝	0.750	¾	15½	1⁷⁄₁₆	⅞
x 60	17.6	18.24	18¼	0.415	⁷⁄₁₆	¼	7.555	7½	0.695	¹¹⁄₁₆	15½	1⅜	¹³⁄₁₆
x 55	16.2	18.11	18⅛	0.390	⅜	³⁄₁₆	7.530	7½	0.630	⅝	15½	1⁵⁄₁₆	¹³⁄₁₆
x 50	14.7	17.99	18	0.355	⅜	³⁄₁₆	7.495	7½	0.570	⁹⁄₁₆	15½	1¼	¹³⁄₁₆
W 18x 46	13.5	18.06	18	0.360	⅜	¹³⁄₁₆	6.060	6	0.605	⅝	15½	1¼	¹³⁄₁₆
x 40	11.8	17.90	17⅞	0.315	⁵⁄₁₆	³⁄₁₆	6.015	6	0.525	½	15½	1³⁄₁₆	¹³⁄₁₆
x 35	10.3	17.70	17¾	0.300	⁵⁄₁₆	³⁄₁₆	6.000	6	0.425	⁷⁄₁₆	15½	1⅛	¾
W 16x100	29.4	16.97	17	0.585	⁹⁄₁₆	⁵⁄₁₆	10.425	10⅜	0.985	1	13⅝	1¹¹⁄₁₆	¹⁵⁄₁₆
x 89	26.2	16.75	16¾	0.525	½	¼	10.365	10⅜	0.875	⅞	13⅝	1⁹⁄₁₆	⅞
x 77	22.6	16.52	16½	0.455	⁷⁄₁₆	¼	10.295	10¼	0.760	¾	13⅝	1⁷⁄₁₆	⅞
x 67	19.7	16.33	16⅜	0.395	⅜	³⁄₁₆	10.235	10¼	0.665	¹¹⁄₁₆	13⅝	1⅜	¹³⁄₁₆
W 16x 57	16.8	16.43	16⅜	0.430	⁷⁄₁₆	¼	7.120	7⅛	0.715	¹¹⁄₁₆	13⅝	1⅜	⅞
x 50	14.7	16.26	16¼	0.380	⅜	³⁄₁₆	7.070	7⅛	0.630	⅝	13⅝	1⁵⁄₁₆	¹³⁄₁₆
x 45	13.3	16.13	16⅛	0.345	⅜	³⁄₁₆	7.035	7	0.565	⁹⁄₁₆	13⅝	1¼	¹³⁄₁₆
x 40	11.8	16.01	16	0.305	⁵⁄₁₆	³⁄₁₆	6.995	7	0.505	½	13⅝	1³⁄₁₆	¹³⁄₁₆
x 36	10.6	15.86	15⅞	0.295	⁵⁄₁₆	³⁄₁₆	6.985	7	0.430	⁷⁄₁₆	13⅝	1⅛	¾
W 16x 31	9.12	15.88	15⅞	0.275	¼	⅛	5.525	5½	0.440	⁷⁄₁₆	13⅝	1⅛	¾
x 26	7.68	15.69	15¾	0.250	¼	⅛	5.500	5½	0.345	⅜	13⅝	1¹⁄₁₆	¾

[a]For application refer to Notes in Table 2.

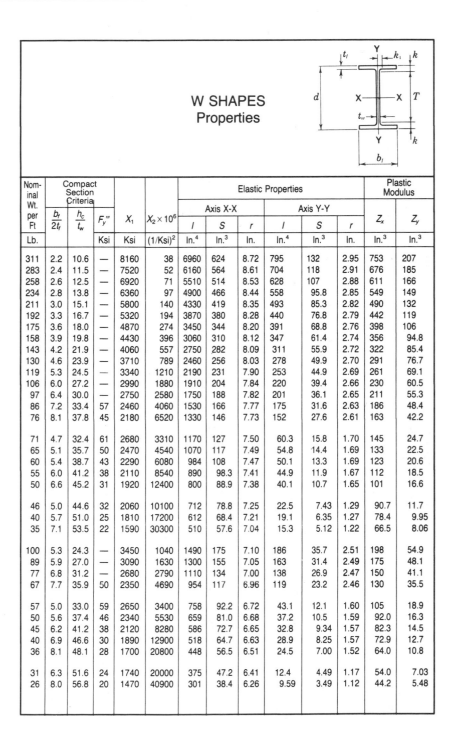

W SHAPES
Properties

Nom-inal Wt. per Ft	Compact Section Criteria					Elastic Properties						Plastic Modulus	
	$\frac{b_f}{2t_f}$	$\frac{h_c}{t_w}$	F_y'''	X_1	$X_2 \times 10^6$	Axis X-X			Axis Y-Y			Z_x	Z_y
						I	S	r	I	S	r		
Lb.			Ksi	Ksi	(1/Ksi)²	In.⁴	In.³	In.	In.⁴	In.³	In.	In.³	In.³
311	2.2	10.6	—	8160	38	6960	624	8.72	795	132	2.95	753	207
283	2.4	11.5	—	7520	52	6160	564	8.61	704	118	2.91	676	185
258	2.6	12.5	—	6920	71	5510	514	8.53	628	107	2.88	611	166
234	2.8	13.8	—	6360	97	4900	466	8.44	558	95.8	2.85	549	149
211	3.0	15.1	—	5800	140	4330	419	8.35	493	85.3	2.82	490	132
192	3.3	16.7	—	5320	194	3870	380	8.28	440	76.8	2.79	442	119
175	3.6	18.0	—	4870	274	3450	344	8.20	391	68.8	2.76	398	106
158	3.9	19.8	—	4430	396	3060	310	8.12	347	61.4	2.74	356	94.8
143	4.2	21.9	—	4060	557	2750	282	8.09	311	55.9	2.72	322	85.4
130	4.6	23.9	—	3710	789	2460	256	8.03	278	49.9	2.70	291	76.7
119	5.3	24.5	—	3340	1210	2190	231	7.90	253	44.9	2.69	261	69.1
106	6.0	27.2	—	2990	1880	1910	204	7.84	220	39.4	2.66	230	60.5
97	6.4	30.0	—	2750	2580	1750	188	7.82	201	36.1	2.65	211	55.3
86	7.2	33.4	57	2460	4060	1530	166	7.77	175	31.6	2.63	186	48.4
76	8.1	37.8	45	2180	6520	1330	146	7.73	152	27.6	2.61	163	42.2
71	4.7	32.4	61	2680	3310	1170	127	7.50	60.3	15.8	1.70	145	24.7
65	5.1	35.7	50	2470	4540	1070	117	7.49	54.8	14.4	1.69	133	22.5
60	5.4	38.7	43	2290	6080	984	108	7.47	50.1	13.3	1.69	123	20.6
55	6.0	41.2	38	2110	8540	890	98.3	7.41	44.9	11.9	1.67	112	18.5
50	6.6	45.2	31	1920	12400	800	88.9	7.38	40.1	10.7	1.65	101	16.6
46	5.0	44.6	32	2060	10100	712	78.8	7.25	22.5	7.43	1.29	90.7	11.7
40	5.7	51.0	25	1810	17200	612	68.4	7.21	19.1	6.35	1.27	78.4	9.95
35	7.1	53.5	22	1590	30300	510	57.6	7.04	15.3	5.12	1.22	66.5	8.06
100	5.3	24.3	—	3450	1040	1490	175	7.10	186	35.7	2.51	198	54.9
89	5.9	27.0	—	3090	1630	1300	155	7.05	163	31.4	2.49	175	48.1
77	6.8	31.2	—	2680	2790	1110	134	7.00	138	26.9	2.47	150	41.1
67	7.7	35.9	50	2350	4690	954	117	6.96	119	23.2	2.46	130	35.5
57	5.0	33.0	59	2650	3400	758	92.2	6.72	43.1	12.1	1.60	105	18.9
50	5.6	37.4	46	2340	5530	659	81.0	6.68	37.2	10.5	1.59	92.0	16.3
45	6.2	41.2	38	2120	8280	586	72.7	6.65	32.8	9.34	1.57	82.3	14.5
40	6.9	46.6	30	1890	12900	518	64.7	6.63	28.9	8.25	1.57	72.9	12.7
36	8.1	48.1	28	1700	20800	448	56.5	6.51	24.5	7.00	1.52	64.0	10.8
31	6.3	51.6	24	1740	20000	375	47.2	6.41	12.4	4.49	1.17	54.0	7.03
26	8.0	56.8	20	1470	40900	301	38.4	6.26	9.59	3.49	1.12	44.2	5.48

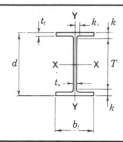

W SHAPES
Dimensions

Desig-nation	Area A	Depth d	Web			Flange			Distance		
			Thickness t_w		$\frac{t_w}{2}$	Width b_f		Thickness t_f		T	k	k_1
	In.²	In.	In.		In.	In.		In.		In.	In.	In.
W 14x730[a]	215.0	22.42	22⅜	3.070	3¹/₁₆	1⁹/₁₆	17.890	17⅞	4.910	4¹⁵/₁₆	11¼	5⁹/₁₆	2³/₁₆
x665[a]	196.0	21.64	21⅝	2.830	2¹³/₁₆	1⁷/₁₆	17.650	17⅝	4.520	4½	11¼	5³/₁₆	2¹/₁₆
x605[a]	178.0	20.92	20⅞	2.595	2⅝	1⁵/₁₆	17.415	17⅜	4.160	4³/₁₆	11¼	4¹³/₁₆	1¹⁵/₁₆
x550[a]	162.0	20.24	20¼	2.380	2⅜	1³/₁₆	17.200	17¼	3.820	3¹³/₁₆	11¼	4½	1¹³/₁₆
x500[a]	147.0	19.60	19⅝	2.190	2³/₁₆	1⅛	17.010	17	3.500	3½	11¼	4³/₁₆	1¾
x455[a]	134.0	19.02	19	2.015	2	1	16.835	16⅞	3.210	3³/₁₆	11¼	3⅞	1⅝
W 14x426[a]	125.0	18.67	18⅝	1.875	1⅞	¹⁵/₁₆	16.695	16¾	3.035	3¹/₁₆	11¼	3¹¹/₁₆	1⁹/₁₆
x398[a]	117.0	18.29	18¼	1.770	1¾	⅞	16.590	16⅝	2.845	2⅞	11¼	3½	1½
x370[a]	109.0	17.92	17⅞	1.655	1⅝	¹³/₁₆	16.475	16½	2.660	2¹¹/₁₆	11¼	3⁵/₁₆	1⁷/₁₆
x342[a]	101.0	17.54	17½	1.540	1⁹/₁₆	¹³/₁₆	16.360	16⅜	2.470	2½	11¼	3⅛	1⅜
x311[a]	91.4	17.12	17⅛	1.410	1⁷/₁₆	¾	16.230	16¼	2.260	2¼	11¼	2¹⁵/₁₆	1⁵/₁₆
x283[a]	83.3	16.74	16¾	1.290	1⁵/₁₆	¹¹/₁₆	16.110	16⅛	2.070	2¹/₁₆	11¼	2¾	1¼
x257[a]	75.6	16.38	16⅜	1.175	1³/₁₆	⅝	15.995	16	1.890	1⅞	11¼	2⁹/₁₆	1³/₁₆
x233[a]	68.5	16.04	16	1.070	1¹/₁₆	⁹/₁₆	15.890	15⅞	1.720	1¾	11¼	2⅜	1³/₁₆
x211[a]	62.0	15.72	15¾	0.980	1	½	15.800	15¾	1.560	1⁹/₁₆	11¼	2¼	1⅛
x193	56.8	15.48	15½	0.890	⅞	⁷/₁₆	15.710	15¾	1.440	1⁷/₁₆	11¼	2⅛	1¹/₁₆
x176	51.8	15.22	15¼	0.830	¹³/₁₆	⁷/₁₆	15.650	15⅝	1.310	1⁵/₁₆	11¼	2	1¹/₁₆
x159	46.7	14.98	15	0.745	¾	⅜	15.565	15⅝	1.190	1³/₁₆	11¼	1⅞	1
x145	42.7	14.78	14¾	0.680	¹¹/₁₆	⅜	15.500	15½	1.090	1¹/₁₆	11¼	1¾	1

[a]For application refer to Notes in Table 2.

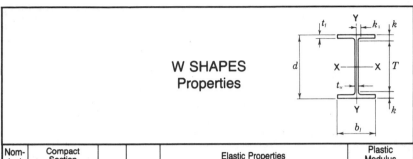

	Compact Section Criteria					Elastic Properties						Plastic Modulus	
Nominal Wt. per Ft	$\frac{b_f}{2t_f}$	$\frac{h_c}{t_w}$	F_y'''	X_1	$X_2 \times 10^6$	Axis X-X			Axis Y-Y			Z_x	Z_y
						I	S	r	I	S	r		
Lb.			Ksi	Ksi	$(1/Ksi)^2$	In.⁴	In.³	In.	In.⁴	In.³	In.	In.³	In.³
730	1.8	3.7	—	17500	1.90	14300	1280	8.17	4720	527	4.69	1660	816
665	2.0	4.0	—	16300	2.46	12400	1150	7.98	4170	472	4.62	1480	730
605	2.1	4.4	—	15100	3.20	10800	1040	7.80	3680	423	4.55	1320	652
550	2.3	4.8	—	14200	4.15	9430	931	7.63	3250	378	4.49	1180	583
500	2.4	5.2	—	13100	5.49	8210	838	7.48	2880	339	4.43	1050	522
455	2.6	5.7	—	12200	7.30	7190	756	7.33	2560	304	4.38	936	468
426	2.8	6.1	—	11500	8.89	6600	707	7.26	2360	283	4.34	869	434
398	2.9	6.4	—	10900	11.0	6000	656	7.16	2170	262	4.31	801	402
370	3.1	6.9	—	10300	13.9	5440	607	7.07	1990	241	4.27	736	370
342	3.3	7.4	—	9600	17.9	4900	559	6.98	1810	221	4.24	672	338
311	3.6	8.1	—	8820	24.4	4330	506	6.88	1610	199	4.20	603	304
283	3.9	8.8	—	8120	33.4	3840	459	6.79	1440	179	4.17	542	274
257	4.2	9.7	—	7460	46.1	3400	415	6.71	1290	161	4.13	487	246
233	4.6	10.7	—	6820	64.9	3010	375	6.63	1150	145	4.10	436	221
211	5.1	11.6	—	6230	91.8	2660	338	6.55	1030	130	4.07	390	198
193	5.5	12.8	—	5740	125	2400	310	6.50	931	119	4.05	355	180
176	6.0	13.7	—	5280	173	2140	281	6.43	838	107	4.02	320	163
159	6.5	15.3	—	4790	249	1900	254	6.38	748	96.2	4.00	287	146
145	7.1	16.8	—	4400	348	1710	232	6.33	677	87.3	3.98	260	133

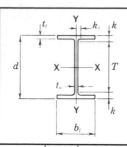

W SHAPES
Dimensions

Desig-nation	Area A	Depth d		Web		Flange				Distance		
				Thickness t_w		$\frac{t_w}{2}$	Width b_f		Thickness t_f		T	k	k_1
	In.²	In.		In.		In.	In.		In.		In.	In.	In.
W 14x132	38.8	14.66	14⅝	0.645	⅝	5/16	14.725	14¾	1.030	1	11¼	1 11/16	15/16
x120	35.3	14.48	14½	0.590	9/16	5/16	14.670	14⅝	0.940	15/16	11¼	1⅝	15/16
x109	32.0	14.32	14⅜	0.525	½	¼	14.605	14⅝	0.860	⅞	11¼	1 9/16	⅞
x 99	29.1	14.16	14⅛	0.485	½	¼	14.565	14⅝	0.780	¾	11¼	1 7/16	⅞
x 90	26.5	14.02	14	0.440	7/16	¼	14.520	14½	0.710	11/16	11¼	1⅜	⅞
W 14x 82	24.1	14.31	14¼	0.510	½	¼	10.130	10⅛	0.855	⅞	11	1⅝	1
x 74	21.8	14.17	14⅛	0.450	7/16	¼	10.070	10⅛	0.785	13/16	11	1 9/16	15/16
x 68	20.0	14.04	14	0.415	7/16	¼	10.035	10	0.720	¾	11	1½	15/16
x 61	17.9	13.89	13⅞	0.375	⅜	3/16	9.995	10	0.645	⅝	11	1 7/16	15/16
W 14x 53	15.6	13.92	13⅞	0.370	⅜	3/16	8.060	8	0.660	11/16	11	1 7/16	15/16
x 48	14.1	13.79	13¾	0.340	5/16	3/16	8.030	8	0.595	⅝	11	1⅜	⅞
x 43	12.6	13.66	13⅝	0.305	5/16	3/16	7.995	8	0.530	½	11	1 5/16	⅞
W 14x 38	11.2	14.10	14⅛	0.310	5/16	3/16	6.770	6¾	0.515	½	12	1 1/16	⅝
x 34	10.0	13.98	14	0.285	5/16	3/16	6.745	6¾	0.455	7/16	12	1	⅝
x 30	8.85	13.84	13⅞	0.270	¼	⅛	6.730	6¾	0.385	⅜	12	15/16	⅝
W 14x 26	7.69	13.91	13⅞	0.255	¼	⅛	5.025	5	0.420	7/16	12	15/16	9/16
x 22	6.49	13.74	13¾	0.230	¼	⅛	5.000	5	0.335	5/16	12	⅞	9/16

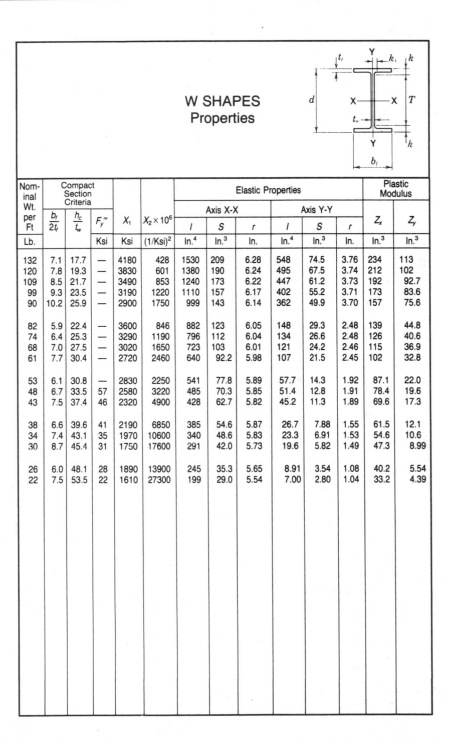

W SHAPES
Properties

Nom- inal Wt. per Ft	Compact Section Criteria			X₁	X₂ × 10⁶	Elastic Properties						Plastic Modulus	
						Axis X-X			Axis Y-Y				
	$\frac{b_f}{2t_f}$	$\frac{h_c}{t_w}$	F_y'''	X_1	$X_2 \times 10^6$	I	S	r	I	S	r	Z_x	Z_y
Lb.			Ksi	Ksi	(1/Ksi)²	In.⁴	In.³	In.	In.⁴	In.³	In.	In.³	In.³
132	7.1	17.7	—	4180	428	1530	209	6.28	548	74.5	3.76	234	113
120	7.8	19.3	—	3830	601	1380	190	6.24	495	67.5	3.74	212	102
109	8.5	21.7	—	3490	853	1240	173	6.22	447	61.2	3.73	192	92.7
99	9.3	23.5	—	3190	1220	1110	157	6.17	402	55.2	3.71	173	83.6
90	10.2	25.9	—	2900	1750	999	143	6.14	362	49.9	3.70	157	75.6
82	5.9	22.4	—	3600	846	882	123	6.05	148	29.3	2.48	139	44.8
74	6.4	25.3	—	3290	1190	796	112	6.04	134	26.6	2.48	126	40.6
68	7.0	27.5	—	3020	1650	723	103	6.01	121	24.2	2.46	115	36.9
61	7.7	30.4	—	2720	2460	640	92.2	5.98	107	21.5	2.45	102	32.8
53	6.1	30.8	—	2830	2250	541	77.8	5.89	57.7	14.3	1.92	87.1	22.0
48	6.7	33.5	57	2580	3220	485	70.3	5.85	51.4	12.8	1.91	78.4	19.6
43	7.5	37.4	46	2320	4900	428	62.7	5.82	45.2	11.3	1.89	69.6	17.3
38	6.6	39.6	41	2190	6850	385	54.6	5.87	26.7	7.88	1.55	61.5	12.1
34	7.4	43.1	35	1970	10600	340	48.6	5.83	23.3	6.91	1.53	54.6	10.6
30	8.7	45.4	31	1750	17600	291	42.0	5.73	19.6	5.82	1.49	47.3	8.99
26	6.0	48.1	28	1890	13900	245	35.3	5.65	8.91	3.54	1.08	40.2	5.54
22	7.5	53.5	22	1610	27300	199	29.0	5.54	7.00	2.80	1.04	33.2	4.39

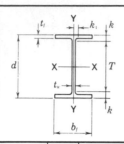

W SHAPES
Dimensions

Desig-nation	Area A	Depth d		Web		Flange				Distance		
				Thickness t_w		$\dfrac{t_w}{2}$	Width b_f		Thickness t_f		T	k	k_1
	In.²	In.		In.		In.	In.		In.		In.	In.	In.
W 12x336[a]	98.8	16.82	16⅞	1.775	1¾	⅞	13.385	13⅜	2.955	2¹⁵/₁₆	9½	3¹¹/₁₆	1½
x305[a]	89.6	16.32	16⅜	1.625	1⅝	¹³/₁₆	13.235	13¼	2.705	2¹¹/₁₆	9½	3⁷/₁₆	1⁷/₁₆
x279[a]	81.9	15.85	15⅞	1.530	1½	¾	13.140	13⅛	2.470	2½	9½	3³/₁₆	1⅜
x252[a]	74.1	15.41	15⅜	1.395	1⅜	¹¹/₁₆	13.005	13	2.250	2¼	9½	2¹⁵/₁₆	1⁵/₁₆
x230[a]	67.7	15.05	15	1.285	1⁵/₁₆	¹¹/₁₆	12.895	12⅞	2.070	2¹/₁₆	9½	2¾	1¼
x210[a]	61.8	14.71	14¾	1.180	1³/₁₆	⅝	12.790	12¾	1.900	1⅞	9½	2⅝	1¼
x190[a]	55.8	14.38	14⅜	1.060	1¹/₁₆	⁹/₁₆	12.670	12⅝	1.735	1¾	9½	2⁷/₁₆	1³/₁₆
x170[a]	50.0	14.03	14	0.960	¹⁵/₁₆	½	12.570	12⅝	1.560	1⁹/₁₆	9½	2¼	1⅛
x152	44.7	13.71	13¾	0.870	⅞	⁷/₁₆	12.480	12½	1.400	1⅜	9½	2⅛	1¹/₁₆
x136	39.9	13.41	13⅜	0.790	¹³/₁₆	⁷/₁₆	12.400	12⅜	1.250	1¼	9½	1¹⁵/₁₆	1
x120	35.3	13.12	13⅛	0.710	¹¹/₁₆	⅜	12.320	12⅜	1.105	1⅛	9½	1¹³/₁₆	1
x106	31.2	12.89	12⅞	0.610	⅝	⁵/₁₆	12.220	12¼	0.990	1	9½	1¹¹/₁₆	¹⁵/₁₆
x 96	28.2	12.71	12¾	0.550	⁹/₁₆	⁵/₁₆	12.160	12⅛	0.900	⅞	9½	1⅝	⅞
x 87	25.6	12.53	12½	0.515	½	¼	12.125	12⅛	0.810	¹³/₁₆	9½	1½	⅞
x 79	23.2	12.38	12⅜	0.470	½	¼	12.080	12⅛	0.735	¾	9½	1⁷/₁₆	⅞
x 72	21.1	12.25	12¼	0.430	⁷/₁₆	¼	12.040	12	0.670	¹¹/₁₆	9½	1⅜	⅞
x 65	19.1	12.12	12⅛	0.390	⅜	³/₁₆	12.000	12	0.605	⅝	9½	1⁵/₁₆	¹³/₁₆
W 12x 58	17.0	12.19	12¼	0.360	⅜	³/₁₆	10.010	10	0.640	⅝	9½	1⅜	¹³/₁₆
x 53	15.6	12.06	12	0.345	⅜	³/₁₆	9.995	10	0.575	⁹/₁₆	9½	1¼	¹³/₁₆
W 12x 50	14.7	12.19	12¼	0.370	⅜	³/₁₆	8.080	8⅛	0.640	⅝	9½	1⅜	¹³/₁₆
x 45	13.2	12.06	12	0.335	⁵/₁₆	³/₁₆	8.045	8	0.575	⁹/₁₆	9½	1¼	¹³/₁₆
x 40	11.8	11.94	12	0.295	⁵/₁₆	³/₁₆	8.005	8	0.515	½	9½	1¼	¾
W 12x 35	10.3	12.50	12½	0.300	⁵/₁₆	³/₁₆	6.560	6½	0.520	½	10½	1	⁹/₁₆
x 30	8.79	12.34	12⅜	0.260	¼	⅛	6.520	6½	0.440	⁷/₁₆	10½	¹⁵/₁₆	½
x 26	7.65	12.22	12¼	0.230	¼	⅛	6.490	6½	0.380	⅜	10½	⅞	½
W 12x 22	6.48	12.31	12¼	0.260	¼	⅛	4.030	4	0.425	⁷/₁₆	10½	⅞	½
x 19	5.57	12.16	12⅛	0.235	¼	⅛	4.005	4	0.350	⅜	10½	¹³/₁₆	½
x 16	4.71	11.99	12	0.220	¼	⅛	3.990	4	0.265	¼	10½	¾	½
x 14	4.16	11.91	11⅞	0.200	³/₁₆	⅛	3.970	4	0.225	¼	10½	¹¹/₁₆	½

[a]For application refer to Notes in Table 2.

W SHAPES
Properties

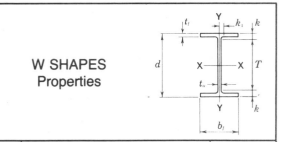

Nom-inal Wt. per Ft	Compact Section Criteria			X_1	$X_2 \times 10^6$	Elastic Properties						Plastic Modulus	
						Axis X-X			Axis Y-Y				
	$\frac{b_f}{2t_f}$	$\frac{h_c}{t_w}$	F_y'''			I	S	r	I	S	r	Z_x	Z_y
Lb.			Ksi	Ksi	(1/Ksi)²	In.⁴	In.³	In.	In.⁴	In.³	In.	In.³	In.³
336	2.3	5.5	—	12800	6.05	4060	483	6.41	1190	177	3.47	603	274
305	2.4	6.0	—	11800	8.17	3550	435	6.29	1050	159	3.42	537	244
279	2.7	6.3	—	11000	10.8	3110	393	6.16	937	143	3.38	481	220
252	2.9	7.0	—	10100	14.7	2720	353	6.06	828	127	3.34	428	196
230	3.1	7.6	—	9390	19.7	2420	321	5.97	742	115	3.31	386	177
210	3.4	8.2	—	8670	26.6	2140	292	5.89	664	104	3.28	348	159
190	3.7	9.2	—	7940	37.0	1890	263	5.82	589	93.0	3.25	311	143
170	4.0	10.1	—	7190	54.0	1650	235	5.74	517	82.3	3.22	275	126
152	4.5	11.2	—	6510	79.3	1430	209	5.66	454	72.8	3.19	243	111
136	5.0	12.3	—	5850	119	1240	186	5.58	398	64.2	3.16	214	98.0
120	5.6	13.7	—	5240	184	1070	163	5.51	345	56.0	3.13	186	85.4
106	6.2	15.9	—	4660	285	933	145	5.47	301	49.3	3.11	164	75.1
96	6.8	17.7	—	4250	405	833	131	5.44	270	44.4	3.09	147	67.5
87	7.5	18.9	—	3880	586	740	118	5.38	241	39.7	3.07	132	60.4
79	8.2	20.7	—	3530	839	662	107	5.34	216	35.8	3.05	119	54.3
72	9.0	22.6	—	3230	1180	597	97.4	5.31	195	32.4	3.04	108	49.2
65	9.9	24.9	—	2940	1720	533	87.9	5.28	174	29.1	3.02	96.8	44.1
58	7.8	27.0	—	3070	1470	475	78.0	5.28	107	21.4	2.51	86.4	32.5
53	8.7	28.1	—	2820	2100	425	70.6	5.23	95.8	19.2	2.48	77.9	29.1
50	6.3	26.2	—	3170	1410	394	64.7	5.18	56.3	13.9	1.96	72.4	21.4
45	7.0	29.0	—	2870	2070	350	58.1	5.15	50.0	12.4	1.94	64.7	19.0
40	7.8	32.9	59	2580	3110	310	51.9	5.13	44.1	11.0	1.93	57.5	16.8
35	6.3	36.2	49	2420	4340	285	45.6	5.25	24.5	7.47	1.54	51.2	11.5
30	7.4	41.8	37	2090	7950	238	38.6	5.21	20.3	6.24	1.52	43.1	9.56
26	8.5	47.2	29	1820	13900	204	33.4	5.17	17.3	5.34	1.51	37.2	8.17
22	4.7	41.8	37	2160	8640	156	25.4	4.91	4.66	2.31	0.847	29.3	3.66
19	5.7	46.2	30	1880	15600	130	21.3	4.82	3.76	1.88	0.822	24.7	2.98
16	7.5	49.4	26	1610	32000	103	17.1	4.67	2.82	1.41	0.773	20.1	2.26
14	8.8	54.3	22	1450	49300	88.6	14.9	4.62	2.36	1.19	0.753	17.4	1.90

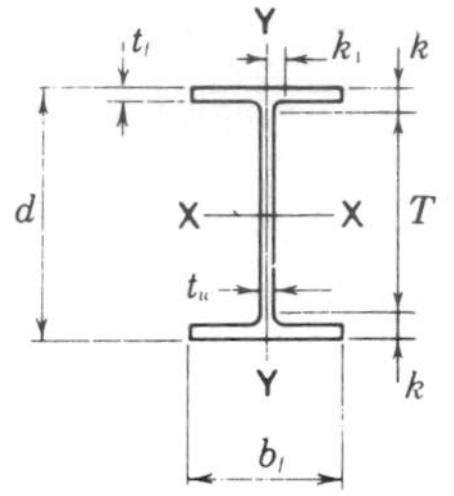

W SHAPES
Dimensions

Designation	Area A	Depth d		Web: Thickness t_w		Web: $\frac{t_w}{2}$	Flange: Width b_f		Flange: Thickness t_f		Distance: T	Distance: k	Distance: k_1
	In.^{2}	In.		In.		In.	In.		In.		In.	In.	In.
W 10x112	32.9	11.36	11 3/8	0.755	3/4	3/8	10.415	10 3/8	1.250	1 1/4	7 5/8	1 7/8	15/16
x100	29.4	11.10	11 1/8	0.680	11/16	3/8	10.340	10 3/8	1.120	1 1/8	7 5/8	1 3/4	7/8
x 88	25.9	10.84	10 7/8	0.605	5/8	5/16	10.265	10 1/4	0.990	1	7 5/8	1 5/8	13/16
x 77	22.6	10.60	10 5/8	0.530	1/2	1/4	10.190	10 1/4	0.870	7/8	7 5/8	1 1/2	13/16
x 68	20.0	10.40	10 3/8	0.470	3/8	1/4	10.130	10 1/8	0.770	3/4	7 5/8	1 3/8	3/4
x 60	17.6	10.22	10 1/4	0.420	7/16	1/4	10.080	10 1/8	0.680	11/16	7 5/8	1 5/16	3/4
x 54	15.8	10.09	10 1/8	0.370	3/8	3/16	10.030	10	0.615	5/8	7 5/8	1 1/4	11/16
x 49	14.4	9.98	10	0.340	5/16	3/16	10.000	10	0.560	9/16	7 5/8	1 3/16	11/16
W 10x 45	13.3	10.10	10 1/8	0.350	3/8	3/16	8.020	8	0.620	5/8	7 5/8	1 1/4	11/16
x 39	11.5	9.92	9 7/8	0.315	5/16	3/16	7.985	8	0.530	1/2	7 5/8	1 1/8	11/16
x 33	9.71	9.73	9 3/4	0.290	5/16	3/16	7.960	8	0.435	7/16	7 5/8	1 1/16	11/16
W 10x 30	8.84	10.47	10 1/2	0.300	5/16	3/16	5.810	5 3/4	0.510	1/2	8 5/8	15/16	1/2
x 26	7.61	10.33	10 3/8	0.260	1/4	1/8	5.770	5 3/4	0.440	7/16	8 5/8	7/8	1/2
x 22	6.49	10.17	10 1/8	0.240	1/4	1/8	5.750	5 3/4	0.360	3/8	8 5/8	3/4	1/2
W 10x 19	5.62	10.24	10 1/4	0.250	1/4	1/8	4.020	4	0.395	3/8	8 5/8	13/16	1/2
x 17	4.99	10.11	10 1/8	0.240	1/4	1/8	4.010	4	0.330	5/16	8 5/8	3/4	1/2
x 15	4.41	9.99	10	0.230	1/4	1/8	4.000	4	0.270	1/4	8 5/8	11/16	7/16
x 12	3.54	9.87	9 7/8	0.190	3/16	1/8	3.960	4	0.210	3/16	8 5/8	5/8	7/16

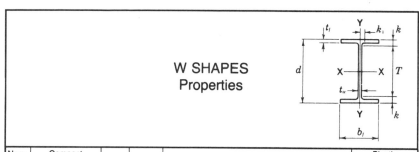

W SHAPES
Properties

Nom- inal Wt. per Ft	Compact Section Criteria			X_1	$X_2 \times 10^6$	Elastic Properties						Plastic Modulus	
						Axis X-X			Axis Y-Y				
	$\frac{b_f}{2t_f}$	$\frac{h_c}{t_w}$	F_y'''			I	S	r	I	S	r	Z_x	Z_y
Lb.			Ksi	Ksi	$(1/Ksi)^2$	In.^{4}	In.^{3}	In.	In.^{4}	In.^{3}	In.	In.^{3}	In.^{3}
112	4.2	10.4	—	7080	56.7	716	126	4.66	236	45.3	2.68	147	69.2
100	4.6	11.6	—	6400	83.8	623	112	4.60	207	40.0	2.65	130	61.0
88	5.2	13.0	—	5680	132	534	98.5	4.54	179	34.8	2.63	113	53.1
77	5.9	14.8	—	5010	213	455	85.9	4.49	154	30.1	2.60	97.6	45.9
68	6.6	16.7	—	4460	334	394	75.7	4.44	134	26.4	2.59	85.3	40.1
60	7.4	18.7	—	3970	525	341	66.7	4.39	116	23.0	2.57	74.6	35.0
54	8.2	21.2	—	3580	778	303	60.0	4.37	103	20.6	2.56	66.6	31.3
49	8.9	23.1	—	3280	1090	272	54.6	4.35	93.4	18.7	2.54	60.4	28.3
45	6.5	22.5	—	3650	758	248	49.1	4.32	53.4	13.3	2.01	54.9	20.3
39	7.5	25.0	—	3190	1300	209	42.1	4.27	45.0	11.3	1.98	46.8	17.2
33	9.1	27.1	—	2710	2510	170	35.0	4.19	36.6	9.20	1.94	38.8	14.0
30	5.7	29.5	—	2890	2160	170	32.4	4.38	16.7	5.75	1.37	36.6	8.84
26	6.6	34.0	55	2500	3790	144	27.9	4.35	14.1	4.89	1.36	31.3	7.50
22	8.0	36.9	47	2150	7170	118	23.2	4.27	11.4	3.97	1.33	26.0	6.10
19	5.1	35.4	51	2420	5160	96.3	18.8	4.14	4.29	2.14	0.874	21.6	3.35
17	6.1	36.9	47	2210	7820	81.9	16.2	4.05	3.56	1.78	0.844	18.7	2.80
15	7.4	38.5	43	1930	14300	68.9	13.8	3.95	2.89	1.45	0.810	16.0	2.30
12	9.4	46.6	30	1550	35400	53.8	10.9	3.90	2.18	1.10	0.785	12.6	1.74

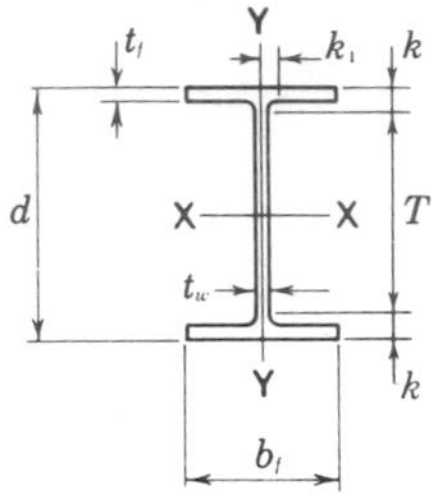

W SHAPES
Dimensions

Designation	Area A	Depth d		Web			Flange				Distance		
				Thickness t_w		$\frac{t_w}{2}$	Width b_f		Thickness t_f		T	k	k_1
	In.^{2}	In.		In.		In.	In.		In.		In.	In.	In.
W 8x 67	19.7	9.00	9	0.570	9/16	5/16	8.280	8 1/4	0.935	15/16	6 1/8	1 7/16	11/16
x 58	17.1	8.75	8 3/4	0.510	1/2	1/4	8.220	8 1/4	0.810	13/16	6 1/8	1 5/16	11/16
x 48	14.1	8.50	8 1/2	0.400	3/8	3/16	8.110	8 1/8	0.685	11/16	6 1/8	1 3/16	5/8
x 40	11.7	8.25	8 1/4	0.360	3/8	3/16	8.070	8 1/8	0.560	9/16	6 1/8	1 1/16	5/8
x 35	10.3	8.12	8 1/8	0.310	5/16	3/16	8.020	8	0.495	1/2	6 1/8	1	9/16
x 31	9.13	8.00	8	0.285	5/16	3/16	7.995	8	0.435	7/16	6 1/8	15/16	9/16
W 8x 28	8.25	8.06	8	0.285	5/16	3/16	6.535	6 1/2	0.465	7/16	6 1/8	15/16	9/16
x 24	7.08	7.93	7 7/8	0.245	1/4	1/8	6.495	6 1/2	0.400	3/8	6 1/8	7/8	9/16
W 8x 21	6.16	8.28	8 1/4	0.250	1/4	1/8	5.270	5 1/4	0.400	3/8	6 5/8	13/16	1/2
x 18	5.26	8.14	8 1/8	0.230	1/4	1/8	5.250	5 1/4	0.330	5/16	6 5/8	3/4	7/16
W 8 x15	4.44	8.11	8 1/8	0.245	1/4	1/8	4.015	4	0.315	5/16	6 5/8	3/4	1/2
x 13	3.84	7.99	8	0.230	1/4	1/8	4.000	4	0.255	1/4	6 5/8	11/16	7/16
x 10	2.96	7.89	7 7/8	0.170	3/16	1/8	3.940	4	0.205	3/16	6 5/8	5/8	7/16
W 6x 25	7.34	6.38	6 3/8	0.320	5/16	3/16	6.080	6 1/8	0.455	7/16	4 3/4	13/16	7/16
x 20	5.87	6.20	6 1/4	0.260	1/4	1/8	6.020	6	0.365	3/8	4 3/4	3/4	7/16
x 15	4.43	5.99	6	0.230	1/4	1/8	5.990	6	0.260	1/4	4 3/4	5/8	3/8
W 6x 16	4.74	6.28	6 1/4	0.260	1/4	1/8	4.030	4	0.405	3/8	4 3/4	3/4	7/16
x 12	3.55	6.03	6	0.230	1/4	1/8	4.000	4	0.280	1/4	4 3/4	5/8	3/8
x 9	2.68	5.90	5 7/8	0.170	3/16	1/8	3.940	4	0.215	3/16	4 3/4	9/16	3/8
W 5x 19	5.54	5.15	5 1/8	0.270	1/4	1/8	5.030	5	0.430	7/16	3 1/2	13/16	7/16
x 16	4.68	5.01	5	0.240	1/4	1/8	5.000	5	0.360	3/8	3 1/2	3/4	7/16
W 4x 13	3.83	4.16	4 1/8	0.280	1/4	1/8	4.060	4	0.345	3/8	2 3/4	11/16	7/16

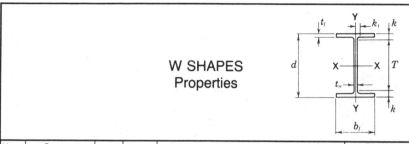

W SHAPES
Properties

Nominal Wt. per Ft	Compact Section Criteria			X_1	$X_2 \times 10^6$	Elastic Properties						Plastic Modulus	
						Axis X-X			Axis Y-Y				
	$\dfrac{b_f}{2t_f}$	$\dfrac{h_c}{t_w}$	F_y'''			I	S	r	I	S	r	Z_x	Z_y
Lb.			Ksi	Ksi	(1/Ksi)^2	In.^{4}	In.^{3}	In.	In.^{4}	In.^{3}	In.	In.^{3}	In.^{3}
67	4.4	11.1	—	6620	73.9	272	60.4	3.72	88.6	21.4	2.12	70.2	32.7
58	5.1	12.4	—	5820	122	228	52.0	3.65	75.1	18.3	2.10	59.8	27.9
48	5.9	15.8	—	4860	238	184	43.3	3.61	60.9	15.0	2.08	49.0	22.9
40	7.2	17.6	—	4080	474	146	35.5	3.53	49.1	12.2	2.04	39.8	18.5
35	8.1	20.4	—	3610	761	127	31.2	3.51	42.6	10.6	2.03	34.7	16.1
31	9.2	22.2	—	3230	1180	110	27.5	3.47	37.1	9.27	2.02	30.4	14.1
28	7.0	22.2	—	3480	931	98.0	24.3	3.45	21.7	6.63	1.62	27.2	10.1
24	8.1	25.8	—	3020	1610	82.8	20.9	3.42	18.3	5.63	1.61	23.2	8.57
21	6.6	27.5	—	2890	2090	75.3	18.2	3.49	9.77	3.71	1.26	20.4	5.69
18	8.0	29.9	—	2490	3890	61.9	15.2	3.43	7.97	3.04	1.23	17.0	4.66
15	6.4	28.1	—	2670	3440	48.0	11.8	3.29	3.41	1.70	0.876	13.6	2.67
13	7.8	29.9	—	2370	5780	39.6	9.91	3.21	2.73	1.37	0.843	11.4	2.15
10	9.6	40.5	39	1760	17900	30.8	7.81	3.22	2.09	1.06	0.841	8.87	1.66
25	6.7	15.5	—	4410	369	53.4	16.7	2.70	17.1	5.61	1.52	18.9	8.56
20	8.2	19.1	—	3550	846	41.4	13.4	2.66	13.3	4.41	1.50	14.9	6.72
15	11.5	21.6	—	2740	2470	29.1	9.72	2.56	9.32	3.11	1.46	10.8	4.75
16	5.0	19.1	—	4010	591	32.1	10.2	2.60	4.43	2.20	0.966	11.7	3.39
12	7.1	21.6	—	3100	1740	22.1	7.31	2.49	2.99	1.50	0.918	8.30	2.32
9	9.2	29.2	—	2360	4980	16.4	5.56	2.47	2.19	1.11	0.905	6.23	1.72
19	5.8	14.0	—	5140	192	26.2	10.2	2.17	9.13	3.63	1.28	11.6	5.53
16	6.9	15.8	—	4440	346	21.3	8.51	2.13	7.51	3.00	1.27	9.59	4.57
13	5.9	10.6	—	5560	154	11.3	5.46	1.72	3.86	1.90	1.00	6.28	2.92

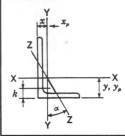

ANGLES
Equal legs and unequal legs
Properties for designing

Size and Thickness	k	Weight per Ft	Area	Axis X-X					
				I	S	r	y	Z	y_p
In.	In.	Lb.	In.^{2}	In.^{4}	In.^{3}	In.	In.	In.^{3}	In.
L 6x6 x1	1½	37.4	11.0	35.5	8.57	1.80	1.86	15.5	0.917
⅞	1⅜	33.1	9.73	31.9	7.63	1.81	1.82	13.8	0.811
¾	1¼	28.7	8.44	28.2	6.66	1.83	1.78	12.0	0.703
⅝	1⅛	24.2	7.11	24.2	5.66	1.84	1.73	10.2	0.592
⁹⁄₁₆	1¹⁄₁₆	21.9	6.43	22.1	5.14	1.85	1.71	9.26	0.536
½	1	19.6	5.75	19.9	4.61	1.86	1.68	8.31	0.479
⁷⁄₁₆	¹⁵⁄₁₆	17.2	5.06	17.7	4.08	1.87	1.66	7.34	0.422
⅜	⅞	14.9	4.36	15.4	3.53	1.88	1.64	6.35	0.363
⁵⁄₁₆	¹³⁄₁₆	12.4	3.65	13.0	2.97	1.89	1.62	5.35	0.304
L 6x4 x ⅞	1⅜	27.2	7.98	27.7	7.15	1.86	2.12	12.7	1.44
¾	1¼	23.6	6.94	24.5	6.25	1.88	2.08	11.2	1.38
⅝	1⅛	20.0	5.86	21.1	5.31	1.90	2.03	9.51	1.31
⁹⁄₁₆	1¹⁄₁₆	18.1	5.31	19.3	4,83	1.90	2.01	8.66	1.28
½	1	16.2	4.75	17.4	4.33	1.91	1.99	7.78	1.25
⁷⁄₁₆	¹⁵⁄₁₆	14.3	4.18	15.5	3.83	1.92	1.96	6.88	1.22
⅜	⅞	12.3	3.61	13.5	3.32	1.93	1.94	5.97	1.19
⁵⁄₁₆	¹³⁄₁₆	10.3	3.03	11.4	2.79	1.94	1.92	5.03	1.16
L 6x3½x ½	1	15.3	4.50	16.6	4.24	1.92	2.08	7.50	1.50
⅜	⅞	11.7	3.42	12.9	3.24	1.94	2.04	5.76	1.44
⁵⁄₁₆	¹³⁄₁₆	9.8	2.87	10.9	2.73	1.95	2.01	4.85	1.41
L 5x5 x ⅞	1⅜	27.2	7.98	17.8	5.17	1.49	1.57	9.33	0.798
¾	1¼	23.6	6.94	15.7	4.53	1.51	1.52	8.16	0.694
⅝	1⅛	20.0	5.86	13.6	3.86	1.52	1.48	6.95	0.586
½	1	16.2	4.75	11.3	3.16	1.54	1.43	5.68	0.475
⁷⁄₁₆	¹⁵⁄₁₆	14.3	4.18	10.0	2.79	1.55	1.41	5.03	0.418
⅜	⅞	12.3	3.61	8.74	2.42	1.56	1.39	4.36	0.361
⁵⁄₁₆	¹³⁄₁₆	10.3	3.03	7.42	2.04	1.57	1.37	3.68	0.303

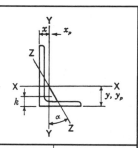

ANGLES
Equal legs and unequal legs
Properties for designing

Size and Thickness	Axis Y-Y						Axis Z-Z	
	I	S	r	x	Z	x_p	r	Tan
In.	In.⁴	In.³	In.	In.	In.³	In.	In.	α
L 6x6 x1	35.5	8.57	1.80	1.86	15.5	0.917	1.17	1.000
7/8	31.9	7.63	1.81	1.82	13.8	0.811	1.17	1.000
3/4	28.2	6.66	1.83	1.78	12.0	0.703	1.17	1.000
5/8	24.2	5.66	1.84	1.73	10.2	0.592	1.18	1.000
9/16	22.1	5.14	1.85	1.71	9.26	0.536	1.18	1.000
1/2	19.9	4.61	1.86	1.68	8.31	0.479	1.18	1.000
7/16	17.7	4.08	1.87	1.66	7.34	0.422	1.19	1.000
3/8	15.4	3.53	1.88	1.64	6.35	0.363	1.19	1.000
5/16	13.0	2.97	1.89	1.62	5.35	0.304	1.20	1.000
L 6x4 x 7/8	9.75	3.39	1.11	1.12	6.31	0.665	0.857	0.421
3/4	8.68	2.97	1.12	1.08	5.47	0.578	0.860	0.428
5/8	7.52	2.54	1.13	1.03	4.62	0.488	0.864	0.435
9/16	6.91	2.31	1.14	1.01	4.19	0.442	0.866	0.438
1/2	6.27	2.08	1.15	0.987	3.75	0.396	0.870	0.440
7/16	5.60	1.85	1.16	0.964	3.30	0.349	0.873	0.443
3/8	4.90	1.60	1.17	0.941	2.85	0.301	0.877	0.446
5/16	4.18	1.35	1.17	0.918	2.40	0.252	0.882	0.448
L 6x3½x 1/2	4.25	1.59	0.972	0.833	2.91	0.375	0.759	0.344
3/8	3.34	1.23	0.988	0.787	2.20	0.285	0.767	0.350
5/16	2.85	1.04	0.996	0.763	1.85	0.239	0.772	0.352
L 5x5 x 7/8	17.8	5.17	1.49	1.57	9.33	0.798	0.973	1.000
3/4	15.7	4.53	1.51	1.52	8.16	0.694	0.975	1.000
5/8	13.6	3.86	1.52	1.48	6.95	0.586	0.978	1.000
1/2	11.3	3.16	1.54	1.43	5.68	0.475	0.983	1.000
7/16	10.0	2.79	1.55	1.41	5.03	0.418	0.986	1.000
3/8	8.74	2.42	1.56	1.39	4.36	0.361	0.990	1.000
5/16	7.42	2.04	1.57	1.37	3.68	0.303	0.994	1.000

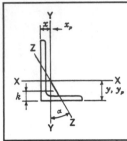

ANGLES
Equal legs and unequal legs
Properties for designing

Size and Thickness	k	Weight per Ft	Area	Axis X-X					
				I	S	r	y	Z	y_p
In.	In.	Lb.	In.²	In.⁴	In.³	In.	In.	In.³	In.
L 5x3½x¾	1¼	19.8	5.81	13.9	4.28	1.55	1.75	7.65	1.13
⅝	1⅛	16.8	4.92	12.0	3.65	1.56	1.70	6.55	1.06
½	1	13.6	4.00	9.99	2.99	1.58	1.66	5.38	1.00
⁷⁄₁₆	¹⁵⁄₁₆	12.0	3.53	8.90	2.64	1.59	1.63	4.77	0.969
⅜	⅞	10.4	3.05	7.78	2.29	1.60	1.61	4.14	0.938
⁵⁄₁₆	¹³⁄₁₆	8.7	2.56	6.60	1.94	1.61	1.59	3.49	0.906
¼	¾	7.0	2.06	5.39	1.57	1.62	1.56	2.83	0.875
L 5x3 x⅝	1	15.7	4.61	11.4	3.55	1.57	1.80	6.27	1.31
½	1	12.8	3.75	9.45	2.91	1.59	1.75	5.16	1.25
⁷⁄₁₆	¹⁵⁄₁₆	11.3	3.31	8.43	2.58	1.60	1.73	4.57	1.22
⅜	⅞	9.8	2.86	7.37	2.24	1.61	1.70	3.97	1.19
⁵⁄₁₆	¹³⁄₁₆	8.2	2.40	6.26	1.89	1.61	1.68	3.36	1.16
¼	¾	6.6	1.94	5.11	1.53	1.62	1.66	2.72	1.13
L 4x4 x¾	1⅛	18.5	5.44	7.67	2.81	1.19	1.27	5.07	0.680
⅝	1	15.7	4.61	6.66	2.40	1.20	1.23	4.33	0.576
½	⅞	12.8	3.75	5.56	1.97	1.22	1.18	3.56	0.469
⁷⁄₁₆	¹³⁄₁₆	11.3	3.31	4.97	1.75	1.23	1.16	3.16	0.414
⅜	¾	9.8	2.86	4.36	1.52	1.23	1.14	2.74	0.357
⁵⁄₁₆	¹¹⁄₁₆	8.2	2.40	3.71	1.29	1.24	1.12	2.32	0.300
¼	⅝	6.6	1.94	3.04	1.05	1.25	1.09	1.88	0.242
L 4x3½x⅝	1¹⁄₁₆	14.7	4.30	6.37	2.35	1.22	1.29	4.24	0.614
½	¹⁵⁄₁₆	11.9	3.50	5.32	1.94	1.23	1.25	3.50	0.500
⁷⁄₁₆	⅞	10.6	3.09	4.76	1.72	1.24	1.23	3.11	0.469
⅜	¹³⁄₁₆	9.1	2.67	4.18	1.49	1.25	1.21	2.71	0.438
⁵⁄₁₆	¾	7.7	2.25	3.56	1.26	1.26	1.18	2.29	0.406
¼	¹¹⁄₁₆	6.2	1.81	2.91	1.03	1.27	1.16	1.86	0.375

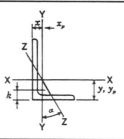

ANGLES
Equal legs and unequal legs
Properties for designing

Size and Thickness	Axis Y-Y						Axis Z-Z	
	I	S	r	x	Z	x_p	r	Tan
In.	In.⁴	In.³	In.	In.	In.³	In.	In.	α
L 5x3½x¾	5.55	2.22	0.977	0.996	4.10	0.581	0.748	0.464
⅝	4.83	1.90	0.991	0.951	3.47	0.492	0.751	0.472
½	4.05	1.56	1.01	0.906	2.83	0.400	0.755	0.479
⁷⁄₁₆	3.63	1.39	1.01	0.883	2.49	0.353	0.758	0.482
⅜	3.18	1.21	1.02	0.861	2.16	0.305	0.762	0.486
⁵⁄₁₆	2.72	1.02	1.03	0.838	1.82	0.256	0.766	0.489
¼	2.23	0.830	1.04	0.814	1.47	0.206	0.770	0.492
L 5x3 x⅝	3.06	1.39	0.815	0.796	2.61	0.461	0.644	0.349
½	2.58	1.15	0.829	0.750	2.11	0.375	0.648	0.357
⁷⁄₁₆	2.32	1.02	0.837	0.727	1.86	0.331	0.651	0.361
⅜	2.04	0.888	0.845	0.704	1.60	0.286	0.654	0.364
⁵⁄₁₆	1.75	0.753	0.853	0.681	1.35	0.240	0.658	0.368
¼	1.44	0.614	0.861	0.657	1.09	0.194	0.663	0.371
L 4x4 x¾	7.67	2.81	1.19	1.27	5.07	0.680	0.778	1.000
⅝	6.66	2.40	1.20	1.23	4.33	0.576	0.779	1.000
½	5.56	1.97	1.22	1.18	3.56	0.469	0.782	1.000
⁷⁄₁₆	4.97	1.75	1.23	1.16	3.16	0.414	0.785	1.000
⅜	4.36	1.52	1.23	1.14	2.74	0.357	0.788	1.000
⁵⁄₁₆	3.71	1.29	1.24	1.12	2.32	0.300	0.791	1.000
¼	3.04	1.05	1.25	1.09	1.88	0.242	0.795	1.000
L 4x3½x⅝	4.52	1.84	1.03	1.04	3.33	0.537	0.719	0.745
½	3.79	1.52	1.04	1.00	2.73	0.438	0.722	0.750
⁷⁄₁₆	3.40	1.35	1.05	0.978	2.42	0.386	0.724	0.753
⅜	2.95	1.17	1.06	0.955	2.11	0.334	0.727	0.755
⁵⁄₁₆	2.55	0.994	1.07	0.932	1.78	0.281	0.730	0.757
¼	2.09	0.808	1.07	0.909	1.44	0.227	0.734	0.759

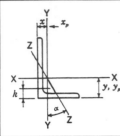

ANGLES
Equal legs and unequal legs
Properties for designing

Size and Thickness	k	Weight per Ft	Area	Axis X-X					
				I	S	r	y	Z	y_p
In.	In.	Lb.	In.²	In.⁴	In.³	In.	In.	In.³	In.
L 4 x3 x⅝	1¹⁄₁₆	13.6	3.98	6.03	2.30	1.23	1.37	4.12	0.813
½	¹⁵⁄₁₆	11.1	3.25	5.05	1.89	1.25	1.33	3.41	0.750
⁷⁄₁₆	⅞	9.8	2.87	4.52	1.68	1.25	1.30	3.03	0.719
⅜	¹³⁄₁₆	8.5	2.48	3.96	1.46	1.26	1.28	2.64	0.688
⁵⁄₁₆	¾	7.2	2.09	3.38	1.23	1.27	1.26	2.23	0.656
¼	¹¹⁄₁₆	5.8	1.69	2.77	1.00	1.28	1.24	1.82	0.625
L 3½x3½x½	⅞	11.1	3.25	3.64	1.49	1.06	1.06	2.68	0.464
⁷⁄₁₆	¹³⁄₁₆	9.8	2.87	3.26	1.32	1.07	1.04	2.38	0.410
⅜	¾	8.5	2.48	2.87	1.15	1.07	1.01	2.08	0.355
⁵⁄₁₆	¹¹⁄₁₆	7.2	2.09	2.45	0.976	1.08	0.990	1.76	0.299
¼	⅝	5.8	1.69	2.01	0.794	1.09	0.968	1.43	0.241
L 3½x3 x½	¹⁵⁄₁₆	10.2	3.00	3.45	1.45	1.07	1.13	2.63	0.500
⁷⁄₁₆	⅞	9.1	2.65	3.10	1.29	1.08	1.10	2.34	0.469
⅜	¹³⁄₁₆	7.9	2.30	2.72	1.13	1.09	1.08	2.04	0.438
⁵⁄₁₆	¾	6.6	1.93	2.33	0.954	1.10	1.06	1.73	0.406
¼	¹¹⁄₁₆	5.4	1.56	1.91	0.776	1.11	1.04	1.41	0.375
L 3½x2½x½	¹⁵⁄₁₆	9.4	2.75	3.24	1.41	1.09	1.20	2.53	0.750
⁷⁄₁₆	⅞	8.3	2.43	2.91	1.26	1.09	1.18	2.26	0.719
⅜	¹³⁄₁₆	7.2	2.11	2.56	1.09	1.10	1.16	1.97	0.688
⁵⁄₁₆	¾	6.1	1.78	2.19	0.927	1.11	1.14	1.67	0.656
¼	¹¹⁄₁₆	4.9	1.44	1.80	0.755	1.12	1.11	1.36	0.625
L 3 x3 x½	¹³⁄₁₆	9.4	2.75	2.22	1.07	0.898	0.932	1.93	0.458
⁷⁄₁₆	¾	8.3	2.43	1.99	0.954	0.905	0.910	1.72	0.406
⅜	¹¹⁄₁₆	7.2	2.11	1.76	0.833	0.913	0.888	1.50	0.352
⁵⁄₁₆	⅝	6.1	1.78	1.51	0.707	0.922	0.865	1.27	0.296
¼	⁹⁄₁₆	4.9	1.44	1.24	0.577	0.930	0.842	1.04	0.240
³⁄₁₆	½	3.71	1.09	0.962	0.441	0.939	0.820	0.794	0.182

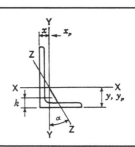

ANGLES
Equal legs and unequal legs
Properties for designing

Size and Thickness	Axis Y-Y						Axis Z-Z	
	I	S	r	x	Z	x_p	r	Tan
In.	In.⁴	In.³	In.	In.	In.³	In.	In.	α
L 4 x3 x⅝	2.87	1.35	0.849	0.871	2.48	0.498	0.637	0.534
½	2.42	1.12	0.864	0.827	2.03	0.406	0.639	0.543
⁷⁄₁₆	2.18	0.992	0.871	0.804	1.79	0.359	0.641	0.547
⅜	1.92	0.866	0.879	0.782	1.56	0.311	0.644	0.551
⁵⁄₁₆	1.65	0.734	0.887	0.759	1.31	0.261	0.647	0.554
¼	1.36	0.599	0.896	0.736	1.06	0.211	0.651	0.558
L 3½x3½x½	3.64	1.49	1.06	1.06	2.68	0.464	0.683	1.000
⁷⁄₁₆	3.26	1.32	1.07	1.04	2.38	0.410	0.684	1.000
⅜	2.87	1.15	1.07	1.01	2.08	0.355	0.687	1.000
⁵⁄₁₆	2.45	0.976	1.08	0.990	1.76	0.299	0.690	1.000
¼	2.01	0.794	1.09	0.968	1.43	0.241	0.694	1.000
L 3½x3 x½	2.33	1.10	0.881	0.875	1.98	0.429	0.621	0.714
⁷⁄₁₆	2.09	0.975	0.889	0.853	1.76	0.379	0.622	0.718
⅜	1.85	0.851	0.897	0.830	1.53	0.328	0.625	0.721
⁵⁄₁₆	1.58	0.722	0.905	0.808	1.30	0.276	0.627	0.724
¼	1.30	0.589	0.914	0.785	1.05	0.223	0.631	0.727
L 3½x2½x½	1.36	0.760	0.704	0.705	1.40	0.393	0.534	0.486
⁷⁄₁₆	1.23	0.677	0.711	0.682	1.24	0.348	0.535	0.491
⅜	1.09	0.592	0.719	0.660	1.07	0.301	0.537	0.496
⁵⁄₁₆	0.939	0.504	0.727	0.637	0.907	0.254	0.540	0.501
¼	0.777	0.412	0.735	0.614	0.735	0.205	0.544	0.506
L 3 x3 x½	2.22	1.07	0.898	0.932	1.93	0.458	0.584	1.000
⁷⁄₁₆	1.99	0.954	0.905	0.910	1.72	0.406	0.585	1.000
⅜	1.76	0.833	0.913	0.888	1.50	0.352	0.587	1.000
⁵⁄₁₆	1.51	0.707	0.922	0.865	1.27	0.296	0.589	1.000
¼	1.24	0.577	0.930	0.842	1.04	0.240	0.592	1.000
³⁄₁₆	0.962	0.441	0.939	0.820	0.794	0.182	0.596	1.000

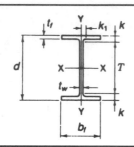

W SHAPES
Dimensions

Designation							Area	Depth	Web		Flange		Distance		
									Thick-ness t_w	$\dfrac{t_w}{2}$	Width b_f	Thick-ness t_f	T	k	k_1
							A	d							
mm	x	kg/m	in.	x	lb/ft		mm²	mm	mm	mm	mm	mm	mm	mm	mm
W	410	x	85	W	16	x	57	10800	417	10.90	5.45	181.0	18.2	347	35	16
W	410	x	74	W	16	x	50	9510	413	9.65	4.83	180.0	16.0	347	33	15
W	410	x	67	W	16	x	45	8560	410	8.76	4.38	179.0	14.4	346	32	15
W	410	x	60	W	16	x	40	7600	407	7.75	3.88	178.0	12.8	347	30	14
W	410	x	53	W	16	x	36	6820	403	7.49	3.75	177.0	10.9	345	29	14
W	410	x	46	W	16	x	31	5890	403	6.99	3.50	140.0	11.2	345	29	14
W	410	x	39	W	16	x	26	4960	399	6.35	3.18	140.0	8.8	345	27	13
W	360	x	1086[a]	W	14	x	730	138000	569	78.00	39.00	454.0	125.0	287	141	54
W	360	x	990[a]	W	14	x	665	126000	550	71.90	35.95	448.0	115.0	286	132	51
W	360	x	900[a]	W	14	x	605	115000	531	65.90	32.95	442.0	106.0	287	122	48
W	360	x	818[a]	W	14	x	550	104000	514	60.50	30.25	437.0	97.0	286	114	45
W	360	x	744[a]	W	14	x	500	94800	498	55.60	27.80	432.0	88.9	286	106	43
W	360	x	677[a]	W	14	x	455	86300	483	51.20	25.60	428.0	81.5	287	98	41
W	360	x	634[a]	W	14	x	426	80800	474	47.60	23.80	424.0	77.1	286	94	39
W	360	x	592[a]	W	14	x	398	75500	465	45.00	22.50	421.0	72.3	287	89	38
W	360	x	551[a]	W	14	x	370	70200	455	42.00	21.00	418.0	67.6	287	84	36
W	360	x	509[a]	W	14	x	342	64900	446	39.10	19.55	416.0	62.7	288	79	35
W	360	x	463[a]	W	14	x	311	59000	435	35.80	17.90	412.0	57.4	285	75	33
W	360	x	421[a]	W	14	x	283	53700	425	32.80	16.40	409.0	52.6	285	70	32
W	360	x	382[a]	W	14	x	257	48800	416	29.80	14.90	406.0	48.0	286	65	30
W	360	x	347[a]	W	14	x	233	44200	407	27.20	13.60	404.0	43.7	287	60	29
W	360	x	314	W	14	x	211	40000	399	24.90	12.45	401.0	39.6	285	57	28
W	360	x	287	W	14	x	193	36600	393	22.60	11.30	399.0	36.6	285	54	27
W	360	x	262	W	14	x	176	33400	387	21.10	10.55	398.0	33.3	285	51	26
W	360	x	237	W	14	x	159	30200	380	18.90	9.45	395.0	30.2	284	48	25
W	360	x	216	W	14	x	145	27500	375	17.30	8.65	394.0	27.7	287	44	24

[a] For application refer to Notes in Table 1.

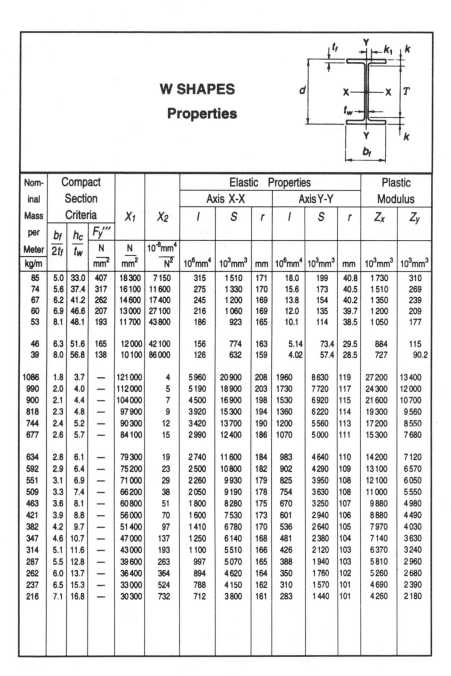

W SHAPES
Properties

Nom-inal Mass per Meter kg/m	Compact Section Criteria $\dfrac{b_f}{2t_f}$	$\dfrac{h_c}{t_w}$	F_y''' $\dfrac{N}{mm^2}$	X_1 $\dfrac{N}{mm^2}$	X_2 $\dfrac{10^{-6}mm^4}{N^2}$	Elastic Properties Axis X-X I 10^6mm^4	S 10^3mm^3	r mm	Axis Y-Y I 10^6mm^4	S 10^3mm^3	r mm	Plastic Modulus Z_x 10^3mm^3	Z_y 10^3mm^3
85	5.0	33.0	407	18 300	7 150	315	1 510	171	18.0	199	40.8	1 730	310
74	5.6	37.4	317	16 100	11 600	275	1 330	170	15.6	173	40.5	1 510	269
67	6.2	41.2	262	14 600	17 400	245	1 200	169	13.8	154	40.2	1 350	239
60	6.9	46.6	207	13 000	27 100	216	1 060	169	12.0	135	39.7	1 200	209
53	8.1	48.1	193	11 700	43 800	186	923	165	10.1	114	38.5	1 050	177
46	6.3	51.6	165	12 000	42 100	156	774	163	5.14	73.4	29.5	884	115
39	8.0	56.8	138	10 100	86 000	126	632	159	4.02	57.4	28.5	727	90.2
1086	1.8	3.7	—	121 000	4	5 960	20 900	208	1 960	8 630	119	27 200	13 400
990	2.0	4.0	—	112 000	5	5 190	18 900	203	1 730	7 720	117	24 300	12 000
900	2.1	4.4	—	104 000	7	4 500	16 900	198	1 530	6 920	115	21 600	10 700
818	2.3	4.8	—	97 900	9	3 920	15 300	194	1 360	6 220	114	19 300	9 560
744	2.4	5.2	—	90 300	12	3 420	13 700	190	1 200	5 560	113	17 200	8 550
677	2.6	5.7	—	84 100	15	2 990	12 400	186	1 070	5 000	111	15 300	7 680
634	2.8	6.1	—	79 300	19	2 740	11 600	184	983	4 640	110	14 200	7 120
592	2.9	6.4	—	75 200	23	2 500	10 800	182	902	4 290	109	13 100	6 570
551	3.1	6.9	—	71 000	29	2 260	9 930	179	825	3 950	108	12 100	6 050
509	3.3	7.4	—	66 200	38	2 050	9 190	178	754	3 630	108	11 000	5 550
463	3.6	8.1	—	60 800	51	1 800	8 280	175	670	3 250	107	9 880	4 980
421	3.9	8.8	—	56 000	70	1 600	7 530	173	601	2 940	105	8 880	4 490
382	4.2	9.7	—	51 400	97	1 410	6 780	170	536	2 640	105	7 970	4 030
347	4.6	10.7	—	47 000	137	1 250	6 140	168	481	2 380	104	7 140	3 630
314	5.1	11.6	—	43 000	193	1 100	5 510	166	426	2 120	103	6 370	3 240
287	5.5	12.8	—	39 600	263	997	5 070	165	388	1 940	103	5 810	2 960
262	6.0	13.7	—	36 400	364	894	4 620	164	350	1 760	102	5 260	2 680
237	6.5	15.3	—	33 000	524	788	4 150	162	310	1 570	101	4 690	2 390
216	7.1	16.8	—	30 300	732	712	3 800	161	283	1 440	101	4 260	2 180

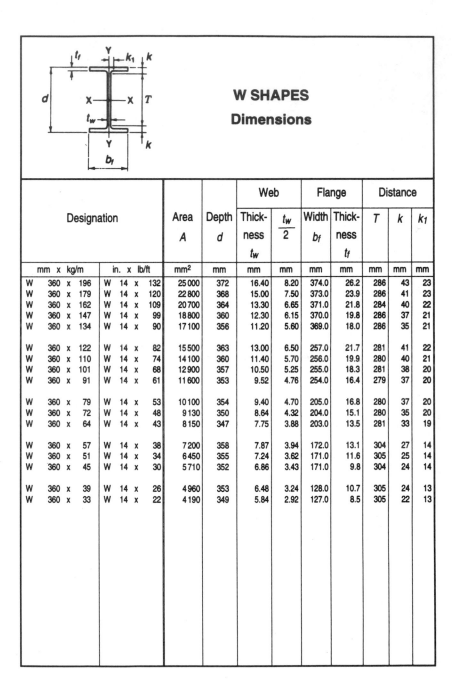

W SHAPES
Dimensions

Designation							Area A	Depth d	Web			Flange		Distance		
									Thick-ness t_w	$\frac{t_w}{2}$	Width b_f	Thick-ness t_f	T	k	k_1
mm	x	kg/m		in.	x	lb/ft	mm²	mm	mm	mm	mm	mm	mm	mm	mm
W	360	x	196	W	14	x	132	25 000	372	16.40	8.20	374.0	26.2	286	43	23
W	360	x	179	W	14	x	120	22 800	368	15.00	7.50	373.0	23.9	286	41	23
W	360	x	162	W	14	x	109	20 700	364	13.30	6.65	371.0	21.8	284	40	22
W	360	x	147	W	14	x	99	18 800	360	12.30	6.15	370.0	19.8	286	37	21
W	360	x	134	W	14	x	90	17 100	356	11.20	5.60	369.0	18.0	286	35	21
W	360	x	122	W	14	x	82	15 500	363	13.00	6.50	257.0	21.7	281	41	22
W	360	x	110	W	14	x	74	14 100	360	11.40	5.70	256.0	19.9	280	40	21
W	360	x	101	W	14	x	68	12 900	357	10.50	5.25	255.0	18.3	281	38	20
W	360	x	91	W	14	x	61	11 600	353	9.52	4.76	254.0	16.4	279	37	20
W	360	x	79	W	14	x	53	10 100	354	9.40	4.70	205.0	16.8	280	37	20
W	360	x	72	W	14	x	48	9 130	350	8.64	4.32	204.0	15.1	280	35	20
W	360	x	64	W	14	x	43	8 150	347	7.75	3.88	203.0	13.5	281	33	19
W	360	x	57	W	14	x	38	7 200	358	7.87	3.94	172.0	13.1	304	27	14
W	360	x	51	W	14	x	34	6 450	355	7.24	3.62	171.0	11.6	305	25	14
W	360	x	45	W	14	x	30	5 710	352	6.86	3.43	171.0	9.8	304	24	14
W	360	x	39	W	14	x	26	4 960	353	6.48	3.24	128.0	10.7	305	24	13
W	360	x	33	W	14	x	22	4 190	349	5.84	2.92	127.0	8.5	305	22	13

W SHAPES
Properties

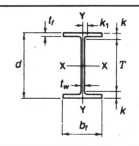

Nom-	Compact					Elastic Properties						Plastic	
inal	Section					Axis X-X			Axis Y-Y			Modulus	
Mass	Criteria		X_1	X_2		I	S	r	I	S	r	Z_x	Z_y
per	$\dfrac{b_f}{2t_f}$	$\dfrac{h_c}{t_w}$	F_y'''										
Meter			$\dfrac{N}{mm^2}$	$\dfrac{N}{mm^2}$	$\dfrac{10^{-8}mm^4}{N^2}$								
kg/m						10^6mm^4	10^3mm^3	mm	10^6mm^4	10^3mm^3	mm	10^3mm^3	10^3mm^3
196	7.1	17.7	—	28 800	900	636	3 420	159	229	1 220	95.7	3 840	1 860
179	7.8	19.3	—	26 400	1 260	575	3 130	159	207	1 110	95.3	3 480	1 680
162	8.5	21.7	—	24 100	1 790	516	2 840	158	186	1 000	94.8	3 140	1 520
147	9.3	23.5	—	22 000	2 570	463	2 570	157	167	903	94.2	2 840	1 370
134	10.2	25.9	—	20 000	3 680	415	2 330	156	151	818	94.0	2 560	1 240
122	5.9	22.4	—	24 800	1 780	365	2 010	153	61.5	479	63.0	2 270	732
110	6.4	25.3	—	22 700	2 500	331	1 840	153	55.7	435	62.9	2 060	664
101	7.0	27.5	—	20 800	3 470	302	1 690	153	50.6	397	62.6	1 880	606
91	7.7	30.4	—	18 800	5 170	267	1 510	152	44.8	353	62.1	1 680	538
79	6.1	30.8	—	19 500	4 730	227	1 280	150	24.2	236	48.9	1 430	362
72	6.7	33.5	393	17 800	6 770	201	1 150	148	21.4	210	48.4	1 280	322
64	7.5	37.4	317	16 000	10 300	179	1 030	148	18.8	185	48.0	1 140	284
57	6.6	39.6	283	15 100	14 400	160	894	149	11.1	129	39.3	1 010	199
51	7.4	43.1	241	13 600	22 300	141	794	148	9.68	113	38.7	895	174
45	8.7	45.4	214	12 100	37 000	121	688	146	8.16	95.4	37.8	776	147
39	6.0	48.1	193	13 000	29 200	102	578	143	3.75	58.6	27.5	661	91.6
33	7.5	53.3	152	11 100	57 400	82.9	475	141	2.91	45.8	26.4	544	71.9

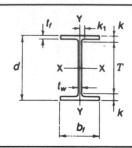

W SHAPES
Dimensions

Designation		Area A	Depth d	Web Thickness t_w	$\dfrac{t_w}{2}$	Flange Width b_f	Flange Thickness t_f	Distance T	k	k_1
mm x kg/m	in. x lb/ft	mm²	mm	mm	mm	mm	mm	mm	mm	mm
W 310 x 500[a]	W 12 x 336	63 700	427	45.10	22.55	340.0	75.1	239	94	38
W 310 x 454[a]	W 12 x 305	57 800	415	41.30	20.65	336.0	68.7	241	87	36
W 310 x 415[a]	W 12 x 279	52 800	403	38.90	19.45	334.0	62.7	241	81	35
W 310 x 375[a]	W 12 x 252	47 800	391	35.40	17.70	330.0	57.2	241	75	33
W 310 x 342[a]	W 12 x 230	43 700	382	32.60	16.30	328.0	52.6	242	70	32
W 310 x 313[a]	W 12 x 210	39 900	374	30.00	15.00	325.0	48.3	240	67	30
W 310 x 283	W 12 x 190	36 000	365	26.90	13.45	322.0	44.1	241	62	29
W 310 x 253	W 12 x 170	32 300	356	24.40	12.20	319.0	39.6	242	57	27
W 310 x 226	W 12 x 152	28 900	348	22.10	11.05	317.0	35.6	240	54	26
W 310 x 202	W 12 x 136	25 800	341	20.10	10.05	315.0	31.8	243	49	25
W 310 x 179	W 12 x 120	22 800	333	18.00	9.00	313.0	28.1	241	46	24
W 310 x 158	W 12 x 106	20 100	327	15.50	7.75	310.0	25.1	241	43	23
W 310 x 143	W 12 x 96	18 200	323	14.00	7.00	309.0	22.9	241	41	22
W 310 x 129	W 12 x 87	16 500	318	13.10	6.55	308.0	20.6	242	38	22
W 310 x 117	W 12 x 79	15 000	314	11.90	5.95	307.0	18.7	240	37	21
W 310 x 107	W 12 x 72	13 600	311	10.90	5.45	306.0	17.0	241	35	21
W 310 x 97	W 12 x 65	12 300	308	9.91	4.96	305.0	15.4	242	33	20
W 310 x 86	W 12 x 58	11 000	310	9.14	4.57	254.0	16.3	240	35	20
W 310 x 79	W 12 x 53	10 000	306	8.76	4.38	254.0	14.6	242	32	20
W 310 x 74	W 12 x 50	9 480	310	9.40	4.70	205.0	16.3	240	35	20
W 310 x 67	W 12 x 45	8 530	306	8.51	4.26	204.0	14.6	242	32	19
W 310 x 60	W 12 x 40	7 600	303	7.49	3.75	203.0	13.1	239	32	19
W 310 x 52	W 12 x 35	6 670	318	7.62	3.81	167.0	13.2	268	25	11
W 310 x 45	W 12 x 30	5 670	313	6.60	3.30	166.0	11.2	265	24	11
W 310 x 39	W 12 x 26	4 930	310	5.84	2.92	165.0	9.7	266	22	11
W 310 x 33	W 12 x 22	4 180	313	6.60	3.30	102.0	10.8	269	22	11
W 310 x 28	W 12 x 19	3 600	309	5.97	2.99	102.0	8.9	267	21	11
W 310 x 24	W 12 x 16	3 040	305	5.59	2.80	101.0	6.7	267	19	10
W 310 x 21	W 12 x 14	2 680	303	5.08	2.54	101.0	5.7	269	17	10

[a] For application refer to Notes in Table 1.

W SHAPES
Properties

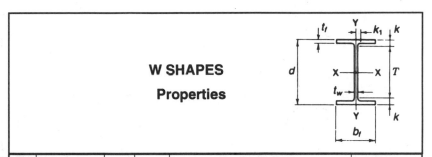

Nom-inal Mass per Meter kg/m	Compact Section Criteria $\frac{b_f}{2t_f}$	$\frac{h_c}{t_w}$	F_y''' $\frac{N}{mm^2}$	X_1 $\frac{N}{mm^2}$	X_2 $\frac{10^{-8}mm^4}{N^2}$	Elastic Properties Axis X-X I 10^6mm^4	S 10^3mm^3	r mm	Axis Y-Y I 10^6mm^4	S 10^3mm^3	r mm	Plastic Modulus Z_x 10^3mm^3	Z_y 10^3mm^3
500	2.3	5.5	—	88 300	13	1 690	7 920	163	494	2 910	88.1	9 880	4 490
454	2.4	6.0	—	81 400	17	1 480	7 130	160	436	2 600	86.9	8 820	4 000
415	2.7	6.3	—	75 800	23	1 300	6 450	157	391	2 340	86.1	7 900	3 610
375	2.9	7.0	—	69 600	31	1 130	5 780	154	344	2 080	84.8	7 000	3 210
342	3.1	7.6	—	64 700	41	1 010	5 290	152	310	1 890	84.2	6 330	2 910
313	3.4	8.2	—	59 800	56	896	4 790	150	277	1 700	83.3	5 720	2 620
283	3.7	9.2	—	54 700	78	787	4 310	148	246	1 530	82.7	5 100	2 340
253	4.0	10.1	—	49 600	114	682	3 830	145	215	1 350	81.6	4 490	2 060
226	4.5	11.2	—	44 900	167	596	3 430	144	189	1 190	80.9	3 980	1 830
202	5.0	12.3	—	40 300	250	520	3 050	142	166	1 050	80.2	3 510	1 610
179	5.6	13.7	—	36 100	387	445	2 670	140	144	920	79.5	3 050	1 400
158	6.2	15.9	—	32 100	600	386	2 360	139	125	806	78.9	2 670	1 220
143	6.8	17.7	—	29 300	852	348	2 150	138	113	731	78.8	2 420	1 110
129	7.5	18.9	—	26 800	1 230	308	1 940	137	100	649	77.8	2 160	991
117	8.2	20.7	—	24 300	1 760	275	1 750	135	90.2	588	77.5	1 950	893
107	9.0	22.6	—	22 300	2 480	248	1 590	135	81.2	531	77.3	1 770	806
97	9.9	24.9	—	20 300	3 620	222	1 440	134	72.9	478	77.0	1 590	725
86	7.8	27.0	—	21 200	3 090	199	1 280	135	44.6	351	63.7	1 420	533
79	8.7	28.1	—	19 400	4 420	177	1 160	133	39.9	314	63.2	1 280	478
74	6.3	26.2	—	21 900	2 970	165	1 060	132	23.4	228	49.7	1 190	350
67	7.0	29.0	—	19 800	4 350	145	948	130	20.7	203	49.3	1 060	310
60	7.8	32.9	407	17 800	6 540	129	851	130	18.3	180	49.1	941	275
52	6.3	36.2	338	16 700	9 130	119	748	134	10.3	123	39.3	841	189
45	7.4	41.8	255	14 400	16 700	99.2	634	132	8.55	103	38.8	708	158
39	8.5	47.2	200	12 500	29 200	84.8	547	131	7.23	87.6	38.3	609	134
33	4.7	41.8	255	14 900	18 200	65.0	415	125	1.92	37.6	21.4	480	59.6
28	5.7	46.2	207	13 000	32 800	54.2	351	123	1.58	31.0	20.9	406	49.1
24	7.5	49.4	179	11 100	67 300	42.8	281	119	1.16	23.0	19.5	329	36.8
21	8.8	54.3	152	10 002	104 000	37.0	244	117	0.986	19.5	19.2	287	31.2

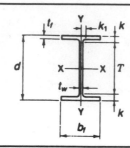

W SHAPES
Dimensions

Designation							Area A	Depth d	Web		Flange		Distance		
									Thick-ness t_w	$\dfrac{t_w}{2}$	Width b_f	Thick-ness t_f	T	k	k_1
mm	x	kg/m		in.	x	lb/ft	mm²	mm	mm	mm	mm	mm	mm	mm	mm
W	250	x	167	W	10	x	112	21 300	289	19.20	9.60	265.0	31.8	193	48	22
W	250	x	149	W	10	x	100	19 000	282	17.30	8.65	263.0	28.4	194	44	21
W	250	x	131	W	10	x	88	16 700	275	15.40	7.70	261.0	25.1	193	41	20
W	250	x	115	W	10	x	77	14 600	269	13.50	6.75	259.0	22.1	193	38	19
W	250	x	101	W	10	x	68	12 900	264	11.90	5.95	257.0	19.6	194	35	19
W	250	x	89	W	10	x	60	11 400	260	10.70	5.35	256.0	17.3	194	33	18
W	250	x	80	W	10	x	54	10 200	256	9.40	4.70	255.0	15.6	192	32	17
W	250	x	73	W	10	x	49	9 310	253	8.64	4.32	254.0	14.2	193	30	17
W	250	x	67	W	10	x	45	8 560	257	8.89	4.45	204.0	15.7	193	32	17
W	250	x	58	W	10	x	39	7 400	252	8.00	4.00	203.0	13.5	194	29	17
W	250	x	49	W	10	x	33	6 260	247	7.37	3.69	202.0	11.0	193	27	16
W	250	x	45	W	10	x	30	5 700	266	7.62	3.81	148.0	13.0	218	24	11
W	250	x	39	W	10	x	26	4 910	262	6.60	3.30	147.0	11.2	218	22	11
W	250	x	33	W	10	x	22	4 180	258	6.10	3.05	146.0	9.1	220	19	11
W	250	x	28	W	10	x	19	3 620	260	6.35	3.18	102.0	10.0	218	21	11
W	250	x	25	W	10	x	17	3 220	257	6.10	3.05	102.0	8.4	219	19	11
W	250	x	22	W	10	x	15	2 850	254	5.84	2.92	102.0	6.9	220	17	11
W	250	x	18	W	10	x	12	2 280	251	4.83	2.42	101.0	5.3	219	16	10

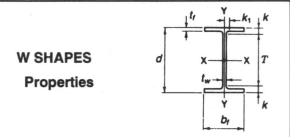

W SHAPES
Properties

Nom-	Compact					Elastic	Properties					Plastic	
inal	Section					Axis X-X			Axis Y-Y			Modulus	
Mass	Criteria			X_1	X_2	I	S	r	I	S	r	Z_x	Z_y
per	$\dfrac{b_f}{2t_f}$	$\dfrac{h_c}{t_w}$	F_y'''										
Meter			$\dfrac{N}{mm^2}$	$\dfrac{N}{mm^2}$	$\dfrac{10^{-8}mm^4}{N^2}$								
kg/m						10^6mm^4	10^3mm^3	mm	10^6mm^4	10^3mm^3	mm	10^3mm^3	10^3mm^3
167	4.2	10.4	—	48 800	119	300	2 080	119	98.8	746	68.1	2 430	1 140
149	4.6	11.6	—	44 100	176	259	1 840	117	86.2	656	67.4	2 130	1 000
131	5.2	13.0	—	39 200	278	221	1 610	115	74.5	571	66.8	1 850	870
115	5.9	14.8	—	34 500	448	189	1 410	114	64.1	495	66.3	1 600	753
101	6.6	16.7	—	30 800	703	164	1 240	113	55.5	432	65.6	1 400	656
89	7.4	18.7	—	27 400	1 100	143	1 100	112	48.4	378	65.2	1 230	574
80	8.2	21.2	—	24 700	1 640	126	984	111	43.1	338	65.0	1 090	513
73	8.9	23.1	—	22 600	2 290	113	893	110	38.8	306	64.6	985	463
67	6.5	22.5	—	25 200	1 590	104	809	110	22.2	218	50.9	901	332
58	7.5	25.0	—	22 000	2 730	87.3	693	109	18.8	185	50.4	770	283
49	9.1	27.1	—	18 700	5 280	70.6	572	106	15.1	150	49.1	633	228
45	5.7	29.5	—	19 900	4 540	71.1	535	112	7.03	95	35.1	602	146
39	6.6	34.0	379	17 200	7 970	60.1	459	111	5.94	80.8	34.8	514	124
33	8.0	36.9	324	14 800	15 100	49.1	381	108	4.75	65.1	33.7	426	99.9
28	5.1	35.4	352	16 700	10 900	39.9	307	105	1.78	34.9	22.2	352	54.7
25	6.1	36.9	324	15 200	16 500	34.2	266	103	1.49	29.2	21.5	306	46.1
22	7.4	38.5	296	13 300	30 100	28.8	227	101	1.22	23.9	20.7	263	38.0
18	9.4	46.6	207	10 700	74 500	22.5	179	99.3	0.919	18.2	20.1	208	28.8

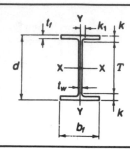

W SHAPES
Dimensions

Designation							Area A	Depth d	Web		Flange		Distance		
									Thick- ness t_w	$\dfrac{t_w}{2}$	Width b_f	Thick- ness t_f	T	k	k_1
mm	x	kg/m	in.	x	lb/ft		mm²	mm	mm	mm	mm	mm	mm	mm	mm
W	200	x	100	W	8	x	67	12700	229	14.50	7.25	210.0	23.7	155	37	17
W	200	x	86	W	8	x	58	11000	222	13.00	6.50	209.0	20.6	156	33	17
W	200	x	71	W	8	x	48	9100	216	10.20	5.10	206.0	17.4	156	30	15
W	200	x	59	W	8	x	40	7580	210	9.14	4.57	205.0	14.2	156	27	15
W	200	x	52	W	8	x	35	6640	206	7.87	3.94	204.0	12.6	156	25	14
W	200	x	46	W	8	x	31	5890	203	7.24	3.62	203.0	11.0	155	24	14
W	200	x	42	W	8	x	28	5320	205	7.24	3.62	166.0	11.8	157	24	14
W	200	x	36	W	8	x	24	4570	201	6.22	3.11	165.0	10.2	157	22	13
W	200	x	31	W	8	x	21	3980	210	6.35	3.18	134.0	10.2	168	21	11
W	200	x	27	W	8	x	18	3400	207	5.84	2.92	133.0	8.4	169	19	11
W	200	x	22	W	8	x	15	2860	206	6.22	3.11	102.0	8.0	168	19	11
W	200	x	19	W	8	x	13	2480	203	5.84	2.92	102.0	6.5	169	17	11
W	200	x	15	W	8	x	10	1910	200	4.32	2.16	100.0	5.2	168	16	10
W	150	x	37	W	6	x	25	4730	162	8.13	4.07	154.0	11.6	120	21	10
W	150	x	30	W	6	x	20	3790	157	6.60	3.30	153.0	9.3	119	19	10
W	150	x	22	W	6	x	15	2860	152	5.84	2.92	152.0	6.6	120	16	9
W	150	x	24	W	6	x	16	3060	160	6.60	3.30	102.0	10.3	122	19	10
W	150	x	18	W	6	x	12	2290	153	5.84	2.92	102.0	7.1	121	16	9
W	150	x	14	W	6	x	9	1730	150	4.32	2.16	100.0	5.5	122	14	9
W	130	x	28	W	5	x	19	3570	131	6.86	3.43	128.0	10.9	89	21	10
W	130	x	24	W	5	x	16	3020	127	6.10	3.05	127.0	9.1	89	19	9
W	100	x	19	W	4	x	13	2470	106	7.11	3.56	103.0	8.8	72	17	10

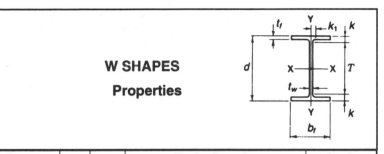

Nominal Mass per Meter kg/m	Compact Section Criteria			X_1	X_2	Elastic Properties						Plastic Modulus	
	$\frac{b_f}{2t_f}$	$\frac{h_c}{t_w}$	F_y''' $\frac{N}{mm^2}$	$\frac{N}{mm^2}$	$\frac{10^{-8}mm^4}{N^2}$	Axis X-X			Axis Y-Y				
						I 10^6mm^4	S 10^3mm^3	r mm	I 10^6mm^4	S 10^3mm^3	r mm	Z_x 10^3mm^3	Z_y 10^3mm^3
100	4.4	11.1	—	45600	155	113	987	94.3	36.6	349	53.7	1150	533
86	5.1	12.4	—	40100	257	94.7	853	92.8	31.4	300	53.4	981	458
71	5.9	15.8	—	33500	501	76.6	709	91.7	25.4	247	52.8	803	375
59	7.2	17.6	—	28100	997	61.2	583	89.9	20.4	199	51.9	653	303
52	8.1	20.4	—	24900	1600	52.7	512	89.1	17.8	175	51.8	569	266
46	9.2	22.2	—	22300	2480	45.5	448	87.9	15.3	151	51.0	496	230
42	7.0	22.2	—	24000	1960	40.9	399	87.7	9.01	109	41.2	446	165
36	8.1	25.8	—	20800	3390	34.4	342	86.8	7.64	92.6	40.9	380	141
31	6.6	27.5	—	19900	4400	31.3	298	88.7	4.10	61.2	32.1	335	93.7
27	8.0	29.9	—	17200	8180	25.8	249	87.1	3.29	49.5	31.1	279	76.0
22	6.4	28.1	—	18400	7240	20.0	194	83.6	1.42	27.8	22.3	222	43.7
19	7.8	29.9	—	16300	12200	16.5	163	81.6	1.15	22.5	21.5	187	35.5
15	9.6	40.5	269	12100	37700	12.8	128	81.9	.870	17.4	21.3	145	27.1
37	6.7	15.5	—	30400	776	22.2	274	68.5	7.07	91.8	38.7	310	140
30	8.2	19.1	—	24500	1780	17.1	218	67.2	5.54	72.4	38.2	244	110
22	11.5	21.6	—	18900	5200	12.1	159	65.0	3.87	50.9	36.8	176	77.6
24	5.0	19.1	—	27600	1240	13.4	168	66.2	1.83	35.9	24.5	192	55.3
18	7.1	21.6	—	21400	3660	9.19	120	63.3	1.26	24.7	23.5	136	38.3
14	9.2	29.2	—	16300	10500	6.84	91.2	62.9	0.912	18.2	23.0	102	28.1
28	5.8	14.0	—	35400	404	10.9	166	55.3	3.81	59.5	32.7	190	90.7
24	6.9	15.8	—	30600	728	8.83	139	54.1	3.12	49.1	32.1	157	74.9
19	5.9	10.6	—	38300	324	4.75	89.6	43.9	1.60	31.1	25.5	103	47.8

C

SIMPLIFIED
FRAME ANALYSIS

| | | | | | | | COLUMNS
W shapes
Design axial strength in kips (ϕ = 0.85) | | | | F_y = 36 ksi
F_y = 50 ksi | |

Designation					W14					
Wt./ft		132		120		109		99		90	
F_y		36	50	36	50	36	50	36	50[†]	36	50[†]
Effective length in ft KL with respect to least radius of gyration r_y	0	1190	1650	1080	1500	979	1360	890	1240	810	1130
	6	1160	1600	1060	1460	960	1320	873	1200	795	1100
	7	1160	1590	1050	1450	950	1310	867	1190	789	1080
	8	1150	1570	1040	1430	946	1300	860	1180	783	1070
	9	1140	1550	1030	1410	937	1280	852	1160	775	1060
	10	1120	1530	1020	1390	927	1260	843	1150	767	1040
	11	1110	1510	1010	1370	917	1240	833	1130	758	1030
	12	1100	1480	999	1350	905	1220	823	1110	749	1010
	13	1080	1450	985	1320	893	1200	811	1090	738	989
	14	1070	1420	971	1290	880	1170	799	1060	728	969
	15	1050	1390	956	1270	866	1150	787	1040	716	947
	16	1040	1360	940	1240	852	1120	773	1020	704	925
	17	1020	1330	924	1210	837	1090	759	991	691	902
	18	997	1300	906	1180	821	1060	745	965	678	878
	19	978	1260	888	1140	804	1030	730	938	664	853
	20	958	1220	870	1110	787	1000	714	911	650	828
	22	916	1150	831	1040	752	943	682	854	620	776
	24	872	1070	791	973	715	880	648	796	589	723
	26	826	997	749	902	678	815	614	737	558	670
	28	780	920	706	832	639	751	578	679	525	616
	30	733	844	663	762	600	688	542	621	493	564
	32	686	769	620	694	561	627	507	565	460	512
	34	639	697	577	629	522	567	471	511	428	463
	36	593	627	535	565	483	509	436	458	396	415
	38	547	563	494	507	446	457	402	411	365	372
Properties											
U		1.34	1.48	1.35	1.49	1.35	1.49	1.36	1.50	1.37	1.51
P_{wo} (kips)		196	272	173	240	148	205	125	174	109	151
P_{wi} (kips/in.)		23	32	21	30	19	26	17	24	16	22
P_{wb} (kips)		520	613	399	471	281	331	222	261	165	195
P_{fb} (kips)		215	298	179	249	150	208	123	171	102	142
L_p (ft)		15.7	13.3	15.6	13.2	15.5	13.2	15.5	13.4	15.4	15.0
L_r (ft)		73.6	49.6	67.9	46.2	62.7	43.2	58.2	40.6	54.1	38.4
A (in.^{2})		38.8		35.3		32.0		29.1		26.5	
I_x (in.^{4})		1530		1380		1240		1110		999	
I_y (in.^{4})		548		495		447		402		362	
r_y (in.)		3.76		3.74		3.73		3.71		3.70	
Ratio r_x/r_y		1.67		1.67		1.67		1.66		1.66	

[†]Flange is noncompact; see discussion preceding column load tables.

F_y = 36 ksi
F_y = 50 ksi

COLUMNS
W shapes
Design axial strength in kips ($\phi = 0.85$)

Designation														
							W14							
Wt./ft		82		74		68		61		53		48		43
F_y		36	50	36	50	36	50	36	50[‡]	36	50[‡]	36	50[‡]	36[‡]	50[‡]

Effective length in ft KL with respect to least radius of gyration r_y

KL	82-36	82-50	74-36	74-50	68-36	68-50	61-36	61-50	53-36	53-50	48-36	48-50	43-36	43-50
0	737	1020	667	926	612	850	548	761	477	663	431	599	386	536
6	705	963	638	871	585	798	523	714	443	598	400	540	357	482
7	694	942	628	852	576	781	515	698	432	576	390	520	347	463
8	682	918	616	830	565	760	505	680	419	552	378	498	337	443
9	667	892	604	807	553	738	494	660	404	526	365	474	325	422
10	652	863	590	781	540	714	483	638	389	498	351	449	312	399
11	635	833	575	753	526	689	470	615	372	469	336	423	298	375
12	618	801	559	724	511	662	457	591	355	439	320	396	284	350
14	579	732	524	662	479	604	428	539	319	379	287	340	254	301
16	538	661	487	598	444	545	396	486	282	319	253	286	224	252
18	495	588	447	532	408	484	364	431	245	263	220	235	194	206
20	450	517	407	467	371	424	331	377	210	213	188	191	165	167
22	406	447	367	405	334	366	297	326	176	176	157	157	138	138
24	363	381	328	345	297	311	265	276	148	148	132	132	116	116
26	321	325	290	294	262	265	233	236	126	126	113	113	99	99
28	280	280	253	253	229	229	203	203	109	109	97	97	85	85
30	244	244	221	221	199	199	177	177	95	95	85	85	74	74
31	229	229	207	207	187	187	166	166	89	89	79	79	69	69
32	214	214	194	194	175	175	155	155	83	83				
34	190	190	172	172	155	155	138	138						
36	169	169	153	153	138	138	123	123						
38	152	152	138	138	124	124	110	110						

Properties														
U	1.98	2.20	1.99	2.21	2.02	2.23	2.03	2.25	2.55	2.83	2.59	2.87	2.62	2.90
P_{wo} (kips)	149	207	127	176	112	156	97	135	96	133	84	117	72	100
P_{wi} (kips/in.)	18	26	16	23	15	21	14	19	13	19	12	17	11	15
P_{wb} (kips)	257	303	177	209	139	163	102	121	98	116	76	90	55	65
P_{fb} (kips)	148	206	125	173	105	146	84	117	88	123	72	100	57	79
L_p (ft)	10.3	8.8	10.3	8.8	10.3	8.7	10.2	8.7	8.0	6.8	8.0	6.8	7.9	6.7
L_r (ft)	43.0	29.6	40.0	28.0	37.3	26.4	34.7	24.9	28.0	20.1	26.3	19.2	24.7	18.2
A (in.^{2})	24.1		21.8		20.0		17.9		15.6		14.1		12.6	
I_x (in.^{4})	882		796		723		640		541		485		428	
I_y (in.^{4})	148		134		121		107		57.7		51.4		45.2	
r_y (in.)	2.48		2.48		2.46		2.45		1.92		1.91		1.89	
Ratio r_x/r_y	2.44		2.44		2.44		2.44		3.07		3.06		3.08	

[‡]Web may be noncompact for combined axial and bending stress; see AISC LRFD Specification Sect. B5.

Note: Heavy line indicates Kl/r of 200.

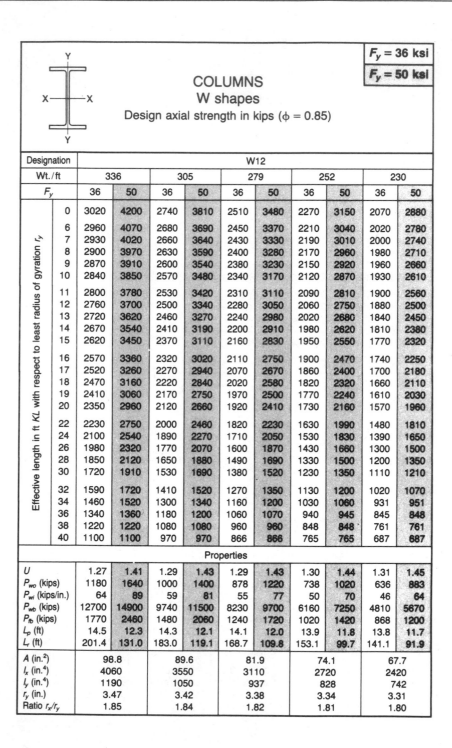

| | | | | F_y = 36 ksi |
| | | | | F_y = 50 ksi |

COLUMNS
W shapes
Design axial strength in kips (ϕ = 0.85)

Designation		\multicolumn{10}{c}{W12}									
Wt./ft		\multicolumn{2}{c}{336}	\multicolumn{2}{c}{305}	\multicolumn{2}{c}{279}	\multicolumn{2}{c}{252}	\multicolumn{2}{c}{230}
F_y		36	50	36	50	36	50	36	50	36	50
	0	3020	4200	2740	3810	2510	3480	2270	3150	2070	2880
	6	2960	4070	2680	3690	2450	3370	2210	3040	2020	2780
	7	2930	4020	2660	3640	2430	3330	2190	3010	2000	2740
	8	2900	3970	2630	3590	2400	3280	2170	2960	1980	2710
	9	2870	3910	2600	3540	2380	3230	2150	2920	1960	2660
	10	2840	3850	2570	3480	2340	3170	2120	2870	1930	2610
	11	2800	3780	2530	3420	2310	3110	2090	2810	1900	2560
	12	2760	3700	2500	3340	2280	3050	2060	2750	1880	2500
	13	2720	3620	2460	3270	2240	2980	2020	2680	1840	2450
	14	2670	3540	2410	3190	2200	2910	1980	2620	1810	2380
	15	2620	3450	2370	3110	2160	2830	1950	2550	1770	2320
	16	2570	3360	2320	3020	2110	2750	1900	2470	1740	2250
	17	2520	3260	2270	2940	2070	2670	1860	2400	1700	2180
	18	2470	3160	2220	2840	2020	2580	1820	2320	1660	2110
	19	2410	3060	2170	2750	1970	2500	1770	2240	1610	2030
	20	2350	2960	2120	2660	1920	2410	1730	2160	1570	1960
	22	2230	2750	2000	2460	1820	2230	1630	1990	1480	1810
	24	2100	2540	1890	2270	1710	2050	1530	1830	1390	1650
	26	1980	2320	1770	2070	1600	1870	1430	1660	1300	1500
	28	1850	2120	1650	1880	1490	1690	1330	1500	1200	1350
	30	1720	1910	1530	1690	1380	1520	1230	1350	1110	1210
	32	1590	1720	1410	1520	1270	1350	1130	1200	1020	1070
	34	1460	1520	1300	1340	1160	1200	1030	1060	931	951
	36	1340	1360	1180	1200	1060	1070	940	945	845	848
	38	1220	1220	1080	1080	960	960	848	848	761	761
	40	1100	1100	970	970	866	866	765	765	687	687

Effective length in ft KL with respect to least radius of gyration r_y

\multicolumn{12}{c}{Properties}
U		1.27	1.41	1.29	1.43	1.29	1.43	1.30	1.44	1.31	1.45
P_{wo} (kips)		1180	1640	1000	1400	878	1220	738	1020	636	883
P_{wi} (kips/in.)		64	89	59	81	55	77	50	70	46	64
P_{wb} (kips)		12700	14900	9740	11500	8230	9700	6160	7250	4810	5670
P_{fb} (kips)		1770	2460	1480	2060	1240	1720	1020	1420	868	1200
L_p (ft)		14.5	12.3	14.3	12.1	14.1	12.0	13.9	11.8	13.8	11.7
L_r (ft)		201.4	131.0	183.0	119.1	168.7	109.8	153.1	99.7	141.1	91.9
A (in.^{2})		\multicolumn{2}{c}{98.8}	\multicolumn{2}{c}{89.6}	\multicolumn{2}{c}{81.9}	\multicolumn{2}{c}{74.1}	\multicolumn{2}{c}{67.7}
I_x (in.^{4})		\multicolumn{2}{c}{4060}	\multicolumn{2}{c}{3550}	\multicolumn{2}{c}{3110}	\multicolumn{2}{c}{2720}	\multicolumn{2}{c}{2420}
I_y (in.^{4})		\multicolumn{2}{c}{1190}	\multicolumn{2}{c}{1050}	\multicolumn{2}{c}{937}	\multicolumn{2}{c}{828}	\multicolumn{2}{c}{742}
r_y (in.)		\multicolumn{2}{c}{3.47}	\multicolumn{2}{c}{3.42}	\multicolumn{2}{c}{3.38}	\multicolumn{2}{c}{3.34}	\multicolumn{2}{c}{3.31}
Ratio r_x/r_y		\multicolumn{2}{c}{1.85}	\multicolumn{2}{c}{1.84}	\multicolumn{2}{c}{1.82}	\multicolumn{2}{c}{1.81}	\multicolumn{2}{c}{1.80}

$F_y = 36$ ksi

$F_y = 50$ ksi

COLUMNS
W shapes
Design axial strength in kips ($\phi = 0.85$)

Designation							W12						
Wt./ft		210		190		170		152		136		120	
F_y		36	50	36	50	36	50	36	50	36	50	36	50
	0	1890	2630	1710	2370	1530	2120	1370	1900	1220	1700	1080	1500
	6	1840	2540	1660	2290	1490	2050	1330	1830	1190	1630	1050	1440
	7	1830	2500	1650	2260	1480	2020	1320	1810	1180	1610	1040	1420
	8	1810	2470	1630	2220	1460	1990	1300	1780	1160	1580	1030	1400
	9	1790	2430	1610	2190	1440	1960	1290	1750	1150	1560	1010	1380
	10	1760	2380	1590	2150	1420	1920	1270	1710	1130	1530	1000	1350
	11	1740	2330	1560	2100	1400	1880	1250	1680	1110	1490	984	1320
	12	1710	2280	1540	2050	1380	1840	1230	1640	1090	1460	966	1280
	13	1680	2230	1510	2000	1350	1790	1210	1600	1070	1420	948	1250
	14	1650	2170	1480	1950	1330	1740	1180	1550	1050	1380	928	1220
	15	1610	2110	1450	1900	1300	1690	1160	1500	1030	1340	908	1180
	16	1580	2040	1420	1840	1270	1640	1130	1460	1000	1290	896	1140
	17	1540	1980	1390	1780	1240	1580	1100	1410	980	1250	864	1100
	18	1500	1910	1350	1720	1210	1530	1070	1360	955	1200	841	1060
	19	1470	1840	1320	1650	1180	1470	1040	1310	928	1160	817	1020
	20	1430	1780	1280	1590	1140	1420	1020	1260	901	1110	793	976
	22	1340	1640	1210	1460	1070	1300	954	1150	846	1020	743	892
	24	1260	1490	1130	1340	1000	1180	891	1050	789	924	692	808
	26	1170	1360	1050	1210	933	1070	827	944	731	832	640	726
	28	1090	1220	973	1090	863	959	763	844	673	742	589	646
	30	1000	1090	895	967	792	852	700	749	617	656	538	569
	32	919	962	819	853	724	750	638	658	561	577	489	500
	34	838	852	745	755	657	664	578	583	508	511	442	443
	36	759	760	674	674	593	593	520	520	456	456	395	395
	38	682	682	605	605	532	532	467	467	409	409	355	355
	40	616	616	546	546	480	480	421	421	369	369	320	320

Effective length in ft KL with respect to least radius of gyration r_y

Properties													
U		1.33	1.47	1.33	1.47	1.35	1.49	1.36	1.51	1.37	1.52	1.38	1.53
P_{wo} (kips)		558	774	465	646	389	540	333	462	276	383	232	322
P_{wi} (kips/in.)		42	59	38	53	35	48	31	44	28	40	26	36
P_{wb} (kips)		3760	4430	2700	3190	2020	2380	1500	1760	1120	1320	815	960
P_{fb} (kips)		731	1020	610	847	493	684	397	551	316	439	247	343
L_p (ft)		13.7	11.6	13.5	11.5	13.4	11.4	13.3	11.3	13.2	11.2	13.0	11.1
L_r (ft)		129.2	84.2	117.3	76.6	105.4	68.9	94.8	62.1	84.6	55.7	75.5	50.0
A (in.²)		61.8		55.8		50.0		44.7		39.9		35.3	
I_x (in.⁴)		2140		1890		1650		1430		1240		1070	
I_y (in.⁴)		664		589		517		454		398		345	
r_y (in.)		3.28		3.25		3.22		3.19		3.16		3.13	
Ratio r_x/r_y		1.80		1.79		1.78		1.77		1.77		1.76	

		F_y = 36 ksi
		F_y = 50 ksi

COLUMNS
W shapes
Design axial strength in kips (ϕ = 0.85)

Designation		W12											
Wt./ft		106		96		87		79		72		65	
F_y		36	50	36	50	36	50	36	50	36	50	36	50[†]
	0	955	1330	863	1200	783	1090	710	986	646	897	584	812
	6	928	1280	839	1150	761	1040	689	947	627	861	567	779
	7	919	1260	830	1140	753	1030	682	933	620	848	561	767
	8	908	1240	820	1120	744	1010	674	917	613	834	554	754
	9	896	1210	809	1100	734	994	665	900	604	818	546	739
	10	883	1190	797	1070	723	973	654	881	595	800	538	723
	11	868	1160	784	1050	711	950	643	860	585	781	529	706
	12	853	1130	770	1020	698	926	631	838	574	761	519	687
	13	836	1100	755	995	684	901	619	814	562	740	508	668
	14	819	1070	739	966	669	874	605	790	550	717	497	647
	15	800	1040	722	935	654	846	591	764	537	694	485	626
	16	781	1000	704	904	638	817	576	738	523	670	472	604
	17	761	968	686	871	621	788	561	711	509	645	460	582
	18	741	932	667	838	604	758	545	683	495	620	446	558
	19	719	895	648	805	586	727	529	655	480	594	433	535
	20	698	858	628	771	568	696	512	627	465	569	419	512
	22	653	783	588	703	531	634	479	570	434	517	391	464
	24	608	708	546	635	493	572	444	514	403	465	362	418
	26	562	635	505	569	455	511	409	459	371	415	333	372
	28	516	565	463	505	417	453	375	406	339	367	305	328
	30	472	497	422	443	380	397	341	355	309	321	277	287
	32	428	437	383	390	344	349	308	312	279	282	250	252
	34	386	387	345	345	309	309	277	277	250	250	223	223
	36	345	345	308	308	276	276	247	247	223	223	199	199
	38	310	310	276	276	248	248	221	221	200	200	179	179
	40	279	279	249	249	223	223	200	200	181	181	161	161

Effective length in ft KL with respect to least radius of gyration r_y

Properties													
U		1.39	1.54	1.40	1.55	1.41	1.56	1.42	1.58	1.43	1.58	1.44	1.59
P_{wo} (kips)		185	257	161	223	139	193	122	169	106	148	92	128
P_{wi} (kips/in.)		22	31	20	28	19	26	17	24	15	22	14	20
P_{wb} (kips)		518	611	378	446	311	366	236	278	181	213	135	159
P_{fb} (kips)		198	276	164	228	133	185	109	152	91	126	74	103
L_p (ft)		13.0	11.0	12.9	10.9	12.8	10.9	12.7	10.8	12.7	10.8	12.6	11.8
L_r (ft)		67.2	44.9	61.4	41.3	56.4	38.4	51.8	35.7	48.2	33.6	44.7	31.7
A (in.²)		31.2		28.2		25.6		23.2		21.1		19.1	
I_x (in.⁴)		933		833		740		662		597		533	
I_y (in.⁴)		301		270		241		216		195		174	
r_y (in.)		3.11		3.09		3.07		3.05		3.04		3.02	
Ratio r_x/r_y		1.76		1.76		1.75		1.75		1.75		1.75	

[†]Flange is noncompact; see discussion preceding column load tables.

F_y = 36 ksi
F_y = 50 ksi

COLUMNS
W shapes
Design axial strength in kips ($\phi = 0.85$)

Designation		\multicolumn{10}{c}{W12}
Wt./ft		\multicolumn{2}{c}{58}	\multicolumn{2}{c}{53}	\multicolumn{2}{c}{50}	\multicolumn{2}{c}{45}	\multicolumn{2}{c}{40}
F_y		36	50	36	50	36	50	36	50	36	50‡

Effective length in ft KL with respect to least radius of gyration r_y	0	520	723	477	663	450	625	404	561	361	502
	6	498	680	457	623	419	566	376	507	336	453
	7	490	666	449	610	408	546	366	489	327	437
	8	482	649	441	594	396	524	355	469	317	419
	9	472	631	432	577	383	500	343	447	306	399
	10	461	611	422	559	369	475	330	424	295	378
	11	450	590	411	539	354	448	317	400	282	356
	12	437	568	400	518	339	421	302	375	269	334
	13	424	545	388	496	322	393	287	350	256	311
	14	411	521	375	474	306	365	272	324	242	288
	15	397	496	362	451	289	337	257	299	228	266
	16	382	471	348	428	271	310	241	274	214	243
	18	352	420	320	381	237	257	210	227	187	201
	20	321	370	292	334	204	209	180	184	160	163
	22	291	322	263	290	173	173	152	152	135	135
	24	260	276	235	247	145	145	128	128	113	113
	26	231	235	208	210	124	124	109	109	96	96
	28	202	202	181	181	107	107	94	94	83	83
	30	176	176	158	158	93	93	82	82	72	72
	32	155	155	139	139	82	82	72	72	64	64
	34	137	137	122	122						
	38	110	110	98	98						
	41	94	94	85	85						

\multicolumn{12}{c}{Properties}
U		1.73	1.92	1.75	1.94	2.18	2.42	2.21	2.45	2.23	2.47
P_{wo} (kips)		89	124	78	108	92	127	75	105	66	92
P_{wi} (kips/in.)		13	18	12	17	13	19	12	17	11	15
P_{wb} (kips)		106	125	94	111	116	136	86	101	59	69
P_{fb} (kips)		83	115	67	93	83	115	67	93	54	75
L_p (ft)		10.5	8.9	10.3	8.8	8.2	6.9	8.1	6.9	8.0	6.8
L_r (ft)		38.4	27.0	35.8	25.6	30.8	21.7	28.5	20.3	26.5	19.3
A (in.²)		\multicolumn{2}{c}{17.0}	\multicolumn{2}{c}{15.6}	\multicolumn{2}{c}{14.7}	\multicolumn{2}{c}{13.2}	\multicolumn{2}{c}{11.8}
I_x (in.⁴)		\multicolumn{2}{c}{475}	\multicolumn{2}{c}{425}	\multicolumn{2}{c}{394}	\multicolumn{2}{c}{350}	\multicolumn{2}{c}{310}
I_y (in.⁴)		\multicolumn{2}{c}{107}	\multicolumn{2}{c}{95.8}	\multicolumn{2}{c}{56.3}	\multicolumn{2}{c}{50}	\multicolumn{2}{c}{44.1}
r_y (in.)		\multicolumn{2}{c}{2.51}	\multicolumn{2}{c}{2.48}	\multicolumn{2}{c}{1.96}	\multicolumn{2}{c}{1.94}	\multicolumn{2}{c}{1.93}
Ratio r_x/r_y		\multicolumn{2}{c}{2.10}	\multicolumn{2}{c}{2.11}	\multicolumn{2}{c}{2.64}	\multicolumn{2}{c}{2.65}	\multicolumn{2}{c}{2.66}

‡Web may be noncompact for combined axial and bending stress; see AISC LRFD Specification Sect. B5.

Note: Heavy line indicates Kl/r of 200.

						COLUMNS W shapes Design axial strength in kips ($\phi = 0.85$)					$F_y = 36$ ksi

Designation		W10								
Wt./ft		112		100		88		77		68	
F_y		36	50	36	50	36	50	36	50	36	50
	0	1010	1400	900	1250	793	1100	692	961	612	850
	6	969	1330	865	1180	762	1040	664	908	588	803
	7	956	1300	853	1160	751	1020	655	890	579	787
	8	941	1270	840	1140	739	999	644	869	569	769
	9	924	1240	824	1110	725	973	632	847	558	749
	10	906	1210	808	1080	710	945	618	822	547	727
	11	886	1170	789	1040	694	916	604	796	534	703
	12	865	1130	770	1010	677	884	588	768	520	678
	13	842	1090	750	970	659	851	572	738	506	652
	14	819	1050	728	931	639	817	555	708	490	625
	15	794	1000	706	892	619	782	537	677	475	597
	16	768	961	682	851	599	746	519	645	458	569
	17	742	915	659	810	577	709	500	612	442	540
	18	715	870	634	769	556	672	481	580	424	511
	19	688	824	609	727	534	635	461	547	407	482
	20	660	778	584	686	511	599	442	515	389	454
	22	604	688	534	605	466	527	402	452	354	398
	24	548	601	483	527	422	458	363	392	319	344
	26	493	518	434	453	378	393	324	335	285	294
	28	440	447	386	390	336	339	287	289	252	254
	30	389	389	340	340	295	295	252	252	221	221
	32	342	342	299	299	259	259	221	221	194	194
	34	303	303	265	265	230	230	196	196	172	172
	36	270	270	236	236	205	205	175	175	153	153
	38	242	242	212	212	184	184	157	157	138	138
	40	219	219	191	191	166	166	141	141	124	124

Effective length in ft KL with respect to least radius of gyration r_y

Properties											
U		1.32	1.46	1.33	1.47	1.34	1.48	1.35	1.50	1.36	1.51
P_{wo} (kips)		255	354	214	298	177	246	143	199	116	162
P_{wi} (kips/in.)		27	38	24	34	22	30	19	27	17	24
P_{wb} (kips)		1210	1430	883	1040	623	735	420	495	293	345
P_{fb} (kips)		316	439	254	353	198	276	153	213	120	167
L_p (ft)		11.2	9.5	11.0	9.4	11.0	9.3	10.8	9.2	10.8	9.2
L_r (ft)		86.4	56.5	77.4	50.8	68.4	45.1	60.1	39.9	53.7	36.0

A (in.^{2})		32.9		29.4		25.9		22.6		20.0	
I_x (in.^{4})		716		623		534		455		394	
I_y (in.^{4})		236		207		179		154		134	
r_y (in.)		2.68		2.65		2.63		2.60		2.59	
Ratio r_x/r_y		1.74		1.74		1.73		1.73		1.71	

F_y = 36 ksi								
F_y = 50 ksi			**COLUMNS**					Y
			W shapes					
			Design axial strength in kips (ϕ = 0.85)					X—X
								Y

Designation		W10										
Wt./ft		60		54		49		45		39		33	
F_y		36	50	36	50	36	50	36	50	36	50	36	50
Effective length in ft KL with respect to least radius of gyration r_y	0	539	748	483	672	441	612	407	565	352	489	297	413
	6	517	706	464	634	422	577	380	515	328	444	276	373
	7	509	692	457	621	416	565	371	497	320	428	269	360
	8	500	675	449	606	409	551	361	478	311	412	261	345
	9	491	657	440	590	401	536	350	458	301	393	252	329
	10	480	638	431	572	392	520	337	436	290	374	243	312
	11	469	617	420	553	382	502	324	412	278	353	233	294
	12	457	595	409	533	372	484	311	388	266	332	222	276
	13	444	571	398	512	361	465	296	364	254	310	211	257
	14	430	547	385	490	350	444	282	339	241	289	200	239
	15	416	523	373	468	338	424	267	315	228	267	189	220
	16	401	497	360	445	326	403	252	290	215	246	177	202
	17	387	472	346	422	314	382	237	266	201	225	166	184
	18	371	446	332	399	301	361	222	243	188	205	155	167
	19	356	421	318	376	288	340	207	221	175	185	144	150
	20	340	395	304	353	275	319	192	199	162	167	133	135
	22	309	346	276	309	250	278	164	164	138	138	112	112
	24	278	299	248	266	224	239	138	138	116	116	94	94
	26	248	255	221	227	199	204	118	118	99	99	80	80
	28	219	220	195	196	175	176	102	102	85	85	69	69
	30	191	191	170	170	153	153	88	88	74	74	60	60
	32	168	168	150	150	134	134	78	78	65	65	53	53
	33	158	158	141	141	126	126	73	73	61	61		
	34	149	149	133	133	119	119						
	36	133	133	118	118	106	106						

Properties													
U		1.38	1.52	1.38	1.53	1.39	1.54	1.75	1.93	1.77	1.96	1.81	2.00
P_{wo} (kips)		99	138	83	116	73	101	79	109	64	89	55	77
P_{wi} (kips/in.)		15	21	13	19	12	17	13	18	11	16	10	15
P_{wb} (kips)		209	246	143	168	111	131	121	142	88	104	69	81
P_{fb} (kips)		94	130	77	106	64	88	78	108	57	79	38	53
L_p (ft)		10.7	9.1	10.7	9.1	10.6	9.0	8.4	7.1	8.3	7.0	8.1	6.9
L_r (ft)		48.1	32.6	43.9	30.2	40.7	28.3	35.1	24.1	31.2	21.8	27.4	19.7

A (in.^{2})		17.6		15.8		14.4		13.3		11.5		9.71	
I_x (in.^{4})		341		303		272		248		209		170	
I_y (in.^{4})		116		103		93.4		53.4		45		36.6	
r_y (in.)		2.57		2.56		2.54		2.01		1.98		1.94	
Ratio r_x/r_y		1.71		1.71		1.71		2.15		2.16		2.16	

Note: Heavy line indicates Kl/r of 200.

D

SIMPLIFIED FRAME ANALYSIS

OPEN WEB STEEL JOISTS, K-SERIES

DEFINITION OF SPAN

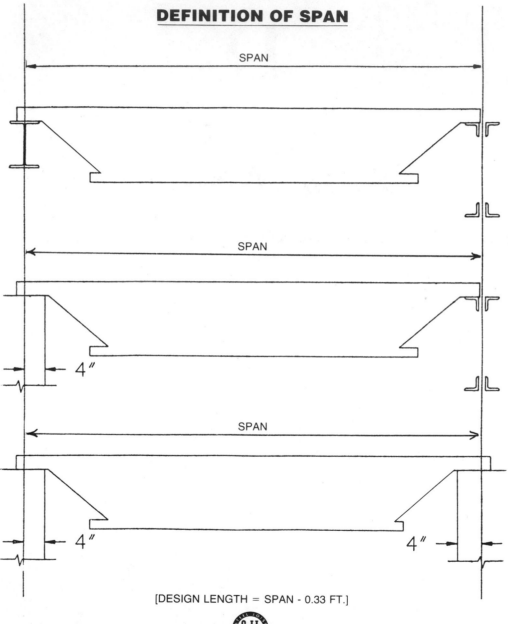

[DESIGN LENGTH = SPAN - 0.33 FT.]

STANDARD LOAD TABLE
OPEN WEB STEEL JOISTS, K-SERIES

Based on a Maximum Allowable Tensile Stress of 30,000 psi

Adopted by the Steel Joist Institute November 4, 1985; Revised to May 19, 1987.

The black figures in the following table give the TOTAL safe uniformly distributed load-carrying capacities, in pounds per linear foot, of K- Series Steel Joists. The weight of DEAD loads, including the joists, must be deducted to determine the LIVE load-carrying capacities of the joists. The load table may be used for parallel chord joists installed to a maximum slope of 1/2 inch per foot.

The figures shown in RED in this load table are the LIVE loads per linear foot of joist which will produce an approximate deflection of 1/360 of the span. LIVE loads which will produce a deflection of 1/240 of the span may be obtained by multiplying the figures in RED by 1.5. In no case shall the TOTAL load capacity of the joists be exceeded.

The approximate joist weights per linear foot shown in these tables do **not** include accessories.

The approximate moment of inertia of the joist, in inches[4] is: $I_J = 26.767 (W_{L.L.}) (L') (10^{\wedge})$, where $W_{L.L.}$ = RED figure in the Load Table; L = (Span - 0.33), in feet.

For the proper handling of concentrated and/or varying loads, see Section 5.5 in the Recommended **Code of Standard Practice (page 65)**.

Joist Designation	8K1	10K1	12K1	12K3	12K5	14K1	14K3	14K4	14K6	16K2	16K3	16K4	16K5	16K6	16K7	16K9
Depth (In.)	8	10	12	12	12	14	14	14	14	16	16	16	16	16	16	16
Approx. Wt. (lbs./ft.)	5.1	5.0	5.0	5.7	7.1	5.2	6.0	6.7	7.7	5.5	6.3	7.0	7.5	8.1	8.6	10.0
Span (ft.)																
8	550 / 550															
9	550 / 550															
10	550 / 480	550 / 550														
11	532 / 377	550 / 542														
12	444 / 288	550 / 455	550 / 550	550 / 550	550 / 550											
13	377 / 225	479 / 363	550 / 510	550 / 510	550 / 510											
14	324 / 179	412 / 289	500 / 425	550 / 463	550 / 463	550 / 550	550 / 550	550 / 550	550 / 550							
15	281 / 145	358 / 234	434 / 344	543 / 428	550 / 434	511 / 475	550 / 507	550 / 507	550 / 507							
16	246 / 119	313 / 192	380 / 282	476 / 351	550 / 396	448 / 390	550 / 467	550 / 467	550 / 467	550 / 550	550 / 550	550 / 550	550 / 550	550 / 550	550 / 550	550 / 550
17		277 / 159	336 / 234	420 / 291	550 / 366	395 / 324	495 / 404	550 / 443	550 / 443	512 / 488	550 / 526	550 / 526	550 / 526	550 / 526	550 / 526	550 / 526
18		246 / 134	299 / 197	374 / 245	507 / 317	352 / 272	441 / 339	530 / 397	550 / 408	456 / 409	508 / 456	550 / 490	550 / 490	550 / 490	550 / 490	550 / 490
19		221 / 113	268 / 167	335 / 207	454 / 269	315 / 230	395 / 287	475 / 336	550 / 383	408 / 347	455 / 386	547 / 452	550 / 455	550 / 455	550 / 455	550 / 455
20		199 / 97	241 / 142	302 / 177	409 / 230	284 / 197	356 / 246	428 / 287	525 / 347	368 / 297	410 / 330	493 / 386	550 / 426	550 / 426	550 / 426	550 / 426
21			218 / 123	273 / 153	370 / 198	257 / 170	322 / 212	388 / 248	475 / 299	333 / 255	371 / 285	447 / 333	503 / 373	548 / 405	550 / 406	550 / 406
22			199 / 106	249 / 132	337 / 172	234 / 147	293 / 184	353 / 215	432 / 259	303 / 222	337 / 247	406 / 289	458 / 323	498 / 351	550 / 385	550 / 385
23			181 / 93	227 / 116	308 / 150	214 / 128	268 / 160	322 / 188	395 / 226	277 / 194	308 / 216	371 / 252	418 / 282	455 / 307	507 / 339	550 / 363
24			166 / 81	208 / 101	282 / 132	196 / 113	245 / 141	295 / 165	362 / 199	254 / 170	283 / 189	340 / 221	384 / 248	418 / 269	465 / 298	550 / 346
25						180 / 100	226 / 124	272 / 145	334 / 175	234 / 150	260 / 167	313 / 195	353 / 219	384 / 238	428 / 263	514 / 311
26						166 / 88	209 / 110	251 / 129	308 / 156	216 / 133	240 / 148	289 / 173	326 / 194	355 / 211	395 / 233	474 / 276
27						154 / 79	193 / 98	233 / 115	285 / 139	200 / 119	223 / 132	268 / 155	302 / 173	329 / 188	366 / 208	439 / 246
28						143 / 70	180 / 88	216 / 103	265 / 124	186 / 106	207 / 118	249 / 138	281 / 155	306 / 168	340 / 186	408 / 220
29										173 / 95	193 / 106	232 / 124	261 / 139	285 / 151	317 / 167	380 / 198
30										161 / 86	180 / 96	216 / 112	244 / 126	266 / 137	296 / 151	355 / 178
31										151 / 78	168 / 87	203 / 101	228 / 114	249 / 124	277 / 137	332 / 161
32										142 / 71	158 / 79	190 / 92	214 / 103	233 / 112	259 / 124	311 / 147

INDEX